THE MOTHER OF MOHAMMED

An Australian Woman's Extraordinary Journey into Jihad

SALLY NEIGHBOUR

MELBOURNE
UNIVERSITY
PRESS

MELBOURNE UNIVERSITY PRESS
An imprint of Melbourne University Publishing Limited
187 Grattan Street, Carlton, Victoria 3053, Australia
mup-info@unimelb.edu.au
www.mup.com.au

First published 2009
Text © Sally Neighbour, 2009
Design and typography © Melbourne University Publishing Limited, 2009

Text design by Phil Campbell
Typeset by TypeSkill
Printed in Australia by Griffin Press, SA

National Library of Australia Cataloguing-in-Publication entry:

Neighbour, Sally.
The Mother of Mohammed: An Australian Woman's Extraordinary
   Journey into Jihad/Sally Neighbour.

9780522856682 (pbk.)

Includes index.

Hutchinson, Rabiah.
Muslim women—Australia—Biography.
Terrorism investigation—Australia.

305.48697092

CONTENTS

PROLOGUE

It was October 2001 and American cluster bombs were raining down on Afghanistan in retaliation for the September 11 attacks on the United States. Al Qaeda and Taliban encampments were being bombarded and their occupants were on the run, fleeing to the mountainous Afghan–Pakistan frontier or escaping across the border into neighbouring Iran.

Among the exodus was an Australian woman named Rabiah Hutchinson, a member of the jihadist elite, known among her fellow fugitives as 'Umm Mohammed'—meaning the mother of Mohammed.

The former country girl turned hippy backpacker would have seemed an unlikely jihadist to those who knew her as a child in Mudgee, New South Wales, or as a dope-smoking teenager on Sydney's northern beaches in the 1970s. But Rabiah Hutchinson was a veteran of the global holy war. She was a trusted insider, known and respected by the Taliban and al Qaeda leadership. She was married to a leading al Qaeda strategist and member of Osama bin Laden's inner circle, and had been handpicked by bin Laden's right-hand man, the Egyptian doctor Ayman al Zawahiri, to set up a new women's hospital in Kandahar. Western intelligence analysts would later call her 'the matriarch of radical Islam'; or—in the words of former CIA field officer Marc Sageman, who worked with the *mujahidin* in Pakistan—'the Elizabeth Taylor of the jihad'.

As she fled across the Afghan countryside, Rabiah certainly didn't look like a Hollywood star. Her *burka* was tattered and caked with dirt; her hair, concealed beneath it, matted and unkempt. She hadn't showered for months. Her four children who were on the run with her looked like a gang of grubby *kuchis*, the Afghan gypsies who roam the country's barren mountains.

In the wake of September 11, the United States and its allies had gone to war in Afghanistan to root out the al Qaeda perpetrators, their Taliban hosts, and anyone who supported or sympathised with them.

'Either you are with us, or you are with the terrorists', US President George W Bush had declared. From the perspective of the US and Australian governments, Rabiah Hutchinson was 'with the terrorists'. Now, like the rest of them, she was a fugitive: hunted from the air by US forces, and on the ground by Afghan troops.

'The next four months—it was just living like you can't imagine', Rabiah recalls. 'Every few days we'd have to move, and the Americans would find out our position and they'd attack. You can't imagine in your wildest dreams—you're fearing rape and torture and mutilation and death. Sometimes the Apache helicopters would come down so low you could see the pilots sitting in them. They were shooting women and children in the back from Apache helicopters while they were running.'

Rabiah and her children spent three months on the run in Afghanistan before escaping across the desert border into Iran, where they were detained under house arrest by the Iranian Revolutionary Guards. Finally, in 2003, they gave themselves up at the Australian embassy in Tehran, and were flown home to Australia. Rabiah's passport was cancelled and she was branded a threat to national security. According to the assessment from the Australian Security Intelligence Organisation (ASIO): 'There is a strong likelihood that further travel by Rabiah Maryam Hutchinson will involve participation in, or support and preparation for acts of politically motivated violence (and) conduct that might prejudice the security of Australia or a foreign country'.

Condemned as a would-be terrorist and placed high on ASIO's watch-list, Rabiah became a virtual prisoner in her home in Sydney's south-western suburbs, where she remains in 2009. She can occasionally be seen striding along the streets of Lakemba, a solitary figure swathed in a black *abaya* and *niqab*, only her eyes visible behind a slit in the fabric. Despite the scrutiny of the Australian authorities, she remains fiercely committed to her beliefs, and dismissive of the reputation she has acquired.

'I'm just a 55-year-old granny with diabetes and arthritis on a disability pension', Rabiah insists. 'What are they so worried about? They've got it wrong. I'm not important. I am absolutely nobody. I just happened to be there.'

But her protestations of insignificance belie the extraordinary life she has lived—twenty years on the frontlines of an ideological war that has reshaped our world. Over the course of those two decades she has been a witness to—and participant in—some of the epochal episodes of our time. She was there in Indonesia during the Islamist uprising against the Suharto regime in the 1980s. She was there at the now infamous Ngruki Islamic boarding school in Java, the crucible for the Indonesian militant group Jemaah Islamiyah, led by her mentor Abu Bakar Ba'asyir. She was there in the *mujahidin* camps of Pakistan during the Afghan holy war in the 1990s. And she was right there in Taliban-ruled Afghanistan at that moment in history when the September 11 attacks on the United States signalled the cataclysmic struggle that has defined our age.

So who is this mysterious black-veiled woman with the broad Australian accent and fiery Scottish temperament, who has Western governments so unnerved? And how did a former Mudgee girl and surf-loving backpacker who set out in her teens on the hippy trail end up at the heart of the global jihad? Clearly, this is no ordinary granny.

* * *

I first met Rabiah Hutchinson in August 2007, in a coffee shop in Bankstown in the south-western suburbs of Sydney. I was waiting at the pre-arranged meeting place when her black shrouded figure appeared, the face concealed behind a veil, the hands encased in black gloves. All I could see of her was her piercing blue eyes—glaring at me with bald hostility.

'I will never trust you', she snapped when we were introduced. I knew full well the reason for her animus. Nine months earlier, I had written an article that was featured on the front page of the the the *Australian* newspaper under an 'exclusive' caption in bold red print and a prominent headline: 'Australian Woman Married to Al-Qa'ida Boss'. The story revealed her marriage in 2001 to the al Qaeda strategist Mustafa Hamid, also known as Abu Walid al Misri, a member of Osama bin Laden's advisory *shura*. It also disclosed her association with bin Laden's deputy, Ayman al Zawahiri, and how he had chosen her to take charge of his hospital project.

An intensely proud and private woman with—I quickly learned—a fearsome temper, Rabiah was furious at my report. Apart from the public opprobrium it generated, it had caused her only sister to finally sever contact with her. 'I'll *never* trust you', Rabiah repeated, to make quite sure I understood.

It was an inauspicious beginning to a meeting I had been working towards for four years. I had first heard about Rabiah in 2003, while making a program for ABC TV's *Four Corners* on the Australian connections of Jemaah Islamiyah (JI), and later while researching my book, *In the Shadow of Swords,* on JI and the Bali bombings. JI insiders had described a gregarious former hippy who had been married to the group's Australian *emir*, the Indonesian Abdul Rahim Ayub. Stories abounded of how, in the 1980s, she had been desperate to join the jihad against the Russians in Afghanistan, but the conservative menfolk of JI would not allow it. She had finally gone off and done it anyway.

For the next four years I tried to track the elusive Rabiah down. I sent her letters and a copy of my book, in which she was briefly mentioned. I knocked on the doors of flats and houses where she had lived, only to find each time that she had moved on. (She has never lived in one place for more than three years.) I contacted her friends and acquaintances and asked them to pass on messages. It was all to no avail. She had no wish whatsoever to speak to me, or to any journalist for that matter. By the time we finally met at the coffee shop in Bankstown, her view had scarcely softened. She was there under sufferance, at the urging of a friend who believed it was time she told her side of the story.

For my part, I was sure it was a story I wanted to tell. I had spent the past four years reporting on terrorism; or, more precisely, the violent struggle being waged worldwide by Islamic militants, some of whom have resorted to terrorism. But what compelled my continuing interest was not the phenomenon of terrorism itself or the appalling details of the individual terrorist acts. What held me fascinated—and still mystified—were the personal stories of the people who have become involved in the jihadist movement, either on its periphery or at its core. Who are these people? Where do they come from? What is it they believe in? And what do they want? Rabiah's story intrigued me. Here was a woman as Australian as me, who had become a footsoldier in the global jihad. Why? It seemed to me that unravelling Rabiah's story might provide some answers to these confounding questions, and perhaps help us understand the magnetism of the Islamist cause, which has made it among the most momentous religious and political movements of our time and spawned some of the most intractable conflicts on the planet. My task now was to persuade her to tell her story.

After venting her hostility, Rabiah relented enough—still under sufferance—to agree to meet me again. Eventually we began meeting once or twice a week, which we did for well over a year. Finally she agreed to co-operate in the writing of this book, which could not otherwise have been written. She agreed because I persuaded her I would tell her story honestly and with integrity, in a way that was faithful both to her life and convictions, and to my journalist ethics. Her condition was that it had to present her side of the story. Mine was that it had to be true, warts and all, and rigorously factual. It was an uneasy relationship at first. We argued often, about world politics, the 'war on terror', the tenets of the Islamic faith (about which I knew nothing, she hastened to point out). She sometimes shouted and harangued me, occasionally wept, tried continually to convert me, and once or twice hung up the phone in my ear. Eventually, she began to trust me, and I began to admire and respect her, not only for her dogged resolve and unflinching conviction, but for her personal qualities as well. I found her funny, warm and compassionate, a great storyteller with an enormous memory for detail, a wry sense of humour, and a strong streak of self-deprecation. She can also be obstreperous and intimidating. The hundreds of hours we spent together were certainly never dull.

I have endeavoured as far as possible to corroborate Rabiah's story, and to ensure that its crucial historical and political context is accurate and factual. I traipsed around her hometown of Mudgee and her teen haunts on Sydney's northern beaches to find relatives, schoolmates, old boyfriends and former neighbours who could illuminate her story. In June and July 2008, I travelled to Indonesia and Afghanistan to visit the locations that feature in her journey and seek out colleagues and mentors who witnessed her role in the Islamist movement. Notwithstanding my efforts, parts of Rabiah's story are impossible to verify; in some instances I have omitted details I could not confirm; in others I have relied on her account. There are also gaps in her story; facts and details that she has not told me, either to guard her own privacy or that of family, friends and colleagues, or to protect people who she fears might suffer from the exposure. I have changed some names throughout the book, either at Rabiah's request, or that of individuals, or at my own discretion. These are explained in the notes at the end.

As a journalist, it has at times been a difficult line to walk, between honouring my professional obligations—truth, fairness, rigour, the pursuit of facts 'without fear or favour'—and honouring the leap of faith she made by entrusting me with her story. Rabiah is a controversial figure. Some of her views are confronting and extreme. They are her views, not mine, but I have chosen to present them as they are, and not to judge her for them. That I leave to readers. Some readers may find me too sympathetic. If I seem so, it is because I respect her right to hold beliefs and opinions that are alien to mine, and admire her tenacity in doing so. It is also because I felt that the normal imperative of journalistic objectivity was less compelling than my undertaking to present an account that is true to Rabiah's experience and beliefs. And finally it is because I believe that such a remarkable story is best allowed to speak for itself.

PART 1

ROBYN

1

ROBIN MERRY HOOD

Mudgee, New South Wales, 1953–1965

Sunday 2 August 1953 was a day of noteworthy events, chronicled faithfully as always in the *Mudgee Guardian*.

Another atomic weapons test to be held at the Woomera rocket range. Three men charged with sedition after a raid on 'red haunts' in Sydney including the printery of the *Communist Review*. Man tells the divorce court that his bride of eleven days knocked him out with a pot of rabbit stew.

And there on page two, tucked between the district cricket results and an advertisement for Kellett's Ironmongery, was a small but eagerly awaited item of news: 'A bonny baby daughter has come to brighten the home of Mr and Mrs Jim Hutchinson of Mudgee'.

Jim and Bessie had been trying for years, since the birth of their son George, now aged seven. Bessie had had four miscarriages and another son, Wayne, born with a hole in his heart, who died at four months. Herself an only daughter, Bessie had longed for a baby girl.

'What do you want to call your sister?' Bessie asked George, who was turning somersaults on the front lawn as his parents arrived home from Mudgee district hospital with their precious bundle.

'Robin Merry Hood', replied George, whose hero was the dashing brigand of Sherwood Forest. Bessie laughed. 'Why Mary?' she asked, not realising that George meant Merry, as in merry men.

'So everyone will know she's a girl.'

In keeping, more or less, with young George's suggestion, the baby was named Robyn Mary Hutchinson. The story of how her name was chosen is a favourite and oft-told anecdote. 'I always loved Robin Hood', she says. 'The principle of stealing from the rich and giving to the poor—not the stealing part, but just the idea of the rich having to give to the poor—really appealed to me.'

Like the legendary Nottinghamshire of mediaeval times, Mudgee in the 1950s was a community of haves and have-nots. Pegged out in the 1830s by the colonial planner Robert Hoddle, and enriched by the New South Wales gold rush, it was a town of wide streets, stately Victorian buildings and leafy parks. When the gold was exhausted, the district's mineral-rich soils and the completion of a rail line to Sydney ensured that it continued to flourish as a producer of fine wool, fat lambs, vegetables, dairy products and wine. By the turn of the century, Mudgee was a bastion of the squattocracy, lorded over by a clutch of wealthy families such as the Loneragans and Kelletts who ran stores, mines and hotels. The divide was keenly felt by working class folk like the Hutchinsons. 'There was a right side of the tracks and a wrong side, and we lived on the wrong side', Robyn would later recall.

Her first recollections were of playing in the yard of the family's home at 51 Horatio Street, a lemon-coloured, cement-rendered bungalow with a Hills Hoist and a treehouse built in a huge old eucalypt out the back. Thursdays were washdays, when Bessie would light a fire under the big copper tub set in bricks in the laundry, and stir the household linen in boiling water and Sunlight soap until it was spotless.

'If I close my eyes I can still the see the house and the white sheets flapping on the clothes line, and Maggie swinging back and forth on the sheets', Robyn remembers. 'Maggie' was her magpie, the first of many wild animals she tamed as pets. 'I have this thing with animals. I think I've always liked animals more than humans, and I got this magpie when I was two years old. It had a damaged wing and we nursed it back, and then it wouldn't leave. I used to dress him up and put little hats on him, and play cowboys and Indians with him.'

When Bessie came out to unpeg her clean linen from the washing line, she would often find a row of dirty claw marks along the bottom of the sheets, and Maggie dangling like a feathered trapeze artist, swinging back and forth in the breeze.

Jim worked two jobs to provide for his young family. By day he was a salesman in the drapery department at Loneragan's department store on a salary of eight pounds a week, and by night a 'steward'—the term used then for a bar tender—pulling beers in the Neptune Bar at the Hotel Mudgee. He was fond of a beer himself and would often stagger home to Horatio Street three sheets to the wind, after a night of bowls at his regular haunt, the Soldiers Club. Jim and a mate were champions in the men's pairs, in which they played 'like infuriated soldier ants' to take the trophy, the *Mudgee Guardian* reported.

Jim and Bessie had married in Sydney in June 1945 at the tail end of World War II, as Lord Mountbatten was declaring victory in Burma and US B-29 bombers were bombarding Osaka in Japan, a prelude to the atomic bombings that would end the war. Bessie was a dark-haired, high-spirited Mudgee girl who had left school in sixth grade and got a job in the coal town of Lithgow. She worked on the production line at the small arms factory, which made Bren machine guns during the war. Jim hadn't been Bessie's first choice. At the height of the war she had fallen in love with an American officer whom she'd met at a dance hall in Sydney while he was on shore leave. They'd become engaged, and at war's end he had bought her a ticket to fly home with him to the United States. But Bessie's mother, Lurline, was bed-ridden with heart disease and Bessie had to choose between leaving with her young fiancé and staying with her dying mother. She chose to stay, nursing her mother until her death at the age of forty-nine, four years after the war. From then on, she wore the air of a woman whose hopes had been dashed.

She married Jim on the rebound. The son of a Lithgow coal-miner, his given name was Kenneth Roy Hutchinson, but everyone called him Jim. He had left school at fourteen, worked variously as a salesman in the Sydney department store Mark Foys, a fruit and vegetable vendor, machinist, and telephone linesman for the Post Master General's Department.

He enlisted in the army in 1943, as a private in the Second Battalion of the Second Australian Infantry Division, but never made it overseas to fight, apparently because of extreme myopia. The closest he got to seeing action was at Townsville in north Queensland, home of the Australian Army's Heavy Anti-Aircraft Battery. His war record was distinguished only by an admonition for going 'AWL'—absent without leave—and another for 'conduct to the prejudice of good order and military discipline', the details of which were not recorded. Because he never saw active service overseas, his father-in-law would often joke derisively about Jim's time in 'the bucket brigade'.

Bessie's father, a dour Scotsman named Archibald Roy McCallum, was the bane of Jim's life. Archibald was the grandson of a Scottish settler, Donald McCallum, who had migrated to the Australasian colonies in 1831, and turned his hand to farming on the fertile plains of the Cudgegong River valley around Mudgee. Donald and his wife Christina had nine children, among them Archibald's father, John McCallum, born in 1845, who listed his occupation as 'maintenance man, farmer, Gold miner'. John himself never struck it rich, but his eldest son, John Alexander, found a nugget the size of a cricket ball, enough to set himself up in comfort.

John junior's brother, Archibald—Robyn's grandfather—was a gifted horseman who turned his skills to training racehorses for a stud at Cullenbone on the Cudgegong River. Robyn recalls that on weekends Archibald would travel to race tracks around the district to cheer on his charges, dressed in his customary navy pinstriped suit and waistcoat, with his silver-grey hair parted neatly down the middle beneath a grey fedora hat. He drove a mustard-coloured Vauxhall with a wooden dashboard and leather seats, which he polished lovingly with saddle wax. Race days were the only time old Archibald abandoned his stiff reserve. Family folklore has it that the most excited he ever got was when one of his rank outsiders came in first, and he slapped Bessie so hard on the back that her false teeth went flying over the railing.

A God-fearing Presbyterian who never drank, cursed or womanised, Archibald (who was commonly known by his second name, Roy) had no time at all for his hard-drinking son-in-law Jim, who was Roman Catholic, to make matters worse. 'My grandfather hated him with a passion', says Robyn. 'He considered my father beneath him.'

Jim wasn't the only one who cringed under Archibald's withering disapproval. 'Everyone was afraid of my grandfather except me and I think that's why he loved me', Robyn recalls. 'He used to call me his wee bonny lassie. He was the person I loved most in my life—I don't think anyone loved him except me.' She called him 'farv' or 'farvie', short for grandfather. While the others tiptoed around the old curmudgeon, she would fiddle with his fob watch, and blow her snotty nose on the starched white handkerchief embroidered with his initials that peeped from his breast pocket. Only his 'wee bonny lassie' was game to tease the peppery patriarch.

'You're Scotch, aren't you?' she would ask with mock innocence, to annoy him.

'Do I look like a bottle of whiskey? I'm a Scotsman', he would indignantly reply.

Archibald's wife Lurline had been a pillar of the Mudgee citizenry, eulogised in the *Guardian* as 'a member of a very old district family … a kindly, charitable lady (who) was held in the highest regard by her neighbours'. After her death, the widower had sold his own property and rented a room in a neat weatherboard bungalow a dozen doors up Horatio Street, owned by an upstanding local family named the Pitts, whom Archibald considered far more respectable than his own unruly brood. 'They were the epitome of what he approved of—husband and wife, mother and father, solid job, own home, family car, church on Sunday. Their little girl was always immaculately dressed with ribbons in her hair', says Robyn. Such was Archibald's scorn for his son-in-law that he refused to set foot in Jim and Bessie's home. When the children wanted to see their grandfather, they would have to walk up Horatio Street to visit him. 'It was very sad for my mum. She had been the apple of his eye—until she married my father.'

When their daughter was still a toddler, Jim and Bessie decided to leave Mudgee and make a new start in the city. Robyn's vague recollection was that her heavy-drinking father had been retrenched from his job; but the urge to escape the pitiless scrutiny of his overbearing father-in-law may also have been a factor in the move. They relocated to the working-class seaside suburb of Narrabeen on Sydney's northern beaches, where Jim and Bessie took over the snack bar in the beer garden of the Narrabeen Hotel. Their new home had an orchid garden and a backyard swimming pool that had been filled with concrete after a child drowned in it. Surrounded by bushland, it was almost like being back in the country.

George was a serious, responsible boy, who could safely be left in charge of his little sister. She was a scrawny, pale-skinned runt, with a shock of frizzy white-blonde hair and an eye-patch she wore from the age of two to correct a severe astigmatism. What she lacked in physical stature she made up for in sheer pluck, as she stumbled through the bush behind her brother like a pint-sized pirate, game for almost anything.

'My mother used to say that poem: "There was a little girl who had a little curl, right in the middle of her forehead, and when she was good she was very very good, and when she was bad she was horrid". She used to throw her hands up in the air and say "Thank God you're not twins", because she never knew what I would do next. I didn't have any fear.' At age two, Robyn recalls packing a toothbrush, face washer and some scraps of food and striding off into the scrub to collect cicada shells in a paper bag, hoping Bessie could bring them back to life. By the time she wandered home several hours later, the local police were leading a search party through the bush to find her.

While Bessie slaved all hours in the hotel kitchen, Jim spent his time propping up the bar and yarning with the regular clientele. Over time, his drinking got steadily worse, as did his volatile temper. Publicly, he was an amiable enough drunk, but at home after a heavy night he would sometimes lash out in violence. 'He never beat my brother and I, but he beat my mum', Robyn remembers.

Her half-brother, Roderick, thirteen years Robyn's junior, paints a sobering picture of their father. Roderick was one of two sons born to Jim Hutchinson's second wife. He made their lives a misery. 'He was always violent', says Roderick. 'I love my father but I'll never forgive him for the alcoholism and the beatings. My dad would come home from the pub each night, and he had two moods—if he whistled he was happy, if he was silent I would cop the beatings. It went on till I was fifteen or sixteen years old. Never once in my life did he tell me he loved me. There was nothing.' Roderick's brother Brett, who was a year-and-a-half younger, committed suicide at the age of twenty-seven. Roderick himself attempted suicide three times and was finally diagnosed with post-traumatic stress disorder, which he attributes to his brutal upbringing.

Fortunately for Robyn, Jim Hutchinson was not yet the extremely cruel man he would become. And in any event, Bessie was not one to tolerate such treatment for long. There were constant arguments, occasional bursts of violence, and money was always tight. By the time Robyn was about three years old, Bessie had had enough; she packed up the children and went home to Mudgee.

'My mother, in the face of damnation, left my father and went back to Mudgee and tried to survive—in a world that did not cater for divorced women. My family was looked down on because Mum had separated. My grandfather wouldn't support her financially, and she was too proud to take welfare. So she worked. She had to do jobs that were normally done by men, because in those days they paid double the wages that they paid to women.'

Bessie and the children moved into the Woolpack Hotel, a gold-rush era bloodhouse that still had the old stables out the back where thirsty prospectors would tether their horses when they stopped for an ale. Now derelict and with its windows painted over, the old pub had ceased trading and was operating as a cheap boarding house. Bessie found work as a 'donkey stoker' at another hotel, shovelling fuel into the coal-fired hot water system known as a 'donkey'. Her other tasks included chopping wood for the hotel fireplaces and cleaning out the stinking black sludge from the cesspool where wastewater from the kitchen and bathrooms stagnated before flowing to the sewer. While George was at school, Robyn would trail around after her mother as she worked. 'I was always at the pub. I hated it', she recalls. Bessie's wage was barely enough to put food on the table for her and the two children. Robyn remembers her mother eating bread and dripping while the children ate meat, and buying cheap Dairy Bell margarine that she wrapped in discarded butter paper so the children would think they were eating butter.

The old teetotaller, Archibald, was horrified at his daughter's new circumstances. In 1950s Mudgee, 'good women' didn't divorce and they didn't go to hotels at all. Those who did were allowed only in the dining room or 'ladies lounge'; the bar was reserved for men. 'My grandfather couldn't bear it, so he shunned her', says Robyn. 'His view was "you are second class". He felt she had brought shame on the McCallum name.'

As best she could under the circumstances, Bessie instilled in her children a strict moral code, which prized good manners, respect for one's elders, adherence to the Queen's English, modesty, frugality and above all honesty. 'My mum was a very strong woman who taught us honesty and truthfulness and that you stand on your principles. She hated gossip, I guess because she was a victim of it all her life. She taught me very strongly that what's important is not how people perceive you, it's how you are yourself. If someone is saying something about you, it's either true or not true; and if it's not true, you don't care what they say. It gave me a very strong sense of self-worth.'

Bessie insisted the children were always neat and clean, even though their clothes were patched and threadbare. 'Being poor is no excuse for being dirty', she would tell the children. They only ever had three sets of clothing each; it was all they needed, according to Bessie—'one on, one off, one in the wash'. A former neighbour, Stephen Gay, remembers Bessie as 'a rough and tough typical Aussie' who enjoyed a laugh and a few beers but was a stickler for her rules, which included forbidding the neighbourhood children from running up and down her hallway. 'She was a genuine old rough diamond', says Gay.

The only occasions Robyn got a spanking were when she told lies. One time was when her mother sent her to the shops to buy a packet of her favourite Capstan cork-tipped cigarettes and Robyn spent the ha'penny change on lollies, lying to her mother afterwards that there had been no money left. Bessie found out and whipped her with the cord from the electric iron.

'Do you know why I'm punishing you?' she asked her whimpering daughter.

'Because I stole money?' sniffed Robyn.

'No, because you looked me in the eye and you lied. And there is nothing on the face of this earth that's worse than a liar.'

Robyn didn't mind the odd thrashing; a far worse punishment in her view was being ignored. 'If my mother beat me, it didn't have much effect, but if she stopped talking to me, it used to kill me. Because for me, to be ignored was just intolerable. It's just my personality—I can't stand to be ignored.'

Aside from the occasional hiding, it was a carefree life for an intrepid child. Robyn had an old red bike with no brakes, on which she would pedal up to the Flirtation Hill lookout with the other kids, wait for a puff of smoke in the distance, and then race the train, careening at full pelt down the hill to the showgrounds. It got so that Bessie refused to buy her another dress; even her 'Sunday best' was constantly being darned. 'It was always ripped, the lace would be hanging off it, because I'd been up a tree, or crawling under the barbed-wire fence, or in the chicken coop playing hospitals with the chickens.' Playing hospitals was Robyn's favorite game, but she was never one for make-believe—all games had to be as real as she could make them. One Christmas, to Bessie's horror, she 'operated' on her brand-new Red Riding Hood doll, cutting a chunk out of its leg with a kitchen knife and then hacking off its hair.

At four years and ten months—'as soon as my mum could get rid of me'—Robyn was packed off to Mudgee public primary school, dressed in a little brown tunic and yellow shirt and lugging an oversized schoolbag, her eye-patch replaced by round tortoiseshell glasses. She came home unimpressed after day one in kindergarten. 'I told my mother it wasn't school, it was play-school. They didn't teach me how to read or write. All we did was sing songs and play games. I said it shouldn't be called a school because we didn't learn anything.'

She devised her own ways of making kindergarten more interesting. One day she led a gang of children to play horses in the yard of the old Mechanics Institute next door, a dilapidated barn of a place with a rusty corrugated-iron fence and overgrown grass. Always a forceful personality, she delighted in being able to get the other kids to do what she told them to.

'We're all wild horses, so first we'll graze and then we'll run', she announced.

Her playmates started pretending to eat grass, which wasn't good enough for Robyn.

'You're not being a real horse', she chided them, 'you have to really eat it, or it won't be real'.

So the children proceeded to eat grass, until one boy began to gag.

'He went blue in the face and nearly choked, then he started crying and the teacher came, and my mother got called up to the school', Robyn recounts. It was the first of many times that Bessie Hutchinson would be summoned to the school about her errant daughter's behaviour. 'Poor mum, I was a shocking child. Not that I was a delinquent, but I was always coming up with the most outlandish schemes and acting them out—and they would have to be as real as possible.' Whenever there was trouble, the teachers knew where to look. 'I always got caught because I wasn't allowed to lie. So if anything was wrong in class, the person they would ask was always me, and I would have to tell the truth.'

During her second year in primary school, the family abruptly packed their bags and moved again. Bessie had a new boyfriend whom she'd met at the pub, a rouseabout who did mustering and shearing on farms around the district. He moved with them to a one-horse town called Wollar, 50 kilometres out of Mudgee, which consisted of a couple of dirt roads, a pub, a bakery, a general store, a one-teacher school and about twenty houses. As Robyn recalls it, their new home was little better than a shack, with dirt floors, no bathroom and no electricity. They used kerosene lanterns and cooked on an open fire. Once a week Bessie would fill a tub with water from the copper and scrub the children in front of the open fire until their skin shone. Robyn's memories are not of grinding poverty but of rollicking, childish adventures. 'I was in my element there. We had all sorts of animals. I used to go rabbit hunting with my brother, and we used to pick wild mushrooms the size of dinner plates and bake them in the oven at the local bakery.'

Weekday mornings, George and Robyn would clump across the paddock from their house to the tiny school, which was elevated on concrete stumps to let the air through and keep the snakes out, or so the children were told. On Saturday nights the townsfolk would dress up in their finery for the weekly square dance at the newly built memorial hall, a large corrugated-iron shed with a fancy cement-rendered Art Deco façade stuck on at the front. Inside was a polished dance floor with bench seats lining the iron walls, and a stage where a local bush band would bash out the latest hoedown tunes on a squeezebox, a banjo and a 'lagerphone'— a broomstick with metal beer-bottle caps nailed down its length, which makes a racket not unlike music when thumped rhythmically on a hardwood floor.

A few months after their arrival, Robyn had something else to amuse her—a baby sister named Susan, whose birth presumably explained the family's hasty departure from Mudgee.

'One day Mum went away and had this baby. I didn't even know she was having a baby. I just got up one morning and she was gone. Our neighbour was there and she said to me, "your mother's gone to get a baby from underneath the cabbage leaf". So she came back with this baby, and after a few hours I said "OK, it's a nice baby but you'd better take it and put it back under the cabbage leaf now". I was very, very jealous, because for seven years I'd been the baby of the family, with no competition.'

Like her father, Jim Hutchinson, Robyn's stepfather was a drinker with a quick temper, 'a bit of a no-hoper', she recalls. She claims that one day when she saw him hitting her mother, she picked up his rum bottle and clubbed him over the head. Not long afterwards, Bessie packed up her three children and their few belongings and returned, yet again, to Mudgee.

Under sufferance, Bessie's father Archibald took his daughter and her young brood in. They moved into a semi-detached bungalow in Lewis Street, Mudgee, which Archibald shared with Bessie's bachelor brother, Noel. Uncle Noel was a simple, good-natured fellow who delighted the children with his first-class yodelling—which drove old Archibald almost to distraction—and took them spot-lighting at night in his ute for rabbits, which he skinned and sold for their pelts. Noel worked for the council as the night-soil collector, doing the rounds of Mudgee each evening to empty the sewage cans from the backyard dunnies of the town. He would regale anyone who would listen with stories like the one about the time he was bailed up by a blue cattle dog with a brimful can on his shoulder and ended up with shit all over him. After school, Uncle Noel would drive Robyn in his pickup truck to the main drag, Church Street, and pull up in front of Wilf Hodges's radio and television shop. Television had just been introduced and Robyn's family could not afford one. They would stand transfixed among a small crowd of townsfolk in front of the store, watching *Rin Tin Tin* without sound through the plate glass window.

The divide between rich and poor was sharply felt by young Robyn. 'The fact that if you didn't have money you weren't as good as someone else was, for as along as I can remember, something I couldn't accept. I used to say to my grandfather, "it's not right, it's not fair". Being rich doesn't make you a better person.' From an early age she bristled at wealth and privilege, smarted over perceived injustice, and flaunted a fierce pride, grounded in her family's strict code of morality and discipline.

For Bessie, the strictures that resulted from living as a divorced single mother in a country town under the same roof as her domineering father made for an oppressive life. 'My grandfather was very, very hard on my mum', says Robyn. 'Whenever she was in Mudgee, she had her father and brother living with her. He was very strict on her; she wasn't allowed any male companionship or Catholic friends. It didn't matter what she did, she couldn't please my grandfather.' For Bessie, the city lights still beckoned, and she would often pack up the children and head off for weekends or holidays in Sydney, to stay with a friend whom the children knew as Auntie Dulce. 'My mother was torn between wanting her own life and looking after her brother and grandfather, so she would come to Sydney, but then the guilt would get to her and she would always go back to them.'

As long as they lived under Archibald's roof, they had to live by his rules. 'If he spoke to you, you spoke. If he laughed, you laughed. If my grandfather put his hat on the hall table and my brother's gloves were underneath it, my brother wouldn't lift that hat. It was farv's hat. We weren't allowed to speak at the dinner table—but I did. I think he liked the rebellion in me. I think I used to shock him and that he secretly approved of my defiance.'

Archibald taught Robyn to play the card game euchre when she was four years old. Occasionally she would beat him, and once she asked if he had let her win. 'He looked at me with this look that said: "how could you even suggest such a thing?" He said something like, "if you truly love someone you can never deceive them". He said, "you'll never achieve any-thing in life except on your own merit". And, like my mother, lying—he abhorred it.'

Archibald's rigid morality had a profound influence on Robyn. 'He was very straight, he was always very sure of what he liked and didn't like, what was acceptable and what wasn't. He was very much a man of princi-ple. I guess he was a black-and-white man.' From the time Robyn could talk, it was maddeningly clear to Bessie that the child had inherited her grandfather's unflinching certitude. 'My mother used to say to me, "Robyn, there *is* grey! It's not all just black and white. There's grey".' On this point, however, Robyn could never be persuaded: 'I don't see grey. It's all black and white to me.'

At the age of eight, Robyn was sent to Sydney to undergo treatment on the astigmatism that her eye-patch had failed to correct. She was a guest of the Royal Far West Children's Health Scheme, a charitable organisation that subsidised medical treatment in the city for the offspring of remote communities in western New South Wales, coupled with 'the holiday of a lifetime by the sea' at its Manly Beach sanatorium. She recalls being there for what seemed like months on end, awaiting surgery on her eye. Notwithstanding the much lauded community service provided by the Royal Far West Scheme, the separation from her family was an ordeal for young Robyn.

'You weren't allowed to have your own clothes', was her abiding memory forty years after the event. 'In the morning when you got up, they'd have boxes of clothes—they'd have socks, singlets, and for the girls, pleated tartan skirts and blouses. You had to line up to get your clothes. Because we had to line up, the little ones got shoved to the back, so by the time you got to the boxes you'd have to wear whatever was left, sometimes it would be odd socks.'

By her own account, the staff found her a trying trouble-maker. 'I got into a lot of strife there. I was always getting into trouble. I remember turning on the industrial polisher and it went berserk and they couldn't get to the plug to turn it off. Another time I found an old wind-up gramophone in a storeroom above the girls dormitory. I took it back and gave it to one of the older girls who was my friend, and convinced her that if we could plug it in we could turn it into an electric one. So I attached an electrical wire to the metal handle and got her to shove the wires in the socket. She got electrocuted—not badly, but her hair stood on end.'

'How do you think of these things? Why don't you just play with blocks like the other children?' she recalls the exasperated matron exclaiming.

The eye treatment she received was ultimately unsuccessful, and Robyn was left legally blind in one eye. She recalls Bessie telling her that after she came home she wouldn't speak, except in monosyllables. She later fell ill with a kidney disease called nephritis, which kept her confined in the Mudgee district hospital for weeks at a time. The main task for the nursing staff was keeping such a hyperactive child occupied; one day, in a fit of boredom, she cut off her eyelashes with a pair of craft scissors. A legacy of her lengthy hospitalisation was an enduring fascination with medicine. She liked to follow the nurses on their rounds, and afterwards joined the Mudgee branch of the Red Cross. In her red cape and white uniform with its Red Cross insignia, marching around the war memorial clock tower on Anzac Day, she fancied herself as a little Florence Nightingale.

'I was always on a mission. There was always some mission or cause—I don't mean stealing from the rich and giving to the poor, but I used to champion causes that I believed were unjust.' The Red Cross ladies auxiliary would organise local families to knit clothing for poor children overseas. Robyn never had much patience with domestic science, and she knitted so tightly that the jumper she was fashioning wouldn't come off the needles, so Bessie finished it for her. When a teacher displayed it in class to show the other children a perfect sample, Robyn was sure she would be struck down dead by a bolt of lightning for the deception.

From as early as she can remember, she was certain there was a God. At weekly scripture classes at Mudgee Primary, she listened rapt to stories of God the Father, God the Son and God the Holy Ghost, in their Kingdom of Heaven. 'They would talk about how wonderful it was that when you belong to this community you're going to heaven. And when I heard about heaven, I knew I wanted to go there.'

Eager to find out more, she pestered her mother to enrol her in Sunday school at Mudgee's Presbyterian Church. Bessie herself had little time for organised religion since the death of her baby son, Wayne, when she was told that her tiny boy would be consigned to purgatory if he wasn't baptised to purge the stain of original sin. 'She still believed in God but she stopped going to church', says Robyn. 'She was very anti church establishment. She said that no God that is just and loving could punish a child for the supposed sins of the mother and father; she said it was impossible for her to believe that. But my mother never imposed her beliefs on us, she had this principle that you had to find out for yourself, especially about personal beliefs.'

So Bessie pulled Robyn's well-darned 'Sunday best' out of the wardrobe and sent her off to the weekly Sunday class at St Paul's. It proved a galling revelation for the girl. 'The Sunday school was filled with the children of happy homes. People like my mum, who was on the fringes of society—she was a divorced woman who worked in a hotel—women like her weren't acceptable. From very early on I could see the hypocrisy and double standards. What you would hear about in Sunday school—that Jesus loves everybody—didn't happen in the real world, in the playground or society at large.'

Robyn's stint at Sunday school ended when she was caught by the teacher gobbling mouthfuls from a jar of Perkins Paste, the glue given to the children to stick together cut-out pictures of Jesus and John the

Baptist that they'd been given to colour in. She liked the smell of the stuff and wondered how it tasted. The teacher sent a note home to her mother, saying Robyn could not come back the following week. The seeming illogic of the punishment confounded her. 'They were telling us Jesus would save us, even the sinners—so if I was a sinner, shouldn't I be going to Sunday school *more*, not less?'

Like much of the Western world since the Reformation, Mudgee society was polarised by a deep sectarian divide. Robyn and her friends used to parade past the imposing Victorian sandstone edifice of St Mary's Roman Catholic Church, chanting 'Catholics, Catholics, march to hell! While the Protestants ring the bell!' But at the age of eleven Robyn underwent her first conversion, after befriending a Catholic girl who lived next door. Her family had moved house again, into a pale-blue weatherboard bungalow in Court Street with a rusting bull-nosed verandah poised on pillars of sun-baked clay bricks. The ceiling was of decorative pressed metal and the interior timber walls were stained a dark smoky brown from decades of wood fires. In the backyard, Uncle Noel kept chooks, cattle dogs, rabbits and a geriatric cockatoo called Cocky, who liked to mimic its master yelling at the dogs, and was once heard screeching at a pair of startled Seventh Day Adventists, 'get up the back, you mongrels!'

Next door lived the Daniels family, who had two girls about Robyn's age. Robyn and Laurette Daniels became fast friends, and the Daniels girls would scramble through a hole in the paling fence to go snake-hunting in the long grass up the back near Uncle Noel's chook shed. Sometimes the kids would borrow George's air rifle to take pot shots at starlings nesting in the eaves. Because Robyn was the littlest of the troublemakers, the older ones always got blamed, even though she was usually the instigator.

Every Sunday morning the Daniels family would head off to St Mary's for Sunday mass, and one week they invited Robyn to go with them. The children sat meekly on the hard wooden pews under a giant crucifixion suspended from the soaring high gothic vaulted ceiling, as the priest, resplendent in snow-white vestments, intoned in Latin the Confiteor, the general confession of sin.

Confiteor Deo omnipotenti, beatae Mariae semper Virgini, beato Michaeli Archangelo …

I confess to Almighty God, to blessed Mary ever Virgin, to blessed Michael the Archangel, to blessed John the Baptist, to the holy Apostles, Peter and Paul, to all the Saints and to you brethren, that I have sinned exceedingly,

In thought, word and deed,

Through my fault, through my fault, through my most grievous fault …

As he uttered the words in Latin—*mea culpa, mea culpa, mea maxima culpa*—the priest would strike his breast three times in a show of sorrow for the sins of the congregation. The ritual absolution was completed with the words: 'May Almighty God have mercy upon you, forgive you your sins and bring you to life everlasting. Amen.'

Eleven-year-old Robyn sat spellbound, as shafts of sunlight pierced the blazing stained-glass windows to illuminate the bleeding heart of Jesus and the graphic images of Christ's agony depicted in the Stations of the Cross lining the walls. The way to heaven seemed brilliantly clear, and she decided Catholicism would be her redemption.

'In the Catholic church there was clarity, perhaps because the mode of worship was more organised', says Robyn. 'I felt it was closer to what God wanted for me. It was clearer—not who God was but what God required of me. I thought, OK, this is what I have to do to obtain salvation. I knew what was expected of me. It was all part and parcel of what I was seeking out.'

When Robyn announced that she was becoming a Catholic, Bessie and Archibald were aghast; it was 'like becoming a Japanese during World War II'. But as usual when it came to his granddaughter, Archibald relented, and bought her a mantilla of white Spanish lace that cost seven pounds, which she wore to mass each Sunday thereafter with Laurette and her family.

Like everything, Robyn took her new faith in earnest. One day they were visited by a middle-aged aunt, who had divorced, lost custody of her children and suffered a nervous breakdown. Robyn decided she needed deliverance from sin. 'So Laurette and I dressed up as nuns. We got a table-cloth and tied it around my head. I was the Mother Superior, Laurette was the novice. We made her repent. We threw water on her and made her kneel at the end of the bed in Uncle Noel's room for hours.' As for why a grown woman would do the bidding of a couple of pint-sized zealots, 'I could always get people to do what I wanted. I was very intimidating. And I had this thing about pretending—everything had to be real.'

Robyn would continue as a practising Catholic for six years. But beneath her characteristic certitude lay a nagging doubt. 'It was always with a fear that I didn't really belong there and I was afraid for people to know who I really was, because the picture of a good Christian—I didn't fit into. I always felt like I was a fake. That picture was mother, father, children, going to church on Sundays, sitting around the table saying grace—all the things my family didn't do.'

Across the road in Court Street lived another family named the Hanchards, who seemed to Robyn to be everything that her family was not. The father was a supervisor in the furniture department at Loneragan's and instructed the Mudgee Girls Marching Squad, of which his daughter, Annmarie, was a proud member. 'She had reddish hair and freckles and she always had these pretty dresses', Robyn remembers. 'She was the epitome of what a little girl is supposed to be. I was so jealous of her. And they had a car. And she had a father. I think it was just green-eyed jealousy because she had everything.'

The marching girls used to line up in three rows of three, a leader with a whistle at the front, and march in formation around Victoria Park, dressed smartly in red tartan vests and berets, white skirts and shiny white boots. They practised on Mondays and Thursdays after school, and marched in local parades and at the annual agricultural show. It made Robyn's blood boil with envy.

One day when the neighbourhood children were playing in the long grass out the back at Court Street, Robyn smuggled her brother's air rifle out of the house, wrapped in Bessie's best embroidered linen tablecloth.

Her quarry was Annmarie, who was up the back near the shed. Both girls would remember the showdown more than forty years later.

'I do remember her bailing me up in the bloody chook shed', says Annmarie. 'There was bloody thistles, or stinging nettles. I think we'd had a fight over a bike or something. They used to go snake-hunting, that's probably why she had the air rifle. I remember she did have a gun.'

As for her memory of what happened next: 'She said she was going to shoot me'.

Robyn's recollection is crystal clear. 'Right, start marching', she ordered, or words to that effect. The air rifle was pointing at Annmarie; and Robyn's faithful accomplice, Laurette, was by her side.

'We made her march around and around in circles until she fainted. It was 47 degrees. She was petrified.' Robyn insists the air rifle wasn't loaded; the object was simply to terrify her unfortunate neighbour. 'I told her after-wards, "if you tell your mother what we've done I'll come in the middle of the night and shoot your toes off and you'll never do marching again".'

At the age of eleven, Robyn Mary Hutchinson was cock of her little roost; a tenacious tomboy borne of harsh material privation, with a rebel's disdain for conformity, a proud contempt for wealth and privilege, an unyielding clarity about right and wrong, and a deep-seated yearning to find her place in the world.

But now childhood was coming to an end, and with it all the certain-ties of her young life so far. Her long-suffering mother Bessie had finally had enough of old Archibald's overbearing ways. 'My mum always hoped her father would soften towards her, but he never did. At heart she was a country girl and hated the city, but the control my grandfather had over her life was stifling and overwhelming.' Determined to shake off the yoke of her father's domination, Bessie decided to pack up and leave Mudgee, this time forever.

2

WILD CHILD

Sydney, 1965–1972

Before the first rays of dawn illuminated the Cudgegong River valley, Bessie piled the children and their luggage into Auntie Dulce's green FX Holden, and they set off on the twelve-hour drive across the Blue Mountains to Sydney. It was nightfall by the time they arrived at Dulce's house in Lagoon Street, Narrabeen, not far from where Robyn had roamed the bush collecting cicada shells as a toddler. It was only when Bessie announced she had found them their own place that Robyn realised to her dismay that this time they would not be going back to Mudgee.

Their new home was a downstairs flat beneath a house propped like an eyrie on the sandstone cliff top at Harbord on Sydney's northern beaches, overlooking a craggy coastline of pounding surf and yellow sand beaches. Eleven-year-old Robyn counted 127 steps as she clambered up the winding stone pathway from the road to the front door, her heart sinking with each footfall.

'They got me up there and I wouldn't come down', she later remembered. 'Moving from the country back to the city was horrific, it disturbed me greatly. I hated it. I was out of my element, I was like a fish out of water with city kids. It was a terrible time.' The only consolation was that her family finally owned a television, so Robyn could spend hours on end watching her favourite programs, the ones starring animals, such as *Lassie* and *Rin Tin Tin*. 'I became very sad and depressed because we'd left the country. I became a recluse. I stayed home, watched television, ate myself silly and was very, very unhappy.'

For an 11-year-old country girl, Sydney in 1965 was another world. It was the swinging sixties, a time of seismic social and political shifts in Australia. The country was still in the grip of Beatlemania, after the Fab Four's riotous tour downunder the previous year. It was the year that British model Jean Shrimpton scandalised polite society by appearing at Melbourne's Flemington racecourse in a sleeveless mini-dress; 'five inches above the knee, NO hat, NO gloves and NO stockings!' as the *Sun News-Pictorial* gasped. The 19-year prime ministership of Robert Gordon Menzies was coming to an end, and a youthful Harold Holt was about to take the helm. Australia sent its first troops to Vietnam, prompting a corps of neatly frocked middle-class mothers to take to the streets with placards demanding 'Save our Sons', the beginning of a massive anti-war movement.

Bessie got a job in the snack bar at the Harbord Diggers Memorial Club, a popular local institution that advertised 'Modern Go Go Dancing for Teenagers', and boasted a lineup of Saturday night entertainment, which featured 'Myleeni the Belly Dancer from the Latin Quarter', and 'Koko, TV's Educated Monkey'. On big nights they would pull headline acts such as Little Patti with Col Joye and the Joye Boys. For Bessie, it was liberation at last from the social straitjacket of Mudgee. The Diggers had a ladies darts club and a ladies indoor bowling club, although they drew the line at allowing women to play billiards and snooker. Here it didn't matter where your father worked, or whether you were married or divorced. And, as Robyn put it, 'If a woman went to the beer garden for a drink on a Sunday it didn't mean she was the dregs of society'.

Robyn and her little sister Susan were enrolled in the local state school, Harbord Public. To Robyn's embarrassment, she was a year behind her classmates, having had to repeat a year at school in Mudgee due to illness. Although she was older, the city girls were streets ahead of her. 'I was a kid from the country. There was no such thing as fashion where I came from. The girls in the city were already into boyfriends and music, they were much more advanced. I found it repulsive. It was just a different world. I hated city life.'

Her brother George had left school years before to get a job and help his mother support the family. A talented athlete and artist, he had abandoned his hopes for a career as a cartoonist to work as a salesman in a menswear store, according to Robyn. He was now lugging furniture for a firm of removalists on Sydney's north shore.

'My brother was very distant, I always looked up to him, he was seven years older so he was the father figure in my life', Robyn recalls. 'He was always the authority figure. He was very matter of fact, not emotional, quite cold—like my grandfather. He picked up a lot from my grandfather—the importance of stability; the man goes to work, saves money, gets married, buys a house, educates his children.' George would pay Robyn pocket money out of his wage, and withdraw it as punishment when she misbehaved, which was often. 'His approval always meant a lot to me. I wanted him to be pleased with me—but he very rarely got the opportunity to be.'

The baby of the family, Susan, was a placid, happy child, devoted to her older sister. 'She was the opposite to me, she's very good-natured, she hasn't got a bad temper, she takes a long while to get angry', says Robyn. The pair of them would clamber down the rocky cliff face every morning to walk the half a dozen or so blocks to school. On one occasion Robyn put Susan in a plastic bucket attached to a rope and lowered her over the balcony, from where it was a sheer 10-metre drop over jagged rocky outcrops to the bottom.

'Are you sure about this, Robby?' a nervous Susan asked her.

'Don't worry about it, just get in, I know what I'm doing', Robyn assured her.

'I always knew what I was doing', she remarks wryly, remembering the event years later.

By dint of sheer chutzpah and a knack for invention, Robyn devised ways to steal a march on the sassy city girls, and her forceful personality soon commanded a following. She formed her own club at school; by way of initiation, would-be members had to take off their shoes and socks and walk barefoot across a line of scalding-hot metal garbage bin lids in the asphalt playground. Those who joined were obliged to do Robyn's needle-work homework for her, and stand in line at the school canteen to fetch her lunch.

But despite her ingenuity, she often felt she didn't belong—even within her own family. Her brother was tall, stern and well behaved. Her sister was petite and amiable. Only Robyn was short, fat and miserable. She felt like a changeling.

'Mum', she said one day, 'I'm grown up now, I'm mature, so I wanted to ask you …'

Bessie sighed and folded her arms. 'Yes, what is it now, Robyn?'

'Am I adopted?'

Bessie put her head on the side and looked at her tubby twelve year old.

'Robyn, if you'd been adopted I would have given you back years ago.'

Her relationship with her mother was close—by virtue of necessity they shared a room and a bed, just as they had done in Mudgee—but frac-tious. Robyn's argumentative nature exasperated her mother. 'If Jesus Christ were to come back tomorrow, you'd argue with him too', Bessie would exclaim. However, Robyn calculated that it wasn't difficult to get her way. 'I learned very early on that my mother carried an awful lot of guilt—about her divorce, about never having her father's approval, about the fact that we didn't have a father. I learned to manipulate her from a very early age. If I wanted something that wasn't good for me, she would say no. And you couldn't argue with my mum. So I would just sit there and stare into space and get a sad look on my face.'

'What's wrong?' Bessie would ask.

'Oh, nothing', would come the dispirited reply.

'Come on, tell me. What's wrong?'

'I was just thinking about how all the other kids at school have fathers.'

With that, a guilt-ridden Bessie would usually relent and give Robyn whatever it was that she was after. When this failed, Robyn would mutter 'I wish I'd gone to live with my father'. One day Bessie called her bluff. 'If you're so keen to live with your father, I'll arrange it', she announced darkly. In no time she had packed Robyn's port and put her on the train to Wentworth Falls in the Blue Mountains to stay with her father, Jim Hutchinson, who had remarried and was now with his new wife running the bar at the historic Hydro Majestic hotel.

'I thought I'd died and gone to hell', Robyn remembers. 'He was still an alcoholic and he would get drunk every day and scream at his wife.' In bed at night, Robyn would cover her head with pillows to block out the thumping sounds from the kitchen. After two weeks she rang Bessie and begged her to be allowed to come home. After that she didn't mention her father again, and the episode was never discussed.

Robyn's pubescent misery ended when she turned thirteen and the family moved down the hill to a block of flats a short walk from Freshwater Beach, a pristine crescent of sand and sparkling ocean that hails itself as the birthplace of Australian surfing. It was here that the legendary Hawaiian Duke Kahanamoku demonstrated his board-riding prowess on a hand-carved timber plank to thousands of rapt spectators in 1915. The board he fashioned out of local hardwood is still proudly displayed at the Freshwater Surf Club. By the mid 1960s, with the advent of Gidget, the Beach Boys and Midget Farrelly's win in the world championships at Bondi, a new surfing craze was in full swing. 'That's when I discovered boys', says Robyn. 'I sure lost all that weight.'

The teenage crowd practically lived at the beach; the boys surfed, while the girls hung out in the sand dunes talking about boys. Robyn had her first marijuana joint at thirteen, in a shelter shed on the grassy dunes of the Freshwater Beach reserve. On weekends they would clamber through the Wormhole, a tunnel blasted by local fishermen through the rocky headland linking Freshwater with its more up-market neighbour, Manly. Freshwater was traditionally a working man's beach, the site in the 1900s of a men-only camping ground, where workers pitched tents on the weekends to enjoy their time off by the sea. Ladies were allowed only on Sundays. Manly was a more genteel resort, with an amusement park at the wharf featuring a ghost train and ferris wheel, and hordes of tourists drawn by its famous slogan: 'Seven miles from Sydney, 1000 miles from care'.

Robyn attended secondary school at Manly Girls High, whose veteran headmistress Miss Simpson was dedicated to grooming virtuous young ladies, regardless of their socio-economic pedigree. The uniform was a pressed fawn pinafore with matching tie, gloves and boater hat. Prefects were stationed at the school gates to impose detention on girls who failed to wear the correct shade of fawn socks. Robyn preferred white: 'Hence, I was always in detention'.

At the weekly assembly, the girls would stand to attention to sing the school anthem, whose lofty morality reflected Miss Simpson's vaulting aspirations for her pupils.

Truth the rock that man must build on
Truth the sword with which we fight
Wisdom gained by patient learning
Turns on truth its radiant light.

Beauty in our thoughts and actions
Beauty in the sky above
And the Glory of the sunlight
Lets us glimpse God's perfect love.

Robyn's strong will and audacity marked her out as a leader among the girls. A former school friend, Deborah Jensen, remembers her as extroverted and charismatic. 'She was an unreal girl, so much fun to be around. She was awesome—very funny, very articulate, she made you laugh.' Deborah says Robyn 'always had a desire to be in the spotlight' and that she liked to 'play roles'. 'She was just a full-on character, she was a wild child.'

On one occasion, while Robyn and Deborah were waiting outside the deputy headmistress's office to be punished for some misdemeanour, Robyn suggested a contest to see who could spit from the farthest distance on the young Queen Elizabeth, who gazed serenely from a framed portrait on the wall. Robyn spat first, as Deborah recalls: 'She did it deliberately to break me up. I do remember it hitting the wall and this big globule dribbling down the wall. And that was the end of me—I was just hysterical; and panicking—because the deputy headmistress was about to come around the corner.' Robyn's version has the headmistress appearing just in time to find a gob of saliva trickling down Her Majesty's face, as a result of which another spell in detention followed.

'I had a very strong personality and I had the ability to get the girls to co-operate with me', says Robyn. 'I don't want to use the word bully, I wasn't really a bully.' Some of her former classmates might disagree; by her own account, she could be tough and intimidating. There was one girl she used to pick on by making her wear her glasses upside down, for no particular reason except 'because I was wicked, because I could'.

Among the teaching staff, Robyn gained a name for herself as a gregarious student who questioned everything and insisted on saying exactly what she thought. She was also known as a ringleader and troublemaker. 'I was always very opinionated', she recalls. 'I wasn't rude or abusive or violent, I was just non co-operative. The deputy principal absolutely detested me, because I was so disruptive.'

She claims her disruptive conduct was often a reaction to some perceived injustice. 'If something happened in class and I deemed it unfair or unjust—that was the end of it; and then I would get other people onto the cause. There was no such thing as "it's not my business" or "I don't want to get in trouble".'

There was a male teacher, Mr Mallard (not his real name), who would sometimes touch the girls inappropriately, according to Robyn. She says she reported him but nothing was done. Mr Mallard's classes were riotous affairs. Picking Robyn out as a leader, he sought her assistance to get the girls under control.

'If you can get the girls in my class to co-operate, I'll let you sit wherever you want.'

'I already sit wherever I want', she responded.

One day Robyn brought a bottle of dishwashing detergent from home and filled up all the disused inkwells in the girls' wooden desks with soapy pink liquid, then instructed her classmates to take the innards out of their ballpoint pens, thus arming themselves with empty plastic tubes, like pea-shooters. When Mr Mallard turned his back to the class and began writing on the blackboard, the twenty-five girls took their cue from Robyn and began blowing bubbles through their pen tubes into the air. The classroom was soon full of inky pink bubbles that exploded when they landed.

Turning back to the classroom, Mr Mallard exclaimed in alarm.

'Where are all these bubbles coming from?'

'Bubbles, sir? What bubbles?' the girls chorused.

Mr Mallard was so rattled he was unable to finish the lesson, by Robyn's account.

Academically, she was an erratic achiever who could succeed or fail depending on the subject and the teacher. Only later she discovered she suffered from dyslexia, an affliction somewhat offset by a near photographic memory. 'My attitude was—and I really regret it now—that if I liked a subject and respected the teacher, I would excel. But if I didn't I wouldn't go to classes.' She claims she could have been a 'straight As' student, except that 'I was always in trouble, always being sent out of class. I spent more time in the assembly hall on detention than in the classroom.' Like the matron at the Far West Children's Home, the headmistress, Miss Simpson, could see the girl had potential. 'You have the ability to do so much', she scolded Robyn. 'Yet you cut off your nose to spite your face.'

Her little sister Susan would spend her own school years living down her older sibling's notoriety. 'Oh, so you're Robyn Hutchinson's sister, are you?' the teachers would ask her. 'She always felt like going "No, no! I'm not like her!"' Robyn recalls.

Robyn's school years ended when she dropped out two years short of completing high school, at the age of fifteen. Failing mathematics put paid to her ambition for a career in medicine; she would later enrol in night school to study for her Higher School Certificate in the hope of becoming a nurse. After leaving school she settled for the nearest thing she could find—a job as an assistant in a pharmacy in Manly. Her favourite task was helping in the dispensary, but she was often admonished for her lack of tact as a saleswoman: on one occasion she advised an elderly lady who was browsing among the anti-wrinkle creams not to bother, because it was like 'shutting the barn door after the horse has bolted'.

On weekends, Robyn and her friends would don the latest psychedelic fashions and persuade their parents to allow them to attend 'The Harbord Bop', a Saturday night dance at the local civic centre. The new craze among the beach crowd was 'the Stomp', which involved literally stamping around the dance floor to tunes such as Little Patti's hit 'He's My Blonde-headed Stompie Wompie Real Gone Surfer Boy'. Robyn was extremely popular among the local boys. 'All the boys loved her', says her friend Deborah Jensen, who recalls Robyn's young admirers painting her nickname 'Hutchy' in 2-metre letters in the driveway of the block of flats where her family lived. At one of the Saturday night dances, Robyn met an up and coming young surfing champion named Ian Goodacre, who didn't dance but walked her home afterwards. Later he invited her to a Christmas party at the factory where he was apprenticed as a silk-screen printer. It was the beginning of a romance that lasted almost three years.

'She was great, she was a really nice person', Ian Goodacre remembers. But headstrong and argumentative as well: 'We did have our moments, we used to fight a bit', he also recalls. Ian's family lived in a neat Edwardian bungalow with a picket fence on Pittwater Road, just up from the Manly Fisherman's Club. His father Jim was a bus driver who had worked for the same company for twenty-five years and drank liquor only on Christmas Day, when he indulged in a single beer. His mother Beryl, a favourite among the surfing crowd, worked at the hamburger joint at Queenscliff Beach.

'It was his family I loved', says Robyn. 'I loved the stability and the decency and the loyalty towards one another, and the caring—all the things I didn't have as a child.' Their house became Robyn's second home. The pair of them would spend hours on Ian's timber verandah printing t-shirts with elaborate silk-screen designs featuring surf scenes and pithy slogans like 'You are a Child of the Universe' from the poems of Khalil Gibran. When Ian went away on surfing trips, Robyn would sometimes stay with his parents and curl up on the couch with them, watching television. 'They treated her like their own daughter', remembers another friend. Robyn called them 'mum' and 'dad'.

Her own home life had grown increasingly turbulent. Bessie had hooked up with a builder's labourer named Fred, another chronic alcoholic with a mean streak. 'Fred was a bit of a nasty type', says Ian Goodacre. 'So she had no stable "father thing" happening. I think she was looking for that stability that she lacked.' Ian would sometimes confuse Fred's name with that of Robyn's beagle, Jack. 'No, Fred is the two-legged dog and Jack is the four-legged dog', Robyn would point out. Bessie spent much of her time playing the poker machines at the Diggers Club, when she wasn't at home drinking with Fred. 'I hated drinking, I hated it', Robyn vehemently recalls.

Around this time, her grandfather, Archibald Roy McCallum, died in the tuberculosis ward of the Manly Hospital from lung cancer, aged seventy-six. Although she had seen little of him in the four years since they had left Mudgee, the death of her beloved 'farvie' was a blow. She was with Ian at a surfing contest in Newcastle when he died, and returned to Mudgee for his funeral at St Paul's Presbyterian Church. 'I remember looking at the coffin and thinking how small it was. I always thought he was so big.' He was buried in the Mudgee cemetery next to the grave that held his wife Lurline and Bessie's baby son, Wayne. There was a final bitter sting for Bessie in the old man's death. In his will he left one hundred dollars for Robyn, nothing for Bessie or anyone else in the family, and the rest to the family with whom he had boarded in Mudgee.

But for Robyn these were heady days, and there was little time for mourning. Ian had won the junior trophy in the New South Wales schoolboys' surfing titles, and was a minor celebrity on the surf scene. They travelled around the country to surfing contests on the Queensland Gold Coast and at Victoria's famed Bells Beach. The Beatles' psychedelic anthem 'Lucy in the sky with diamonds' was in the charts and many in the surf crowd were doing drugs, mostly marijuana, hashish and LSD, though a few later graduated to heroin. Robyn and Ian holidayed in Byron Bay where they picked magic mushrooms in a paddock and cooked up a hallucinogenic omelette. There were constant parties, tickets to rock musicals such as *Hair* and *Jesus Christ Superstar*, and concerts with bands such as Daddy Cool and Billy Thorpe and the Aztecs. The former Mudgee girl basked in her share of the limelight. 'I never understood how I ended up in the "in crowd". I was the beach bunny of this surfing idol. You'd walk down the street and people would say, "there goes so-and-so's girlfriend".' Looking back later as a devout Muslim, these memories would seem surreal. 'When I talk about these things it's almost like I'm talking about a different person.'

A friend from those days, surfer turned journalist Steve Warnock, remembers Robyn as a fixture on the scene, a happy extrovert who was always up for a party. 'She smoked dope, she drank alcohol, she knew how to party and kick on. She was always a friendly, outgoing person. She was very easy to get along with—she was a good person.' Warnock says Robyn was well known and liked in her own right, not just as Ian's girlfriend. 'She had a strong personality, she wasn't a weak person, that's for sure. She picked her own man when she wanted to. She wasn't afraid to pick a guy. And she'd stick up for herself, she wasn't afraid to have a fight. She was a bit of a street fighter, Robyn.' Not physically, Warnock hastens to add; she was too small for brawling. 'She wasn't a spitfire, but she was proud. She had confidence, and she was strong.' Warnock says she seemed 'very honest and open', but never let on how harsh a background she had come from.

Warnock also recalls that 'Goody' and 'Rob' stood out as one of few steady couples in a fraternity where romantic entanglements tended to unravel quickly. For all her temerity, Robyn's most deeply held wish was to marry and settle down, although it would not have been the done thing to admit it at the time. 'When I think back, I was never ever happy or satisfied with the "sex, drugs and rock 'n' roll" life. The majority of girls I knew really just wanted to get married, although they didn't say it openly; it wasn't politically correct.' At seventeen, Robyn naively believed she had found her future with her teenage sweetheart. 'I thought we'd get married and have children, and all be one big happy family.'

Her own domestic circumstances were anything but the 'big happy family' she craved. Robyn rarely saw her own father, Jim Hutchinson, after he caught her smoking marijuana at the age of sixteen during a visit, according to her half-brother, Roderick. 'Their relationship was distant, frosty to the point of—he disowned her when she got into the drug scene', Roderick recalls.

Meanwhile life at home with Bessie and Fred was becoming unbearable. Robyn and Bessie argued constantly, and she couldn't bear her nasty drunkard of a stepfather. Their alcohol-fuelled domestic chaos inflamed her own volatile temper. She recalls that as a teenager she was 'always throwing things'. One night she came home around 2 a.m. to find her mother and Fred in a heavy drinking session with 'some other loser' and arguing loudly. She retreated to the bedroom she shared with Susan, to find her little sister awake and crying in bed. She went back out to confront the trio in the lounge room.

'It's time you went to bed', she announced.

'Have some respect for your mother', the visitor snarled, taking Robyn by the arm.

Robyn recounts that she shook her arm free and punched the man in the jaw, then threw a chair after him as he staggered from the room. As Fred stumbled out the door, she picked up a can opener and hurled it, piercing his neck with the metal spike. Fortunately no one called the police, or Robyn might have found herself the one being arrested.

In her mid teens, Robyn moved out of home and into a dilapidated share house in Manly with a crowd of surfie friends who lived in a haze of dope smoke and on a diet consisting largely of lentils and tequila. They all believed the house was haunted, because it was rumoured someone had committed suicide upstairs. After each night of partying they would line the empty liquor bottles up along the picture rail, only to come out in the morning to find them all neatly laid out on the floor. Bessie was mortified that Robyn had left, and would ring and leave tearful messages, begging her to come home. As Bessie herself had been with her own mother, Robyn was torn between loyalty to her parent and the urge to break free.

In answer to Bessie's entreaties, she would usually relent and return home, only to move out again a few weeks later.

Throughout her tumultuous teen years, the Catholic Church provided one comforting constant in Robyn's life. Every Sunday, after a morning at the beach, she would towel off and stroll to St Mary's at Manly to attend afternoon mass. Among the teenage surf crowd this was decidedly not 'cool', but Robyn was not the kind of girl people made fun of, at least not within earshot.

But as she grew older the dogma of Catholicism no longer rang true. 'I had a very analytical mind and there were things that just didn't make sense, like the Holy Trinity.' How could God be three beings at once—the father, son and holy spirit? It simply didn't make sense, 'because I'm a very practical person, and things have to be real, and three into one doesn't go'. She used to wonder, if Jesus was God, who was he calling out to when he was on the cross—'Oh Father, Father, why hast thou forsaken me?' 'Who was he speaking to? If he was talking to himself, why did he need to scream out? Wouldn't he already know what he was thinking?' It troubled her that the statues which were supposed to represent divinities were always different—sometimes Jesus would have blue eyes, sometimes brown; apart from which, it seemed pointless genuflecting before a painted concrete idol. She was deeply disillusioned by the sweeping changes that followed the Second Vatican Council in the 1960s. 'Suddenly you could eat meat on Fridays, and it was not necessary to cover your head in church. Before we'd been told we would go to purgatory, that it was a major sin to enter a church with your head uncovered. It started to bother me. I thought, so what about all those people who did it when it wasn't allowed, and they're now in purgatory? Those things were devastating to me.'

Later, when she became a Muslim, the belief that God's laws are immutable would become an article of faith. 'I think non-Muslims don't understand this. It's absolutely impossible for Muslims to entertain or contemplate the idea of changing Allah's laws—because they are Allah's laws.'

In the Catholic Church, she found that answers to her questions were never forthcoming. 'When you asked those questions, you were told "It's a matter of faith. If you don't believe, you're not a Christian". And when I was told "It's just faith, you don't have to understand it, you just have to believe it", I couldn't accept that. That's when the church and me parted ways.'

Robyn was still sure there was a God, but she now knew the Catholic Church was not where she was going to find Him. 'At seventeen I said, "I believe in God, but I can't accept a system that's going to regulate my life when I'm not expected to understand it". And it was not only the fact that you didn't understand, but there was no necessity for you to understand. The view was, "You don't need to know, and that's the test of faith". So I said, "Well, God, I know you exist, but unless you show me what you want from me, I can't be blamed for not worshipping you".'

At eighteen, Robyn was heartbroken when her romance with Ian Goodacre came to a tempestuous end. 'We used to fight a bit, that's what split us up', says Ian. 'She was going through a difficult time. It was a bit of a rough passage. She was a nice person, she was looking for something to cling onto. It comes back to that family thing. I could see she had a good core, a good base, and she was reaching out for something. But for me, just being young and into surfing all the time, I didn't want that responsibility.'

'I was devastated', Robyn recalls. She had lost not only her first love, but her place in a stable loving family who had treated her like one of their own. A friend remembers she seemed most shattered at losing the adoptive parents whom she had called mum and dad. After the breakup she was admitted to a private clinic on Sydney's north shore where she was treated for depression for several weeks. Ian describes it as 'a bit of a mental breakdown'. Robyn says, 'I don't know if it was really a breakdown, I think I was trying to get him back. I like to get my own way, and when I didn't, that depressed me.' Their split would have an enduring impact. 'After my relationship with Ian when I'd thought we'd get married and have children and all be one big happy family, and it didn't happen like that, my whole concept of love and marriage and children changed. I lost my illusions about a Cinderella Hollywood fairytale kind of love.'

Never one for moping, Robyn set herself a new mission—to travel the world. It was the early 1970s and young Australians were hefting backpacks and setting off around the globe, to South-East Asia, India and Europe. A local surfboard maker had been to Bali and reported back that it was 'a magical tropical island where they sold magic mushrooms and hash cookies in the restaurants', Robyn recalls. She and two girlfriends decided to travel first to Bali and then hit the hippy trail, making their way across Asia and north through India, then on to Europe and London.

With her usual fixity of purpose, Robyn threw herself into the task, taking on three jobs to save for the trip. She worked mornings at the pharmacy in Manly, afternoons at an electronics factory in Dee Why, and nights as a barmaid at Manly's Steyne hotel, a riotous drinking barn with beer-soaked carpets whose doors would overflow with brawling vomiting drunks every Friday and Saturday night.

After abandoning Catholicism, she continued to explore the meaning of life and the nature of God, a popular pastime in the 1970s. She became a vegetarian, took up causes such as animal rights, and later joined in protests against the Vietnam War. 'I always had a mission, like Save the Pigeons on the Corso, or Save the Koalas, or Save the Gum Trees', she says. She was briefly intrigued by the 1968 cult hit *Chariots of the Gods*, which hypothesised that ancient religions and technologies were delivered by space travellers who were welcomed on Earth as gods. She was always game for an adventure. Once she and two girlfriends hitchhiked to Adelaide to try a pie-floater (a meat pie served upside down in a bowl of mushy green peas with tomato sauce), which they had heard about but thought sounded too disgusting to be real. Her friends ended up leaving her beside the highway on the Nullarbor Plain because she refused to get on a truck carrying live sheep, objecting to their inhumane treatment.

'She was quite a character', says another friend from this era, Lynn Collins. 'She was kind of a bit hippy-ish, a little bit "out there".' When Lynn gave birth to her first child, Robyn came to visit her at Manly Hospital, apologising that she had knitted a bonnet for the baby but had to leave it at home because she'd spilt lentils on it. 'I remember her being quite funny. She had a great sense of humour. She was very outspoken, and strong—she was a strong girl, she knew what she wanted.'

Looking back on this period, Robyn would later see her 'hippy days' as a transitory phase. Beneath the bohemian exterior lay a deeply old-fashioned girl who shared the abstemious morality of her mother and grandfather. 'I grew up in the days of Germaine Greer—burn your bra, women taking over the world. But I laugh when people say I was a hippy. No way I could have been a hippy—I was too clean, and I didn't even really like smoking dope. I don't like to lose control—chemically, socially, politically, or any other way. I did it because everybody else was doing it.'

At this stage, the thought of becoming a Muslim could not have been further from her mind. 'Before I went to Indonesia I didn't know anything about Islam, except that men can have as many wives as they want and women have no rights. So I disliked it intensely.'

Robyn's travel plans were expedited when her mother Bessie enjoyed a long-awaited change of luck, winning $16 000 in a lottery, a small fortune in those days. Her partner Fred had treated himself to a new car, and the rest was fast being squandered on alcohol and the pokies, so Robyn decided a donation to her travel fund would be a good cause.

'I need some money—and if you don't give it to me, I'll just have to sell drugs to get it', she announced to her mother. She says she had no real intention of dealing in drugs, but 'knew which buttons to press'. Bessie gave her $1500, enough to facilitate an immediate departure. Robyn's friends were still saving and asked her to wait for them, but her patience had run out and she told them she would meet them in London.

She was unusually apprehensive as she prepared to embark on her travels. 'I was absolutely paranoid. I had never been out of the country. The only time I had ever flown was on a Fokker Friendship from Sydney to Mudgee when I went back to spend the school holidays with Laurette.' Her own attack of nerves paled compared with Bessie's dread of what might happen to her daughter in remote Bali. 'Mum thought they were still cannibals and they would probably eat me. My mother was paralysed with fear. She never flew in her life. She used to say, "If God had meant us to fly he would have given us wings".'

However, Robyn had little time for any of her mother's advice as they bade one another farewell. She had long since sworn not to follow Bessie's path in life. 'I used to say to my mother, "I'll never make the mistakes you made". I had visions of getting a university degree, being happily married, having a profession.' Never in her strangest dreams could she have imagined how different from that idyllic vision her future would be.

3

GOD IS GREAT

Indonesia, 1972–1974

The 'island of the Gods' appeared through the window of the Qantas jumbo like a postcard picture of emerald rice terraces, volcanic peaks swathed in jungle, and white sand beaches shimmering in an azure sea.

In the early 1970s, Denpasar airport consisted of a strip of baking tarmac and a shed. The first thing that struck Robyn as she stepped off the aircraft was a wall of tropical heat so thick she felt faint. The next was the cacophony from a swarm of hotel touts and *bemo* drivers that descended like locusts on the sweaty backpackers crowded around the luggage carousel. 'You want taxi? Cheap hotel? My friend give you special price!'

Bali was still largely untouched by mass tourism. The palm trees were taller than the buildings, and much of the island had no electricity. Women worked bare-breasted in the rice paddies and cock-fighting was the most popular form of amusement. Travellers stayed in family guesthouses known as *losmens*, built around courtyards lush with banyan trees and the scent of frangipani, and featuring carved stone statues of Hindu deities to whom the residents made daily offerings of sticky rice, flowers, incense and Balinese coins, to honour the good spirits and appease the bad.

'It was surreal', Robyn remembers. 'You could sleep with your door open. You never paid for food—they would write it on a board for weeks, and you would pay later. Ceremonial dances were done in the open fields, not for the tourists, but as part of religious ceremonies. Balinese women didn't cut their hair in those days. And there was no such thing as prostitutes.'

For three months Robyn became one of the resident crowd of backpackers, hippies and itinerant surfers for whom Bali was a home away from home. They spent long days at the beach or lounging in bamboo chairs on the verandahs of their *losmens*, playing chess, swapping remedies for Bali belly, drinking Bintang beer and passing around marijuana joints. In the evenings they hung out at Mama's café, which was popular for its mountainous smorgasbords, and The Garden restaurant, famed for its 400-rupiah 'special' omelettes and pizzas, whose not-so-secret ingredient was Bali's famously psychotropic mushrooms. As the law decreed the death sentence for narcotic drug use, the specials didn't appear on the menu; you had to know what to order. Robyn recalls that one night a pair of elderly British tourists came in, apparently clueless about the local specialties, and told the waitress, 'we'll have what everybody else is having'. They ended up in such a stupor they had to be taken to hospital.

In Bali, Robyn discovered a talent that had eluded her during her interminable French classes at high school—a knack for languages. She picked up Balinese easily, and became sufficiently fluent to be called upon by her fellow travellers in minor emergencies as a translator. On one occasion she was summoned to a *losmen* where some Australian surfers were staying, to explain to them that the square concrete tank in the courtyard was the family's water supply, used for cooking, washing and cleaning their teeth, and was not intended to be used as a bath. Some callow youth had simply climbed in and begun lathering up with soap, and when Robyn arrived the distraught owner was crying 'He put his bum in it!'

It sounded like another planet to Bessie when Robyn rang home from the Kuta telephone exchange.

'How are you, darling? How's the food?'

'I'm great, Mum, and I'm eating like a horse.'

'Oh my God, she's eating horse!' she heard Bessie exclaim.

Robyn was intrigued by Bali's intense spirituality and the exotic rituals of its Hindu faith. The final bastion of the great Majapahit Hindu dynasty, which crumbled in Java in the fifteenth century as Islam spread across the archipelago, Bali retained a vibrant Hindu culture, overlaid with its own plethora of indigenous spirits and gods. There were temples by the thousands, and shrines in every rice paddy and family courtyard. Once a year during the Nyepi festival, villagers would parade through the streets hoisting a huge monster doll called the *ogoh-ogoh*, which was chased by a mob with flaming torches and finally incinerated in a mighty bonfire to purge its evil spirit.

For a country girl from Mudgee, it was all intoxicatingly picturesque. Many who followed the hippy trail would embrace the Hindu culture, returning home wearing nose studs, saris and bindis on their foreheads. But to Robyn the animistic rites and pantheon of gods—including Hinduism's own trinity of Brahma, Shiva and Vishnu—were exotic, but made no sense. 'I was never attracted to Hinduism, because it's totally illogical', she says. 'If a woman doesn't produce children in this life she comes back reincarnated as a cockroach or something. And they beat up on dogs because they're believed to be an incarnation of someone or other. And the gods—some of them are elephants with lots of hands. I wanted to know all the ins and outs, and to know the Balinese people as much as humanly possible as an outsider. But I was never interested in it as an alternative religion.'

As for Islam, what little she had seen of it at this stage had done nothing to quell her distaste. 'I hated Islam. I had watched *1001 Nights* and *Ali Baba*, and I thought Islam was a religion where a man could have as many wives as he wanted to and they had absolutely no rights. It was never a religion I thought of looking into.'

After three months in Bali, Robyn was ready to move on. Her plan was to travel overland across Java to Jakarta, then fly to India en route to London. The next stop on the backpacker route was the Javanese city of Jogjakarta, renowned for its ancient walled citadel housing the sultan's palace, the *kraton*, guarded by giant carved dragons and sacred banyan trees, where in feudal times white-robed petitioners would await an audience with the king. At a cockroach-infested *losmen* in Jogja, she met a Frenchman called Thomas who was working as an English teacher in Jakarta. He told her it was easy to get a job; there was such a thirst to learn

English that they were employing virtually anyone who was a native speaker. It seemed like an easy way to replenish her travel funds, so Robyn travelled with him by train to Jakarta to try her luck.

They arrived in the capital after nightfall, and Thomas took Robyn to stay at the home of a journalist friend in the upmarket residential suburb of Kebayoran Baru. Drained after the eight-hour train trip, she fell into bed, oblivious of the mosque next door.

'I went to bed in a spare room, not knowing that the loudspeaker of the mosque was directly above my window', she recounts. 'So at four o'clock in the morning I was sound asleep and the *azan* (call to prayer) went off. I was so petrified I literally levitated off the bed. I thought it was World War III.'

'What's going on?' she yelled, stumbling out of bed.

'Don't worry, it's just the Muslims going to pray', her host called back.

'Who do they think they are?' she snapped. 'They don't have to wake the whole world up. It's so inconsiderate.' The racket only confirmed her distaste for Islam.

The next morning, to her annoyance, she was startled awake again before sunrise by the call to prayer. On the third morning she woke early, just as the *muezzin* was climbing the minaret to begin the *azan*.

'I was lying in bed and I started to listen to it, and it was incredibly beautiful', she recalls. This time she heard the intricate pattern of the melodious chanting with its rhythmic pauses, repetition of phrases and haunting tone.

Allahu Akbar, Allahu Akbar
Ash-hadu alla ilaha illallah
Ash-hadu anna Muhammadar rasulullah
Hayya alas-salat

God is great
I bear witness that there is no God except Allah
I bear witness that Mohammed is Allah's messenger
Hasten to the prayer

As she lay listening in the pre-dawn light, her contempt for Islam turned to curiosity. 'I can remember after that asking more about it', she says. It would prove to be a profound awakening.

Through Thomas, Robyn got a job with Intensive English Course (IEC), a language institute established in the 1960s, which would eventually grow into a conglomerate with fifty branches across Indonesia. Headquartered in east Jakarta, the school provided lodging for foreign staff in the quarters occupied by the owner and his family. Robyn was allotted a room to share with the director's daughter and niece. Just as Thomas had promised, her own lack of schooling was no obstacle. 'They were employing anybody and everybody, as long as you were white and you could speak English.' She was given a book called 'English 500' and told to simply follow the instructions. When a student asked a question about grammatical structure that she couldn't answer, she would reply knowledgeably, 'Oh, you're talking about *American* English. I only speak *British* English.' Her characteristic certitude made up for her lack of qualifications. 'I had a cultural arrogance, I thought I knew more than they did, that what I knew was right and they should learn from me. And that anything I did was better than them.'

Among the students in her classes were three army officers who told her they had been enrolled for a crash course in English before being sent to Egypt to be trained in controlling political unrest. It was seven years after General Suharto had seized power amidst a storm of political turmoil that culminated in vicious anti-Communist massacres across the country, sparked by accusations of Communist complicity in a failed coup. After years of bloody foment, Suharto's takeover and the resulting restoration of order and stability had been widely welcomed. But the initial relief at his ascendance was now giving way to rising discord over the endemic corruption and nepotism of his New Order regime. In late 1973, resentment over economic inequality erupted in the form of anti-Chinese riots in the hill town of Bandung, West Java, in which looters trashed hundreds of shops and houses. The unrest would soon spill over onto the streets of the capital.

But at this stage Indonesian politics was of little concern to Robyn. One night a few weeks after arriving in Jakarta, she was out at a city discotheque with a British friend from IEC. The Tanamur disco in the nightclub district of Tanah Abang was a favorite haunt of working expatriates and Indonesia's brat-pack, the spoiled sons and daughters of the military and political elite. Among the crowd that night was a young man named Malik Sjafei, whose father was a former military doctor and Health Minister in the Sukarno Government before Suharto took power. Malik was nineteen years old, the same age as Robyn, and just as outgoing.

'I just saw a *bule* (white person) in the disco, she was one of the foreigners', Malik remembers. He asked her to dance—'we were flirting a little bit'—and then introduced her to his companions. Malik's friends were the children of Indonesian businessmen, politicians and serving army brass. Some of them were at university, while others like Malik, who had just finished high school, were too busy studying the nocturnal goings-on at their regular hangout, the Tanamur. 'We used to call it school because we go there every day—it was like going to school', Malik recounts. (He would eventually attend university at Bandung and graduate with a degree in communications.) Another member of their group was a girl named Liliek Soemarlono, the vivacious daughter of an army captain who was in her first year at the University of Indonesia studying English literature. Robyn and 'Lili', as her friends called her, hit it off immediately.

Three decades later and now living in Australia, Lili remembers Robyn fondly. 'She had a good heart, she was very nice, a lovely kind of person. She's very gentle. I was attracted to her gentleness. She was very kind and caring. And she likes good times, and she's not boring. She's lovely—but she's not boring. You can find a lot of lovely people who are boring—but she's not boring.'

For their own amusement, Malik and his friends had launched a pirate radio station, which they set up in one of their bedrooms, using fifty watts of power, a turntable and one microphone. 'It was felt that the gang needed an identity as radio broadcasters', they later explained. They called it Prambors FM, an acronym derived from the streets in which they lived in Jakarta's upscale Menteng district, which were all named after temples. The station was illegal at the time, but they were able to secure a licence thanks to their fathers' influence and the patronage of the Governor of Jakarta, Ali Sadikin, who lived in a mansion in Borobodur Street just down from Malik's house. Prambors was an instant sensation among Jakarta's entertainment-starved youth. Its formula was a mix of the latest Western rock 'n' roll and Indo-pop hits, interspersed with edgy and irreverent commentary from its enthusiastic band of student DJs. They ran a weekly music request segment, pioneered talkback radio and launched a panel chat show called 'Warkopi', short for *warung kopi*, meaning coffee shop. Prambors FM would become the most successful youth radio station in Jakarta, with Malik Sjafei eventually appointed as its CEO.

Malik and Lili invited Robyn to come with them the next day to see their setup, which by this time had moved into its own small studio in Menteng. The privileged rich kids of Prambors became Robyn's new best friends.

'It was like the surfing scene, except it was very much upper class', she recalls. 'They were the cream of the crop. They used to drive around in their fathers' jeeps, or sometimes their fathers' army drivers would drive us around. They paid cash for everything, I got to be in the in-crowd because I was white. I was the only white person. They always treated me as though I was as rich as them—they assumed all foreigners were rich.'

Lili and Robyn became constant companions. 'We were very close together', says Lili. 'I still feel very warm towards her—it was a short time, but very meaningful.' Robyn taught Malik to speak English—'just flirting English', in his words. 'She was fun. She's like every teenager, no responsibility, just like water—going with the flow.' They spent most nights at the Tanamur, often till 4 or 5 a.m., dancing to the latest disco hits by The Jackson Five and Kool & the Gang. They attended functions like the eighteenth birthday party of the governor's son, held in his mansion in Jalan Borobodur, which was shielded from the street by a small rainforest and boasted an indoor Japanese garden complete with bridges and babbling streams. 'I just used to gape, but they thought that sort of thing was normal', says Robyn. They smoked cigarettes and shared marijuana joints with the staff of the US embassy with whom they socialised. Lili recalls a night when 'some of the guys' in their crowd put LSD in her tea as a joke. She says Robyn took care of her and made sure she got home safely. Lili describes Robyn as fun-loving but practical and responsible.

'She's probably "wild" as in being adventurous, but she's not "wild wild". She's the kind of person who'd got her life together. She wasn't a "hippy hippy" type. She's clean, she's got her finances together, she just had her life together.' Lili says Robyn never talked about her previous life, but she could tell her new friend was searching for something, just as Lili was herself. 'She probably wasn't happy with something. Me, I always wanted to live outside Indonesia—looking for something else. That's what she was like too.' She got the impression that Robyn was eager to make a new life, and wanted to really 'belong' in Indonesia. 'She was very open to Indonesians. She was willing to adapt to the new place she was in.'

The Prambors crowd were not political activists by any means. Aware that their broadcasts were monitored by the authorities, they steered well clear of politics except for the odd foray into oblique satirical commentary on issues such as corruption. 'We were not political; sometimes we were critical of government policies and action, but it had to be very, very soft, because in the Suharto era there is no critic', says Malik. Robyn recalls the introduction of a new regulation that limited the number of people who could assemble at the station at any given time, lest they gather to plot political intrigue; after that, if more than five of them wanted to meet, they had to sneak in.

'Everything in Indonesia was considered subversive. Never mind freedom of speech—freedom of thought was not allowed. Was it subversive? Yes and no. They were uni students, so they were the thinkers of society, but they weren't allowed to think. There was no such thing as criticising Suharto. They were afraid to.' The anti-Communist massacres in which hundreds of thousands of people had been slaughtered were still vivid in the national psyche, and the authorities constantly revived the menace of Communism as a curb on dissent. 'You didn't talk openly about anything, because there was a fear that expressing any dissatisfaction was seen as treason, and the only people who would do that were Communists.'

But even for the rich kids of Prambors, the discontent seething beneath the surface of Indonesia's body politic was becoming too blatant to be ignored. One weekend Robyn and her friends made a trip to the hill town of Bandung, the scene of riots targeting Indonesia's affluent Chinese merchant class. When they returned to Jakarta late in the evening, protesters were burning cars in the streets and a curfew was in place. Lili, whose brother had joined the rioters, remembers that she and Robyn had to sleep at the bus station for the night because it was too dangerous to make their way home.

Despite the growing political discord, after six months in Indonesia the country had got under Robyn's skin, and she felt an overwhelming urge to stay. 'I felt drawn to the Javanese people, in a way that I didn't feel in Bali. I admired them for their hospitality and their politeness and their ability to forego individual desires for the good of the group. It was something you didn't see in Western society. They genuinely cared about each other. And their concept of extended family—I liked it and wanted to be part of it.'

The values that seemed important to the Indonesians were reminiscent of many of those instilled in her from childhood by her mother and grandfather, such as the importance of family, modesty, respect and personal discipline. But in contrast to her Sunday school days in Mudgee, here it seemed that the people lived what they preached. And the more she saw of this, the more she believed—to her surprise—that their religion was at the heart of what she most admired. Her friends from Prambors, although mostly Muslims, were hardly devout; they drank liquor and forgot to pray, and some of them were reformed drug addicts. But Robyn noticed that the ones who did pray and spurned alcohol were treated with a special regard. And the fabric of the broader society appeared to be woven together by its faith.

'I thought religion had influenced Indonesia's character; I thought they got it from religion. I saw things in Muslims that I didn't see in the Hindu Balinese—respect for women, personal hygiene, respect for the mother. I also saw things my mother had taught me to respect which, in our society, some of them had disappeared. I was drawn by the honesty and modesty, by their consideration and kindness to each other, their politeness and calmness. I saw a people who had characteristics that I recognised and I wanted to be a part of a society that held those principles. And through doing that I found out that the reason for it was Islam. I had thought it was the Javanese people I was drawn to—but it was actually Islam.'

She found herself entranced by the simple rituals of the faith she had previously derided. 'I noticed that people would carry a prayer mat over their shoulder. And when the *azan* sounded, the women would put on a white skirt and scarf—they were beautifully embroidered, very ornate. And when you watched them stand in line and move in unison, it did something to your heart.'

She bought a prayer mat herself and learned to perform *wudu*, the ceremonial washing of the face and hands and wiping of the head and feet done by Muslims before prayer, although she didn't know yet how to perform the ritual *salat*, or daily prayers. 'I used to do *wudu* and then sit on my mat, I just wanted to be part of what was going on.'

As she began to delve into Islam, she was struck first by its simplicity, embodied in the 'five pillars' that Muslims must observe: uttering the *shahadah*, or profession of faith, which states that there is only one God and Mohammed is his messenger; praying five times a day; fasting during Ramadan; paying *zakat*, or charity for the poor; and making the *haj* pilgrimage to Mecca at least once in a lifetime. She liked the lack of inexplicable mysteries like the Holy Trinity, which depicted God as three beings. Compared with Catholicism, she found it all so clear—it all made sense. 'When I was a Catholic, I couldn't get my mind and heart to correspond. But in Islam there was never anything I couldn't reconcile. In Islam I have never found anything where the heart and mind don't correspond.'

One day the television was on and an elderly man was speaking. Her Indonesian was still patchy but she was mesmerised by his tone of speech and charisma. The speaker was a famous Muslim intellectual known as Buya Hamka, a champion of the 'modernist' school of Islam, which sought to harmonise modern civilisation with a purified form of Islam cleansed of its Javanese cultural accretions. The modernist wave was part of an Islamic revival movement which was sweeping the world, based on a return to the fundamentals of the Quran and *Sunnah*, the Islamic holy book and the customs of the Prophet Mohammed. Robyn asked a friend what the old man was saying, and her companion explained that he was talking about the fasting month of Ramadan.

'What's Ramadan?' Robyn asked.

'It's a time of year when Allah puts all the human beings on Earth on an equal footing, no matter where they are in the world', she recalls her friend explaining. 'Whether you're poor or rich, white or black, whether you live in the United States or the North Pole, at this time of year you go without eating, without drinking, without sexual intercourse during the day. There's no swearing, no smoking—it's a shutdown of all your desires.' The egalitarian quality of the practice instantly appealed to Robyn. 'I was shocked that (a religion) that I had thought was so unjust would have a facet in it that was so just.'

She decided to try it herself, with mixed results. 'The first fast I ever did, I would fast and if I got really hungry I would go into my room and eat without telling anybody.' Incapable herself of going hungry, she was struck by the serenity of those around her who endured the fast until sunset each day when they gathered for an evening meal. 'Instead of people being angry and depressed and sad, they seemed to exuberate (with) joy. I couldn't understand it—the camaraderie of eating together, the joy of giving food to the poor. I thought it was terrible. I just got migraine headaches.' Her conversion to Islam was off to a faltering start.

During university holidays, the Prambors crew would flee the heat of Jakarta for cooler retreats such as the hill town of Bandung or the island of Bali. During one such trip to Bali, Robyn and Lili were dining with a group of friends at Mama's café in Kuta Beach when a handsome young stranger came over to their table to say hello to one of their group. He wore jeans and a checked cowboy-style shirt, and had long jet-black hair, a jocular manner and spoke good English. He was introduced as Bambang.

Raden Bambang Wisudo was the son of a respectable Javanese family who was well known among the progeny of Indonesia's upper crust. His father, Amir Andjilin, was a medium-level functionary in Suharto's New Order regime, in charge of customs at Bali's international airport. His mother was a member of the aristocratic *priyayi* class who claimed descent from Javanese royalty, a haughty matriarch with manicured fingernails and a penchant for mahjong who carried the title *raden ayu*, which denoted her place in the nobility. Bambang's honorific, *Raden*, signified his own, albeit diluted, upper-class blood. His family called him 'Wisha', a variation on his Hindu family name which means 'to graduate' or attain success; everyone else called him 'Boy'.

When Robyn met him, Bambang was twenty years old. He was the favoured eldest son among six children, who had dropped out of private Catholic college and had not yet found anything to do. 'He was spoilt rotten', she would later conclude. While content to have his family support him, Bambang treated their elaborate etiquette with casual disdain. His sister told Robyn that he had earned his stripes in the brat-pack at the age of sixteen, by riding a motorbike given to him by his father through the front doors of the family home and into the dining room. He spent his time writing songs and poetry, smoking hash and playing blues guitar in all-night jam sessions with his friends. He also liked to befriend foreign tourists in Kuta Beach and squire them around on his motorbike to restaurants, bars and tourist traps where they would invariably pick up the tab.

Bambang was smart, good-looking, funny and a non-conformist like Robyn. But Lili, who was there the night they met, thought them an unlikely pair. She says he was 'cute' but looked no older than seventeen. 'Bambang strikes me as a nice boy. He strikes me as a "mummy's boy" really. He always had a clean shirt, well ironed, just nice. To me he's just a boy so I didn't pay much attention to him. He's always in the background. I never thought she would end up marrying him.'

'It wasn't a wild, passionate falling in love', says Robyn. 'Marriage in Indonesia was still very much based on social compatibility. Our compatibility was that he was intelligent, he was decent, he wasn't unattractive, he was funny. I found him interesting, we had the same sense of humour, we had a lot in common—unfortunately that we smoked dope and liked music. But the fact that he was taking drugs didn't bother me, because so was I.'

For all her devil-may-care exterior, Robyn was at heart a conservative girl whose most heartfelt aspiration was to settle down and have a family of her own. The painful breakup with her first love, Ian Goodacre, less than two years earlier had left her cynical about romance. She simply wanted to marry, make a home and have children, and the highly ordered, family-centric society in which she found herself seemed an ideal place to do so. 'I was disillusioned with the Cinderella stories, the Romeo and Juliet nonsense about love. I could see myself getting married, having children and staying in Indonesia.' The clincher, however, was that her visa was about to expire.

'If we got married, you'd get a visa', suggested Bambang. So they did.

'We never thought about it, it was on the spur of the moment', Robyn says. 'It was not a "visa marriage" as in a deception, but that was one of the things that motivated us. He liked me and wanted to help me out. So it was just a case of "why not?" It wasn't really something that either of us thought about the long-term consequences of.'

In order to marry, Robyn had to formally convert to Islam, a straightforward procedure that required her merely to swear the profession of faith, the *shahadah*, in front of two witnesses. On 1 February 1974, she and Bambang rode on his motorbike to the Department of Religion at Ubud, where, in the presence of a pair of government officials, she declared: 'There is no God but Allah and Mohammed is his messenger'. Later, when she told her family she had become a Muslim, she recalls that their response was: 'Oh here she goes again, I wonder how long this will last'.

Bambang dreaded the florid formalities of a Javanese society wedding. 'He wasn't into the whole cultural Javanese thing—so we actually ran away and got married', Robyn recounts. The signing of their Islamic marriage contract took place with virtually no ceremony at the religious affairs office in Ubud. But their subterfuge was short-lived. When Bambang went home and told his parents he had married a foreigner they hadn't laid eyes on, his mother was appalled; it simply wasn't the done thing for the scion of a blue-blooded clan. His family insisted on a full Javanese wedding to solemnise the union.

The nuptials were held in the city of Magelang, Central Java, the family's maternal ancestral home. First they needed the blessing of their forebears, which entailed a trip to the cemetery where Bambang's grandparents were buried.

'We have to seek permission for you to get married', Bambang's mother explained.

'But they're dead', Robyn pointed out. Dead or not, the betrothed couple were obliged to prostrate themselves and sprinkle water on the grave to secure the ancestors' dispensation, which was apparently granted.

Forty days of elaborate preparations followed. The bride-to-be was bathed in perfumed water and rose petals, and anointed with a potion of herbs and saffron concocted to whiten the skin, notwithstanding Bambang's protestations: 'But she's already white!' Bambang's mother oversaw the preliminaries in her customary imperious style. Robyn was a young woman who was not easily intimidated, but her mother-in-law was 'scary', she later recalled. Fortunately the matriarch was satisfied with her son's choice of wife, because marrying a foreigner was a mark of prestige. Bambang's father, as usual, had little say in the matter. Amir Andjilin was a wise, kindly man who preferred to avoid domestic drama, and did so by demurring to his wife's whims. As a result, their home was her dominion.

The family prized their colonial-era provenance. They liked to speak Dutch at home and their children called them 'mami' and 'papi', in the Dutch style. When the servants walked past their masters, they were expected to stoop so the tips of their fingers trailed on the ground, to signify their lowly station. When leaving a room they were required to back out bowing. Bambang's mother used the royal 'we' in Javanese, and liked to reminisce about how her father, an officer in the colonial regency, used to stride around the royal palace escorted by a minion bearing an umbrella to spare him from the tropical sun; and how, until her marriage, she had never so much as spooned the rice onto her own plate.

On the day of the wedding, Robyn's forehead was adorned with painted designs and gold ornaments were woven through her hair. She was dressed in a ceremonial *kain kebaya*, an ornately embroidered blouse worn with a long swathe of batik wrapped tightly around the lower body and legs, and held in place by a sash called a *setagan*, which is bound so firmly that the bride can only totter in tiny steps. Rendered virtually immobile, she was then seated on a throne-like chair on display for several hours, with eyes downcast and wearing the expression of blank forbearance encouraged in a Javanese bride. For Bambang, attired in similar ceremonial fashion, it was an ordeal to be endured only to humour his mother. But Robyn was in awe of the solemn rites. 'I took all the rituals seriously. I thought that they were all part of being a Muslim.' On their wedding night, the matriarch laid an offering of flowers, food and incense under the bridal bed, in an appeal to the gods to sanctify their union. It was supposed to stay there for seven days but Bambang threw the whole thing out the window when the rotting banana started to stink in the tropical heat. Robyn hastily retrieved it and put it back, lest the gods be offended.

The newlyweds returned to Bambang's family home in Bali, an imposing colonial-style manse in the Krunang district of Denpasar, which boasted seven bedrooms, three lounge rooms, two dining rooms, two kitchens and an expansive garden pavilion for entertaining. The family sitting room, known as the 'blue room', featured ornate curtains in peacock blue, and a gold inlaid coffee table 2 metres long, which was made from an ancient temple door. Bambang's father had been transferred to a new customs post at Medan on the island of Sumatra, so the newlyweds shared the house with three of Bambang's sisters, a retinue of servants, and a passing parade of visiting relatives. In the matriarch's absence, Bambang's eldest sister ran the household with the same magisterial authority as her mother. The servants slept on mats in the kitchen and there were locks on the fridges so they couldn't steal the food. While the family reclined on lounges to watch television of an evening, the hirelings would sit on the floor behind them awaiting their next command.

Robyn quickly discovered that the fact of their marriage had transformed her hitherto casual relationship with Boy. 'When Bambang and I were just hanging out together, we were friends. But when we got married our roles changed. Being a husband and wife in Indonesia, you are not "friends". You have separate lives and defined roles.' It was no longer acceptable for her to call Bambang by his given name, because for a wife to do so was considered disrespectful. So while he continued to call her Robyn, she was expected to address him as *Mas*, which literally means 'gold' but in common usage means 'older brother', and is employed as a generic term of respect for a man.

After their marriage, Robyn lost touch with her friends from Prambors, even her close friend Lili. It was not the last time she would leave an old life behind to fashion a new one. Lili was not offended; she believed Robyn had simply found what she'd been looking for. 'We lost contact because our interests were different. I was always interested in foreigners, all my boyfriends were foreigners. She was very into Indonesian guys.' Lili saw Robyn just once after she married, when Robyn came to visit Lili's mother's home in Jakarta. She was struck by the change in her friend, who appeared to have morphed into a new role.

'I thought she had become more and more not like an Australian girl. She was very Indonesian in her behaviour. She had become demure—like a typical Indonesian wife, married to an Indonesian guy. That was my impression.' Lili saw this as a natural consequence of Robyn's Javanese marriage. 'Once you're married, you belong to your husband's life, you don't have your own life', she explains. Nor was she completely surprised by the new 'demureness' that she saw in her friend. 'I think it's easy for Robyn because she's quite soft inside. I can see that side of her. She's very soft. If she meets someone who can nurture that softness in her, she would probably succumb to that.'

However, finding her place in the hierarchy of Bambang's family proved a challenge. She was expected to stay out of the kitchen, which was considered the servants' preserve; apart from which her habit of clattering the pots and pans was considered 'low class'—as was any unnecessary noise. 'From the time I arrived in Indonesia, my mother-in-law used to say I even walked too loud', she recalls. Navigating the elaborate protocols of a traditional Javanese household was fraught with pitfalls. 'I had terrible trouble with the servants because I didn't have the ability to manage them or interact with them. I had this idea from my hippy days that everyone is equal. I later realised that everyone is equal in worth, yes, but not in status. You have to have an employer–employee relationship. If you try to behave as though you are the same as them, they think you're stupid.' When she took her plate and sat on the kitchen floor one day to eat with the servants, they were so alarmed they ran out.

Robyn would later look back and laugh at these experiences, although by her own account it sounds like a lonely ordeal. It reminded her of the famous scene from the science fiction spoof movie *Spaceballs*, in which the Darth Vader look-alike Dark Helmet announces to the young hero, Lone Starr: 'Before you die, there is something you should know about us … I am your father's brother's nephew's cousin's former roommate'. 'What does that make us?' asks Lone Starr. 'Absolutely nothing.' That was how Robyn felt about the value she was assigned in the arcane pecking order of her marital home: absolutely nothing.

But that was about to change. Within weeks of her marriage, Robyn fell pregnant. Having longed to settle down and start a family, she felt elated, but also deeply apprehensive. Suddenly her own home and family seemed a long way away. As mother-to-be of her Indonesian family's first grandchild, she found her place in the family hierarchy suddenly elevated. But at the same time, her activities were dramatically circumscribed. A whole array of hitherto daily tasks and amusements became *pantang*—not allowed—in her delicate condition. There was no such transformation for Bambang. 'My role changed—I was having a baby, I would have to stay home and play house. But he had no reason to change. He wasn't pregnant. His attitude was, "You're my wife, you're pregnant, and of course you can't be riding on the back of the motorbike, coming to Kuta and taking drugs". I think that was my first reality check, and it was a shock when I sat down and thought about it, that I was really married and so many people were involved in our life now. It changed me and I thought, how long were we going to be able to stay in Kuta Beach smoking dope, eating magic mushrooms and living off his parents?'

Robyn found herself spending long days at home alone with the domestic help. Left to her own devices, she befriended a servant girl named Muna who was about her own age. Muna was a devout Muslim and follower of a hardline new organisation called Islam Jamaah (which is not to be confused with Abu Bakar Ba'asyir's group, Jemaah Islamiyah, founded in 1993). She wore a hijab (headscarf) to cover her hair, which was rare in Indonesia at the time. She took Robyn to the mosque and to lectures by the group's leaders, who preached that Islam in Indonesia must be purged of its Javanese 'impurities'. They had begun burning books they deemed to be impure and branded those who didn't join them as infidels. Islam Jamaah would later be banned as a heretical sect. It was from Muna that Robyn learned that the offerings made to gods and spirits in Bali and the statues of divinities like those revered by Bambang's family were *haram*, or forbidden, because Muslims are meant to worship God alone, not cement idols. Robyn and Muna would sit and discuss Islam for hours, until Bambang's family found out and the girl was dismissed from the household. 'You can't have the *majikan* (master) fraternising with the servants', they explained.

While Robyn was making her new life in Bali, more trouble was brewing in Jakarta. At the start of 1974, simmering anger over corruption and economic inequality had boiled over in the streets of the capital. Student protests demanding price cuts and curbs on corruption turned to riots in which shops were looted and cars burned. In response, Suharto's troops opened fire, killing about a dozen people. The upheaval shook the New Order regime and ushered in a new era of repression in which hundreds were arrested and tried, newspapers shut down, student activism squashed and moderate military leaders purged from the armed forces.

Meanwhile Robyn was growing restless and homesick, and felt reluctant to entrust her own fate and that of her unborn infant to Indonesia's rudimentary health care system. So at the end of 1974 the couple decided to travel to Sydney to await the birth of their child. Bambang was characteristically nonchalant about what lay ahead. 'He was from a privileged family', says Robyn. 'He lived a privileged life and did whatever he pleased. His father had always supported him. His family thought, he's in Australia now, her family will take care of him.'

4

A JAVANESE WIFE

Indonesia & Australia, 1974–1977

Robyn was six months pregnant when she and Bambang landed in Australia around the end of 1974. Bessie was waiting eagerly at Sydney airport to meet her exotic new son-in-law, whom she had hitherto seen only in wedding photos, resplendent in ceremonial attire.

'How will you recognise him?' one of Bessie friends had asked.

'I'll just look for the guy in the dress and tall hat.'

To her disappointment, Bambang was wearing his habitual blue jeans and checked shirt when he and Robyn emerged through the customs gates.

'How ya going, love? You haven't got your skirt on? Oh no, of course you wouldn't.'

A welcoming party of curious friends and relatives lay in wait at Dee Why on Sydney's northern beaches, where Bessie made cups of tea and sandwiches while Robyn did the introductions: 'Susan, this is Bambang, Bambang this is Susan' and so on around the room. Among the gathering was Bessie's friend Gladys, whom the children called 'aunty'. 'Aunty Glad, this is Bambang, Bambang, this is Aunty Glad', Robyn continued. Bambang shot her a glance of alarm, but held his tongue until they were alone in the bedroom.

'Far out! I thought I knew you Westerners pretty good, but you people really are incredible!'

'What do you mean?' she asked, puzzled.

'You don't have any shame.'

'What are you talking about?'

'Well in Indonesia, if we thought someone was a *tante girang* we'd never say it to her face.' In Indonesian, the term *tante girang* is used to refer to a woman who goes with younger men; the English translation is 'aunty glad'.

It was a foretaste of the culture shock that lay in store. This was Bambang's first foray out of Indonesia, his first encounter with any existence other than his own rarefied world. 'He was from a privileged family, he had never worked a day in his life', says Robyn. 'They assumed that all white people are rich and that my family would look after him. So coming to Australia and living in Dee Why in a fibro house, where we were very much a working-class family—it was a total shock.'

Bessie had split up with Fred and was living with her younger daughter, Susan, in a two-bedroom fibrocement house at the industrial western end of Dee Why. They lived frugally on Bessie's supporting mother's pension, supplemented by a part-time job making breakfasts at a motel around the corner. Bessie's health was poor; she suffered from chronic asthma and was in the early stages of emphysema, yet to be diagnosed and no doubt aggravated by smoking two packets of cigarettes a day. Thirteen-year-old Susan was a sweet, good-natured girl, who was now in her second year at Manly Girls High, where she was still living down the notoriety of being Robyn Hutchinson's younger sister.

Polite, laid-back and affable, Bambang was an instant hit with the family. 'Bambang had an incredible ability to fit in wherever he was', says Robyn. 'He was extremely funny. I don't know anybody who met him who didn't like him. He had my mum wrapped around his little finger.'

However, a rude jolt was in store for Bambang when Robyn found an advertisement in the 'situations vacant' page of the *Manly Daily* for a process worker at a chemical warehouse in Dee Why West. Bambang suddenly found himself packing chemicals into bulk bags for distribution in return for a wage of $120 a week. Fortunately the boss took a liking to him, he got on well with his workmates, and at least he was earning an income. But getting up at 6 a.m. each day to be at the factory by seven was an unaccustomed tribulation for a Javanese aristocrat whose life had been governed thus far by *jam karet*—Indonesian 'rubber time'. 'He didn't like how everything here was time driven', says Robyn. 'He used to say *jam karet* and "time is money" just don't go together.'

In February 1975, about two months after their arrival in Australia, Robyn went into labour with their first child. Bambang had been startled to learn that it was now commonplace in Australia for fathers to be present for childbirth, a practice that was virtually unheard of in Indonesia and which struck him as quite bizarre. 'He had no idea what it was like and didn't want to know', Robyn recalls. So they agreed he would accompany her to hospital but leave before the birth. However, the event did not proceed according to their plan.

'It was a 17-hour labour', says Robyn. 'By the time the baby's head crowned, I was so exhausted and in such a state I couldn't have cared less who was there. I remember him bending down and saying, "OK, I'm going out now". I couldn't have cared less. I was screaming.'

But as Bambang headed for the door, he was rounded on by the duty midwife, a hard-boiled Dutch matron whose delivery room was her domain; she would decide who left and who stayed.

'Oh, is this what they do in your country? They desert women in their hour of need? It took two to make this child, didn't it?' the midwife harangued him. A speechless Bambang felt compelled to stay for the whole bloody ordeal. 'He was absolutely and utterly horrified', says Robyn, 'even though he was delighted with his newborn daughter. He leaned down and said to me, "Never again, I will never see you go through that again". He was so traumatised he swore I would never have another child.'

The baby was a golden-skinned girl with a thatch of black hair, who weighed 3.2 kilograms. They called her Devi (pronounced *Day-vee*) Suni Wisudo Putri, a Hindu name meaning 'goddess of the sun and daughter of Wisudo'.*

---

* See note on page 319.

'Devi was my firstborn', says Robyn. 'You love all your children and they're all different and you love them all in different ways. But your firstborn has something special and she was my firstborn.'

When they arrived home at Dee Why, to Bessie's horror they brought the after-birth wrapped in a plastic bag, which Robyn placed carefully in the freezer compartment of the fridge. Bambang would happily have left it behind to be disposed of at the hospital, but Robyn wished to bury it in keeping with a Javanese custom that deems the placenta to be the *adik ari ari*—the 'little brother' (*adik* means little brother and *ari ari* means umbilical cord) of the newborn child, thus necessitating a respectful burial. She dug a little plot in a garden bed beside the driveway, in view of the next-door neighbour's lounge room window, and buried the placenta in the soil. A lamp placed over it was to be lit each evening for forty days to keep away evil spirits. She wrongly assumed this was an Islamic practice. 'The type of Islam I was practising was very much confused with Javanese beliefs, and had so much Hinduism in it that it's hard to know where the Hinduism ended and the Islam began.'

One evening at *maghrib*, the time around sunset when Muslims pray, Robyn asked Bambang to go out and light the lamp in the garden. Wondering why he was taking so long, she looked out the kitchen window a few minutes later, and saw him dancing around the tiny grave in a seemingly trance-like state, chanting some strange incantation.

'What on earth were you doing?' she asked, when he came back in chuckling.

'I couldn't help myself. The neighbours were looking out the window. I didn't want to disappoint them, so I gave them a show.'

Despite the social revolution of the 1970s, Australia remained a deeply conservative country, in which a quick scratch on the surface of polite society was enough to expose a rich seam of xenophobia beneath. It was only two years since the last vestiges of the White Australia Policy had been dismantled by the new Whitlam Labor Government. The fall of Saigon and the Communist victory in Vietnam would soon send a wave of refugees washing onto Australian shores, reviving the nation's latent suspicions towards the 'yellow hordes' of Asia to its north. Intermarriage between white Australians and Asians was still rare. After Devi's birth, a nurse pushing a trolley-load of newborns through the maternity ward had glanced at Robyn, then at her baby, and kept on walking past her bed, assuming the tawny infant could not be the white mother's child. At the infant health centre in Manly, a kindly nurse mistook golden-skinned Devi for an adopted Vietnamese orphan.

Robyn contacted her father, Jim Hutchinson, whom she hadn't seen in years, eager to show off her firstborn. Jim and his new wife Yvonne drove over to Dee Why to visit with their two sons, nine-year-old Roderick and his little brother Brett. Roderick recalls that Robyn and her father were soon arguing, about what he doesn't recall, while Bambang sat quietly in the lounge room playing his guitar. 'They didn't get on', says Roderick. 'My father really disapproved of the marriage. He didn't want his white Anglo-Saxon girl marrying another race. My father did not approve of mixed marriages.' Roderick had only met his half-sister a couple of times. He was struck by her forceful personality and her strident voice and behaviour. 'She was loud, very strong, she was a pretty ballsy type of girl too, she didn't take any crap from anyone. It was that voice—anyone's got a voice like that has to be ballsy.'

When news of Devi's birth made it to the surfing fraternity, Robyn's old friends came bearing gifts of baby bonnets and fluffy toys. The crowd had thinned somewhat while she had been away; Ian Goodacre had moved to Queensland, and some of the others had travelled overseas. The drug culture had grown more insidious, as heroin had crept onto the scene. A few of the boys had been conscripted to serve in Vietnam and returned as hardcore addicts, and there had been a rash of heroin overdose deaths.

Robyn's own days of frequent drug use were over, since she had become pregnant and then begun breastfeeding. It was a past she was happy to leave behind in favour of the settled domesticity she yearned for. 'I had changed because I had a kid', she remembers. 'Most of my friends didn't work, and sold dope to support their habits. A lot of people were getting busted. I didn't want that life any more.'

Another old friend, Steve Warnock, saw a marked change in the carefree party-girl of old. 'She was certainly different. Her life had changed radically at that time. Where she had come from was no longer the place she was at. She found something in Asia and came back with a whole new perception. I think she went looking for that. She wasn't a Sydney girl from the northern beaches any more; she had found a new life. She dumped her roots, and I don't blame her—it was a pretty ordinary life she was leaving behind.'

But the life that lay ahead was uncertain as well, and the stability she longed for would prove elusive. Their living conditions with Bessie and Susan in the fibro house at Dee Why were cramped and for Bambang, the novelty of bagging chemicals eight hours a day to support his wife and child had quickly worn off.

'Some days I would wake him up and he'd say, "No, I'm not going to work today". I would say, "What do you mean you're not going to work? This isn't Indonesia, you'll get the sack".'

Australia had fallen on troubled times. A global downturn combined with the adventurist policies of the Whitlam Labor Government had sent unemployment soaring and inflation spiralling to 16 per cent. The deprivations of childhood, when her mother had slaved as a donkey stoker and eaten bread and dripping, were still vivid in Robyn's memory, whereas Boy had never known privation of any kind. He would simply roll over and fall back to sleep, while Robyn fretted over how they would pay the rent. When he wasn't sacked, he would say, 'See, you didn't have to worry'.

'It didn't matter what you did with Bambang, he just used to live from day to day. It was always "Don't worry about it, it'll be alright". His whole life had been spent just doing what he wanted, when he wanted, how he wanted. In Indonesia there were no consequences because his mother and father always took care of him.' With his lackadaisical attitude and fondness for marijuana, Bambang fitted well into the surf crowd. 'Boy was a sweet guy. People wanted to be around him because he was a lovely bloke', remembers Robyn's friend Deborah Jensen. 'But unfortunately he got a bit involved in smoking dope and taking pills. When she brought him to Australia he just wanted to be like the Australian boys.'

Their precarious domestic equanimity was shattered when Robyn's mother found a bag of marijuana seeds on top of a cupboard. If there was one thing Bessie couldn't abide, it was drugs. She gave them an ultimatum: the drug use must stop or she would tell Robyn's brother, George. It's unclear exactly what George would have done, as he was married by now with his own domestic affairs to attend to. But the mere thought of her brother's reaction was enough to send Robyn and Bambang packing. 'My brother was seven years older than me. I'd always looked up to him like a father figure. He was always very straitlaced and very law abiding, and it was always very important to me what he thought. Not that he would have done anything, but just the fact of him knowing about something he disapproved of would have been very difficult for me.'

Robyn, Bambang and the baby moved into a two-bedroom flat in Ashburner Street, Manly, around the corner from Manly's famous South Steyne beach and a block from the Royal Far West Children's home where Robyn had been billeted as a child. Bambang had developed an allergy to the chemicals and quit his job at the factory, leaving them reliant on unemployment benefits, a good part of which he spent on marijuana, which he now smoked daily. 'We used to fight about it', says Robyn. 'Well, I used to fight and he would ignore me. You couldn't fight with him. And he didn't stop. He saw every reason why I shouldn't smoke, but he wouldn't stop himself.' Occasionally, in the face of her persistent nagging, the normally acquiescent Bambang would snap and erupt in a rage. He usually stormed out before it got physical.

Ashburner Street was a well-known drug dealers' haunt, where junkies and dope peddlers would skulk beneath the streetlights to do their deals, then slink off into the shadows when a police patrol car cruised by. On 23 July 1976, Robyn and Bambang were at home at about ten in the morning, when two police officers appeared at the open front door, presumably in response to a tipoff. Bambang was in the lounge room chatting to a neighbour, while Robyn was in the bedroom changing Devi's nappy. On the dressing table next to her was a plastic bag containing six 30-gram packets of Indian hemp. 'When they came through the door, the marijuana was in a plastic bag on the dresser', says Robyn. 'I saw the police coming and tried to throw it out the window, but I wasn't a very good shot, and it landed in the baby's cot.'

When the police found the incriminating package, Bambang was arrested and taken to the Manly police station, where he was charged with smoking and possessing Indian hemp and possessing a homemade pipe for the purpose. Robyn went along later to bail him out with a $200 bond and three days afterwards his case was heard in the Manly magistrates court. It was so rare to have a Muslim defendant in those days that they had to send out for a Quran so that Bambang could be sworn, and Robyn was asked to help out with translation because there was no Indonesian interpreter. Bambang was relaxed as usual, calling out a cheery 'How are you?' to the magistrate from the dock.

But for Robyn, always a proud young woman and now a wife and mother intent on settling down, the episode was sheer humiliation. 'The fact that we were raided for drugs is bad enough. But it was made out as though I was some sort of negligent drug-crazed mother, which wasn't true. I was really paranoid they were going to take Devi away.' Much was made of the drugs having been found in the baby's cot, and the magistrate recommended the Department of Child Welfare investigate the child's care. 'With a father who is a previous drug-user, it must be ascertained the child is being properly looked after', instructed stipendiary magistrate Mr LJ Nash.

To make matters worse, a week later the story was reported in the Sydney tabloid newspaper, the *Sunday Mirror*, under a headline in bold upper case letters: 'DRUG FAMILY MAY LOSE BABY'. It featured a photograph of 'Mrs Robyn Wisudo, 22' holding her doe-eyed 17-month-old daughter, beside a subheading 'We love our little girl'. Robyn was smiling but reportedly 'distraught' with fear that her baby would be taken away.

'The court thought we had hidden the drugs in Devi's cot and that we couldn't care less about her. But that is all so far from the truth', Robyn was quoted as saying. 'Bambang and I love our daughter dearly. The reason the drugs were in the cot was because I had them in my hand when the police arrived and I panicked and threw them there.' She said Bambang was also distressed. 'When I told him our baby could be taken away he just shook his head and said, "They cannot do that. It is wrong".'

The story was written by a former friend from the surf scene, Steve Warnock, who was now working as a junior journalist at the *Mirror* and had volunteered to interview Robyn after spotting the case in a court report in the *Manly Daily*. Warnock remembers visiting the flat in Ashburner Street to find Robyn furious over what had happened. 'She was pissed off, she was angry, defiant.' Her ire was reserved mostly for Bambang, who sat chastened, like 'an unassuming Asian guy', while Warnock interviewed his wife.

While Robyn stood by him publicly, she never forgave Bambang for the shame, and for finally shattering her cherished domestic idyll. 'It was the straw that broke the camel's back. I was so angry because that was my whole point. I had been trying to tell him this was irresponsible behaviour. And him being caught for marijuana paled into insignificance compared to the slight on me as a mother. I was the one who ended up on the front page of the newspaper. I wasn't even smoking at the time. No one even remembered it was him who had the drugs. It was all about what kind of mother was I.'

Her family was mortified. Bessie said she literally fell off her bar stool when she came across the 'DRUG FAMILY' headline while reading her Sunday morning newspaper at the motel. Robyn's brother George refused to talk to her for years afterwards. Her father, who abhorred illicit drugs and disapproved of her Asian husband, was 'livid', according to Robyn's half-brother Roderick. He remembers asking some time afterwards whether they would be going to visit Robyn again. 'No. As far as I'm concerned she's no daughter of mine', his father replied.

Bambang was fined $900 and placed on a two-year good behaviour bond. But there was worse to come. In the aftermath of his conviction, a letter arrived from the immigration department announcing that his residency visa had been cancelled and he would face deportation. Bambang's family moved quickly to head off the mounting scandal after being discreetly informed of their son's predicament by an Indonesian diplomat in Canberra who was a family friend, according to Robyn. Bambang's father, Amir Andjilin, paid for their tickets and they were soon on a flight to Jakarta, before Bambang could be bundled out of the country.

* * *

The ignominy of the drug bust and Bambang's narrowly averted deporta-
tion was politely ignored when they arrived back in Jakarta with 18-
month-old Devi a few weeks after the event. Had the scandal occurred in
Indonesia it would have caused immense loss of face for Bambang's
family, but Sydney was far enough away for the matter to be discreetly put
behind them. His parents were happy to accept their son's assurance that
the incident in Australia had been a trivial infringement. 'I think for his
parents it was just accepted that boys would do all these weird things, be
totally irresponsible, get into trouble, then grow up and "get over it"', says
Robyn. 'They certainly cared about his drug use—most definitely, but
there was a lot of denial. If he told them the sun shone at night and the
moon came out in the morning, they would believe him.'

By the time they returned to Jakarta, Bambang's father had been
transferred to a new position at Indonesia's busiest port, Tanjung Priok,
and the family had moved into a four-bedroom government house in an
expansive residential compound for customs department officials and
their families in the affluent suburb of Pondok Bambu, East Jakarta.
Bambang's three unmarried sisters still lived at home, as did his younger
brother, Eddy, the family's equally pampered second son, a budding artist
who would later join a national dance company.

Robyn had always got on well with Bambang's father, known in the
family as 'papi'. 'His children loved and respected him; but they feared
their mother—she was the strong one', says Robyn. The matriarch had
lost none of her regal aplomb. In addition to her role as mistress of the
household, she was an enterprising wheeler and dealer who traded in
land, gold and precious stones and an inveterate gambler who spent long
days playing mahjong at the gambling dens in Chinatown. On her return
home each afternoon, chauffeured by a neatly uniformed driver in the
family Mercedes, she would run her manicured fingers along the carved
timber furniture checking for dust, to ensure the servants had not neglected their chores. While Robyn and Bambang had been in Sydney, his
mother had set up her own beauty salon, after obtaining certification from
the French cosmetics house Lancôme. She ran it from an enclosed pavilion

attached to their home, where the well-heeled wives and daughters of Jakarta society would come to be exfoliated and coiffured. The salon was named 'Devi Suni' in honour of her granddaughter.

'Mami' was besotted with her long-awaited first grandchild, who was doubly treasured for having been sired by the family's eldest son. She explained to Robyn that grandchildren born from sons are known as *cucu* (pronounced *choo choo*) *dalam*, which means 'incoming grandchild', denoting the family's ownership of the child, while those produced by daughters are known as *cucu luar*, or 'outgoing grandchild', as they are automatically deemed to be on their way 'out' of the family to become part of the paternal clan.

Bambang's eldest sister had married and had two children of her own, who were designated as *cucu luar*, which made them effectively second-class grandchildren, it seemed to Robyn. 'The way they were treated, it was just shocking. They weren't even allowed to eat the same food as my daughter. If they sat down to eat chicken, my daughter would get the best piece and as much as she wanted, while they got one piece each.' The family's attitude, as Robyn saw it, was: 'Devi belongs to us', whereas 'the other children didn't count'.

She was disturbed to learn that the family's claim of ownership over her firstborn went even further, according to the tradition as it was explained to her. 'The first child of the first son goes to the grandparents to be brought up. My daughter was the first grandchild of the first son, therefore my mother-in-law felt she had the right to take her. It's very common in Indonesian culture that children don't necessarily live with the parents; children are not individual possessions, they are part of the family. My mother-in-law wanted to exercise her right to take Devi and bring her up, which was the custom.'

There was no way Robyn was handing over her child, so mami had to content herself with lavishing gifts and special treatment on Devi. By Robyn's account the child slept in her own double bed, and if she wanted ice cream the chauffeur would be instructed to take her out in the car to get some. The contrast with Robyn's own spartan upbringing could hardly have been more stark. 'The decadence was just shocking. It was gross.

I hated it', she says. The family's extravagance seemed to contradict the basic tenets of their purported faith—such as egalitarianism, temperance and charity. And Robyn now knew that their animist rituals and indulgent habits were not condoned by Islam. Mami placed charms around the house to ward off evil spirits, dabbled in black magic and gave thanks to her dead ancestors for their food at mealtimes. When Bambang's uncle came back from the *haj* pilgrimage to Mecca, he sat down with papi over a glass of Bintang beer to tell him all about it.

Despite the growing tensions in the household, Robyn was determined to be a good Javanese wife, and threw herself into the role.

'I did reach a stage where I lost myself', she remembers. 'I tried so hard to fit in that I actually lost myself. I was just fulfilling the role of a Javanese wife—when I wasn't a Javanese wife. Even Bambang used to say, "Why do you try so hard to be one, when you're not?"' Over time, she would reach the reluctant conclusion that, try as she might, she would never completely belong. 'In a culture like Indonesia they never really accept you. You're always an outsider. You will always be an *orang bule*— a white person.'

Not long after settling in at Pondok Bambu, they discovered that Robyn was pregnant with their second child. Her joy was quickly tempered by Bambang's horror at the prospect of having to endure the ordeal of another birth, if only as a witness; apart from which, he simply didn't want another child. He urged Robyn to terminate the pregnancy using a herbal concoction that replicates a morning-after pill.

'Just tell my mother and she'll get the herbs for you to drink', he advised.

But the suggestion was anathema to Robyn, whose conservative personal morality and years as a Catholic would not allow her to contemplate an abortion, regardless of her husband's view.

'He was adamant, and I was just as adamant, because even before I was a Muslim I was pro-life. I think that it's murder.'

Tired of his obstinate spouse and overbearing family, Bambang decided to return to Bali, preferably without Robyn, telling her it would be best for her to remain in Jakarta with his family until the birth.

Anticipating the arrival of another *cucu dalam*, Bambang's mother was happy for Robyn and her beloved Devi to stay. Mami was sure that sooner or later Boy would grow up and accept his responsibilities as a husband and father, and that Robyn should wait patiently like a faithful Javanese wife until he did so. But Robyn was having none of it. 'I was expected to stay in Jakarta and be looked after and play the part, while he could do whatever he wanted. I put on a scene—no way was I getting left behind and stuck there with them. So I went too.'

On the subject of her pregnancy, Bambang had made his position quite clear. 'He told me, if you continue with this pregnancy, consider it your child and not mine. Don't tell me about it, don't speak about it, I want nothing to do with it. I was not allowed to mention it or talk about it; for all intents and purposes it was like it didn't exist.'

Despite his denial and the awkward relations with her in-laws, Robyn says the thought of leaving Bambang and returning to Australia did not occur to her. 'I know the negative effects on children who come from broken homes', she explains. But their marriage was clearly doomed. 'That was the beginning of the end for us. From this point it was much more blatant: you have your life and I have mine. And mine was being a mother and responsible for two human beings.'

Leaving Jakarta to go back to Bali meant Robyn had to quit her job as an English teacher, which she had resumed on returning to Indonesia. This left the couple without an income. Bambang's parents paid the bills, the servants' wages, and the costs of maintaining their property in Denpasar, which included a supply of staples such as rice, cooking oil and kerosene. But the cash flow from the family coffers effectively ceased.

'His mother wanted to smoke me out, so she stopped sending money', says Robyn. 'We were still supported—there were clothes and food, but no cash. There was this massive house in Denpasar; we had electricity and water because the bills were paid, but there was no money. Bambang just saw it as them wanting something, trying to control him, as always.' His mother would visit once a month from Jakarta, bringing gifts for Devi, and always making it clear that if they returned to live with the family they would be looked after. Proud and stubborn as ever, Robyn refused to ask her for anything.

In Bali, Bambang returned to his familiar life of late-night jam sessions with his musician buddies in their old hangouts at Kuta Beach.

'Where the bloody hell have you been?' Robyn would bawl at him when he came home.

He was always perplexed at her fury. 'Yeah, I haven't been home for three days—and?'

He would simply pick up his guitar and start quietly strumming. 'It was like talking to an alien', she recalls.

During one of her visits from Jakarta, Robyn's mother-in-law offered some maternal advice.

'Why don't you try one day to do it like a Javanese woman?'

'What do you mean?'

'Well, if you were a Javanese woman and your husband did that, when he came home you would not even let on that you knew he had been gone for three days. When he came through the door you would smile and ask him how he was and talk about the weather, then you'd go and make him a cup of tea—with your own hands, not ask the servant to do it.'

She went on to explain the Javanese psychology behind her advice. 'If you do it this way, when he comes through the door, it will make him very nervous and anxious. You show him he's not very important because you didn't even notice he was gone. And by making him a cup of tea yourself, you don't give him any reason to blame you, to say that you are the problem in his marriage. And then later you say to him, "you know, I do worry when you don't come home". And then you say nothing else. And he will feel so guilty, he won't do it again—at least for another three or four months.'

So the next time Bambang came home after a night of partying, Robyn said nothing, set her jaw and made him a cup of tea. He was waiting in the blue room on a sofa beside the gold-inlaid coffee table, with his mother and sister.

'I was gritting my teeth, trying to smile', she recounts. 'I made this cup of tea, and I could feel the spoon grinding on the bottom of the cup.

I came in with the cup of tea and went to put it down on the coffee table. Then for one fleeting second, I glanced up, and they were all smiling at me—and I lost it.'

She smashed the cup on the coffee table, sending shattered china flying. 'Where the bloody hell have you been?' she screamed.

Eventually Bambang's nocturnal revelry became so conspicuous that even his parents grew concerned. In a rare show of paternal authority, Robyn's father-in-law, Amir Andjilin, paid a visit to the house in Denpasar, to put a stop to it. 'He came to Bali and decided to take Bambang back to Jakarta with him because of how Bambang was behaving. He was basically taking him back for detox. For whatever reason, the offer was not extended to me.'

Six months pregnant, Robyn was left alone in the house in Denpasar with two-year-old Devi and a servant girl. Other than the usual supply of staple foods and kerosene, there was little else in the house. Robyn survived on her child endowment pension of $14 per month, paid by the Australian government into her bank account at home, supplemented by the odd cash gift sent by her mother.

Two months before her due date, Robyn went into premature labour and had to rush herself to Denpasar's Sanglah Hospital. Normally a solid young woman, her weight had dropped by 8 kilograms to 47 kilograms. 'It was really terrible, I nearly lost the baby, I was in a terrible condition, extremely underweight. I was in the public ward; it was the filthiest place I've ever seen. It was disgusting—there were no sheets on the beds, there was blood on them from the previous patients, there were nits in the pillows. You had to bring your own drinking water; that's how bad it was. And there were rats as big as cats in the bathroom.'

After she was stabilised and the contractions stopped, a pair of nurses came around to take sterile urine samples from all the maternity patients, armed with a metal kidney bowl, a 'not so stainless' steel jug, and a mouldy-looking orange tube. 'The sight of this antiquated equipment was almost enough to make you lose the baby', says Robyn, who was in the bed closest to the door. With minimal ceremony, the nurses inserted the tube in Robyn's urethra and deposited a urine sample in the metal bowl. Then they sloshed some water from the jug on the tube to clean it, made their way to the neighbouring bed and repeated the procedure, continuing around the ward until all the maternity patients were done. 'I have never been so glad to be the first in line, and I refused to think about where it had been before me', says Robyn.

After seven days, she was discharged, under orders to have complete bed rest until the birth of the baby. She arrived home at the house in Denpasar to be greeted by her mother-in-law, who announced she was taking Devi back to Jakarta to look after her for the duration of the pregnancy. 'Her opportunity had come because the doctor had said I had to have bed rest and was not allowed to pick anything up. So instead of arranging for me to be looked after, she said, "I'm going to take Devi back with me because you won't be able to look after her". I was so ill I couldn't fight her. So she took Devi and promised to bring her back two to three weeks before the baby was born. She had finally got what she wanted—she had her granddaughter living with her. I was an afterthought. She, for all intents and purposes, became Devi's mother, because she was the matriarch.'

Before leaving with her granddaughter, Mami arranged to have the house in Denpasar more or less cleared of furniture and valuables, which were placed in locked rooms. 'So they took Devi and left me and the servant in the house with no money', says Robyn. 'They took the furniture, the cutlery, the statues, everything. They left a couple of plates, spoons, glasses and two chairs. The rest they put in the other half of the house and locked it up.' It was never explained why this was done. Robyn assumed it was to prevent her from selling the family's belongings or the servant from stealing them.

In May 1977, Robyn went into labour with her second child. Unbeknown to her, she was suffering from a complication known as placenta praevia, where the placenta is in the lower part of the uterus and may become detached, causing severe bleeding and blocking the entrance of the womb. She was haemorrhaging badly, and due to her relatively rare RH-negative blood type, there were no blood supplies available for transfusion. Lying on the delivery-room table, she remembers hearing the obstetrician commenting calmly in Balinese: 'We've only got about half an hour. We have to decide whether to save the baby.' She looked around, wondering who they were talking about. 'There was no one else in the labour ward, only me.' Robyn's cervix was only 4 centimetres dilated. The obstetrician told her afterwards she was losing so much blood that he believed a caesarian section would be the only way to deliver the child alive, but that she would almost certainly not survive it.

She remembers placing her life in God's hands. 'I started praying and asking Allah to help me. I said that I trusted him, and that whatever he had planned for me I would accept.' The next thing she remembers is an overwhelming urge to push. 'The baby's coming, the baby's coming!' she yelled. A few moments later, the baby emerged, with the placenta wrapped around his feet.

It was a boy, weighing just over 2 kilograms. They gave him the names Mohammed, after the Prophet, and Firmansah, which means 'that which comes from Allah'. He was placed in a makeshift humidicrib—a wooden box with a glass lid, lit by electric light bulbs—while Robyn was left in the recovery ward. When her sister-in-law arrived at the hospital, she started screaming; Robyn hadn't realised she was lying in a pool of blood. The doctor told her afterwards it was a miracle she hadn't died.

'Medically it was against all the odds. Technically I should have died, because I had lost so much blood. But I survived—thanks to Allah.'

After a brief visit from her sister-in-law and Bambang, Robyn lay in hospital waiting for someone to come and take her home. 'The family came and visited, then for three days they didn't come. No one came to get me out.' She says the hospital staff wouldn't allow her to leave with the baby because the bill hadn't been paid. All she had was a platinum and diamond ring given to her as a gift by Bambang's father, so she left the ring as a surety and walked home with the baby, returning later to redeem the ring and pay the bill herself with money sent from home by Bessie.

Despite mami's promise to bring her back before the birth of the baby, two-year-old Devi was still in Jakarta where the family was resisting Robyn's entreaties to return her to Bali. She says they only relented three weeks after Mohammed was born, when she threatened to report them to the Australian embassy.

The next seven to eight months passed in a blur. Bambang had returned from Jakarta but was seldom at home. There was no regular income and not much food in the half-empty house in Bali. Robyn found a job teaching English at a Chinese-run language college in Denpasar, whose owners had a sideline distributing baby formula and supplemented her salary with powdered milk. Because of her RH-negative blood type the doctor had instructed her not to breastfeed, not realising that baby Mohammed had the same blood type. 'It was just a time of intolerable living conditions', Robyn remembers. 'I tried to work and look after the kids, and I managed to feed them, but I was extremely skinny and ended up quite ill.' Word of her predicament filtered back via the travellers' grapevine to her friends in Sydney.

'She went through a really, really bad time', says her old friend Deborah Jensen. 'After Boy disappeared into Kuta Beach, she had a shocking time. She was living on nothing in this house. A lady stayed with her as a servant, but they had barely enough to eat. This was after the horrible ordeal of giving birth to Mohammed. It was just a horrible ordeal until she got back.'

One day, as she was walking down the main street of Denpasar on her way home from working at the English-language school, Robyn bumped into an old acquaintance from Manly Girls High. The woman was a born-again Christian who was honeymooning in Bali with her husband who ran a surf shop at Avalon on Sydney's northern beaches. They had known each other at school and on the surf scene, but were not close friends.

'Oh my God, Robyn, what's happened to you?' the woman exclaimed.

Robyn was pale and emaciated. By this stage her milk had dried up, so she couldn't breastfeed, even if she wanted to. Later the woman came to visit at the house in Denpasar, where Robyn was feeding baby Mohammed weak tea from a bottle, having run out of powdered milk.

'Why have you only fed your son tea?' she asked.

'Because I don't have any milk.'

Before she left, Robyn's Christian friend made a solemn promise.

'I swear by God that when I get back to Australia, I'll help you get out of here.'

She was as good as her word. Three months later she sent enough money to Jakarta to buy plane tickets home to Sydney for Robyn and the two children. Robyn later wondered about the motivation for her act of kindness. 'I'm not saying she didn't do it out of the goodness of her heart, but I think the fact that I'd become a Muslim and needed "saving" was also in there somewhere.' When Robyn told Bambang she was leaving, he offered no objection; he even took them to the airport to say goodbye. 'Take care of yourself and look after the baby' were his parting words, as Robyn, Devi and baby Mohammed left to return to Australia.

5

THE DEATH OF ROBYN

Sydney, 1978–1980

Two weeks after touching down in Australia, and after visiting her local GP for a checkup, Robyn was admitted to the Mona Vale hospital on Sydney's northern beaches. She was diagnosed with malnutrition, immune deficiency caused by blood loss, and a raging uterine infection, which had gone untreated since Mohammed's birth and had spread to spawn secondary infections in her liver and kidneys. She was hooked up to a drip and fed antibiotics intravenously then discharged after ten days.

Robyn and the two children, three-year-old Devi and Mohammed, now aged seven months, moved in with Bessie and her younger daughter Susan, who were living in a granny flat in the backyard of their old fibro house in Dee Why West. They had vacated the house and moved into the bungalow in the garden when Robyn and Bambang had left hurriedly for Indonesia after the drug bust. But two adults, a teenager and two small children was more than the little flat was built to hold, and not long after their arrival the owner told them they had to leave.

Reliant for income on her single mother's pension, Robyn rented a room in a dilapidated doss house on the waterfront at Manly Wharf near the aquarium. She and the children slept in the same bedroom and shared a common kitchen and bathroom with a motley collection of junkies, drug dealers and winos. 'It was a terrible place, it was gross', she recalls. The linoleum flooring was thick with grime. 'The baby was crawling by this stage but I wouldn't let him on the floor at all; I either carried him or he was in bed.' Despite their mean accommodation, Robyn was elated to be home. 'She was just relieved to be back. She always had this amazing smile—and she was just all smiles', remembers her old classmate Deborah Jensen. Her friends in the surf crowd passed a hat around to raise money for a bond and helped her find a garden flat at Narrabeen overlooking the lagoon.

About a year after her return to Australia, Robyn received a phone call out of the blue from Bambang's mother in Jakarta. Bambang had been arrested for possession of drugs and was in a Denpasar prison. His parents were beside themselves. Apart from the public shame for the family, serious drug offences could carry the death penalty, and his father's money, rank and clout were proving insufficient to get Boy out of this particular fix. They believed an appeal for mercy from his *orang bule* wife and mother of his children might just be enough to save him. 'They wanted me to come to set up the impression that he was a good family man who had gone a bit off the tracks, and to give assurances to the judge that he's going to come back to Australia and start a new life.'

After borrowing the airfare from her mother, Robyn left the children with Bessie and Susan and flew to Jakarta. She was greeted by her father-in-law, Amir Andjilin, who took her first to the jail to see Bambang and then to the home of the judge presiding over his case, to pay their respects and beg for clemency. Bambang was a fine upstanding husband and father who had seen the error of his ways and wished only to be reunited with his family in Australia where he could start a new life, Robyn assured the judge. Apparently convincing in the role of tearful supplicant, Robyn's performance combined with his father's connections—and no doubt an appropriate token of the family's appreciation—was enough to secure Bambang's release.

Robyn returned to Australia and next petitioned the immigration department to overlook Bambang's previous drug conviction in Sydney and renew his residency status so he could be reunited with his family. No mention was made of his latest infringement in Indonesia, of which the Australian authorities were presumably unaware. Once again Robyn's entreaties had the desired effect. A new visa was issued and Bambang flew back to Australia, 'with all the promises in the world that he was going to wake up to himself', she recalls.

But Bambang's penitence—and their reunion—proved short-lived. Unqualified and reluctant to return to factory work, he remained unemployed and they made do on social security benefits. Robyn thought he had stopped taking drugs, but while rummaging through the medicine cabinet she found a stash of the benzodiazepene Rohypnol. She knew enough about narcotics from the surf scene to know that Rohypnol was the prescription drug of choice for heroin addicts. When she confronted him, she says he admitted he had graduated to heroin.

Not long after this, Robyn was hanging the washing on the line in the garden when two-year-old Mohammed woke up crying. Bambang, apparently in a drug-induced stupor, gave the baby a dose of Rohypnol—or else the child took it himself after finding it on the bedside table, as Bambang claimed. Either way, the toddler fell unconscious and had to be rushed by ambulance to the Mona Vale hospital. Robyn was enraged.

'When I leave this hospital and take my son home, you will not be there', she told him. 'If you promise to leave us alone, I will tell them it was an accident. If you don't, I will tell them you did it on purpose, and you will be charged with attempted manslaughter—or manslaughter if the baby dies.' When Robyn and baby Mohammed came home from hospital three days later, Bambang had packed his things and gone.

She was now twenty-six, and the life of Robyn Mary Hutchinson was not going according to plan. She had envisaged a career, a stable home life and 'a big happy family'. Instead she was separated from her drug-dependent husband, bringing up two children alone, and working night-shift as a barmaid at the Steyne Hotel, where one night an obnoxious drunk tipped a beer over her head. It was looking far too much like her mother Bessie's life for Robyn's liking. Unlike her mother, she had by now sworn off drugs and alcohol for life after seeing their ravages at close quarters. She briefly tried a career in drug and alcohol rehabilitation, but her brusque intolerance proved ill-suited to counselling; asked to advise on a couple of heroin addicts who had hired their eight-year-old son out for sex to fund their habits, she wrote: 'Stand them up against a wall and shoot them'.

Robyn felt angry and betrayed at the direction her life had taken. At times she despaired of the future. It was a struggle to maintain her faith. 'My practice of Islam had almost disappeared. I still believed in God, but I had no real knowledge of Islam, other than "there is no God but Allah and Mohammed is his messenger", and that was it.'

One summer evening a workmate from the Steyne came over to take Robyn out for a night on the town. She had lined up a babysitter and they were heading for a disco in the city. Her friend had brought a pizza to share before they went.

'I can't eat it', said Robyn, pushing the cardboard carton away.

'Why not?' asked her friend.

'It's got pig in it. I don't eat pig. It's my religion.'

Her friend rolled her eyes.

'What kind of religion is that—when the only thing you don't do is eat pig? I've known you long enough, and as far as I've seen that's the only thing you don't do. What kind of religion is that?'

Four-year-old Devi was sitting under the table playing with a doll.

'Mummy', she piped up, for no apparent reason, 'when I was a little girl, you taught me to say something before we ate. What was it?'

'*Bismilla hir Rahman nir Rahim*', Robyn recited. In the name of Allah, the most gracious, the most merciful.

Looking back years later, Robyn would recall this instant as an epiphany.

'When I said it, I felt like I'd been hit over the head—it was physical pain. A feeling came over me like I was going to die. I felt like this was my last chance—Allah wasn't going to give me any more chances. Either I was going to be true to this religion of Islam or else I would be lost for ever.'

Shoving aside the pizza box, Robyn fumbled for the White Pages phone book, looked under 'm', and found a number for a mosque at Surry Hills, in Sydney's inner eastern suburbs. Her call was answered by a caretaker who spoke little English and listened, bewildered, as she blurted out that she needed help. He wasn't sure what he could do.

'You don't understand', she insisted. 'I've been a really bad Muslim and I'm going to die.'

'You come', was his reply.

She called a taxi, bundled up Devi and baby Mohammed, and took them to the mosque, where the caretaker was waiting for them.

'You come with me', he repeated, lifting the children into the back of his car.

Robyn had no idea where he was taking them, as they motored south-westwards in the fading light through a trail of shabby suburbs strung out along Sydney's Parramatta Road. Eventually they reached a shopping strip in Haldon Street, Lakemba, which is known for being Australia's Muslim heartland. In the middle of the shopping centre they pulled up outside a bookshop with a sign in Arabic and a display window full of books, prayer mats, clothing and Islamic paraphernalia. It was owned by a couple of Australian Muslim converts, Silma and Siddiq Buckley.

Silma Buckley (now Ihram) was a well-known figure in the Australian Muslim community. Like Robyn, she and her husband Siddiq had trav-elled to Indonesia on the hippy trail in the 1970s and converted there to Islam. She had returned to Australia to become the youthful doyenne of a small but growing band of converts—or 'reverts', as they preferred to call themselves, believing that Islam is the universal religion and that those who discover it are simply reverting to their natural faith. She and Siddiq had set up the Muslim Services Association in an office in Haldon Street, with a shopfront that housed the Muslim Women's Shop and Centre.

Silma recalls the day an extremely agitated Robyn showed up on her doorstep and poured out her story. 'You don't know me but you would have read about me—I'm the marijuana baby's mother', Robyn announced.

'I remember when she came in, because she spent a fair bit of time talking to me, and she was obviously having a really hard time', says Silma. 'She told me how her husband had left the country, and how the police had found the dope in the cot. She was very bitter about the media and what they had done to her, and she was bitter about her husband.' Silma could see that Robyn was vulnerable, depressed and angry, but at the same time determined to take control of her life. 'I found her overpowering in some ways. I'm quite an outgoing person, but I found her a bit intimidating. But she was obviously someone in need.'

Robyn was taken by Silma's attire—a full-length, loose-fitting dress with a scarf tied around her hair. It reminded Robyn of the outfit worn by her former servant girl, Muna, in Indonesia.

'What's that you're wearing?' Robyn asked her.

'It's called a hijab', Silma replied.

'Why are you wearing it?'

'Because it's a requirement for all Muslim women.'

'Well, you'd better give me one too.'

Wrapped in the folds of fabric, she felt relief wash over her. 'I felt like I'd come home. I felt an incredible sense of peace. I was at peace.'

Silma and Siddiq persuaded her to move with the children to Lakemba, where they assured her it would be easier to maintain her faith among a large Muslim community. They likened it to the Islamic tradition of *hijrah*, 'where you leave something for the sake of Allah, something that's bad for you, and you take a journey to something that's good for you', in Robyn's words. The original *hijrah* was the Prophet Mohammed's historic journey from Mecca to Medina in the seventh century, to escape his enemies and take shelter in the safe haven where he established his Islamic realm.

Robyn packed a single bag with three sets of clothing for herself and each of the children. 'I left the rest behind—clothes, furniture, toys, everything I owned. It was quite a statement. I didn't care any more. I just wanted that feeling of peace.' She knew that this time there would be no going back. 'I feel now that everything before that was a prelude to what I would become. This was the beginning of the real me—who I was and what I really believed in, and I felt it very intensely. And I made a promise to Allah that to the best of my ability I would try to learn this *deen* (religion) of Islam with everything that I had.'

She took to Islam with a convert's zeal, redoubled by her own characteristic intensity and desperate need to order her life. Silma Buckley had already seen what happens when 'vulnerable people' convert to Islam. 'When they find out there's a way they can sort themselves out, they seize onto it like someone who is drowning seizes onto life support. Converts are often high maintenance, they have high emotional needs. They're people on the outskirts of society. You find the same kind of person in a whole range of religious and alternative organisations—like Scientology, or Pentecostalism. Because they're not your mainstream, conservative kinds of people. You have to be really at the edges of society before you're able to make the jump to Islam, because it's so unacceptable to mainstream Australians. It's more acceptable to become gay than to become a Muslim.'

Through Silma and Siddiq Buckley, Robyn was welcomed into the tight-knit convert community. They were caring and supportive; they called each other 'brother' and 'sister'; it was like the big happy family she had craved.

In keeping with Muslim tradition, Robyn's friends suggested that she Islamise her name. One of the women at Lakemba suggested the moniker of a legendary eighth-century Iraqi teacher and ascetic named Rabiah al Adawiyah. According to Robyn: 'She was a pious woman in the time when the men were very lax and didn't do their Islamic duty. She led men into battle.' The history books give a somewhat different account, describing the original Rabiah as a Sufi scholar, mystic and saint, who formulated an ideal of selfless worship, inspired purely by love of God, rather than by hope for paradise or fear of hell. One famous story tells how she ran through the town of Basra with a bucket of water and a torch, to symbolically douse the fires of hell and set paradise ablaze, so that people would devote themselves to worship for Allah's sake alone. Her legendary fortitude and unyielding faith were recounted in many such tales:

One night Rabiah al Adawiyah was praying in the hermitage when she was overcome by weariness and fell asleep. So deeply was she absorbed that when a reed from the mat she was lying on broke in her eye so that the blood flowed, she was quite unaware of the fact. A thief entered and seized her *chaddur* (veil). He then made to leave, but the way was barred to him.

After several attempts to steal Rabiah's veil—a symbol for luring her away from Islam—the thief heard a voice from the corner of the hermitage:

Man, do not put yourself to such pains. It is so many years now that she has committed herself to Us. The Devil himself has not the boldness to slink around her. How should a thief have the boldness to slink around her *chaddur*? Be gone, scoundrel!

And thus in 1980, at the age of twenty-six, Robyn Mary became Rabiah Maryam Hutchinson. It was a propitious choice of name, because her single-minded sense of mission would prove every bit as staunch as that of her intrepid namesake.

But it was more than just a change of name. As she saw it, it was her life starting over—the transformation was complete. 'Robyn died that day, the day I went back and got my belongings and moved to Lakemba. I just literally walked out and left that person behind. It reminds me of the cicadas I used to go and collect as a child. What I left behind was a shell, and it was empty because that wasn't the person I was. The life that I had lived as Robyn was false, it wasn't really me. I wasn't leaving behind who I really was; it's exactly the opposite—it was me becoming who I really am.'

PART 2

RABIAH

6

BECOMING RABIAH

Sydney, 1980

Allahu Akbar, Allahu Akbar
Ash-hadu alla ilaha illallah
Ash-hadu anna Muhammadar rasulullah
Hayya alas-salat

The pre-dawn wail of the *muezzin* wafted across the terracotta rooftops of suburban Lakemba, calling Muslims to pray at the Arabian-themed mosque in Wangee Road. The mellifluous chant that had merely piqued her curiosity the first time in Jakarta now filled Rabiah with a joyous relief and sense of belonging.

In the name of Allah, the most gracious, the most beneficent,
All praise and thanks be to Allah, the Lord of the worlds ...
You alone we worship
You alone we ask for help
Guide us to the straight way
The way of those on whom you have bestowed your Grace,
Not the way of those who have earned your Anger nor of those who
went astray.

Veiled in white and surrounded by hundreds of fellow Muslims, prostrated and praying in unison, their feet lightly touching to signify their communion, Rabiah knew for certain that she had found the true faith—and her true self.

'The transformation was profound. It was so drastic. One day I was somebody and the next day I was somebody else. The way I dressed, the way I spoke, the way I looked.' And unlike her childhood epiphany under the stained glass of the Catholic church in Mudgee, this time there was not a shadow of doubt. 'The person I was when I was Robyn wasn't real. I never felt comfortable and I always felt like I was looking for something, not something I'd lost but something I wanted to see and experience. When I found Islam it was so clear that that's what I had been lacking all my life.'

Praying beside her was one of her new Muslim friends, an American convert named Rahmah McCormack, who was a member of the cohort formed around Silma and Siddiq Buckley. Rahmah's journey had much in common with Rabiah's own. She was born Suzanne into a Catholic family in New Jersey, but abandoned the church at the age of thirteen; much like Rabiah, she found there were too many esoteric mysteries that made no sense. 'It was not intellectually satisfying for me. I was asked to accept a lot in faith without any intellectual backup and it was very frustrating', she explained later. She studied education at university, obtained a masters degree in teaching, married an atheist, bought a home and explored eastern religions. 'I had everything I was supposed to want. But I was still very confused. People of my mother's generation had stability, but in my generation we were left on our own to decide. We really did not know what to do. I began to reject my lifestyle. My marriage was falling apart.'

It was then she met Robert McCormack, an Australian travelling in the United States who had become a Muslim and taken the name Abdul Wasi. She converted, changed her name to Rahmah, and they married and moved to Australia in 1979. They settled in Sydney's Lakemba—whose large Lebanese Muslim population had earned it the nickname 'Lebkemba'— where the shops stocked *halal* food and there was a huge mosque, built in the mid 1970s with a gift of $300 000 from the King of Saudi Arabia, supplemented by donations from Libya, Kuwait and other benefactors. Lakemba was the natural home for an ever-widening circle of about 200 Australian Muslim converts.

It was by this same community that Rabiah was embraced when she arrived at Lakemba a year after Rahmah, with five-year-old Devi and Mohammed, now aged three. The McCormacks invited Rabiah and the children into their home, a tidy brick house in nearby Dulwich Hill. The children slept in bunk beds while the adults slept on mattresses on the floor, as the Prophet Mohammed had done, and instead of chairs in the lounge room there were velvet cushions and mats draped in Indian prints.

With all the mettle of her namesake, Rabiah now set about mastering Islam. She was determined to really *become* Rabiah, not just go by the name. 'I call this my sponge stage. When I moved here I kept my promise to Allah to try to the best of my ability to learn this *deen* of Islam. And it was the most incredible time for me. For the next six months I hardly slept. It was six months of striving to understand Islam. All I did was clean, cook, look after my kids and read. I just read anything and everything I could get my hands on.'

Having overcome her childhood dyslexia to become a voracious reader, she now consumed every Islamic text she could find in English. In the space of a few days, she read a four-volume compilation of the *hadith*, the collected sayings and deeds of the Prophet Mohammed, which make up the body of knowledge known as the *Sunnah*, the customary ways of the Prophet, used by Muslims as a guide to how they should live. With her near photographic memory, she says: 'I remembered every word I read. If there was something I didn't understand or it didn't make sense, I would go back to the original text. I'm a very thorough person, I keep going till I get the correct interpretation.' Her fixation with finding the 'correct' interpretation was reminiscent of the obsession with realism evident in her childhood games, playing horses with her schoolmates in Mudgee or playing nuns with Laurette to convert their hapless visiting auntie to Catholicism. 'That's always been part of who I am and what I am, that if I do something I want to do it right. I mean I made those kids eat grass, and that poor deranged auntie was kneeling at the foot of that bed for hours.'

The year 1980 was an exhilarating time to be a Muslim. The Iranian revolution led by Ayatollah Khomeini had recently toppled the corrupt American-backed Shah of Iran and established an Islamic state which Muslims the world over were inspired to emulate. The Soviet Union had invaded Afghanistan, prompting the nation's mullahs to declare a jihad (holy war) against the infidel aggressors. Muslims around the globe were rallying to support the *mujahidin* (holy warriors) in their fight against the Russians, enthusiastically backed and bankrolled by the United States and its allies.

On Tuesday nights, Rabiah and her new friends would congregate at Silma and Siddiq's bookshop, which also served as a drop-in centre and welfare office where English-speaking Muslims gathered to discuss and seek guidance on the tenets of their faith. The converts were a bunch of enthusiastic idealists who were captivated by Islam's strong sense of com-munity, egalitarianism and social justice. They attended lectures on Islam at the universities and Sunday talks in the Domain by celebrated converts such as the firebrand former Communist trade union leader Mohammed John Webster.

Rabiah was drawn to Jemaah Tabligh, a missionary sect established in India in the early 1900s to promote the spiritual revival of Islam through strict observance of the *Sunnah* (customs) of the Prophet. Jemaah Tabligh's Lakemba chapter was the most organised and active Muslim group in Australia at the time, and its adherents the most conspicuously devout. The men wore long Arab-style robes, with their pants above their ankles and their beards the length of a man's fist, in the style of the Prophet. They took their sleeping bags to Friday *jummah* (communal prayers) so they could spend the entire weekend at the mosque. Their movement eschewed politics and the use of violence, believing that Muslims could only wage jihad once they had perfected their practice of Islam. Their stark literalism and blatant religiosity appealed to Rabiah. 'It was something I admired because of their outward display of Islam. It's a strong statement: "I am a Muslim". I saw them as the epitome of good Muslims.'

For Rabiah, a potent part of the allure of Islam was that nothing was left to chance; every aspect of a Muslim's life was prescribed in the Quran and *Sunnah*. 'Once you become a Muslim, everything—from how long your fingernails are to how you go to the toilet; how you live your life twenty-four hours a day to how you rule a country—is governed by Islam.' After a life marked by domestic tumult, it spoke powerfully to her longing for discipline, order and clarity.

'She was very motivated to have a clear grasp of Islam', Siddiq Buckley recalls. 'Her attitude seemed to be: "OK, I can hang onto this— it's very clear, it's transparent, I can have no doubts about this". She wanted everything to be clear. I think she was always looking—even in those days—for the "right" kind of Islam.'

Having found her own salvation, Rabiah was eager to spread the word. In November 1980, she and Rahmah McCormack were interviewed by the *Sydney Morning Herald* newspaper, for a story about Muslim converts in Australia. (The *Herald* sent its 'ethnic affairs reporter', reflecting the prevailing view that a story about Muslims constituted 'ethnic affairs', even though the article was about mostly Australian-born devotees.) The story appeared under the headline 'Two women converts explain Islam's "simplistic" appeal'.

'The two women are young and attractive', the reporter wrote. 'Between them, they have tried the Roman Catholic, Anglican, Baptist and Presbyterian faiths and now, they say, they are committed Moslems [*sic*] ... They are no longer confused, aimless or unhappy. The Koran tells them what to do and they do it, happily, in the knowledge of Islam.'

'I was looking for the truth. I found the truth through Islam', Rabiah told the newspaper. 'Moslems [*sic*] say there is a way to live your life and make it easier to live with one another, and this is the way', her friend Rahmah explained. 'It is a simplistic direction. You are not confused, you are directed.'

Rabiah was pictured wearing a yellow Indian-style kaftan with a flowing headscarf held in place by a black band around her hair, 'like a Muslim hippy', she later observed. She wore her trademark grin as she and Rahmah were photographed strolling along a street in Dulwich Hill. 'I looked like a stupid Cheshire cat and she looked like the Virgin Mary.'

The two neophytes were eager to emphasise that Islam was not a culture but a faith, that they were Australian *and* Muslim. They insisted that contrary to popular perception Islam was not oppressive, and the primitive customs followed in some Muslim countries were a reflection of their cultures, not of the true Islamic faith. As Rabiah explained it: 'Islam is not a mantle of another culture. As converts we do not have cultural ties. People look at the culture of Afghanistan or Iraq or Iran and blame Islam. (But) we look to pure Islam. Practices in Arab countries such as female circumcision or wearing veils are local practices done in ignorance of Islam.'

Rabiah's own experience as a Muslim and her study of the scripture had transformed her previously low opinion of Islam's treatment of women. Like many female Muslims, she embraced those parts of the Quran and *Sunnah* that extol the dignity, honour and rights of women. The *hadith* record the Prophet Mohammed telling his followers: 'You will be held to account for how you treated the women'. When asked by one man, 'To whom do I owe my loyalty?' the Prophet replied 'your mother'. 'And then?' the man asked him. 'Your mother', the Prophet replied again. 'And then?' 'Your mother.'

Rabiah's role models were the iconic heroines of Islamic lore such as Mohammed's first wife, Khadija, a respected businesswoman fifteen years his senior, who remained his sole partner until she died; and his third wife, Aisha, who accompanied Muslim forces into battle after the Prophet's death. It was Aisha who inspired Mohammed to enjoin his followers: 'Take half of your religion from this woman', an order that is widely read as acknowledging women's equality in religious matters. This equality is alluded to in the Quran, which addresses itself to both 'men who believe and women who believe, men who obey and women who obey'.

For the women of seventh-century Arabia, the revelations set down in the Quran were an enormous step forward. Previously, women had had the status of mere chattels who could be taken as war booty, and newborn girls were often left to perish in the desert. Wives were routinely beaten and there was no limit on how many spouses a man could take. The Quran ordered an end to female infanticide and established that a man could take a maximum of four wives, but only if he treated them equally, stressing: 'If you shall not be able to deal justly, (take) just one'. The Prophet discouraged domestic violence, chastising his followers: 'Some of your wives came to me complaining that their husbands have been beating them. I swear by Allah those are not the best among you.' The Quran instructed that a disobedient woman should first be admonished, then banished from her husband's bed; if she continued to disobey him she could be beaten as a last resort, but never on the face. When a follower asked him what kind of beating was allowed, the Prophet replied that he could hit his wife only with a *sewak*, or tooth stick. This was a twig cut from a desert Arak tree, which was soaked in water and chewed until the fibres separated, creating a natural toothbrush that was (and still is) widely used by Muslims. While to a modern reader this may seem brutal, in the context of its time the Quran was a force for women's liberation rather than oppression; indeed in some respects it afforded them rights that were well ahead of those enjoyed by European women at the time. It was this that Rabiah and her fellow converts grasped.

'I had been reading a lot of *hadith* and my reaction was—look at all these rights that Islam has given women', says Rabiah. 'Don't forget I had just been through Germaine Greer and the "burn your bra" period. A lot of things that women were fighting for, Muslim women had had for 1400 years: the fact that a Muslim woman doesn't become "Mrs" anything; you are not the property of your husband; your husband has no right to your money; a man doesn't have the right to beat his wife black and blue; he is responsible for her upkeep.' She had read in the *hadith* that a man was supposed to provide his wife with a slave if he could afford one, that women were not obliged to do menial chores, and that the Prophet used to sew his own clothing. 'I thought all these things were wonderful', she says.

The fact that the Quran allotted women half the inheritance rights of men (again, a progressive step in seventh-century Arabia) and gave their legal testimony only half the value of that of men could be simply explained, according to Rabiah. Men were obligated to financially support their wives and sisters, so they needed a greater share of wealth. And women were known to be more emotional than men, hence their testimony was deemed less reliable. The same explanation applied to the divorce rules, which allow a man to end his marriage by simply saying 'I divorce thee' three times, whereas a women must go to a judge to seek a formal annulment.

Herself hot-tempered and impulsive by nature, Rabiah felt this made perfect sense. 'I'm not going to be apologetic about it—Islam teaches us that women are more emotional than men. The reason it (the power in divorce) is given to men is because of the nature of the female. When she gets very upset she gets more emotional, and is likely to say "Well, divorce me then!" It's a safety net against emotional decisions.'

For all her rebelliousness in childhood and her teens, Rabiah remained an old-fashioned girl at heart. She held motherhood and family life as her most cherished values and had no time at all for political correctness. Despite her flirtation with the 'burn your bra' movement, to Rabiah the 'equality of the sexes' was nothing more than a slogan. 'Men and women aren't "equal". It's like saying a cup of coffee and a cup of tea are "equal"— yes they're both hot, they're both in a cup. But the mere term "equal" connotates "the same". Men and women are so different, in the shape of their body and the functions of their brain. Is one better than the other? No. Which one is more capable? It depends what you're talking about. Which one is kinder? A woman. Which one is stronger? Usually a man.'

To her it was self-evident that their distinctive qualities should be recognised in separate roles. As she saw it, Islam offered a different kind of 'liberation'. 'It's liberating in that it allows you to be a woman and it liberates you from unreal expectations and untrue stereotyping. It liberates you from the wrong concepts about being a woman. And Islam liberates women *and* men from the servitude of any human being.'

When Rabiah's old buddies on the surf scene saw her spouting her views in the *Sydney Morning Herald*, they were gobsmacked. The day she had packed up and moved to Lakemba, she had left without saying good-bye, severing all contact with previously close friends, some of whom had been oblivious of her conversion.

'I picked up the newspaper one day and there's Robyn in her Muslim regalia as "the spokesperson for the Muslim community"', remembers Deborah Jensen, her old schoolmate from Manly Girls High. 'Two weeks prior she'd been working as a barmaid at the Steyne Hotel in Manly. She had an argument with a customer and he threw a beer in her face so she quit her job and went back to being a Muslim again.'

Deborah was furious and rang the journalist at the *Herald* to pour scorn on the story. Next she rang her former friend to let her have it. 'I was angry with her because she was being a hypocrite. I spoke to her on the phone afterwards, and I said, "Robyn, you know me very well and you know I don't like hypocrites. Robyn, you're a hypocrite".' It was the last time they ever spoke. Twenty-eight years later, Deborah, who volunteers that she has little time for organised religion, remains cynical about her friend's metamorphosis. 'I didn't see it as a betrayal, I just saw it as bullshit. There wasn't a religious bone in her body. She just went on a mission. That's Robyn. Being a Muslim—I think it drew attention to her, it made her feel valued, important. It was an unusual thing for an Australian woman to be a Muslim, and she liked that. It made her feel more important and better about herself. Robyn had a hard life. She wanted to be noticed—Robyn wanted to be noticed.'

Normally thick-skinned, Rabiah was mortified at her friend's reaction. 'I was really embarrassed. It made me sound like I was on some sort of scam, pretending to be something I wasn't. According to Deborah and the people who'd known me in Manly, I was an Aussie chick who did everything everyone else did, and now I was pretending to be a Muslim. In fact it was the other way around. I was a Muslim and I was pretending to be that Aussie chick—not pretending, but I'd slipped back into that way of life.'

Determined to reinvent herself, Robyn had left the 'Aussie chick' behind, once and for all—discarded like a cicada shell—along with her old friends. 'I never "wiped" them. It was just that they stayed with Robyn— my friends stayed with Robyn. It wasn't that I didn't need them any more, like I discarded them because they weren't useful. It was more a case of— I'm going somewhere and I can't take you with me. And in any case, they wouldn't recognise me any more. They didn't know Rabiah, they didn't know Rabiah existed. And they have no idea Robyn doesn't exist any more. And you could not be Robyn and Rabiah at the same time.'

This belief in the all-consuming nature of her conversion was underscored, a few months after her move to Lakemba, when her sister Susan got married in a service at the Uniting Church in Dee Why followed by a reception at the Diggers Club. Rabiah baulked at attending the church service but went along to the reception, albeit reluctantly, having been told that devout Muslims regard music as *haram*, or forbidden. She bought herself a new outfit and draped her headscarf to look like an exotic fashion rather than religious attire. 'From the minute I got there I wanted it to be over. I went out of duty, love and respect for my sister, but it was terrible. I felt like the biggest hypocrite. It was like knocking on a door and someone answers it and they think you're someone else, and because they insist you're that person you try to accommodate them. Everyone else thought it was Robyn. But it wasn't Robyn who went to that wedding, it was Rabiah. I just didn't belong.'

Her family, long accustomed to her knack for reinvention, was sanguine about her latest incarnation. Despite her own ambivalence about religion, Bessie took it in her stride. 'I think in the beginning Mum just thought, oh well, here she goes again. Then it was: oh well, she may dress funny but as long as she's improving herself. Because my mum saw the change in me—that I was being focused, not going out to nightclubs or drinking alcohol and taking drugs. She didn't really care if I was wearing something on my head, just as long as I was better, a better person.'

Aside from the strange clothing and rituals, Rabiah's core beliefs had changed little from the values Bessie had drilled into her as a child. 'There's fundamental things about me that are still the same—the values instilled by my mother that are a part of my character. *And* the negative things: bad-tempered, stubborn, authoritarian. I didn't turn from a devil into an angel. The only thing I haven't found to be true is that she taught me there was grey. I don't see grey, it's all black and white to me.'

Since Rabiah now avoided the northern beaches, Bessie often made the long trip by public transport across the Harbour Bridge to Lakemba to visit her daughter and grandchildren, Devi and Mohammed, on whom she doted. Eventually she moved in and lived with them for three months. She remained entirely mystified by Islam, but when Rabiah went out and Bessie was left to babysit she always made sure the children said their prayers, as instructed. 'I don't know what they said but they said something', she would report on Rabiah's return.

The family had moved out of the McCormacks' house and into a one-bedroom flat, where the only furniture was a fridge and bunk beds for the children. Rabiah rejected repeated offers of furniture from helpful friends, preferring to sit and sleep on the floor as the Prophet Mohammed had done. She was a fastidious housekeeper who couldn't stand mess or dirt. 'I think it's just me, I like things to be in order, I think it's because I'm a control freak', she explains. She liked to hang the laundry in order on the washing line; her own clothes, Devi's and Mohammed's in separate— preferably colour co-ordinated—groups; she also used to colour-code the pegs until a friend told her it was a sign of obsessive compulsive disorder. Bessie lost her temper one day after hanging out the washing when she found Rabiah rehanging it 'correctly'. 'You can go naked for all I care', her mother snapped.

Rabiah's style of parenting owed much to Bessie's own no-nonsense firmness, with echoes of her grandfather's severity. 'Mum was a lot softer than me as a person, not as severe', she says. The children were drilled each morning to wash their face, hands and feet, fold their pyjamas and place them under their pillows. They had to finish every scrap of food on their plates; Rabiah couldn't abide waste and continually lectured them about all the poor children starving overseas. For all her efforts as a disciplinarian, it was clear early on that her children had inherited a streak of rebellion, which she put down to her own draconic temperament and the absence of a father. 'It affects children, not to have a father figure, and to have an authoritarian mother; it tends to make them more unconventional, to want to rebel.'

Five-year-old Devi came home from her first day at school refusing to go back because she hadn't been taught to read and write.

'If you don't go, the police will come and take you', Rabiah warned.

As strong-willed as her mother, Devi tried a new tack the following day.

'Don't forget your lunch', Rabiah reminded her.

'No thank you, I don't want any lunch today.'

'Why not?'

'Well, you know all those children who die from not eating? Well if I don't eat, I'll die, then I won't have to go to school.'

Three-year-old Mohammed was a similarly forthright child. One day, while Bessie was staying with them, they were about to walk to the shops when Mohammed darted into his mother's bedroom and came out with a headscarf, which he handed to his grandma.

'Oh no, darling, I don't wear that', laughed Bessie.

'But Muslims have to wear it', replied Mohammed, echoing his mother's oft-repeated words.

'I'm not a Muslim, darling', explained Bessie.

'Well you'll have to leave then', said a solemn-faced Mohammed.

The education of their children was a pressing concern for the small but vocal convert community, which lobbied the New South Wales government to introduce Islamic education into the state's public schools. In those days there were no exclusively Islamic schools; most Muslim children attended government public schools where they were expected to take part in Christmas nativity scenes and Easter passion plays. Islam rarely rated a mention, even though in some schools in south-western Sydney 80 per cent of the students came from Muslim families. Finally, a program was launched under the auspices of the Islamic Council of New South Wales to teach Muslim scripture in certain schools. Rabiah was among the volunteers who offered to take the classes.

She showed up on day one at the Hampden Park Public School in Lakemba where the teachers had rounded up about sixty children, aged seven to ten, and herded them into the assembly hall for their first Islamic scripture class.

'They were totally out of control', Rabiah recalls. 'It was like being in a zoo, they were running and screaming, it was absolute bedlam.' She first tried cajoling them into some semblance of order. When that failed she resorted to the bootcamp approach.

'I got 'em all in there and I literally screamed at them. I made them stand up against the wall. I threatened them—"I know who your father is".' The children came from mostly Lebanese families who hailed principally from impoverished rural villages or were refugees from the country's civil war of the 1970s. Many of their parents were on social security benefits or in poorly paid manual work, and most spoke English as a second language and felt like second-class citizens in Australia. 'They were ashamed to be Muslim, most of them. I wanted them to be proud of being Muslims, to give them back their self-esteem', Rabiah recounts. After haranguing them into submission, she taught them how to perform *wudu*, the ritual washing, and how to recite *salat*, the five obligatory daily prayers. She taught them Islamic songs and games. Then she delivered an ultimatum.

'Right, now it's up to you. Which one did you like better—when I was screaming at you and punishing you, or when we were doing fun things?'

'When we were doing fun things, Miss', they chorused.

'OK, well this is the rule. We'll do fun things as long as you behave. If you misbehave, you get out.'

Silma and Siddiq Buckley remember Rabiah as always an eager volunteer. Siddiq says she had 'a lot of determination, a lot of energy'. Silma recalls: 'If there was a challenge, she would do it. If they told her that to be a Muslim she would have to climb Mount Everest, she'd do it. She would do it in the morning, and then she'd go back and do it again in the afternoon. That's how determined and committed she was. She had a lot of respect in the community.'

Rabiah could often be found proselytising with gusto on the streets of Lakemba, issuing instructions to hapless passers-by on the 'correct' practice of Islam in her usual stentorian tone.

'Oh no, here comes Rabiah with her *shariah* stick', people would mutter as they spotted her striding down the street.

'Excuse me, brother', she would yell across the road in her strident Australian accent, if she spied a man standing in the shopping strip having a drink.

'Do you know you're not a Muslim any more, because the Prophet said Muslims don't stand up to drink?'

Or if she saw someone eating with their left hand, she would berate them: 'You know you're not going to paradise, don't you?' Looking back, she shakes her head at the memory of her younger self in full flight, 'screaming at the top of my lungs from one side of the street to another'. 'In a very short time I had acquired—I wouldn't call it knowledge, but massive amounts of information. Sometimes this is good, but sometimes it can be a disaster, if there's no method or rhyme or reason to it—like someone who loves science but turns out to be the mad professor. I think I was a bit dangerous, I had no qualms.'

She dates her zeal to the evening of her pizza epiphany when she had been gripped by a sensation of dying, as a result of which she carried a burning conviction that God had saved her. 'That feeling I had of dying has never left me. Since that day I thought Allah was going to take my soul from me, that has stayed with me. It has made me very intense. People find me intense and scary.'

This assessment is confirmed by those who know her. 'She was very stern about everything, not just religion, that was just her character', Siddiq Buckley says. 'Everything for her was serious, and she had an opinion about everything, no matter how big or small it was. If she saw things a certain way then that was how it was; it was either right or wrong, there was no grey area in between the two. She had very pessimistic views about Australia, even though she was a dinky-di Aussie. We were all concerned about the lax moral attitudes, but she expressed herself more forcefully than most people. And once she had an opinion it was very hard to shift her, because she was very firm in her conviction. People are generally happy and enthusiastic about becoming a Muslim. Most of the people who came to Islam were much softer in their approach to Islam. They didn't seem to have a chip on their shoulder about doing something to change the world, they were more interested in changing themselves. She seemed to be an angry young woman. I wasn't sure if she was angry about herself, or angry at others, or angry at life in general. Not angry as in violent, but she was not happy.'

Silma Buckley recounts an occasion when she was looking after Devi and Mohammed, of whom Rabiah was fiercely protective. When Rabiah arrived to pick them up, she was furious to learn that Silma had given them biscuits that she believed were not *halal*. Silma remembers: 'She went off. "How can you give the kids biscuits? I've heard there's liquor in these!" She was very angry and upset that she had been violated and her kids had been violated.'

The split between them deepened during a debate over the 'correct' interpretation of a particular *ayat* (verse) of the Quran. At one of their Tuesday night meetings, Silma was reading from a verse that states that Jews, Christians and non-believers will be judged by Allah alongside Muslims on the Day of Resurrection. Silma told the gathering that the meaning of this verse was that other 'People of the Book' could gain entry to paradise, along with Muslims. Rabiah was taken aback.

'Hang on a sec, do you mean to tell me that I could still be a Christian, and drink and party, and I don't have to wear this, and it's acceptable? And I can still go to paradise?'

'Well that's what it's saying.'

'But that doesn't make sense. Why would someone become a Muslim if they can just be a good Christian and it's acceptable to Allah?'

Rabiah resolved to seek a second opinion from an Egyptian friend who spoke fluent Arabic and could therefore check the original text, rather than rely on a translation. The woman consulted a book on *tafsir*, the study of interpreting the Quran, by a renowned eighth-century scholar named Ibnu Kathir. His view, her friend explained to Rabiah, was that the only Jews and Christians who could enter paradise were those who lived in pre-Islamic times. Rabiah announced her discovery at the next meeting.

'What we said last week was wrong. Here's the correct interpretation', she explained to the gathering. But Silma stood her ground.

'Well Ibnu Kathir's got his opinion and I've got mine.'

Rabiah was shocked by Silma's seeming renunciation of a renowned Islamic scholar, who she assumed must be correct.

'It's like saying, "Well, Rabiah's got a scalpel and the brain surgeon's got a scalpel, so I might as well just let Rabiah do my brain surgery".'

The differences between the two women would prove irreconcilable over time. 'I couldn't accept that interpretation—that only Muslims can go to paradise. I've simply never accepted it', says Silma. 'People like Rabiah have one view, they can't countenance alternative views.' Rabiah believes there can be only one interpretation of the Quran because it is unthinkable for a mere human to change the laws of God.

Rabiah also parted company with Jemaah Tabligh, deciding the group was cult-like and that its eschewal of politics—including the waging of jihad—meant denying an elemental part of Islam. 'Their concept was that you have to be a perfect Muslim before you can defend Islam, which is wrong. And this business of not being involved in politics. I mean Islam is a way of life. You can't separate the political side of Islam from ritual devotion because it's a way of life. If Islam teaches us how to go to the toilet, how can it be that it doesn't teach us how we should be ruled? It doesn't make sense. There's no such thing as politicised Islam and non-politicised Islam. If you have un-politicised Islam, then you've only got half of it.'

Political Islam was now the fastest growing ideological movement in the world. The Iranian revolution had fuelled a global surge of Muslim pride and a resolve to replicate the Ayatollah's *shariah* state in other Islamic countries. Iranian women had taken to the streets wearing the face-covering *chador*—which had been banned by the Shah of Iran's father—as a symbol of protest against the corrupt Western-backed regime. After meeting an Iranian woman whose husband was studying in Australia, Rabiah abandoned her hippy-style kaftan and headscarf, and began wearing a more austere Iranian-style hijab, which she teamed with a grey *abaya*, the flowing cloak-type garment designed to conceal a woman's body shape, in keeping with the Quranic *ayat* that says women should 'draw their veils over their bosoms and not display their finery'.

Another front in the Islamic revolution had been opened in Afghanistan following the Soviet invasion of 1979. Volunteers from all over the Islamic world had begun trekking to Afghanistan to join the *mujahidin*, and donations were pouring in from Muslims around the globe, a contribution soon eclipsed by the billions funnelled from the United States and matched dollar for dollar by Saudi Arabia. Rabiah didn't know much about Afghanistan, except that the Russians were 'filthy Communists' who had invaded a Muslim land. On Fridays, she and her friends would spend hours at the mosque collecting money for the *mujahidin*. Women would hand over their gold necklaces, bracelets and rings, sometimes thousands of dollars worth in a day. The proceeds were handed over to a roving representative of the *mujahidin*, an Afghan doctor named Abdul Aziz, who had been given the use of an office in Lakemba by the Lebanese Muslim community.

On one of his visits, Dr Abdul took a shine to Rabiah's boy, Mohammed, an intrepid youngster who was by now four and a half years old.

'Do you want to come to Afghanistan with me?' Dr Abdul asked the boy. 'You could come and live in Afghanistan and be a Muslim soldier.'

Mohammed's eyes lit up. 'My son thought he was serious', Rabiah recounts. 'When Dr Abdul left and went back to Afghanistan without him, he was devastated. After that Mohammed used to say "One day I'm going to Afghanistan".'

Rabiah herself was growing restless. Like her own mother, she had never really settled down, and had never lived in one place for more than three years (she still never has). In late 1981, she decided to make the *haj* pilgrimage to Mecca, a journey that Muslims are expected to make at least once in a lifetime as one of the 'five pillars' of Islam. She booked the trip through a tour group in Lakemba and arranged for Bessie to mind the children while she was away. But two days before their scheduled departure, Rabiah was seized by a sense of foreboding. Seeking guidance, she performed an *istikharah* prayer, a special supplication that Muslims make to solicit Allah's advice.

'I'm not going', she announced to her fellow pilgrims' dismay.

'But you have to go.'

'No, I've prayed *istikharah*. That's it, I'm not going.'

The *hajis* left the following Saturday. On the Sunday, Rabiah's mother collapsed and was rushed to hospital where she was diagnosed with chronic emphysema, which would eventually take her life. After a week or so in hospital, Bessie was discharged and went to stay with her younger daughter, Susan, at her home on Sydney's northern beaches.

Having missed out on the trip to Mecca, Rabiah resolved instead to take the children to Indonesia so they could see their grandparents and she could study Islam. 'I couldn't bear it any more—sitting around with a translation of the Quran saying, "I think this" or "according to me, that". A lot of the time it was just empty talk. The reality was we weren't putting into practice even the things we knew. I didn't know how or where, but I just knew I wanted to go back and study.'

Before returning to Indonesia, there was one outstanding matter that she wished to resolve—her marriage to Bambang Wisudo, which had not yet been annulled. Neither she nor the children had seen him since he left Australia and returned to his family in Indonesia after their separation two years earlier. She was confident she had grounds for a divorce based on Bambang's drug use and failure to support her financially, and wanted to have the marriage dissolved before going back to Indonesia. She travelled to Canberra to visit an Indonesian cleric, Amin Hady, who was then *imam* of the Canberra mosque and recognised as a religious authority by the Indonesian embassy in Australia. However, he refused to grant her a divorce, having not heard Bambang's side of the story. Legally she was still Mrs Robyn Wisudo, a situation she resolved to remedy on her return to Indonesia.

7

AN ENEMY OF SUHARTO

Indonesia, 1981–1984

Arriving back in Indonesia in early 1981, Rabiah was startled to find Bambang there to greet her. When she had phoned from Australia to tell his parents she was bringing Devi and Mohammed to see them, they had told her Bambang was in Bali; but there he was in Jakarta, doing rehab and staying at the house in Pondok Bambu. With customary Javanese inscrutability, the family embraced Rabiah and the children as though nothing had changed, and ushered them to Bambang's room. 'The crazy thing was they just automatically assumed I was still his wife—and technically I was', she says. When she raised the issue of a divorce with him privately, Bambang was uncharacteristically obdurate. 'He told me "I'll never give you a divorce". The family view was that divorce was shameful. I was his wife, and legally he had rights over me.'

She could have gone to an Islamic *kadi* (judge) to seek a divorce, but with Bambang trenchantly resisting, it was unlikely one would have been granted. So Rabiah decided to give her recalcitrant spouse a final chance— on one condition.

'I can't stay with you if you don't pray', she told him.

'OK, you teach me to pray', he replied.

So Rabiah taught Bambang to pray. The novelty of being an observant Muslim and the imperative of maintaining domestic harmony proved sufficient for him to persist, for about three months. He learned to say the *salat* (daily prayers), fasted through Ramadan and read books on Islam. He also exercised his conjugal rights, and almost immediately Rabiah fell pregnant with their third child. Despite their tempestuous history, she clung stubbornly to her hopes of settled domesticity. 'I didn't hate him, I still don't', she explains. 'There was still compatibility there, intellectually, we had the same principles … If he had turned into a good Muslim and taken care of me and the children and stopped his habit, I would have stayed with him, because he was the father of my children.'

They must have made an odd-looking pair. On returning to Indonesia Rabiah had modified her attire, replacing her *abaya* with a long skirt, a loose buttoned blouse that hung to her knees, and a Malay-style 'triangle hijab', which fastens in the centre beneath the chin and covers the upper body. But in a country unaccustomed to Muslim *orang bule* (white people), she was still conspicuous enough that passers-by would walk into trees as they craned their necks to gape after her in the street. A photograph taken at the time showed a piously outfitted Rabiah beside Bambang in leather pants and tie-dyed t-shirt, sporting short cropped hair with a plaited rats tail at the back, and new homemade tattoos.

Rabiah's assertive piety alarmed her father-in-law, Amir Andjilin, who remained a faithful functionary in the Suharto establishment. After obliterating the Communist Party in the massacres of the mid 1960s, the regime had come to regard the Islamic movement as the most potent threat to its hold on power. As Suharto consolidated his rule and sup-pressed political opposition, Indonesians turned to their mosques and prayer groups as an alternative forum for venting their views and aspirations. Islamic discussion groups were mushrooming and Jakarta's bookstores were doing a brisk trade in the works of Islamic radicals such as Hasan al Banna and Abul a'la Maududi, founders of the Egyptian Muslim Brotherhood and Pakistan's Jamaat-e-Islami, who advocated political activism twinned with a return to pure Islam as the salvation of the Islamic world. Across Indonesia, a bold new religiosity was flourish-ing. The hijab was increasingly viewed, particularly among students, as a symbol of covert protest against the regime.

Amir Andjilin couched his disquiet about Rabiah's attire in theological rationale. 'In Islam, the aim of covering yourself is so that a woman does not draw attention. But you getting around like this has the opposite effect', he pointed out.

Rabiah agreed to wear her headscarf tied at the back of her neck, affecting a more Western look, but only for a while.

The expectant couple's reconciliation was predictably fleeting. Emboldened by her newfound conviction and Muslim identity, Rabiah was no longer prepared to play the docile Javanese wife. Nor would she stay silent about what she saw as the pagan practices of her mother-in-law, who secreted lucky charms around the house and performed monthly rituals with her treasured Javanese *kris*, a ceremonial dagger believed to be spiritually potent. When Rabiah challenged her, sparks flew. 'I felt it was my duty to go back and convince them that the type of Islam they were practising was not right. And that was about as popular as an in-grown toenail with my in-laws', she recalls. The inveterate party boy, Bambang, soon lost interest in getting out of bed before dawn every day to pray, and took to sleeping through the day and rising in the evening to avoid his demanding family. Rabiah thought he had reformed until the day she found a stash of drugs, which she flushed down the toilet. Bambang flew into a fury and lashed out as if to strike her, but his father intervened to stop him.

Five months pregnant, she announced she was leaving, and Bambang didn't stand in her way.

Rabiah and the children moved into a cramped shanty in the shabby backblocks of Pondok Bambu. Their new abode was one of a ramshackle row of attached dwellings known as *petak*, which means 'square' or 'compartment'. The walls were made of cement at the bottom and *bedek*, woven palm leaves, at the top. Their 'compartment' consisted of a single room that doubled as living space and bedroom, a tiny enclosed porch with a louvre window and chicken wire instead of glass and a lean-to kitchen-cum-bathroom with a concrete squat toilet in the corner. Outside the back door were an open drain and a pump that fed water into a square concrete tub, with a plastic ladle that was used to scoop out the water for cooking and washing. The floors were of cement, the roof of tin, and the thatch ceiling was home to a menagerie of insects and boisterous rats. At night, Rabiah would lay a pathway of 'rat strips'—oblongs of plastic covered with a strong, sticky adhesive—from the front door to the mats where the family slept, to stop the rats in their tracks before they started gnawing on the children. One night she woke to see a large rodent creeping sideways along the wall. She screamed, waking Devi, who jumped out of bed and got stuck on the rat paper. Their neighbours were intrigued that a pregnant *orang bule* with two young children should be living in such penury. 'The concept of white people being poor had never occurred to them. Indonesians can't get their heads around poor white people', she recalls.

They had been there two months when Rabiah went into premature labour and took herself by taxi to the R. S. Ciptokusumo public hospital in Central Jakarta. The delivery was mercifully quick because the baby was so tiny, born two months premature and weighing less than 2 kilograms. Rabiah herself weighed only 42 kilograms, even less than when she had given birth to Mohammed. The nurses wrapped the newborn in a face washer for a nappy and placed her in a humidicrib, top and tailed with another infant because there weren't enough cribs for all the premature births. Rabiah named the child Rahmah, which means 'mercy', from the opening verse of the Quran.

When her in-laws showed up at the hospital, they were in no mood for celebrating. Because Rabiah had only returned from Australia seven months earlier, they assumed it was not Bambang's child. 'They accused me of being pregnant when I went to Indonesia—that was the most devastating thing', she remembers. After two days, she and baby Rahmah were discharged. Indonesia was still a third-world country where intensive care for premature babies was unheard of; infants simply survived or they died. Rabiah had had no time or money to buy baby clothing so baby Rahmah was sent home to their shack in Pondok Bambu in hospital-issue swaddling clothes.

Now with four mouths to feed and in need of an income, Rabiah made her way to Jakarta's business district and traipsed in and out of the city office blocks housing multinational corporations until she found a position teaching English to the Indonesian staff of a large joint venture company. The salary was US$700 per month, a small fortune by Indonesian standards at the time, and it was enough for the family to move out of their shanty and into a spacious house in Pondok Bambu where Rabiah could now afford servants of her own to help care for the children. Her new employer sent a car with a chauffeur to drive her to and from work each day.

In what spare time she had, she set out to teach herself Islam, relying on a vast array of Islamic literature, mostly in Indonesian, which was stocked in Jakarta's bookstores. Much of the material available was from the Shafi'i school of Islamic jurisprudence, one of the four schools of Islamic law and the prevalent school in Indonesia. Its pioneer was an eighth-century scholar, Imam al-Shafi'i, who believed the Quran should be interpreted purely according to the sayings and deeds of the Prophet Mohammed as recorded in the *hadith*. At all hours of the night in her house in Pondok Bambu, Rabiah could be found poring over books on *tawhid*, the fundamental belief of the Islamic faith, which holds that God is the one and only entity to be worshipped, and that his sovereignty extends to all creatures and all aspects of human life, including governance and the law. She read works by the Pakistani ideologue Maududi and the Arabian theologian Muhammad ibn Abd al-Wahhab, whose allegiance with the House of Saud had transformed Arabia into a bastion of Islamic puritanism. Many of these tracts were deemed politically subversive under the Suharto regime.

Rabiah soon resumed wearing her hijab fastened at the front, to the consternation of her in-laws, whom she continued to visit with the children despite their strained relations.

'I thought we agreed you wouldn't wear it like that', Amir Andjilin chastised her.

'But I read this book and it says that Islamically you have to wear it at the front.' When she showed him the book she was reading, her normally mild-mannered father-in-law was furious.

'This book is illegal! Do you know that to be found with this book you can be accused of collaborating with the enemies of the state?'

His warning was more prescient than he knew.

One afternoon in Jakarta, Rabiah was on a bus travelling home. She had left work early, passing up on the chauffeur-driven ride. As always, the pale-skinned *orang bule* in the hijab was an eye-catching figure, attracting curious stares and whispered comments. She was startled to hear a young man's voice close behind her.

'*Salam Alaikum, Ibu* (Peace be with you, mother). Forgive me for speaking to you and please don't turn around. I'm going to leave a phone number on the seat next to you. It's the telephone number of a group of sisters who are interested to know how you became a Muslim.' The young man dropped a scrap of paper beside her and alighted from the bus.

Busy with her job, three children and her studies, it was several weeks before she rang the number. '*Selamat Pagi* (good morning), my name is Rabiah', she said in Indonesian to the young woman who answered the phone. 'I am a Muslim from Australia. I got your number from an *adik* (brother) who asked me to ring you.'

The woman on the other end of the phone was a twenty-one year old named Nuraini, a student in the engineering faculty at the University of Indonesia (UI). She invited Rabiah to attend a meeting at her father's home and talk to a group of students—'about how I became a Muslim and were there any more like me on the planet'.

Rabiah arrived in the evening at Nuraini's house in Pondok Jeruk, a district of East Jakarta, where about twenty-five students had assembled for a lecture on Surah al Nur, the twenty-fourth chapter of the Quran. This is the chapter that sets out the rules on adultery (100 lashes for an offender and 80 lashes for a false accuser; stoning to death was not pre-scribed in the Quran) and the dress code for Muslim women, enjoining them 'to draw their *jilbab* (cloak) over their bosoms and not to display their finery except to their husbands'. The women in attendance all wore headscarves, and males and females sat in separate rooms with a PA system set up so that everyone could hear. It was the first time Rabiah had witnessed segregation of the sexes, inspired by a *hadith* which recorded that in the Prophet's time men and women sat separately in the mosque.

The male and female students avoided mingling and making eye contact, in keeping with the Quranic injunction on both sexes to 'lower their gaze' when they meet. Most of the crowd were students from either UI or the local Islamic universities. Some had graduated, mostly in engineering or medicine, while others had dropped out.

'They were very intelligent, very articulate', says Rabiah. 'When I met these students it was amazing because it was the epitome of what I'd read about how Islam should be practised.'

After the lecture, Rabiah was invited to the podium to speak about her experience as a Muslim convert. She related the story of how she had first been woken by the *azan*, and how her initial irritation had been replaced by curiosity and finally devotion. The students were intrigued by the seemingly worldly, affluent foreigner who was exuberant and pious in equal measure. Among the group was a 20-year-old street vendor named Pujo Busono, a fervent young Muslim who worked with his family selling drinks in the market and had latched onto the student movement. Pujo was especially taken by the ardent *orang bule*, ten years his senior. 'She was beautiful, she was a Westerner, she was also a Muslim and wearing hijab, and her *akhlaq* (Islamic behaviour) was very good', Pujo reminisced when I met him in Solo, Central Java, in 2008.

The gathering Rabiah joined in Jakarta was part of a clandestine student movement that bloomed from the early 1980s to evade the regime's crackdown on political dissent. Suharto had introduced a program of so-called Campus Normalisation in 1978 to repress political activity and protests in universities. So students had begun flocking to campus mosques and Islamic study groups, known as *pengajian*, as an outlet for their grievances and aspirations. The campus activism was promoted by the Middle-Eastern-funded Indonesian Council for Islamic Propagation and was loosely linked to the movement known as Darul Islam (meaning 'Abode of Islam'), which was formed in the 1940s to campaign for an Islamic state. The students, however, were not plotting to overthrow anyone. As one commentator wrote, their focus was on 'personal morality, piety and discipline', and an 'inner rejection' of Suharto's New Order and the un-Islamic practices of modern Indonesia.

'The students were not initially coming together because they were strong Muslims', says Rabiah. 'It was because of disaffection with Suharto, (the state ideology) Pancasila and corruption. Then they said, "Well hang on, we're Muslims, we have a perfect system". It went from being a student movement to an Islamic movement in a very short period of time. And when they turned to Islam—that's when Suharto realised he had a major problem.'

Rabiah became an enthusiastic champion of the students' cause. 'I didn't have to be convinced the Suharto Government was rotten and needed replacing. The corruption, the poverty—there was something really rotten. And since the majority of Indonesians are Muslims, the most logical answer was Islamic rule.'

The student activists followed a highly literal reading of the Islamic texts, inspired by jurists such as the thirteenth-century scholar Ibn Taymiyya, who was an early champion of the Islamic revival and the leading proponent of the concept of jihad as military struggle, as opposed to the gentler definition of personal 'striving'. In keeping with Ibn Taymiyya's teachings, some of the students sought to emulate the ways of the earliest Muslims, known as the *Salaf al-Salih*, or 'pious predecessors'. (Hence the revival movement known as Salafism.) The students called Suharto the *fir'aun*—a modern-day pharaoh bent on wiping out the believers—and saw the Islamic *shariah* (way) as a pure alternative to the corrupt and oppressive New Order state.

To avoid detection, the new movement used a cell structure pioneered by the Egyptian Muslim Brotherhood known as *usroh*, meaning 'family', meeting in private venues in small groups of around a dozen at a time. 'Sometimes you would have a group that didn't even know who the other groups were', says Rabiah. 'It was underground and secret only because they couldn't do it openly. There were lessons taking place all over Jakarta. There would be an initial lecture, then those who had attended would go out and lecture to another ten people, then another ten. It was spreading very rapidly. It was momentous. It was growing week by week, (and) it scared the government.'

Rabiah became a regular attendee at the secretive trysts held at ever-changing locations around Jakarta. She soon became a minor celebrity in the movement, because her zeal was even greater than that of the students. She was highly regarded by key organisers such as Irfan Awwas, a student activist who later spent nine years in jail for subversion after publishing a magazine critical of the Suharto Government. Awwas remains a high-ranking figure in the Islamist movement as Secretary-General of the Indonesian Mujahidin Council, of which Abu Bakar Ba'asyir was the *emir* (leader) until 2008.

Irfan Awwas shared his memories of Rabiah during an interview in his office in Jogjakarta in July 2008. 'Rabiah was very famous among young Muslims because she was very motivated', Awwas says. 'When she joined the *usroh* movement, people were very surprised—why this woman is more motivated than them in practising Islam. She was very motivated, very energetic. It was really surprising how this convert was so devoted to Islam.'

Rabiah was even closer to Awwas's brother, Fihiruddin, who is widely known within the Islamist movement as Abu Jibril. He was also a senior organiser in the *usroh* movement, and later a founding member of Jemaah Islamiyah (JI) and senior lieutenant to Abu Bakar Ba'asyir. Abu Jibril famously featured in a JI recruitment video, brandishing a Quran and a gun, and declaiming: 'No one can fight a jihad without the holy book in their left hand and a weapon in their right hand'. Abu Jibril was arrested in Malaysia in 2001 and detained for three years under that country's Internal Security Act, before being deported to Indonesia where he has maintained his close ties with Ba'asyir.

'We were quite close, I was her *ustadz* (teacher)', says Abu Jibril, who recalls being struck by her 'aggressive spirit' and insatiable desire to learn. 'She was really curious and eager to know everything about religion. She wanted to be the best Muslim. And once she learned something about Islam, she couldn't wait to practise it. She was young and excited, and we were excited as well, so we worked well together.' Abu Jibril recalls that when she first joined their movement, Rabiah still smoked the occasional cigarette, an unbecoming habit for a devout Muslim woman.

'We challenged her—how can you become a *mujahidah* (female holy warrior) if you cannot give up smoking?' He says that 'after three nights of training' she had quit.

Not long after meeting the students, Rabiah resigned from her highly paid job as an English teacher, having decided it was Islamically unacceptable to be teaching mixed classes of male and female students. She says the company offered to segregate the classes but she now found the job repugnant anyway. 'I hated it because people who learn English want to be as Western as they can, and the more Islamically aware I became, the more distasteful that was.' She told the company the job was no longer consistent with her beliefs. 'I didn't tell them "I'm an enemy of Suharto".'

Rabiah's home in Pondok Bambu became a meeting place where the young zealots could canvas their radical politics out of their parents' earshot. Many of the older generation were alarmed at how the youth were scorning the Indonesian cultures of their forebears in favour of a puritanical form of Islam rooted in mediaeval Arabia. Young women who had been disowned by their families for donning the hijab began turning up on Rabiah's doorstep, and visitors from the provinces coming to attend lectures could always find a spare mat on her floor. The female students displayed posters of Iran's revolutionary leader, Ayatollah Khomeini, and pictures of women with black *chadors* clutched tightly around their faces demonstrating in the streets of Teheran.

Rabiah was seen as a role model and mentor for young women in the Islamist movement, and helped to popularise a new, more pious mode of dress, which quickly became de rigueur among the female students. Traditionally, Indonesian Muslim women had worn Malay-style long-sleeved blouses over ankle-length skirts with separate scarves. Rabiah encouraged them to don the all-enveloping *abaya*, a cloak-style garment commonly worn in more conservative Muslim societies.

'That was the first time Muslim women in Indonesia wore long thick dresses', says Pujo Busono, the young market vendor who had joined the movement. 'She was followed by other women in the community. This idea to change the dress of all Muslim ladies in Jakarta came from Rabiah.'

Inspired by their Iranian revolutionary sisters, some of the student activists took the radical step of donning the *niqab*, the Arabian-style veil (a variation on the *chador*), which covers a woman's entire face except for her eyes. This practice, followed by those who seek to emulate the ways of the *Salaf al-Salih*, is based on a particular reading of Surah al Nur in the Quran, which urges women to 'draw their *jilbab* (cloak) over their bosoms'. As the original *jilbab* included a head covering, Salafists reason that pulling it down over the bosom would mean it covers the face as well. The prononents of this reading also cite a *hadith* which recorded that the Prophet's wives dressed like 'black crows', clad head to foot in black.

Abu Jibril remembers that Rabiah was the first among the Indonesian activists to cover her face with a veil. 'At a time when there was nobody wearing *chador*, she already wore it.' Where once she had seen the veil as a sign of cultural subjugation, she now saw it as a symbol of religious and political defiance. It was a highly provocative move—so much so that the movement's leaders persuaded the women to desist from wearing it, for fear it would draw the attention of the authorities.

The stories of Rabiah's zeal are still recounted with enthusiasm within the Islamist movement in Indonesia. One oft-told anecdote recalls an occasion when she was travelling on a train with a group of activists. While her companions took their seats in the crowded carriage, Rabiah insisted on sitting on the floor. 'Why do you sit on a chair when the Prophet never did?' she demanded of one of her fellow travellers. For the entire all-day journey Rabiah sat on the floor of the train, while her friends sat on seats. One of them recalls joking that because an *ayat* in the Quran refers to the 'throne' of Allah it must be acceptable for Muslims to use chairs. Abu Jibril cites this incident as proof of his student's superior conviction, although Rabiah recalls that at the time he chided her for being fixated on technicalities, saying 'She has accepted Islam but faith hasn't entered her heart'.

Rabiah's conspicuous activism was bound to bring her to the attention of the Indonesian authorities. Irfan Awwas says that because of her involvement in the Islamist movement she was 'watched by the government' and as a result 'she was in danger'.

But for now the student movement was not the government's greatest concern. A more pressing worry was the revival of the old Darul Islam campaign for an Islamic state, and the emergence in its midst of a clique of charismatic new leaders. Among them were two clerics from Solo in Central Java, a charismatic preacher named Abdullah Sungkar and his loyal lieutenant Abu Bakar Ba'asyir.

Darul Islam had been formed in the 1940s and campaigned for Islamic law to be made the foundation of the new Republic of Indonesia. Its quest had failed when founding president Sukarno opted instead for a secular democracy and refused to include Islamic law in the constitution. Infuriated by this perceived betrayal, a rebel commander named SM Kartosuwiryo declared his own Islamic state based in West Java in 1949. It was known variously as Darul Islam—meaning 'the Abode of Islam'— or Negara Islam Indonesia, the Islamic State of Indonesia. A 13-year rebellion was crushed when Kartosuwiryo was captured and executed and his embryonic state collapsed in 1962.

Darul Islam was resurrected in the 1970s, and covertly supported by the Indonesian intelligence apparatus, which hoped to flush out its enemies and co-opt them with money and protection in return for a pledge of loyalty. Among those who joined the revived Darul Islam were Abdullah Sungkar and Abu Bakar Ba'asyir. They were both students of Yemeni heritage who had joined the Indonesian Islamic Youth Movement in the 1960s and set up their own pirate radio station to promote Islamic law; it was deemed subversive and was shut down by the government. They went on to establish a *pesantren*, or Islamic boarding school, in the village of Ngruki on the outskirts of Solo. It was modelled on Ba'asyir's alma mater, the esteemed Gontor *pesantren* in East Java, which embraced the 'modernist' school of Islamic thought, combining a rigorous modern curriculum with a puritanical teaching of the Islamic texts.

But as the renascent Darul Islam blossomed in the late 1970s, the Suharto regime sensed it had grown out of control and a full-scale crackdown was launched, with some 700 Muslim 'extremists' arrested.

They included Sungkar and Ba'asyir, who were charged in 1978 with subversion.

'The charges were standard fare for the time', wrote Sidney Jones of the International Crisis Group. 'Broadly worded accusations against two men who dared to criticise the Suharto government, with nothing to suggest that they advocated violence or were engaged in criminal activity.' At their trial, Abdullah Sungkar made an impassioned oration, which cemented his status as a champion of the Islamist struggle. He accused the Indonesian government of hijacking its opponents, rigging elections and stacking the parliament with military appointees, and alleged systematic torture of Muslim detainees, including an associate who he said had been electrocuted thirty-one times. He claimed he himself had been prevented from sleeping for three days and three nights, and had been made to stand for hours while being questioned until he confessed, which he called 'a violation of fundamental human rights'. Despite his dissertation, he and Ba'asyir were sentenced to nine years in prison, reduced on appeal to three years and ten months.

By the time they were freed in 1982, Sungkar and Ba'asyir were renowned as heroes of the Islamist cause, and their school at Ngruki had become a beacon of resistance to Suharto. The pair had begun regrouping their followers, using Ngruki as their base and adopting the *usroh* model of clandestine cells. Ba'asyir referred loosely to those who joined them as their *jemaah islamiyah*, or Islamic community. Rabiah had not yet met the two dissident clerics, but it was inevitable that their paths would soon converge, as the pair were gaining iconic status among the students in Jakarta.

However, for Rabiah to be accepted in the Islamist movement, there was one awkward anomaly to be resolved: her marital status. Her husband Bambang had finally relented and given her a divorce after meeting another woman. So she was now a *janda*, or widow, a term used for any woman who has 'lost' her husband, whether through death or divorce. Among devout Muslims it was considered unseemly for a woman to remain alone, especially a middle-aged mother of three. (Rabiah was now thirty years old.) Marriage is considered an integral duty in Islam, as the Prophet Mohammed instructed Muslims: 'marriage is half your *deen* (religion)'. Furthermore, pious women were expected to travel with a *mahram*, a husband or male relative to act as chaperone. There was no shortage of eager suitors for the attractive *mujahidah* from Australia. One was a taxi driver; another a wealthy businessman turned Muslim activist whose home was used as a meeting place by the *usroh* groups. A third was the headmaster of an Islamic primary school in Jakarta who had written a book on Quranic study and sent a copy to Rabiah, followed by a proposal of marriage. Furious that an Islamic gift should come with such strings attached, she returned his book and spurned his proposal.

The least likely among those paying her court was Pujo Busono, the young drinks seller who had listened rapt to her tales of conversion at the first students meeting she attended in Jakarta. Pujo was the son of poor market vendors, a man of little education or experience and meagre means. His circumstances appeared to have changed little when I met him in 2008, outside a small neighbourhood mosque in Solo. Sitting cross-legged on the verandah and at times misty-eyed with nostalgia, Pujo was eager to share his memories of Rabiah. He pedalled me in the rickshaw he now rode for a living to his extremely modest home nearby, where, in the company of his new wife and baby son, he recounted how his first marriage came about.

Pujo knew he was the least prepossessing of Rabiah's admirers, but knew also that what he lacked in worldly goods he could make up for in spiritual fervour. Not only did he find Rabiah extremely attractive; he calculated as well that marrying the single mother of three was his Islamic duty.

'I read a *hadith* that said "the best of you are those who help orphans and widows"', Pujo recounts. After visiting several times at her home in Pondok Bambu, he summoned up the courage to propose marriage. Taken by his sweet nature, humility and youthful enthusiasm, Rabiah accepted, to the bewilderment of their peers.

'People were very surprised why this woman with very wide experience would want to marry this very ordinary man', says Irfan Awwas. At first, he says, 'people questioned her motives, they were suspicious. But then they became convinced about her Islam, and the facts swept away their suspicions.' The fact that it was essentially a practical arrangement made it Islamically sound, as far as Awwas was concerned. 'She needed a man to accompany her to go anywhere. Pujo was physically fit, although economically poor. So Rabiah married him for Islamic reasons alone. It's part of how she was able to maintain her belief.' For Abu Jibril, who married them, Rabiah's choice was further proof of her conviction. 'She didn't care what kind of husband he was. What was important to her was that her husband was a good *mujahid*, even though his situation was very poor.' Pujo himself was clearly proud of being chosen: 'She liked Pujo because he's also strict and very brave, including doing jihad', he later proclaimed.

In keeping with custom, they had spent no time together alone and barely knew each other. He was just twenty, soft-hearted and naive. She was in her thirties with three children, fiery, strict and uncompromising. He called her *Ibu*, which means 'mother' or 'Mrs', reflecting the gap in their age and experience. She renamed him 'Mohammed'.

'Poor Pujo, it was a disaster from the first day', says Rabiah. 'Not because he wasn't a nice person—it was just a horrible mistake. I mean it was a big mistake on my part because I was totally unaware of the fact that in an Islamic marriage compatibility has to be established beforehand and that includes social status, intelligence, education and culture. I was still in my black-and-white stage and I thought if a man's a good Muslim and a woman's a good Muslim then there won't be any problems. He was decent and kind, but we were like chalk and cheese.'

By her account, he was extremely jealous and tried to make her stay at home. He also assumed he could spend her money as he saw fit, which Rabiah insists is 'Islamically not allowed' because in Islam a woman's money is her own. By his account, she was a difficult woman to please. When he was unemployed, she complained that he was always hanging around the house; when he went to look for work, she complained that he was always going out. 'So doing this is wrong, and doing this is wrong. If there was a small problem or a big problem, it always became a big problem, even when it was not supposed to be big', says Pujo. They argued often; once he struck her and was mortified afterwards. The marriage would prove short-lived, though not through want of devotion on the part of Pujo, which he was still professing more than twenty years later.

Not long after their marriage, Rabiah learned that a group of students were planning to travel to Central Java for a weekend study session in Solo, the hometown of Abdullah Sungkar and Abu Bakar Ba'asyir. She eagerly accepted an invitation to join them. They set off one Friday morning in early 1984, Rabiah and her three children squeezed in among a busload of about fifty students, for the bumpy 500-kilometre journey. Pujo was not invited.

It was an intensive weekend of Islamic study. They attended lectures, talks and prayer sessions for nine or ten hours a day and late into the evening, then slept for a few hours before rising for the *fajr* (dawn) prayer, and studying all day again until *isha*, the evening prayer. On the second day, there was a special guest speaker—Abu Bakar Ba'asyir, the former political prisoner and renowned co-founder of the Ngruki school. Rabiah couldn't see him speak; she was in a separate room with the women students, while Ba'asyir was in the room reserved for men. She was captivated nonetheless. His subject was Tawhid al Hakimiya—the concept that God alone is the law-maker, and that only His laws must be obeyed, as laws made by men are an abrogation of His sovereignty.

For Rabiah, this idea of a universal, God-given regime, which rendered irrelevant the unjust and arbitrary whims of humans, was profoundly appealing. It was a radical and empowering prescription: only God's laws must be obeyed; the laws crafted by mere mortals can be ignored. And the crystal clarity with which Ba'asyir spelt this out left no room for doubt.

'I thought it was the beginning of finding what I had been looking for for a long time, because he spoke with knowledge and certainty, and you could tell he knew what he was talking about. He was so calm and sure about it, that's what affected me. It's like being sick and going to a series of doctors, and having a lot of tests, and you know there's something horribly wrong with you, and finally you meet a specialist who says, "OK, there is something seriously wrong with you, but we've got the medicine and all you have to do is learn how to use it".'

Afterwards, Rabiah fell into conversation with an *ustadzah* (female teacher) who taught Arabic at the Ngruki school, and at whose house the students were staying for the weekend.

'What brought you to Indonesia?' the teacher asked her.

'I want to study Islam and learn Arabic, but until now I haven't been able to find the right place', Rabiah replied.

'Why don't you come and live here? You could study and get a job teaching English.'

The *ustadzah* said she would ask her husband to raise the matter with Ba'asyir, who was in charge of the school.

Back in Jakarta, Rabiah told Pujo she wanted to move to Solo. He was enthusiastic, apparently presuming he would be going too. By his account, he arranged a letter of recommendation from one of the leading activists in Jakarta, Ibnu Thoyib, addressed to Abdullah Sungkar and urging him to 'receive this family'. Ibnu Thoyib (whose real name is Abdullah Anshori, and who is also known as Abu Fatih) would later become a leading lieutenant in JI, as head of Mantiqi 2, the branch that covered most of Indonesia.

Three weeks later, Rabiah received a message in Jakarta, relayed on behalf of Sungkar and Ba'asyir, advising her: 'come down to Solo'. The brevity of the dispatch belied its import. Rabiah was to be the first—and only—Westerner admitted into the inner sanctum of their *jemaah islamiyah*, or Islamic community.

8

TRUE BELIEVERS

Indonesia, 1984–1985

O n the outskirts of Solo in Central Java, a narrow road crosses a bridge
over a muddy creek then weaves through the backblocks of the village of Ngruki to a dusty cul-de-sac and a set of imposing wrought-iron
gates, where a sign announces the entrance to the Al Mukmin Islamic
boarding school. Inside lies a rambling compound of classrooms, office
blocks, dormitories and a modest flat-roofed mosque. Back in the 1980s
it was surrounded by luminous green rice paddies, which have since been
overrun by the clutter of suburbia.

After being ushered through the gates, Rabiah and her companions
were shown to a modest cement block house, the home of the *pesantren's*
co-founder and principal, Abu Bakar Ba'asyir. He emerged to greet them,
a tall sinewy figure in a white robe, large wire-rimmed glasses and silver-
flecked beard. With him was his wife, whom he introduced as Mbak
(sister) Ecun, a small, bright-eyed woman with a warm smile. Like her
husband she had the strong nose, Arab complexion and forthright
manner of her Hadhrami forebears, the seafaring traders from Yemen
who first brought Islam to Indonesia.

'*Salam Alaikum*', Ba'asyir greeted the newcomers. 'Welcome to
Ngruki, please take a seat', gesturing towards a cluster of bamboo chairs
in his living room.

Rabiah was taken aback.

'Why have you got chairs?' she scolded him. 'Why don't you sit on the floor according to the *Sunnah* (custom) of the Prophet?'

Ba'asyir chuckled quietly and slowly nodded his head.

'*Sah, sah*', he replied; in English, 'that is correct'. By the next time she visited, he had got rid of the chairs.

The earnest preacher and the intense convert from Australia formed an immediate bond. They shared the same unflinching certitude and all-consuming sense of mission. Like his students, Rabiah called him *ustadz* (teacher) Abu. She recalls a very different man from the heartless fanatic described in Western media reports in later years, after the Bali bombings of 2002.

'*Ustadz* Abu was very humble and gentle', says Rabiah. 'He was quietly spoken and very calm. He was always very approachable, he had a way of making you feel at ease.' As for his impression of her: 'I don't know if he'd ever met a Western woman before. He was shocked by a lot of things I said.'

Ba'asyir had already vetted Rabiah via phone calls to Muslim contacts in Australia and references from colleagues in the Islamist movement. Now he quizzed her about the Muslim community in Australia, her knowledge of Islam, plans for further studies and reasons for wishing to move to Ngruki. Rabiah told him she wanted to learn Islam 'the correct way'. He warned her that the school was under constant surveillance and her presence would be noted by the authorities, and pointed out the salary would be a meagre $15 per month, supplemented by a supply of rice, tea, sugar, cooking oil and kerosene.

'If you're doing it for monetary reward, then Ngruki is not the place for you. You must be doing it for the sake of Allah', Ba'asyir advised.

Rabiah and her companions stayed for a week as guests in Ba'asyir's home. The cleric and his wife vacated their bedroom for the visitors, sleeping in their children's room for the duration of their stay. In the course of that week Rabiah began a lasting friendship with Ba'asyir's wife, Ecun (pronounced *ee-choon*), a lively, curious woman with a keen sense of humour, who found the convert's bluntness refreshing and amusing compared with the unfailing politeness of the Javanese.

'She was really enthusiastic, very highly motivated and energetic', Ecun remembered, when I met her at their home in the Ngruki school-grounds in 2008. 'And she was very direct. Rabiah will say anything. If she likes something, she says so. If she doesn't like it, she says so as well.'

At the end of the week, Ba'asyir doubted that Rabiah would want the job. 'You should go home, pray *istikharah*, think about it and decide if this is what you want', he told her. But she felt no need for guidance. 'I knew instantly it was where I wanted to be. I didn't have to make up my mind, I already knew.' The school *shura* (council) approved her appointment. Like her marriage to Pujo, it was essentially a practical arrangement, according to Wahyuddin, who was the son-in-law of Abdullah Sungkar and a council member. 'She was unemployed and had no place to stay, (and) the school needed her knowledge of English because she was a native speaker.' The fact that the paltry salary did not deter her only enhanced her credentials in Wahyuddin's eyes. 'She was a very established woman, with money. So to live in this poverty, she had to be strong.'

Rabiah returned briefly to Jakarta to pack up her possessions and the children, nine-year-old Devi, Mohammed, now aged eight, and Rahmah who was eighteen months. She told Pujo he could join them later. He would visit them from time to time in Solo in the coming months, but for all intents and purposes their marriage was over when she moved to Ngruki.

Ba'asyir's wife, Ecun, found her new friend a house around the corner from the *pesantren* gates and 100 metres down the road from the girls school, which at the time was in a separate compound. Their new home was palatial compared with their tiny *petak* in Jakarta. It was freshly built of unpainted grey cement with tiled floors and boasted two bedrooms, a family room, guest sitting room, bathroom and a large kitchen overlooking the headstones of the cemetery next door. The rent was cheap because the Javanese disliked living beside the *kuburan*, 'the place of graves'. Rabiah had no such superstitions. With her savings she hired two servants to keep house and look after baby Rahmah, while she began her new job teaching English at the Ngruki girls school.

It was early 1984 and these were heady times at the Al Mukmin *pesantren*, a crucible of the Indonesian Islamic revival and the increasing resistance to Suharto. The campus was the focal point of a community of 1000 to 1500 people, comprising students, teachers, staff and followers of Sungkar and Ba'asyir. Within the straitened confines of Suharto's Indonesia, it was its own separate world, where the law of God and the customs of the Prophet prevailed over the fiat of the dictator, in an atmosphere of brazen defiance.

'The jihad atmosphere dominated our campus', recalled one pupil from around this time. The *santri* (students) would march around the schoolyard railing against the Soviet occupation of Afghanistan and handing out leaflets urging support for the Afghan *mujahidin*. They called themselves *al Mukmin*, the moniker the clerics had chosen for their school. While a Muslim is someone who merely submits to Allah (the word Islam means 'submission', and *muslim* means 'one who submits'), a *mukmin* is a true believer who strives to put all of his or her beliefs into practice. Many of them were the children and grandchildren of Darul Islam devotees, who had sworn to carry on the quest of their martyred hero Kartosuwiryo to have *shariah* law enshrined in Indonesia. In the meantime they were dedicated to living it themselves. Despite being a political neophyte, Rabiah was thrilled to be a part of it. 'The whole thing was exciting, it was exhilarating. It was huge, there were hundreds of people. It was like a mini *dawlah* (Islamic state)—except of course they didn't kill people as punishment. All the women covered. The etiquette and *akhlaq* (behaviour) was totally Islamic. Everyone I knew who lived there—teachers, students, administrators, cooks—truly wanted to live their Islam, in every way, shape and form.'

The school day began well before sunrise, when the *muezzin*'s first call to prayer rang out over crackling loudspeakers from the mosque. At Ngruki there were two morning *azans*, a custom copied from the time of the Prophet. The first was at about 3.30 a.m., to wake those who were fasting so they could eat before daybreak and those who wished to perform a voluntary pre-dawn prayer. Another *azan* about an hour later announced the compulsory *fajr* (dawn) prayer, heralded by the 'the first thread of light' on the horizon, as stipulated in the Quran.

Classes commenced at 7 a.m. and continued until 11.30 when they broke for lunch and to rest through the harshest heat of the day, then resumed from three until 6 p.m. The students were compelled to speak in only English and Arabic. Any child who spoke in Indonesian or their native dialect was penalised with detention or 100 lines: 'I will not speak Javanese. I will not speak Javanese. I will not speak Javanese ...' While the school taught mathematics, science and English, its focus was on Islamic studies, which included the philosophy of *tawhid*, the 'one-ness' of all things under God; the 'science' of *tafsir*, interpreting the Quran; and *fiqh*, or Islamic jurisprudence, which was taught by Ba'asyir. Although secular subjects were part of the curriculum, the notion of a secular system of government was spurned. 'They used to say anybody who graduates from Ngruki and then becomes a government employee, it means their education has failed', says Rabiah.

Ibu (mother) Rabiah, as she was known to the students, taught English six days a week, typically taking between two and four classes per day. For her, the job was merely a means to an end—furthering her own studies of Islam. 'I hated teaching English. I had to do it to be there, but I would have much preferred to be *in* the classes, not teaching them.'

Every morning after the dawn prayer and before classes started, a two-hour lecture was held for the teachers, usually given by Abdullah Sungkar. 'Aba' (father), as he was universally known among staff and students, did not teach in the school, but regularly lectured to the teachers and in the mosques of Solo. Sungkar travelled frequently to raise funds and sponsorship, run the businesses associated with the school *yayasan* (foundation), and do *dakwah*, or proselytisation. In his absence, Ba'asyir would conduct the morning lecture instead, and an additional talk for the teachers three afternoons a week. While Sungkar's speeches were invariably political, Ba'asyir's were devoted to the letter of Islamic law. Their styles were a study in contrasts.

'Abu Bakar Ba'asyir and Abdullah Sunkgar were like chalk and cheese', says Rabiah. '*Ustadz* Abu (Ba'asyir) was a very humble man, very quiet; whereas Aba (Sungkar) was loud, someone who would always say what he thought. He was boisterous, he would laugh and make jokes, he always kept you on your toes. Abdullah Sungkar was extremely intelligent, he had a very strong personality, he was charismatic but daunting, and he commanded respect. He was a bit more scary, he just had this aura about him. You automatically got a feeling that you wouldn't want to make him displeased.'

Abdullah Sungkar had used his nearly four years in prison to memorise the Quran, which he could now quote chapter and verse, Ba'asyir had spent his confinement studying the *hadith*, committing hundreds of the Prophet's sayings and deeds to memory. Ba'asyir was thin, thoughtful and cautious. The product of his formal training, he was the scholar of the pair; the bespectacled headmaster and organiser; bookish and methodical, respected for his superior mastery of the minutiae of *shariah*, by nature modest and reserved. Sungkar was imposing in both physique and voice; tall, solidly built and loud, 'more like an Arab than an Indonesian' as Rabiah recalls. Self-taught in Islam and prone to bombastic rhetoric, he would often stand correction by Ba'asyir on the finer points of Islamic law. Rabiah recalls they were always arguing. The two men had a profound influence on Rabiah as leaders, teachers, mentors and friends. 'I love them both and I respected them both, but for different reasons. I respected *ustadz* Abu's knowledge. And you couldn't know Abdullah Sunkgar and not be impressed by his passion, by his unwavering conviction. Not that *ustadz* Abu didn't have that too, but they had very different methodology. They were the first of a long line of many people I've met in my life since I became a Muslim, who live their Islam to the extent that there isn't anything they love more in the world than Islam.'

Of the two it was undoubtedly Sungkar who was the leader, entrepreneur and demagogue; he would electrify the congregation in the mosque with his thundering orations. Sungkar believed there was no room for compromise with the *kafr* (unbeliever) Suharto and Indonesia's state ideology, Pancasila ('five principles'), which prescribed belief in one God, justice and civility, unity, democracy and social justice, but made no mention of Islamic law. Rabiah recalls one memorable sermon by Sungkar in a Solo mosque.

'A person who compromises is like a fly that gets up in the morning, and flies off to find whatever sustenance Allah has provided him', Sungkar opined.

'If he finds milk, he will consume milk. If he finds meat, he will consume meat. If he finds sweets, he will consume sweets. And if he finds shit, he will consume shit.'

The congregation sat awestruck as Sungkar bellowed his finale. 'And that's what a Muslim does when he consumes Pancasila! Because Pancasila is shit!'

In his lighter moments, Sungkar affected an air of casual informality, riding around the campus in a safari suit on his motor scooter yelling 'Salam Alaikum' and waving at passing students and staff. But he also enforced a code of strict discipline and obedience to the concept of *ta'at*, which asserts that Muslims are compelled to obey their leader as long as he conforms to God's laws.

Sungkar demonstrated the point in his inimitable style during a lecture when he called a trainee teacher before the class, and instructed him to take his motorbike and dispatch a letter to a nearby post office.

'Did you post the letter as I told you to?' he asked, when the young man returned fifteen minutes later.

'Yes, *ustadz*', the teacher replied.

Sungkar glared at his watch.

'Stand up and I'll ask you again. Did you post that letter as I told you to?'

'Yes, *ustadz*', his victim gulped nervously.

'Are you blatantly lying to me?' boomed Sungkar. 'I told you to go to the post office on Jalan Gajah Mada and post the letter. You've only been gone for fifteen minutes. I gave you a motorbike, not a jet. It's impossible for you to have done it in that time.'

'*Ustadz*, you forgot', the young man stammered. 'There is a post office that is closer, on the way to Gajah Mada, so I posted it there to save time.'

Sungkar feigned fury to demonstrate his point.

'You have not obeyed me! You have supposed that you knew better than me', he thundered, his point being that the young man should have obeyed his orders. The offending teacher was sent to Coventry for three weeks, forced to sit alone for meals, the other staff forbidden to speak to him. The lesson for all who witnessed it was that the orders of the leader must be obeyed, as long as they do not conflict with the word of God.

In contrast to his redoubtable colleague, Abu Bakar Ba'asyir was unfailingly approachable, according to Rabiah. Although male and female students were taught separately, the Ngruki leaders did not impose the strict segregation observed by the students in Jakarta, and the door to Ba'asyir's home was always open. 'Ngruki was a family', Rabiah says. 'I was very close to *ustadz* Abu's family, especially his wife. I used to see them on a daily basis. I would often go and sit with he and his wife and I used to visit Mbak (sister) Ecun regularly. You could just go and visit whenever you wanted. If you had a question you could just go and knock on the door and say "Is *ustadz* here?" Sometimes I would go to *ustadz* Abu's house and he would be doing the washing for his wife—Abdullah Sungkar would never do that.'

On Fridays, the Muslim day of rest, Rabiah would often take her children to visit Ba'asyir's family at his home. Ba'asyir would sit on the floor and play games with his sons' toy cars with baby Rahmah, having got rid of his bamboo chairs after Rabiah's pointed comments the first time they met. Their children were around the same age. Rabiah's girl Devi would play dolls and cooking games with Ba'asyir's daughter, Zulfur, while Mohammed played in the rice fields with Ba'asyir's two sons, Rashid and Abdul Rohim. Ecun remembers the boys coming home after chasing eels in the paddy fields looking like a trio of little water buffalo, covered head to toe in mud, which they traipsed through the house. Rabiah was furious at the mess; Ecun's view was 'they're children, let them play', although she couldn't help but be impressed by Rabiah's fixation with cleanliness amid the dirt and dust of rural Indonesia.

While the children played, Rabiah would bombard Ba'asyir with questions about the intricacies of *shariah* law, which she was determined to master. She describes a patient and mild-mannered teacher, reluctant to rush to judgement, who would sometimes express reservations about the dogmatic zeal of the students in Jakarta. He disapproved of their enthusiasm for the controversial doctrine of *takfir*, the practice of denouncing as infidels Muslims who are deemed to have strayed from 'pure' Islam. Rabiah says his view was 'you can't just go around saying "you're *kafr*"', as the students tended to do. '*Ustadz* Abu would say: "No, if someone believes in Allah, even though they may be ignorant of many things in Islam, that is not the basis to say they are outside of Islam".'

Within a month of arriving at Ngruki, Rabiah volunteered to swear a *bai'at*, or oath of allegiance, to Abu Bakar Ba'asyir. The *bai'at* is an Islamic tradition based on a pledge of loyalty sworn by the companions of the Prophet Mohammed who accompanied him on his historic *hijrah* from Mecca to Medina, to escape his enemies and establish the Islamic faith. As Rabiah tells it, she repeated after Ba'asyir words to the effect of: 'I swear to hear and obey to the best of my ability all things pertaining to the word of Allah and the way of the Prophet'.

The practice of swearing *bai'at* was later used in Indonesia as evidence against many of Ba'asyir's followers who were arrested in the 1980s for subversion. However, Amnesty International, which called these detainees 'prisoners of conscience', reported that taking the *bai'at* was not evidence of subversive intent: 'Such pledges of obedience are common in many different kinds of organisations in Indonesia, most of which are perfectly legitimate. An oath by itself need not entail acceptance of the authority of the organization's leadership over that of the state.' Amnesty found that the oaths taken at Ngruki, which varied in wording but were broadly similar to the one described by Rabiah, were 'more in the nature of a declaration of faith' than a vow of obedience.

Rabiah saw her *bai'at* as akin to a verbal contract of employment, signifying that while she was at Ngruki she would defer to Ba'asyir's authority in matters of her daily life and religion. '*Ustadz* Abu was responsible for me. I did it with him because I worked at Ngruki and he was the director. In terms of what was *halal* and *haram* ("allowed" and "forbidden") for me, he had limited authority. For example, he would advise me on issues like marriage, but I was free to make my own decision.'

After settling in at Ngruki, Rabiah decided to formally end her marriage to Pujo Busono, whom she had seen little of in the months since they had wed. She believed their marriage had been a mistake and in practical terms had no further need of him as provider or chaperone.

When he came to visit one day she took him to see Abdullah Sungkar and announced she wanted a divorce. Dismayed, Pujo argued against it.

'Do you want to be married to him?' Sungkar asked Rabiah.

'No', she replied.

'Has he provided for you?'

'No.'

'Do you have work?' Sungkar asked Pujo.

'No', the young man said.

'This is ridiculous', Sungkar erupted with his usual brusqueness. 'The thing is she doesn't want to be married to you, so give her a divorce and stop this nonsense.' Pujo remained a committed activist after their divorce, joining the Islamic Defenders Front, the Indonesian Mujahidin Council, and Ba'asyir's security detail, by his own account.

Rabiah's children were too young to attend the Ngruki *pesantren*, which did not have a primary school at the time. Keen to have her first-born learn Arabic, she enrolled nine-year-old Devi in an Islamic boarding school on Madura island off the northern Java coast. However, Abdullah Sungkar ordered her removal from the school, after learning that its principal was a follower of Iran's Ayatollah Khomeini, whose Shia creed Sungkar abhorred. Seven-year-old Mohammed attended the same local Islamic primary school as Ba'asyir's sons. Mohammed's schooling was abruptly interrupted one day while the children were standing to attention at assembly to salute the Indonesian flag. For his salutation Mohammed turned his back and slapped his bottom in the direction of the ensign. In an echo of her own mother's frequent forays to Mudgee public school, Rabiah was summoned to explain her son's behaviour. This was no minor infringement—failing to honour the flag was tantamount to treason. Rabiah explained that the boy was simply being naughty. But when pressed to insist that he salute the flag in future she refused to do so, instead withdrawing him from the school and arranging to have him home-schooled instead.

'I taught my children there is no law except the law of Allah', she says. 'I told him he was naughty and that it was a rude thing to do. But I wasn't prepared to tell him he had to salute the flag.'

Rabiah became well known at Ngruki for speaking her mind. On one occasion she reprimanded Ba'asyir's wife Ecun, who came from a family of well-off batik merchants and had her own line of clothing, for selling hijabs with lace trimming. Rabiah was sure this breached the Quranic *ayat* urging women not to 'display their adornments'.

'You can't sell these, it's *haram* (forbidden)', Rabiah reproved her friend.

Mba Ecun disliked an argument and, in any event, it was hard to argue with Rabiah.

'When *ustadz* comes home I'll ask him', she diplomatically replied.

She raised the issue with Ba'asyir that evening. 'Rabiah is saying this business I'm doing, that Allah will be displeased with me, and the money's *haram*.'

Ba'asyir nodded with a quiet laugh. '*Sah, sah*', he replied. 'That is correct.'

Ba'asyir himself used to wear a black *kopiah*, a traditional Malay-style box-shaped hat, until Rabiah took him to task.

'*Ustadz*, it's not right that you wear that hat. It's a symbol of nationality. You should wear a Muslim hat.'

From then on he took to wearing a soft crocheted cap of the kind worn by men who have done the *haj*, which on windy days would go flying off his head as he rode around on his motor scooter. He would shake his head in mock sorrow, muttering '*Rabiah, Rabiah, aduh!*' (*Aduh* is a mild exclamation, akin to 'oh dear'.)

Abdullah Sungkar's safari suit also attracted Rabiah's ire. After leading a government delegation on an inspection tour around Ngruki, Sungkar asked Rabiah whether she had seen the official party which included Defence Minister Benny Murdani, who had come to ensure the dissidents knew the government was keeping an eye on them.

'Did you see our visitors?' Sungkar asked Rabiah.

'Yes', she replied. 'I was watching out the window when the delegation went past. I couldn't distinguish you from them because you dress the same.'

The next time she saw him, she says, he had abandoned his safari suit in favour of more orthodox Islamic attire.

To her students, Ibu Rabiah was foremost a disciplinarian. 'She was very strict and not very patient. She sometimes clashed with the students, so some of the students didn't like her very much', Ecun remembers. One former student, Sri Murtiah, recollects that Rabiah was 'very strong and very strict' but 'funny' at times and a 'good teacher'. 'Sometimes when the students couldn't follow her English, we would laugh and she would laugh as well. But when the students were undisciplined, she became angry. If she was serious, the students should be serious too. She didn't scream at us, but she had a very loud voice.'

Rabiah was such a stickler for Islamic etiquette that she was appointed by Ba'asyir as 'house mother' to monitor the female students' *akhlaq*, or Islamic behaviour. In scenes reminiscent of a younger Rabiah with her '*shariah* stick' patrolling the streets of Lakemba, she would stride around the dormitories where the girls slept six to a room, laying down the law. Her pet hate was the wasting of food; if she found food discarded among the rubbish she would whack the bin with a stick and harangue the nearest suspect. Another aversion was the female students' habit of forgetting to collect their laundry from the clothesline, which often meant it ended up blowing around the schoolyard. Rabiah believed some of the girls had too many clothes anyway; as her mother used to say, no one needed more than three sets—'one on, one off, one in the wash'. Any girl who forgot to bring in her washing would get two warnings. The third time, she was punished. 'I used to make them put all their clothes on at once. Whatever clothes they had they'd have to put them all on top of each other, because they didn't appreciate what Allah had given them, and they had more than they needed anyway. It was very successful, very successful.'

But in a country where merely raising one's voice is considered unbecoming, some of Rabiah's colleagues disapproved of her mode of discipline. 'The Indonesian teachers were absolutely horrified at my methods. They wouldn't say anything to me, but they used to complain about me', she says. Any expression of anger was frowned upon as not only culturally inappropriate but Islamically suspect as well. A *hadith* records that when an early Muslim asked the Prophet, 'Messenger of Allah, teach me some words which I can live by', the Prophet replied, 'Do not be angry', repeating the advice three times. But curbing her volatile temper was a challenge Rabiah had never mastered, although she claims to have made some headway. 'That is the biggest struggle I've had. But from someone who used to pick up a chair and throw it, to someone who only becomes irate and raises their voice, I *have* made progress.'

Among her disapproving colleagues was Abdullah Sungkar's son-in-law, Wahyuddin, who was then a teacher and later became headmaster of the *pesantren*, a position he still held in 2008. Wahyuddin admired her strictness but frowned on her tirades, recalling, 'She easily became angry and the students bore it'. After one outburst, a complaint was made to Abu Bakar Ba'asyir. By Rabiah's account, Ba'asyir took her side, telling the complainant: 'If you have come here to tell me that she lost her temper for other than the sake of Allah, I will listen. Otherwise, make this the last time you stand before me.' Rabiah did not hear of any further complaints. Ecun recalls that in contrast to Rabiah's own impatience, Ba'asyir was unfailingly patient with her.

'*Ustadz* Abu was always very loyal to me', says Rabiah. 'People would complain about me and *ustadz* Abu would always maintain that as long as my behaviour was not un-Islamic it was alright. He always gave me an excuse if it was anger for the sake of Allah. He would say, "If her behaviour is un-Indonesian or un-Javanese, that's OK, because she's not Indonesian or Javanese".'

However, Ba'asyir's patronage and her friendship with Ecun did not help endear Rabiah to some of her colleagues, particularly the women on the staff. 'The female teachers in Ngruki didn't take kindly to outsiders', she says. 'Some of the female teachers never accepted me because I was never a *santri* (*pesantren* student), I was an outsider, I was a *bule*, I couldn't speak Arabic. I wasn't even married when I was there and that was another problem.' Wahyuddin confirms that her status as a *janda* ('widow' or divorced woman) was a source of discomfort to the other female teachers. He says some of the women felt 'uncomfortable' about her habit of approaching the male teachers to seek their advice on Islamic issues. 'The wives of the *ustadz* were not happy with it', Wahyuddin says. Rabiah's position as 'house mother' was supposed to include the provision of a house inside the school-grounds but, apparently because of these rumblings, her move was blocked, and Wahyuddin and his wife took the house instead.

While Rabiah was at Ngruki, Ba'asyir and Sungkar were in a crucial phase of their campaign for an Islamic state in Indonesia. Using the *usroh* model of an ever-expanding cell structure, the small groups of followers they established proliferated from their base in Solo across the island of Java to the capital Jakarta. They urged their supporters to implement *shariah* within these groups, using a series of manuals written by Ba'asyir, as a precursor for an eventual Islamic state.

'I never saw or heard anything from Abdullah Sungkar or Abu Bakar Ba'asyir that suggested some massive underground movement plotting a military takeover of the government', says Rabiah. 'It was just Muslims saying there is no alternative but the law of Allah and the way of the Prophet. Even when they broke into cells, that was still the target. It was underground and done in secret only because they couldn't do it openly.'

This account is supported by an analysis of Ba'asyir's manuals done by Amnesty International in the 1980s. The manuals set out forty duties for *usroh* (family) members such as physical health, cleanliness, education, honesty, abstinence from alcohol, charity and obedience, with the aim of creating an 'Islamic brotherhood'. They describe the three foundations of *usroh* as knowledge, education and jihad. Jihad is defined as 'struggle by education, struggle in both body and soul for the greatness of Islam, struggle through politics, and struggle through the use of one's wealth'. There was no mention of violence or military struggle at this stage in their campaign.

Sungkar and Ba'asyir's growing popularity led to rumblings of disaffection in the wider Darul Islam movement, which had long been riven by personal rivalries and doctrinal disputes. 'There were rumours in Jakarta that Abdullah Sungkar had deserted Darul Islam and breached the chain of command, that he was creating divisions in the *umma* (community) and setting himself up as a rival to Darul Islam', says Rabiah. 'They were saying he was doing it because he wanted to set himself up as the new *caliph* (Muslim leader) of Indonesia.'

Rabiah was now such a trusted insider that she was chosen as an emissary to travel to the capital to try to find out who was behind the sniping at her mentors. It transpired that much of the gossip was emanating from a particular Islamic study group in Jakarta. Students of this group were taught a method known as *nukil*, in which they learnt to read the Quran in Arabic by translating it word for word into Indonesian and writing the Indonesian words next to the Arabic text. The classes attracted members from a range of rival groups and had become a hotbed of gossip and intrigue, much of it directed against the two clerics in Solo.

With the twin aims of learning Arabic and gleaning intelligence on the rumblings, Rabiah joined the *nukil* study group in Jakarta. It was there she met a Javanese undergraduate named Abdul Rahim bin Ayub, a jovial twenty year old who had studied engineering at the Catholic Jayabaya University in Jakarta but had abandoned his degree to become a full-time student activist. He had mastered *nukil* himself and was now teaching it to others. Abdul Rahim had a twin brother, Abdul Rahman, who was studying Arabic at the Saudi-funded Institute of Islamic and Arabic Language Studies in Jakarta.

An acquaintance of Abdul Rahim was a religious teacher named Zainal Arifin, who later migrated to Australia. Arifin remembers Rabiah as the 'Abdullah Sungkar woman' who showed up one day in Jakarta in around mid 1984. He describes her as a 'strong woman', 'very fanatic' and also 'very good looking'. Once again, according to Arifin, she soon had a throng of admirers eager to marry her, including Abdul Rahim.

However, Rabiah had no interest in remarrying at this point. She was there to sort out the dissent against her mentors, and it turned out that Abdul Rahim was among the most vocal detractors who felt Sungkar and Ba'asyir had deserted the broader Darul Islam movement. Rabiah persuaded him to travel to Ngruki to meet the clerics for himself, as a result of which he transferred allegiance and joined them. Unbeknown to either

Rabiah or Abdul Rahim, his switch came at a critical juncture in both of their lives, and in the history of the Islamist uprising in Indonesia.

* * *

By the mid 1980s, the tensions between the Islamist movement and the Suharto regime were coming to a head. In the preceding years the government had been tightening the noose on the movement seen as the most potent threat to its hold on power. Activists including the son of Darul Islam founder Kartosuwiryo were arrested and put on trial, accused of reviving the campaign for an Islamic state. The Muslim youth group run by Rabiah's colleague Irfan Awwas was raided and his newspaper shut down. Awwas himself, who had infuriated the government by publishing Abdullah Sungkar's courtroom denunciation of Suharto, was arrested and would soon be sentenced to thirteen years imprisonment for subversion. He and others were accused of belonging to an illegal group named Komando Jihad, meaning Holy War Command. Amnesty International wrote: 'The Indonesian government has regularly accused radical Muslims in recent years of being members of a Komando Jihad aiming to set up an Islamic state in Indonesia, but often the evidence for such a link presented at their trials has been insubstantial. Many commentators have doubted whether a Komando Jihad exists or ever existed, and have suggested that these accusations were used to stifle radical Muslim activity.' Amnesty denounced Awwas's trial as unfair, and suggested he had been detained 'for peacefully exercising his internationally-recognized right to express his political and religious beliefs'.

The Ngruki school was by now under close surveillance and government spies were suspected of infiltrating the *pesantren*. Secret police posed as *becak* drivers outside the front gates, although they were easy to pick, says Rabiah: 'The real *becak* drivers were barefoot or wore thongs. The secret police wore army boots.' Their presence at the mosque in Solo merely inflamed Abdullah Sungkar, who would announce at Friday prayers: 'All you secret police stationed outside the mosque, don't stay outside, come in! I'll give you a few minutes to make your way in. And may Allah guide you to the truth.' Sungkar's sermons became ever more inflammatory. Rabiah remembers him fulminating in public: 'Suharto is going to hell! And anyone who follows him is going straight where he's going!'

Rabiah had by now joined the speakers' circuit herself, accepting invitations to give talks for women in private homes or in the mosques. Her usual topic was Islamic dress, which she advocated passionately. 'The reason they asked me to speak was because I was a white convert who wore hijab. It was the shock impact—here's this Western woman who should be wearing a bikini saying, "I want to live under Islam". I would get better results (than an Indonesian woman) because I was a Westerner and I had chosen it, so that made a greater impression on them.'

Rabiah was also a vocal advocate of polygamy, an Islamic practice that the Suharto government had moved to restrict.

'As we all know, the government has said, "don't have two wives". Well, I'm here to tell you: don't have two—have three or four!' Rabiah would urge her audience. For her, the argument for polygamy was black and white: it is part of God's law, laid down in the Quran, which cannot be altered by humans. At this point, her support for polygamy was largely theoretical, though she would later embrace it in practice as well.

It was only a matter of time before Rabiah's displays of bravura brought her to the attention of the authorities. That time came on Indonesia's national day, 17 August 1984, when patriotic citizens were expected to fly the Indonesian flag as proof of their allegiance to the republic. The flagpole outside the *orang bule*'s home at Ngruki remained conspicuously bare. The next day there was a knock on her door. It was the local *rukun tatanga*, the Indonesian equivalent of a neighbourhood-watch man who doubled as a spy for the government. He was carrying a letter from the district commander of the Komkamtib, the Central Command for Security and Stability, instructing Rabiah to present herself at its local headquarters the following morning.

Rabiah took the letter to show Abu Bakar Ba'asyir.

'You have no choice, you have to go or they'll drag you', he said gravely, then walked with her to Abdullah Sungkar's home to inform him.

'It's obvious someone has reported her, maybe it's one of the neighbours', said Ba'asyir, adding in a hushed voice: 'Maybe there is an informer'.

Rabiah recalls that Sungkar was uncommonly quiet. 'I think I know who informed on her', he said, as the room fell silent. 'I think it might have been me.'

The week before, during his Friday sermon at a public mosque in Solo, Sungkar had berated his congregation for failing to stand up to the regime, and held Rabiah up as an example.

'Don't you Indonesians know the meaning of shame?' he had hectored them. 'We've got this *orang bule* teaching at Ngruki—she's a convert and she refused to put up the flag on national day.'

As he recounted the story, Abdullah Sungkar looked sheepish. 'Maybe that's got something to do with them calling her in.'

The next morning Rabiah presented herself to the Komkamtib as instructed, carrying two-year-old Rahmah on her hip, and was questioned for several hours. What was she doing in Indonesia? Was she a spy for the Australian secret service? Was she a follower of Abdullah Sungkar? Did she support an Islamic state? Why had she not flown the flag? She was sent home at nightfall but ordered to return the following day to be questioned again. She played dumb and told them nothing, apparently with the desired effect. At the end of her interrogation, a frustrated commander snapped at his subordinate in Javanese, apparently assuming Rabiah would not understand: 'Get this woman out of here, she's an idiot'.

The simmering showdown between the government and Islamic activists came to a head in September 1984, after the introduction of a new law requiring every organisation in the country to recognise the much maligned state ideology, Pancasila, as its 'sole ideological basis'. It was a deliberate affront to the Islamic movement. A prayer meeting-cum-rally was organised in the port district of Tanjung Priok in north Jakarta. Rabiah was invited to speak at the event, and travelled to the capital ahead of time. But the day before the rally the organiser who had arranged her attendance was detained by the police, and Rabiah was advised to stay away for her own safety.

On the day of the rally, the mood was incendiary. Several days earlier an army sergeant had walked into a local mosque with his shoes on and smeared water from an open sewer on the walls. His action sparked a riot in which the crowd set his motorcycle on fire and four men were arrested. As the rally got underway one of the speakers declared that, unless the detainees were released by that night, there would be a 'bloodbath'. When the deadline passed, a crowd of about 1500 set out to march on the north Jakarta police station and the district military command headquarters. According to eye-witness accounts cited by Amnesty International, the organisers urged the crowd not to use violence: 'Listen, brothers! We don't want a fight with the Armed Forces. We will come and ask for our four friends … Brothers, I ask you, don't do any damage! Brothers, behave like Muslims!'

The marching mob was met by a column of soldiers with armoured vehicles and tanks, who blocked the road and surrounded the crowd in a pincer movement, said the eyewitness accounts. Then they opened fire. The official death toll was eighteen; witnesses said they saw sixty to one hundred people killed.

An estimated two hundred people were arrested on charges ranging from spreading false information to subversion and destruction of property. Many of those scooped up in the dragnet were bystanders who had been shot and were later dragged from their hospital beds for interrogation. Amnesty International reported that they included a 21-year-old banana seller who followed the crowd, was shot in the stomach and buttocks, and then spent seven months in detention with bullets still festering in his body. Another was a 19-year-old student caught up in the march while running an errand at the market. He was shot in the head, leaving half his body paralysed, then interrogated while barely conscious. He signed a confession without having read it. A third was a 16-year-old ice seller who had heard the crowd and gone to see what was going on. After falling in the chaos, he was beaten unconscious by a soldier with a rifle, and later agreed to whatever his interrogators wanted him to say.

In the months after the infamous events at Tanjung Priok, the crackdown was widened to include scores of *usroh* activists across Java, who were arrested and charged under Suharto's anti-subversion law. Several dozen were convicted and sentenced to jail terms of between four and eleven years, not for crimes of violence, but for undermining the Suharto regime. In the single case that was heard on appeal, the conviction was overturned, in a rare show of independence by the Indonesian Supreme Court, which judged that *usroh* activity did *not* constitute subversion. Amnesty International called the detainees 'prisoners of conscience, detained for their non-violent religious activities or their concern about government policies', and called for their immediate release. As usual Suharto ignored their calls.

Many of the detainees were followers of Sungkar and Ba'asyir; some were Rabiah's friends and colleagues. She describes the case of a teacher at Ngruki who was arrested in the crackdown. 'After Tanjung Priok his wife and daughter were raped by soldiers. While they were interrogating him they put a table with metal legs on his foot and the soldiers sat on it. They kept adding soldiers to it until it pierced his foot, then they did the other foot. They did horrific things, young men aged only seventeen and eighteen years old had their hair ripped out. They used electrodes, and drugs.'

Other methods documented by Amnesty International included 'beatings, submersion in water, threats on their lives, denial of food, and confinement for up to three months in cells without sunlight and without any exercise allowed'.

As Suharto's crackdown continued, some of Sunkgar and Ba'asyir's followers retaliated with violence. In the months that followed, a home-made bomb was set off at the Borobodur Buddhist temple in central Java, and explosive devices erupted on a bus and at a Christian church. A teacher at the Ngruki school would later be convicted of supplying the explosives and sentenced to fifteen years in jail.

While Rabiah was still in Jakarta, an order went out from Ngruki that Sungkar and Ba'asyir's followers should stay wherever they were and suspend all travel to avoid arrest. Rabiah was told that her name had been on a list of speakers at Tanjung Priok which was now in the hands of the authorities. It was considered unsafe for her to return to Solo. 'I was told not to go back to Ngruki because they would probably pick me up. They were picking up people by the hundreds. And the government was saying they were going to re-arrest Abdullah Sungkar and Abu Bakar Ba'asyir.'

She spent the next three months in virtual hiding, moving from place to place in Jakarta to avoid detection. She was desperate to get back to Ngruki, having left her children there in the belief she would be gone only a few days. It was several weeks before she was finally able to make her way back to Solo, in late 1984, chaperoned by her Quranic studies teacher, Abdul Rahim Ayub. When they arrived in Solo, Abdul Rahim proposed marriage, to Rabiah's professed surprise. At thirty-one, she was ten years his senior and, mindful of her disastrous union with the similarly youthful Pujo, she baulked at the suggestion. 'I thought he was delusional, because of the age difference', she says. But Abdul Rahim was persistent, pointing out that being married was a central tenet of their faith and that age was no barrier in Islam. 'He reminded me that you have to follow Islam in everything you do and that I should at least consider it and pray *istikharah*. And if the only reason I didn't find him suitable was that he was younger than me then that wasn't a proper reason, because the Prophet Mohammed was fifteen years younger than Khadija (his first wife).'

While Rabiah had no great wish to remarry, there were persuasive practical reasons to do so. In devout Islamic society the peer-group pressure to marry was extreme. She didn't want to return to Australia and could not resume working at Ngruki in the tense political climate. In order to stay in Indonesia she needed financial support for her and the children and a male companion to accompany her on her travels. Apart from their age disparity, Abdul Rahim was a suitable candidate. He came from a religious family: his father was a clerk in the Department of Religion, while his mother worked in an Islamic hospital in Jakarta; his twin brother was an equally devoted student activist and his sisters wore hijab. He was also genial, intelligent and sincere. And he had the imprimatur of Sungkar and Ba'asyir.

They were married by Abdullah Sungkar at the Ngruki *pesantren* in early 1985. The minimal formalities consisted of a simple ceremony to sign the Islamic marriage contract known as an *akad nikah*. The bride herself did not attend. 'It was not necessary for the woman to attend because it was just the legal signing of a contract which was done by men, so there was no need for the woman to go. *Ustadz* Abu (Ba'asyir) was my *wali* (male representative) so he went on my behalf', Rabiah explains. Afterwards there were two separate wedding parties—one for the men held at the Ngruki school, another for the women at Rabiah's home.

Abdul Rahim's family could barely conceal their consternation when their son brought home his new *orang bule* bride. 'His family didn't approve of him marrying a divorced woman with three children and ten years older than him', says Rabiah. 'It was a big shock to them. But they said, it's not *haram* (forbidden) and if that's what Allah has written for you, then we accept it. I don't think I would have been their number-one choice as a daughter-in-law, but after the initial shock I was welcomed into their family.'

In the prevailing climate of confusion and uncertainty Rabiah made a decision that is hard for an outsider to fathom, and which she would later profoundly regret. It is not an episode she discusses willingly as it has been the cause of deep angst within her family. In early 1985, she arranged for her 10-year-old daughter Devi to be contracted to marry 21-year-old Abdul Rahman Ayub, the twin brother of her own husband, Abdul Rahim. 'It was only a betrothal', she hastens to explain. 'It was Islamically legal (and) it was a way I thought I could keep the family together.'

In conservative Islamic tradition, girls are considered mature enough to marry from nine years old, the age of the Prophet Mohammed's third wife Aisha when they married. In some societies girls are betrothed before school age, although the union may not be consummated until after the girl reaches puberty, at which point she is supposed to be asked whether or not she wishes to continue the marriage. There are two parts to an Islamic marriage. The first is the signing of the formal contract, the *akad nikah*, which denotes that the couple are betrothed; it is akin to the Western tradition of becoming engaged. The second stage of the marriage occurs when the couple starts living together as man and wife, which occasions a more festive celebration known as a *walima*.

Abdul Rahman was about to travel overseas to study Islam in Saudi Arabia or Pakistan. Rabiah's explanation is that she believed that by arranging his marriage to her daughter it would help cement their family. It was agreed that Devi would stay with her until she was several years older and Abdul Rahman had completed his studies and returned to Indonesia. While she maintains it was 'Islamically legal', Rabiah's decision was greeted with dismay and anger within their community. 'It was not accepted by anyone. No one could understand why I would do something like that. Even *ustadz* and Aba (Ba'asyir and Sungkar) disapproved. Aba thought it was ridiculous. But I was insistent, that's what I wanted. I didn't think about the implications, I underestimated the negative effects it would have on her and I never took into account the potential problems due to the fact that they were brothers. I honestly thought it would be a way we'd all be able to be together and extend the family.' She typically ignored the objections and the signing of the marriage contract proceeded, although it would prove short-lived.

Rabiah was eager to resume her teaching duties at the Ngruki school. But the clerics insisted it was too dangerous for her to stay, and told her to return to Jakarta and lie low there until it was safe to come back to Solo.

So in early 1985, during a school break at Ngruki, she bade farewell to Abdullah Sungkar and Abu Bakar Ba'asyir.

'What are your plans?' Sungkar asked her.

'I'm not really sure but I'll be back here before school starts', she assured him.

Ba'asyir and his wife gave her gifts to take to their friends in Jakarta.

'Mbak (sister) Rabiah, you must have patience', Ba'asyir counselled her, before turning to Abdul Rahim. 'Sometimes she loses her temper, but the good in her outweighs the bad', he said with a grin.

Ba'asyir's wife, Ecun, and Rabiah embraced. 'May Allah reward you both', said Ecun to her friend; and to Abdul Rahim, 'Pak (father) Rahim, you are a brave man'.

It was the last time Rabiah would see her mentors for more than five years. Within days of her departure from Ngruki, the Supreme Court of

Indonesia heard a belated appeal by the Suharto Government against the reduction in the prison sentences meted out to Sungkar and Ba'asyir after their arrest in 1978, which had seen them serve only three years and ten months instead of the original sentence of nine years. The court upheld the government's appeal and ordered the two clerics be re-arrested to serve another five years in jail.

But this time, Sungkar and Ba'asyir were a step ahead of the regime. By the time the military police arrived to arrest them they had fled, accompanied by a small band of supporters. Abdullah Sungkar later boasted to Rabiah and others of how they had made good their escape thanks to a tipoff. 'An army officer sent a message to Aba (Sungkar) that they were going to be arrested again. They left that day. Aba rode out while the soldiers were there—he rode straight past them.' Sungkar told Rabiah he thought of her as he rode to freedom on his motor scooter through the green wrought-iron gates, disguised in a pair of blue jeans and a lairy short-sleeved batik shirt: 'Rabiah reckoned the safari suit was bad—if only she could see me now'. By nightfall he and Ba'asyir were on a fishing boat to Malaysia, which would become their home in exile for the next thirteen years.

When she learned of their escape, which they likened to the Prophet Mohammed's historic *hijrah* from Mecca to Medinah, Rabiah wanted to follow them.

'Of course I wanted to go to Malaysia but it wasn't possible. They reminded me I was an *orang bule*, I was too recognisable. They were going there to hide and blend in.' Key lieutenants including Abu Jibril were among those who would follow the clerics into exile, without Rabiah. 'I remember Abu Jibril saying the only way we can take you to Malaysia is if you wear a motorbike helmet for the rest of your life.'

There was more bad news to follow. The men left in charge of the *jemaah* believed it was now too dangerous for Rabiah to remain in Indonesia, and that she should return home to Australia. She protested but to no avail.

'I was devastated', she remembers. 'That was a very sad time for me because as much as I wanted to be part of it, at the end of the day I wasn't an Indonesian. I didn't really belong, I was different. I was always accepted as a Muslim, but what was happening in Indonesia and what Abdullah Sungkar and Abu Bakar Ba'asyir were calling for was an internal thing. It was not that I was rejected, but for me it was a choice, while for Muslims in Indonesia there was no choice.'

In the autumn of 1985 Rabiah boarded a plane to return to Australia with her three children—and a fourth on the way; she was now pregnant with her and Abdul Rahim's first child. He was to follow them a few weeks later after his visa was approved. Their lives were about to take a very different course. 'When Abdul Rahim and I married, I had no intention of coming back to live in Australia. I had no desire to come back and I certainly didn't intend to bring my children up here. The decision to come to Australia was not one that we made. It was forced upon us. So from the outset it was something that caused major problems between us.'

9

MUHAJIRIN

Australia, 1985–1990

The *imam* of the Darwin mosque was startled to find a heavily pregnant Australian woman in a hijab with a clutch of small children on his doorstep, demanding shelter. Rabiah and her tribe had got off the plane and gone straight to the mosque. They had no money and didn't know anyone in Darwin. They had flown to Australia's northernmost city because it was the closest and cheapest to get to from Indonesia.

'I'm a *muhajir*, and it's your duty to look after me. I'm going to stay here at the mosque because I don't have anywhere else to go', Rabiah announced. A *muhajir* is a Muslim pilgrim, named after the companions who accompanied the Prophet Mohammed on his *hijrah* from Mecca to Medina, to escape their persecutors and find a safe haven for the Islamic faith. The mantle of *muhajirin* was also donned by Ba'asyir and Sungkar when they fled into exile in Malaysia. Islamic tradition obliges Muslims to provide sanctuary to *muhajirin*, as the perplexed imam was well aware.

'As a spiritual leader I had to accommodate her and look after her children', remembers the Indian-born imam, Abdul Qudus. 'There is a covenant in Islam that if a Muslim has nowhere to go or needs assistance, they can go to the mosque. It is the duty of the community to take care of them.' Abdul Qudus recalls Rabiah as a 'very good lady' and a 'loving, caring mother'. He gave them clothes and blankets and spread out prayer mats for them to sleep on in the ladies section of the mosque, where they stayed for two or three weeks. After that, he arranged for them to stay with an Indonesian family, the Siregars, who lived with their 13-year-old daughter in suburban Wagaman nearby. The Siregars remember little except that Rabiah was heavily pregnant, 'very outspoken', and liked to regale them with stories of her life in Indonesia 'even without being asked'. Later a hat was passed around at Friday *jummah* prayers, to help pay the first month's rent on a small flat found by the imam for Rabiah and her family across the road from the giant Casuarina Shopping Square and a short walk from the mosque.

Rabiah enrolled Devi and Mohammed in the local public school system, where they were streamed into a special 'ESL' school for children who spoke English as a second language. After three years in Java, the children spoke better Indonesian and Arabic than English. Ten-year-old Devi was a bright, diligent pupil who adjusted easily and was soon back in the mainstream. But eight-year-old Mohammed, who had been born and spent most of his life in Indonesia, struggled to adapt.

'Mohammed just hated Australia', says Rabiah. 'When he lived in Ngruki he used to spend his time playing in the streets or in the rice fields. He didn't speak English. It was just a culture shock.' It was later learned that the boy was severely dyslexic. He compensated by playing the class clown, amusing his classmates with outrageous stories and antics. It was never the dog that had eaten his homework; more likely a sabre-toothed tiger that had snuck out of its underground cave to devour his project book. In an echo of her own troubled school days, Rabiah was often summoned by the principal because her son was being 'disruptive'. It was little wonder the boy was unsettled, given his chaotic life so far.

'Devi and Mohammed had absolutely no stability in their lives', Rabiah admits. 'They went through dramatic changes. They were there in the "Robyn turns to Rabiah" stage—it was traumatic for me so it must have been for them, there's no denying that, because I went through such a transition in a short period of time.'

Two months after they landed in Darwin, Rabiah's husband, Abdul Rahim Ayub, was still in Indonesia waiting for a residency visa. The

Australian authorities wanted proof that the couple were legally married under Australian law and had urged them to formalise their union with a civil ceremony in Jakarta before she left, which she refused to do. 'My principle was that I was married under Islamic law in Indonesia—it was recognised and legal. So I refused, and the more they told me "just do it", the more I dug my heels in.' Apart from the principle, she did not want a marriage certificate that would indicate her unborn child had been conceived out of wedlock. Hence, Abdul Rahim was still waiting in Jakarta when their son Abdullah Mustafa (known among the family by his second name, Mustafa) was born on 21 October 1985. The birth was quick and relatively painless. She left the children at the mosque with the imam, got a lift to Royal Darwin Hospital, gave birth, was discharged, fetched the children and went home, all in the same day. Abdul Rahim arrived three days later, with a fresh 'permanent resident' stamp in his Indonesian passport.

They settled well enough into Darwin's polyglot community of Asian migrants, Pacific Islanders, asylum seekers and illegal immigrants, and were allocated a subsidised housing commission home at Casuarina, still within walking distance of the mosque. It was a typical breezy 'Darwin house' with cyclone shutters and a big yard with mangos, coconuts and a frangipani tree. If you closed your eyes and inhaled the fragrant steamy air, you could almost be in Indonesia. The large and tight-knit Indonesian diaspora welcomed newcomers and the mosque was a popular hub where Friday *jumaah* was more a social than a religious event; 'like Christians going to church on Sunday', as Rabiah recalls.

In keeping with their role as *muhajirin*, whose duty is to propagate Islam, Rabiah and Abdul Rahim threw themselves into life at the mosque. Abdul Rahim was soon teaching the Quran to children while Rabiah took classes for women. As in Indonesia, the novelty factor made her a drawcard. 'I was a bit of a phenomenon because I was white, I wore hijab and spoke Indonesian. The Indonesians in Darwin were not particularly religious. Our behaviour was very foreign to the Muslims in Darwin because they had missed out on the Islamic revival.'

Fresh from the maelstrom of Islamist politics in Indonesia, Rabiah was fired up to continue the struggle against Suharto and expected the local diaspora to rally to the cause. But the Indonesians in Darwin had grown comfortable; they were 'very liberal, easy going, very casual', says Abdul Qudus. Most still had families in Indonesia and many commuted back and forth; some had arrived illegally or overstayed their visas and had no wish to attract attention. So Rabiah's fulminations were met mostly with embarrassed silence or mild alarm. She sums up their reaction: 'we don't want to talk about it, we can't talk about it, and please don't make trouble for us'.

The imam grew accustomed to Rabiah barging into his office to harangue him about his failure to enforce *akhlaq*, correct Islamic behaviour. 'I'd march down to the mosque, and the imam would see me coming and try to hide', she remembers. One pet aversion was women from the Indian subcontinent wearing saris to the mosque, exposing bare flesh. 'I'd go to the imam and say things like, "Why are you letting naked women into the mosque? You can't let it happen".' Abdul Qudus was unperturbed. 'She can't push me—I was the imam', he later pointed out.

Abdul Rahim, who had never before been out of Indonesia, tried as best he could to absorb the double-barrelled culture shock of marriage to Rabiah and life in Australia. A short, stocky man with a wispy beard and dimpled grin, he was, by several accounts, amiable and well liked. But he had come from a devoutly religious family, was one of twelve children and a twin, and had never been apart from them before. In Indonesia, he had been a talented engineering student, respected Quran teacher, political activist and devotee of Islamic law. Here he was just another unqualified migrant with hardly any English and a wife and four kids to support. He got a job as a kitchen hand and dishwasher in an Indonesian *halal* restaurant called Warung Pojok (the Corner Stall) in Darwin's CBD. The café's owner, an Australian-born convert, Luqman Landy, who now runs schools and charities in Indonesia, recalls Abdul Rahim and Rabiah as 'concerned and compassionate' people who were devoted to Islam. He and Abdul Rahim tried to establish an Islamic school in Darwin but failed because of 'insufficient material support from the local Muslims'.

'From the beginning it was a disaster', Rabiah says of their life in Australia. 'He never wanted to come here in the first place. He had given up his studies, upset his family (by marrying her) and all of a sudden he's in Darwin. So you can imagine, coming into a society that didn't see any difference between men and women. I can remember him turning on the television and seeing naked people. He was quite shocked.'

The contrast in their personalities was more starkly apparent now that Rabiah was back in her homeland and no longer bound by Javanese etiquette. The Siregars recall that Abdul Rahim was 'very very quiet', while 'she was not—she was an Australian girl', and a particularly loud one at that.

'He didn't speak a word of English, so wherever we'd go of course I'd have to do all the talking', says Rabiah. 'Also because I was older, I think he found that intimidating. He was not comfortable with the role he was forced into because I took over the dominant role of the family in every respect.'

The simplest excursion could turn into an ordeal. One day they were pushing Mustafa in his pram around the supermarket when an old lady leaned over to chuck the baby's cheek, and cooed, 'Aren't you a cute little monkey?' Abdul Rahim had gleaned enough English to pick up the word 'monkey', which to an Indonesian is a grievous insult—like calling someone an 'ape'. 'What did she say?' he asked, his eyes wide with alarm and shaking his head in consternation. 'I could imagine his brain was exploding', recalls Rabiah. 'Why would a nice old lady come up and smile, and then say something so terrible? And every day was like that.'

In her conservative Islamic attire, Rabiah found herself the butt of curiosity and sometimes derision, but not yet the intense hostility that would come in later years. 'People in the 1980s didn't hate Islam. They'd say, "Where's your camel?" or "Do you know you're in Australia now?" I'd turn around and say, "Have you got a problem, mate?" And they'd hear my Aussie accent and say, "Are you Australian? Oh, sorry".' But sometimes the fact that she was Australian only made it worse. 'There was an underlying sense that you've defected, or become a traitor.'

For Abdul Rahim the shock of life in Australia was compounded by the plight of the Northern Territory's indigenous population, many of whom lived in squalor exacerbated by rampant alcohol and drug abuse and domestic violence. 'The drunkenness and the state of the Aborigines really concerned and shocked him, and so did the society as a whole. He was totally dumbstruck by what he saw as the moral decay', says Rabiah. He was horrified when he learned of a news report about a father who had raped his 18-month-old child and been sentenced to a short prison term. 'He was just devastated. His mind couldn't comprehend it. In Indonesia, if that man had been dragged out and beaten to death, nothing would have happened, it would have just been the natural thing.' Australia's idea of justice simply did not compute. 'He hated it. It traumatised him. It was constantly like this—"What am I doing here?"'

About a year after his arrival in Australia, Abdul Rahim travelled to Malaysia to pay the family's respects to a 'brother' who was dying of cancer and to visit Abdullah Sungkar and Abu Bakar Ba'asyir in their new home in exile. He had nothing better to do in Australia, and suburban domesticity was proving a strain, according to Rabiah: 'So I asked *ustadz* Abu (Ba'asyir) if he could go for a visit, to give him something to do, make him feel important'. She had fallen pregnant again and while Abdul Rahim was away she gave birth to a stillborn son, born two months premature and mildly deformed, apparently as a result of undiagnosed gestational diabetes. She named the boy Azhar and buried his tiny body under the frangipani tree in the backyard.

'Of course I was sad but I had peace in my heart', she says, 'because any child who dies will wait for you at the gates of paradise, because they are sinless. And when Allah says, "Enter into *jannah* (paradise)", the child will say "No, I want to wait for my mother and father".' When Abdul Rahim rang from Malaysia and learned the news he offered to return immediately, but Rabiah told him there was no need, so he stuck to his schedule and came back four weeks later.

Around this time, Rabiah received word from Sydney that her mother Bessie was dying from the emphysema that had been diagnosed four years earlier. She bundled up baby Mustafa and four-year-old Rahmah, so that Bessie could see her two newest grandchildren for the first time. When they arrived in Sydney, Bessie was in an aged-care facility opposite her younger daughter Susan's home on the upper north shore. Her emphysema was so advanced that when they wheeled her across the road to Susan's house they had to carry an oxygen tank to keep her breathing.

Rabiah faced her mother's death with trepidation. She believed firmly that Bessie would be barred from paradise because she was not a Muslim, a conviction that angered her sister who later said she wanted nothing to do with a religion that deemed her mother unworthy of heaven. On the last day Rabiah saw her mother, a Muslim friend in Sydney asked if he could try to persuade Bessie to convert to Islam before she died. But Rabiah could see Bessie was exhausted. 'I said to him, "Mum's not well today, she's tired, leave it for another time". So it was never said. I still ask Allah to forgive me.'

Rabiah was back in Darwin a few weeks later when her brother George rang to say Bessie had passed away. Rabiah didn't return to Sydney for the funeral. It was her mother's wish to be cremated, and Rabiah had told her she could not attend because cremation is regarded as sacrilege in Islam. And in any event, according to Rabiah: 'You're not permitted to pray for forgiveness for people who die in disbelief. She was my mum and I loved her. But at the end of the day she didn't choose to acknowledge Allah. And if she didn't attain paradise, then it was her choice.'

A few months after her mother's death, Rabiah gave birth to another son, Mohammed Ilyas (known in the family simply as Ilyas), her third delivery in barely two years. He was a large baby and became stuck in the birth canal, a complication known as 'failure to descend'. Rabiah's blood pressure was dangerously low and the baby was in foetal distress. She remembers it like a scene from a movie: fluorescent lights whizzing overhead and a doctor yelling 'we're losing her!' as they raced her down a corridor on a hospital trolley to the operating theatre for an emergency caesarean. The doctor who performed it recommended she have her fallopian tubes tied afterwards, as it could be life threatening to have another child. After seeking religious advice on the matter, she decided instead to leave her fate in the hands of God.

Ilyas was nearly one year old when Rabiah and Abdul Rahim decided to leave the Northern Territory after three years. 'We left Darwin because it was a dead end, we'd done enough', is how Rabiah explains it. She and Abdul Rahim had grown dispirited among the laid-back Muslim crowd with its culture of 'barbecues at the mosque', while Rabiah's aggressive proselytising had got some people's backs up. Some of the women who attended her classes had begun wearing hijab, prompting complaints that she was having an 'extreme' influence, and her lessons were brought to a stop. 'Wherever Abdul Rahim and I went, there was always opposition', Rabiah says. 'The imams of the mosques would either say "Yes, yes we know you're right, but it's too hard", or they would oppose us and say "These people are extremists".'

After leaving Darwin, they moved for a while to Brisbane, but never really settled there. Abdul Rahim was out of work and they were living on his unemployment benefits and her child welfare payments, a meagre income with seven mouths to feed. Her eldest children, Devi and Mohammed, never got on with their stepfather. Twelve-year-old Mohammed was still struggling and behaving disruptively at school and was referred to a child psychologist. The marriage was under growing strain. 'Australia wasn't a good time for us. He was depressed, I was frustrated, basically we just didn't want to be here. All that travelling around was about trying to find an Islamic environment that was going to be, if not good, at least not so detrimental to the children and ourselves. We kept moving because we were unhappy here. It's not hard to see a pattern with me—that's been my life. When I come up against difficulties, you know the saying: "a change is as good as a holiday". I think that was invented for me.'

After a few months in Brisbane they packed up and moved again, to Melbourne. Abdul Rahim went first to find them a place to live, while Rabiah—who was pregnant again—followed on the train with the five children. She got a sleeper carriage and 'kept a couple of kids hidden' to save on the fares. By the time they got there, Abdul Rahim had rented a house in Footscray in Melbourne's working-class western suburbs, sandwiched between the railway line, the Footscray produce market and the Western Oval football ground, home to the Bulldogs Australian Rules team. The house had mouldy carpets, clumps of asbestos hanging from a hole in the fibrocement wall and a World War II–model refrigerator. A friend described it as 'the cheapest house in the cheapest suburb in Melbourne' with a hallway floor that 'went up and down like the Scenic Railway at Luna Park'. It was owned by a niggard named Bellado who refused to spend money on repairs. 'Mama, bloody Bellado's here', three-year-old Mustafa would call out, mimicking his mother, when the landlord came to collect the rent.

Despite the grungy accommodation, Melbourne proved a more comfortable fit for Rabiah and Abdul Rahim. The city was home to a proud Salafist community, presided over by a Jordanian-born cleric, Sheikh Mohammed Jamal Omran, known among his followers as Abu Ayman. From his base at the Michael Street mosque in suburban Brunswick, Omran oversaw a community-based organisation, the Ahlus Sunnah wal Jamaah Association (roughly translated as 'people of the *Sunnah*'), and its offshoot, the Islamic Information and Support Centre of Australia. Omran's group became known as the most pro-active 'fundamentalist' outfit in the country, its members conspicuous for their pious dress; the men in long beards and Arab-style robes, the women shrouded in black, in the style of the original Muslims, the *Salaf al-Salih*, or 'pious predecessors'.

In June 1989 in Melbourne, aged thirty-five, Rabiah gave birth to her sixth living child, a girl named Aminah, who was delivered by emergency caesarean. Mother and child spent a fortnight in hospital recovering, and afterwards Rabiah had her fallopian tubes tied to prevent further pregnancies.

Two months after the birth, Rabiah enrolled at Melbourne University to study Arabic. She also volunteered as the co-ordinator of a neighbourhood house run by the Footscray council, which provided language lessons for immigrants, mother and child play groups, cooking and arts and crafts classes. Rabiah arranged for local Muslim women to use the neighbourhood house every Sunday afternoon, and got approval to run a weekend Islamic school for children. Classes were held at the community house every Saturday and Sunday from 9 a.m. to 3 p.m. Rabiah took the children for Islamic lessons and games, while Abdul Rahim taught them the Quran. An Indonesian immigrant who had studied at Abu Bakar

Ba'asyir's alma mater, the esteemed Gontor Islamic boarding school in East Java, was roped in to take classes in *nukil*, translating the Quran from Arabic to Indonesian. Sometimes they took the children on excursions to the local swimming pool, because 'Muslim children *are* allowed to have fun', Rabiah points out, as long as they wore proper Islamic attire and girls and boys were kept apart. On Sundays she held religious classes for their mothers at the council facility, instructing about a dozen women in the *hadith* and Islamic law.

'They loved her down there', says a friend from this time, Nadia Aboufadil, another Australian-born convert. 'They were just happy that a Muslim woman was active and organising the community and getting things together.'

Nadia had grown up in leafy middle-class Glen Iris and was a student in the film and television course at Melbourne's Swinburne University. On a trip to Europe to attend the Cannes Film Festival, she had met a Moroccan man who took her to his homeland where she 'fell in love with Islam'. She married, had two girls, and returned to Melbourne, where her husband had recently died of cancer. She met Rabiah at a gathering held by the Islamic Council of Victoria. Rabiah's energy and charisma made a huge impression on Nadia, who was a 'bit of a feminist' by her own description.

'Rabiah wasn't like the other women', Nadia remembers. 'I admired her. She knew everybody, she was very articulate and confident, she had a humanity, an openness and she made friends easily … She was quite dynamic and a powerful woman. People have this impression of Muslim women all being submissive women who obey their husbands, but Rabiah was completely the opposite. She was too outspoken even for some of the men.'

Nadia recalls that at their meetings the women, who were predominantly Indonesians and other immigrants, would be in the kitchen cooking or sitting demurely with their husbands paying little attention to what was being discussed. 'And here was Rabiah rattling off all these *hadith* by heart. She was really passionate. Compared to the others she was just really interesting.'

Nadia says Rabiah became 'the organiser of a circle of women'. Also among its members was another Australian convert, Charmaine Johnston, who had taken the popular Muslim name Khadija. Her background had much in common with Rabiah's. She was a country girl who had grown up at Cooranbong in New South Wales and attended Booragul High School on the picturesque northern shores of Lake Macquarie. Charmaine's brother was the Australian soccer legend Craig Johnston, who played his first game for Booragul High then went on to star for Liverpool in the United Kingdom. Khadija was 'a beautiful person' in Nadia's words, a loveable 'former hippy' who made her own bread and kept bees for honey. She and Rabiah met at a mutual friend's home where Rabiah had given a talk one evening. Afterwards Rabiah bundled the children into the car but miscounted and left three-year-old Mustafa behind. As Rabiah tells it, it was this that inspired Khadija to seek her out as a friend, curious about 'what kind of weirdo would leave her child behind'.

As they got to know each other, Khadija confided: 'My husband's a sheikh'.

'I'd like to meet him as well', said Rabiah.

Khadija's husband was the leading Salafi cleric in Melbourne, Sheikh Mohammed Jamal Omran. He and Khadija had met and married in 1984 while Omran was visiting Sydney from Fiji where he ran a mosque at the time. Omran was looking for a wife, and a friend introduced him to Khadija. (By Rabiah's account his proposal at their initial meeting was straight to the point: 'What have you decided? Because I've got other women to see.' Khadija told Rabiah she was so stunned by his directness that she accepted.) After Khadija introduced her to Sheikh Omran, Rabiah persuaded him to take her as a student for weekly classes at his home, despite the fact that he usually did not take female students. Nadia recalls: 'He used to teach only men. Rabiah was the only woman who insisted on being a part of whatever was going on.'

For Rabiah's children, Melbourne was their fourth new home in as many years. Fourteen-year-old Devi—'a fiery teenager with a mind of her own', according to Nadia—attended the local high school. Her brother

Mohammed had struggled through primary school devising ever more inventive excuses for not doing his homework. On one occasion Rabiah was summoned to the school after Mohammed told his teacher that he had been unable to finish his project because his mother had woken him for breakfast at 3 a.m. so he could fast through the day, and as a result he was too exhausted. Rabiah indignantly insisted it wasn't true. The younger children attended the Footscray state primary school where they became known as the pupils whose mother would not allow them to do music, dancing or go on excursions, which she regarded as *haram* (forbidden). 'The school found me uncompromising', Rabiah volunteers.

Their life in Melbourne was a constant whirl of activity, and the strain of it showed. Abdul Rahim was studying computer science and applied physics at the Victoria University of Technology but didn't work while they lived in Melbourne. Nadia Aboufadil recalls that he was 'pleasant' but 'very quiet and kept to himself'. 'He seemed to admire Rabiah but they rarely spoke to each other.' She recalls her friend saying they were 'having problems'. By her own description, Rabiah was not an easy woman to be married to—domineering, tempestuous and a relentless perfectionist. One habit that grated on Abdul Rahim was her insistence on crisply folded 'hospital corners' on their bed sheets. One night they arrived home late after a function. It was almost midnight and Abdul Rahim was ready to collapse—but first the bed had to be correctly made. Exhausted, he put his face in his hands and begged, 'please, please don't make me do hospital corners'. Of course she did.

Abdul Rahim's crisis of confidence over his diminished role had not abated, and having to rely on government benefits to feed a family of eight didn't help. 'Rabiah told me that her six children were only allowed to eat one piece of fruit per day', says Nadia. 'Every day she'd cook up a few cups of rice in her electric rice cooker. There was never much to go with it.' However, Rabiah blames the stresses in their marriage primarily on the difficulty of maintaining an Islamic lifestyle in secular Australia. 'There was never a problem in our compatibility as husband and wife—we were very compatible. The problem was being in Australia. The social structure of this society placed a lot of outside pressures on our marriage and on his identity as a man and a husband. The fact of having four kids in four years—it should have been joyous. But instead people thought: they breed like rabbits, or: they're doing it to get money from the government.'

In her inimitable fashion, Rabiah came up with an idea that she thought might solve their marital problems. She raised it with her friend Nadia Aboufadil.

'Will you be my co-wife?' she asked, to her friend's astonishment.

'No thanks', Nadia replied.

It was not the first time Rabiah had suggested that Abdul Rahim take a second wife. She had proposed it while they were living in Brisbane, suggesting an Indonesian woman his family knew in Jakarta. Abdul Rahim was unenthused. 'No, you're enough—just having you is like having four wives', he told her. Undaunted, she rang the family in Indonesia, who was aghast at the suggestion. 'Apart from the fact that now most people shy away from polygamous relationships, they said, "Tell him to look after the one he's already got"', she recounts.

Rabiah had long held that polygamy must be accepted simply because it is part of God's law. She could now see practical advantages as well, particularly for a youthful husband with a healthy libido and an extremely busy first wife. 'I had so many children and so many things to do, and he was younger than me. One of the benefits of polygamy is that if there's another wife there are so many days in the week when you don't have to cook or clean for the husband because someone else is looking after him. It means the woman has more time to herself.'

The issue of polygamy was a source of much debate among the women in her circle. Her friend Khadija dreaded the thought of Sheikh Omran taking a second wife, which they used to joke about.

'You wouldn't want to see your co-wife crossing the road or you'd be tempted to run her over in your car', said Rabiah one day.

'Don't be bloody ridiculous—I'd drive up onto the footpath to run her over', Khadija replied.

Rabiah's proposal for a second wife rejected, the tensions in her marriage continued to simmer. Abdul Rahim's frustrations came to a head one day while they were sitting in a traffic jam with three of the children in the back of the car. Beside them in the traffic was a very large 'Aussie guy' in a Mini Minor who was glaring at Abdul Rahim. As the traffic started moving, his vehicle veered towards them and sideswiped their car, seemingly on purpose.

'I saw something in Abdul Rahim's face—it was the straw that had broken the camel's back', Rabiah recalls.

'Just try to get away', she urged him.

'Shut up, I'll handle this', he replied.

Abdul Rahim stopped the car dead in the middle of the street.

'I'm ordering you to stay in the car and whatever happens, do not interfere, do not get out of the car.'

When he confronted the other driver, the stranger took a tyre lever from his car and hit Abdul Rahim over the head, causing blood to spurt from his skull. A life-long martial artist, Abdul Rahim swiftly floored his assailant then grabbed the tyre lever and was about to strike him, when Rabiah stepped in.

'As he brought up the tyre lever, I came from behind and pulled it out of his hand—and he never forgave me.'

Abdul Rahim required treatment in hospital for the gash to his head. Doctors found an aneurism in his brain that required surgery and later diagnosed post-traumatic stress disorder. The police were called but Abdul Rahim declined to press charges. He eventually received a small compensation payment but he never fully recovered, according to Rabiah—either from the physical trauma or the humiliation of being stopped from defending himself by his wife. 'He became very moody, very angry. He used to get incredible headaches and was unable to sleep. And the fact that I had effectively taken away his manhood in front of the inhabitants of Footscray—it affected our relationship terribly. No matter how much I tried to tell him—he would have gone to jail, he would have been charged with manslaughter—he said, "It would have been worth it to keep my manhood".'

Because of the injury, Abdul Rahim had to give up his studies and was unable to work, and they were forced to discontinue their weekend Islamic school. His despair worsened. Once, when leaving the house, he muttered, 'You'd better give me your hijab, I've got to go out'. When she asked what he meant, he replied, 'Well, I've turned into a woman'.

One day when the children's rowdy horseplay woke him while he was trying to sleep off a migraine, Abdul Rahim lashed out and gave Mohammed a hiding. The boy was so sore and bruised he had to be kept home from school. When he returned to school three days later, a teacher asked him why he was bruised. 'Because my father beat me', Mohammed replied. The school called the government department responsible for child welfare who ordered that Mohammed be removed from his family. Rabiah was mortified. Even worse to her than her son being taken was the fact that he was placed with a non-Muslim foster family. At her insistence, he was transferred to a Muslim family, who kept him for a month before he was allowed to go home.

'We got Mohammed home with a very stern warning', says Rabiah. 'They tried to make out it had happened because of Islam, that it was normal for Muslim men to bash their children and wives, that he was power-drunk and an egotistical excuse for a human being. They gave me the benefit of the doubt because I was an Aussie—"poor thing, poor oppressed thing". They made it clear that if it happens again, you won't just lose this child, you'll lose all of them.'

* * *

Throughout the five years they lived in Australia, Rabiah had stayed in contact with Abdullah Sungkar and Abu Bakar Ba'asyir, still living in exile in Malaysia. There they had begun building a new *jemaah* (community), which would later form the foundations for the organisation they called Jemaah Islamiyah, with branches in half a dozen countries. The clerics had established a new Islamic boarding school in a jungle clearing in Johore, the southernmost state of Malaysia, and appointed as its principal one of their loyal followers, a young Indonesian named Ali Gufron bin Nurhasyim, who was a former student and teacher at their Ngruki school. Ali Gufron would later become infamous by his *nom de guerre* Muklas, as the spiritual leader of the 2002 Bali bombings. He had been at Ngruki at the same time as Rabiah but she says she never met him, because single males were housed separately from women and families and were barred from entering the girls school where she taught.

Rabiah had been agitating to move to Malaysia with her family so her children could attend the new *pesantren*. But Ba'asyir and Sungkar had insisted to her frustration that she stay put, arguing that it was her duty as a *muhajir* to spread the message of Islam in Australia. 'When they established the school in Johore, I was still complaining and whingeing— "Australia is no good for us, we don't want to be here". I wanted to move to Malaysia with Abdul Rahim and the children. But Aba (Sungkar) wanted me to stay here to continue the work I was doing, and send the children to Malaysia.' The new *pesantren* took children as young as three years old, but Rabiah wanted to keep her children with her, so all of them stayed in Australia.

One day she was on the phone to her old friend Ecun, Ba'asyir's wife, lamenting the parlous state of the Indonesian Muslim diaspora in Australia and its lack of Islamic guidance. 'The Indonesian community here is lost—they are mostly young students, there is no Indonesian mosque and no scholars', she recalls telling Ecun. 'Could you ask *ustadz* Abu (Ba'asyir), does he have anyone—a student maybe—who he could send to Australia to guide us?'

When they spoke a few days later, Ba'asyir feigned chagrin.

'So you want one of my students, you don't want me?'

'Would you come? Can you really come?'

'Yes, we will come', he replied. 'But you know we don't have money.'

Rabiah and Abdul Rahim solicited donations from the Indonesian Muslim community to raise the $1000 or so that was needed in those days for two return economy airfares from Malaysia to Australia. Rabiah could barely wait to see them. She showed her friend Nadia a report from Amnesty International documenting the torture and arrest of *usroh* activists in Indonesia, and told of how her mentors had escaped by boat to Malaysia to avoid capture. 'She kept talking about her *ustadz* (teacher). She said to me, "Come and meet my *ustadz*"', Nadia remembers.

Ba'asyir and Sungkar arrived in Melbourne in April 1990 on the first of a dozen trips they would make to Australia through the 1990s. They stayed for a week with Rabiah and Abdul Rahim in their home in Footscray, sleeping in one of the children's bedrooms while the children all piled in together. Their reunion was a polite affair, in keeping with Indonesian custom and Islamic *akhlaq* (behaviour). But it was soon just like the old days, with Rabiah berating them as she had done at Ngruki for paying insufficient heed to 'correct' Islamic practice. It was the fasting month of Ramadan, the timing of which is calculated in Australia by computer calculations of the lunar cycle, rather than the traditional method based on the first sighting of the new moon.

'I remember having a big fight with *ustadz* Abu because they were praying according to the computer readout instead of sighting the moon', says Rabiah. In keeping with the maxim 'when in Rome', Ba'asyir was willing to go along with the local custom, pointing out to Rabiah that Islam allows for minor technicalities to be overlooked in the interests of a greater good such as preserving community harmony. But Rabiah wouldn't hear of it: 'I told *ustadz* Abu I wasn't going to pray, and that coming to Australia had corrupted him'.

Just like Abdul Rahim five years earlier, the two clerics were gobsmacked by their first taste of Australia. They had travelled to Malaysia, Singapore and Saudi Arabia, but never to a Western country. They were impressed by the cleanliness, order and affluence, commenting on the lack of beggars on the streets, and scandalised by the sight of women wearing shorts.

Ba'asyir was a fitness enthusiast and creature of habit whose daily routine mandated a brisk walk after morning prayer. He returned on the first morning after striding around the streets of suburban Footscray, clearly perturbed. '*Aduh* (Oh dear), Rabiah! The people here are not embarrassed, are they? Even the women—sticking their heads out the windows, looking at me.' For a woman to display blatant curiosity towards a strange man was unheard of in Ba'asyir's milieu, and it hadn't dawned on him that a man with a scraggly white beard wearing a sarong and a *haji* hat might be worth a second glance. He soon dispensed with his morning walk, deciding 'it was too traumatic to go out in the daytime', according to Rabiah. Abdullah Sungkar was even more voluble, particularly about Australian feminine attire. 'This is because we don't live under Islam and that's why you have all these naked women running around!' he pontificated.

After five years in exile together in Malaysia, Ba'asyir and Sungkar resembled an old married couple. A companion who had travelled with them told of how they'd spent the entire journey doing silent battle over the air-conditioning vent above their seats. Sungkar would reach up and turn it on, then settle back for a snooze; as soon as his eyes were shut Ba'asyir, who couldn't stand air-conditioning, would reach up and turn it off. Nor could the health-conscious Ba'asyir abide Sungkar's habit of chain-smoking clove cigarettes. 'They were always fighting over it', Rabiah recollects. Ba'asyir believed that smoking was *haram* because self-harm is forbidden to Muslims, while Sungkar had decided it was merely *makru*, which means disliked by Allah, but not necessarily *haram*. But he had learned to keep his *kreteks* on his person as they tended to mysteriously disappear if left lying around.

The preachers' first visit to Australia was kept deliberately low key. They travelled under aliases they had assumed to avoid detection in Malaysia: Sungkar was known as Abdul Halim, Ba'asyir as Abdus Samad Abud. The visit was a private affair, with no public sermons or political speeches; those would come on subsequent visits as their confidence and enmity towards Suharto grew, along with their reputation among the Australian Muslim community as fearless dissidents who dared to speak out against the tyrannical Suharto regime. They attended Friday *jummah* at the Preston mosque where they met other clerics including Sheikh Mohammed Omran, whose Salafist ideology was a close match with Ba'asyir's and Sungkar's beliefs. Sheikh Omran said later he found Ba'asyir to be 'a very peaceful man'.

During their visit Rabiah arranged for Abdullah Sungkar to deliver a private lecture at an Indonesian family's home in Melbourne's northern suburbs. The neophyte Nadia Aboufadil remembers being impressed to meet such a knowledgeable cleric: 'I thought it was really cool, here's this guy who's memorised the Quran'. Starting with this visit, Ba'asyir and Sungkar would build a strong following among the community they referred to as their Australian *jemaah*. 'The Indonesians here fell in love with them', Rabiah says.

Ba'asyir and Sungkar were not yet preaching violent resistance; they still believed their goal of an Islamic state in Indonesia could be achieved through peaceful means. However, they had by now begun preparing for the eventuality of having to fight for it. Since 1984, they had been sending selected recruits for military training in Pakistan to build up their group's military preparedness. Nadia Aboufadil remembers Sungkar delivering a fiery lecture on chapter eight of the Quran, 'Sura Al-Anfal (The Spoils)', which contains this clarion call to jihad:

Your Lord bade you leave your home to fight for justice ... God revealed his will to the angels, saying ... 'I shall cast terror into the hearts of the infidels. Strike off their heads, strike off the very tips of their fingers! ... Make war on them until idolatry shall cease and God's religion shall reign supreme ... Muster against them all the men and cavalry at your command, so that you may strike terror into the enemy of God.'

While Sungkar thundered on in Indonesian, Rabiah would sit with Nadia whispering the English translation into her ear. Nadia recalls Sungkar's orations about jihad had an electrifying impact on her friend.

'Rabiah also began talking about jihad a lot. Her eyes would light up when she spoke about it. She had this whole romantic notion that Muslims defend themselves with jihad. It was just this fantastic thing that you aimed for.' Rabiah says the jihad to which Sungkar was alluding and which so inspired her was the ongoing *mujahidin* struggle in Afghanistan to defeat the infidel Communists and establish an Islamic state.

Ba'asyir and Sungkar's visit to Melbourne only seemed to exacerbate the growing tensions in Rabiah's marriage. As a student radical in Jakarta, Abdul Rahim had been habituated to segregation of the sexes, which was practised by the students but had never been enforced at Ngruki. While living in Australia, he and Rabiah had practised segregation, as far as practicable, in their own home, with discreet sitting rooms for men and women to socialise separately. Now here was his wife entertaining the two visiting luminaries, vigorously debating the finer points of *shariah* with two men unrelated to her *and* in the same room. By Rabiah's account, it only reinforced Abdul Rahim's place on the periphery—a position not unlike the one her two previous husbands had endured. As she tells it, Abdul Rahim was just 'Rabiah's husband' to Sungkar and Ba'asyir.

'Their familiarity with me was difficult for him because of my long association with them. They didn't know Abdul Rahim very well. I had lived at Ngruki. Abdul Rahim came to meet them because I introduced them. He never lived there.' Rabiah would later dismiss reports that her husband and his twin brother were significant figures in the Islamist hierarchy: 'Abdul Rahim and Abdul Rahman were wannabes. They were more important to themselves than to anyone else.'

While Ba'asyir and Sungkar were staying with them in Footscray, Rabiah decided to end her marriage to Abdul Rahim. From her perspective it was a pragmatic decision, in keeping with her view of marriage as an essentially practical arrangement.

'An Islamic marriage is a contract between two consenting adults, and the function of the man and woman are very different', she says. 'If you marry someone who doesn't demonstrate the ability to lead and instil confidence and bring about a feeling of contentment, then you cannot fulfil your duties as a wife.'

Rabiah is quick to add that her utilitarian view of marriage does not rule out romantic love, which ideally will develop *after* marriage if the couple is well matched. But the contractual obligations must be met, and as far as she was concerned Abdul Rahim had demonstrably welched on his end of the bargain by failing to provide and care for her and the children, which meant she could not honour her own obligations as a Muslim spouse. In her meticulous study of the *hadith* Rabiah had made it her business to know exactly what her rights were under Islamic law and she now insisted on her right to a divorce.

She raised the issue with Abdullah Sungkar, whose unsentimental approach had facilitated the end of her previous marriage to Pujo Busono six years before. Once again Rabiah persuaded Sungkar that it was within her rights under Islam to demand a divorce. 'I told him I didn't want to continue the marriage. He looked at all the evidence and thought it was better for both of us (to separate).' Sungkar took the opportunity also to terminate the ill-conceived marriage contract between Rabiah's daughter, Devi, and her brother-in-law, Abdul Rahman Ayub. They had never lived together as man and wife. Since the signing of the marriage contract Devi had been in Australia with her family while Abdul Rahman was doing military training in Pakistan. Sungkar had opposed their union from the outset and persuaded Abdul Rahman to agree to a dissolution.

When Sungkar and Ba'asyir left to return to Malaysia, Abdul Rahim moved out of their marital home in Footscray. But within days he was back, insisting the marriage was not over because he had not actually agreed to a divorce. His attempts to effect a reconciliation ended dramatically not long afterwards, when he was again woken from an afternoon sleep by the children, lost his temper, and raised his hand to strike his stepdaughter, Devi. For all their differences, Rabiah insists Abdul Rahim was not normally a violent man. 'He used to get terrible headaches, no amount of medication would help. It was just circumstances, he was physically not well. When he got these headaches he didn't know what he was doing.' When Rabiah stepped between them to stop him hitting Devi, he struck her instead. The children started screaming and Devi rang the police.

'I arrived just in time to see the police roughly grabbing Abdul Rahim and dragging him out of the house', recalls Nadia Aboufadil. She describes a rather comical scene, as 'this tiny shrimpy little Indonesian guy' was manhandled by two burly constables. In those days 'domestic' disputes were frequently ignored by the authorities, but the Footscray police had no sympathy for Abdul Rahim, given his previous history. 'You might be able to do that in your religion, mate, but you're in Australia now. If you don't leave, we'll have to remove the children', they told him. 'The next day the department of child welfare came and told me that if he moved back into the house they would take the children', Rabiah recounts.

Finally, Abdul Rahim agreed to a divorce. Rabiah says she still harbours regrets over the failure of their five-year marriage. 'Anybody who's been divorced knows the loss and the regret and it's something that no person, man or woman, could do easily.' Despite its contractual formality, marriage in Islam is considered a sacred duty, which constitutes half a Muslims's *deen* (religion), as decreed by the Prophet.

'When I look back, I don't think I ever married for the right reasons', Rabiah reflects. 'When I married it was always for a reason other than that. And getting married for any other reason—visas, or monetary reasons, or convenience—is not the correct intention. I got married or accepted proposals because I thought it would solve a particular problem I had, not because it was pleasing to Allah. It was always a way out of something. And if you marry with those intentions, how could you have the patience and tolerance and unselfishness that's needed to live with someone else as a partner?'

Ultimately though, she maintains it was out of her hands: 'Why did I get married and divorced so many times? Because that's what Allah wrote for me. And wisdom and good came out of all those marriages.'

Their divorce was amicable. Rabiah and the children moved out of the dingy house in Footscray and into a spacious new housing commission home at Sunshine in Melbourne's western suburbs. Abdul Rahim stayed in Footscray and had the children on weekends. Not long after this, Rabiah sent 15-year-old Devi off to Malaysia to attend Ba'asyir and Sungkar's new Islamic boarding school in Johore.

Rabiah was now comfortably ensconced in a brand-new, solid brick, four-bedroom home in Australian suburbia—but it was the last place she wanted to be. It was 1990 and the global jihad beckoned. In Afghanistan, the *mujahidin* had finally defeated the Soviet Union and formed their own Afghan Interim Government, which was preparing to take power as soon as the despised President Najibullah, installed by the departing Soviets, could be defeated. After ten years of war, Afghanistan was in tatters, with millions of its people displaced into sprawling refugee camps across the border in neighbouring Pakistan.

The defeat of the mighty Soviet Union had inspired jubilation across the Muslim world. 'The myth of the superpower was destroyed', in the memorable words of a young Saudi named Osama bin Laden, an emerging icon of the Islamist struggle. A new wave of Muslim volunteers was converging from around the world, to join the jihad, help out in the relief effort, and be part of the new Islamic state of Afghanistan.

Among those heading for the sub-continent were two friends of Rabiah's: an Aboriginal convert named Aisha, and her husband, a Syrian-born religious teacher, Hassan. They had moved to Peshawar in north-west Pakistan where Hassan planned to start a new school. In the meantime he had made a standing offer to members of the Muslim community in Australia to take their sons back with him to study in Islamic *madrassas* (religious schools) in Lahore. During a visit from Peshawar, Hassan put a proposition to Rabiah.

'Remember how your boy Mohammed always wanted to go to Afghanistan? Well, I'm going to open a school in Peshawar, and if you want Mohammed can come with me and go to school with my kids.'

Thirteen-year-old Mohammed leapt at the adventure—anything to get out of regular school—and Rabiah accepted.

'Is there anything else I can do for you, sister?' Hassan asked her.

'Yes. Say a *duah* (prayer) that Allah will give me a chance to go there too.'

Hassan rang back a few days later and told her he had contacts with two of the Afghan *mujahidin* warlords, Gulbuddin Hekmatyar and Abdul Rab Rasul Sayyaf, both of whom presided over large communities of Afghan refugees loyal to their organisations. They had assured him that any volunteers would be welcomed.

'They're crying out for women who can work in the hospitals and with the refugees', said Hassan. 'If you want to go I can arrange it. You would be given a house and taken care of.'

Rabiah rang Abu Bakar Ba'asyir in Malaysia to seek his blessing.

'I don't know, a woman alone … I don't know if I approve', he pondered.

She argued forcefully that she would be fulfilling her duty of *hijrah*, migrating for the benefit of Islam.

'Let me think about it and pray *istikharah*', said Ba'asyir. 'Oh, and I'll talk to Aba.'

Abdullah Sungkar was dead against it. The pair had been sending their own recruits to Pakistan for military training in the warlord Sayyaf's camp for six years, but they were young, single men; a woman travelling alone with six children was an entirely different matter, Rabiah was told. 'Aba didn't approve of me going to Pakistan. He believed it wasn't a place for a woman alone. Who was going to take responsibility for me?'

But Ba'asyir knew she was desperate to go and that she was more than capable of taking care of herself, Islamic convention notwithstanding; apart from which, once she had made her mind up, there was no dissuading her. After checking on exactly where she was going, what she would be doing and who would be responsible for her, Ba'asyir cautiously gave his imprimatur, on the proviso that the Indonesians in Pakistan would not be able to look after her because they were all unmarried men. She would effectively be on her own, reliant on a bunch of notoriously fickle *mujahidin* warlords whom she had never met.

'It happened very quickly', Rabiah remembers. 'Within a very short time, I borrowed the money for the tickets, and within three weeks we were on a plane to Pakistan. I had absolutely no money. I had the tickets—and nothing. But I knew Allah would look after us.'

PART 3

UMM MOHAMMED

10

JOINING THE JIHAD

Pakistan, 1990–1994

The tribal town of Peshawar in Pakistan's North West Frontier Province was like a scene from some exotic film set where mediaeval Central Asia meets the Wild West. Gnarled war veterans in black turbans with limbs missing sat cross-legged sipping green tea and swapping war yarns in the Street of Storytellers. Gun smugglers and gem merchants rubbed shoulders with spies, aid workers and sheikhs in the Smugglers Bazaar, where AK-47s and slabs of sticky black opium were sold alongside fridges, VCRs and treasures looted from the Afghan national museum. In a hotel lobby frequented by war correspondents and warlords, a polite sign advised: 'Hotel guests are asked that their bodyguards kindly deposit all firearms at front desk'.

Peshawar was the gateway to the legendary Khyber Pass, the perilous mountain switchback that leads to Afghanistan. Throughout the 1980s, the city had been Jihad HQ, the home base for the seven mujahidin parties that had fought for ten years to oust the Soviet Union's forces from Afghanistan. By 1990 that war had been won, and the fractious warlords had united to form the so-called Afghan Interim Government, to continue their struggle against the pro-Moscow regime of President Najibullah, installed in Kabul by the Soviets before their last tank rumbled home across the border in February 1989. The decade-long conflict had left between one and two million Afghanis dead and had displaced two-thirds of the population. More than three million had spilled across the border into Pakistan, and on the outskirts of Peshawar squalid tent cities teeming with refugees stretched as far as the eye could see.

Peshawar had also become a magnet for thousands of foreign Muslim volunteers who had flocked from all over the world to join what was seen as a holy struggle. They were known as the 'Afghan-Arabs', although many of them were neither Afghan nor Arab in origin. As well as the Persian Gulf, they came from Egypt, Algeria, Libya and Sudan; Uzbekistan, Turkmenistan and western China; Bosnia and Chechnya; Bangladesh, Indonesia, Malaysia and the Philippines; in fact from virtually every Muslim community in the world, even Australia. Some called them 'the brigade of strangers'. In the words of one jihadist, 'Peshawar was transformed into this place where whoever had no place to go went'.

Thirty-seven-year-old Rabiah Hutchinson landed in Peshawar in August 1990 accompanied by her five youngest children. Mohammed was thirteen years old, and eager to become a junior holy warrior. Rahmah was coming up to her eighth birthday, a polite, well-behaved child but as determined as her mother. The elder of Abdul Rahim's two sons, Mustafa was a serious-faced boy who would soon turn five, while his little brother Ilyas was a precocious two years and nine months. The baby of the family, Aminah, had just turned one and was still being breastfed. The family's belongings bulged from a dozen 'Chinese samsonites', the durable striped plastic sacks used by budget travellers the world over. They contained pillows, doonas, electric blankets, fitted sheets, three sets of clothing per person, a bucket of Lego blocks, and a jar of Vegemite stuffed into each bag.

They were greeted in Peshawar by a man who introduced himself as Abu Ubeidah, who was apparently a representative of the *Maktab al-Khadamat* (MAK), or Office of Services, a bureau set up to cater for the thousands of foreign volunteers arriving in Peshawar. MAK had been founded in the 1980s by the man known as the 'godfather' of the jihad, the charismatic Palestinian scholar Abdullah Azzam, and funded by his young assistant, the Saudi billionaire's son, Osama bin Laden.

Abu Ubeidah drove Rabiah and her family to the new suburb of Hayatabad on Peshawar's outskirts, where MAK had a guesthouse and where many of the Afghan-Arabs had made their homes. A colony of gaudy two- and three-storey 'poppy palaces' built from the proceeds of the opium trade had grown up there alongside the traditional Pashtun houses carved from dung-coloured mudbrick. Beyond Hayatabad the road led west to the anarchic frontier regions where tribal law prevailed, and where anti-aircraft guns could be spotted on the roofs of some of the fort-like houses.

'I was put in this house and left. We were told, don't go outside, it's dangerous', Rabiah remembers. 'We could hear automatic gunfire and we'd go out at night on the roof and you could see explosions. Everyone had guns, you could hear the gunshots—it was so exciting!'

The excitement evaporated when the children fell violently ill from dysentery, which left them with uncontrollable diarrhoea and vomiting. It was the middle of summer with temperatures in the high thirties, sauna-like humidity and an air-conditioning system that worked if and when the sporadic power supply flickered into life.

After a few days, Abu Ubeidah came back, with a surprise announcement. 'Now you're here, you have to get married. It's not feasible for a woman alone, you need someone to protect you.'

Rabiah was furious. 'What are you talking about? I don't want to get married. I didn't come here to get married.'

'Well, you can't stay here by yourself. If you don't get married you have to go back.'

He told her he would return in two days to hear her answer.

Left to her own devices, Rabiah's first resort was to pray for guidance. 'I said to Allah, "I came here for your sake. You know my intention. If it's pleasing for you, open the way for me to stay without getting married".'

Next, she got dressed in her black *abaya* and hijab and covered her face with the Arab-style black veil, the *niqab*, which was customary attire for many Afghan-Arabs. Then she ventured up onto the flat roof of their house to survey the scene beyond its 3-metre-high mudbrick walls.

'The children were sick, I was stranded and alone, and I thought, what am I gonna do?'

She knew her brother-in-law Abdul Rahman Ayub, the twin of her former husband Abdul Rahim, was out there somewhere. Abdul Rahman had left Indonesia for Pakistan in 1986, among the fourth batch of recruits sent by Abdullah Sungkar and Abu Bakar Ba'asyir for military training with Sungkar's old friend the Afghan warlord Abdul Rab Rasul Sayyaf, the leader of one of the seven main jihadist parties in Afghanistan. Abdul Rahman had completed his training at Sayyaf's Camp Sadda, which was the first training camp set up for foreign volunteers. It was located about 100 kilometres west of Peshawar in the Kurram Agency, one of the Pashtun tribal zones that straddles the Afghan border. After finishing the three-year program, Abdul Rahman had graduated to become an instructor at Sayyaf's grandly named Military Academy of the Mujahidin of Afghanistan at Camp Sadda. He taught Islamic theology and also special-ised in traditional Indonesian self-defence including fighting with knives, according to a comrade. Rabiah knew he was out there; the question was how to find him.

From the rooftop, she spied a young man who looked like an Arab walking along the street. Her children spotted the familiar steely glint in her eye and asked nervously, 'Oh mama, what are you going to do?' (It was a question they would ask many times. 'I was always a constant source of embarassment to my children', she remembers. 'It got worse as the boys got older. They would say "Oh, no, what are you gonna do *now*, mama?"')

Downstairs, she strode across the dirt courtyard and out onto the dusty street to accost the young passer-by.

'*Salam aleikum*! Excuse me, brother', she called out in English. The young man looked up, startled to see a strange woman with a broad foreign accent gesticulating wildly. It was most uncommon for a woman dressed in the Salafi style to be so forward with a man she didn't know. The Arab put his head down and kept walking.

'Wait, brother, do you speak English?' Rabiah persisted.

'Little bit', the flustered young man replied.

'Are you a mujahid?' she demanded to know.

The Arab was plainly alarmed.

'He had this look on his face, like he was asleep and having a nightmare, or he'd eaten something bad—he just couldn't believe it was happening', Rabiah recounts. 'He was looking at me, like—"Is this woman CIA?" He didn't know what to do. He kept looking around as if to say, "Please don't let anybody see me".'

Evidently sensing that his inquisitor was not to be put off easily, the Arab came closer. 'Yes, I'm a mujahid', he muttered.

'Well if you are a mujahid you have to help me. I'm a woman alone, I have five children in here, and I'm in big trouble. Do you know any Indonesian mujahidin?'

The Arab was wary. 'Maybe yes, maybe no.'

'All right, listen to me. I've done *hijrah*, right? And that means Allah has given me special rights. The people who brought me here are trying to make me get married and I don't want to get married. So you have to go and find my family for me.'

She handed him a scrap of paper with Abdul Rahman's name scribbled on it.

'If you can find this man, tell him I'm here with all his nieces and nephews, and he must come because we are in trouble.'

The mujahid took the paper but looked doubtful, so she gave him a parting warning. 'If you don't do anything, and if me and my children die here, you'll be responsible before Allah on judgement day.'

Within twenty-four hours Abdul Rahman had received the message and came knocking on the door of the house. The younger boys, Mustafa and Ilyas, Abdul Rahim's sons, were beside themselves with excitement; they had never met their father's identical twin and thought it was their father himself come to see them. After Rabiah explained their predicament, Abdul Rahman left again to speak to his superiors. The next day he returned with a Toyota pickup truck, loaded Rabiah and the five children onboard and set off into the arid wilderness.

Their destination was the sprawling mujahidin encampment of Pabbi, about 20 kilometres east of Peshawar, which was now a major base for the foreign volunteers who had flocked to Pakistan and Afghanistan. Pabbi was the stronghold of Abdul Rahman's commander, Abdul Rab Rasul Sayyaf, a principal protagonist in the Afghan jihad.

Sayyaf was a former professor of Islamic law at the Shariah faculty at Kabul University. After studying at Cairo's Al Azhar University, the intellectual hothouse of the global jihad, he had become a leading light in Afghanistan's nascent student Islamist movement, as deputy head of the Muslim Youth Organisation in the 1970s. He spoke fluent classical Arabic and followed the Wahhabi creed of Saudi Arabia, which made him a favourite of the Saudi establishment, whose petro-dollars were helping to bankroll the jihad. He was a wily politician with a flowing white beard and an imposing 1.9-metre frame, which he habitually draped in colourful Afghan *batu*, lengths of woollen fabric that doubled as blankets or shawls. It was Saudi support and funding that enabled the creation of Sayyaf's party, Ittehad-e-Islami (Islamic Union), which was closely aligned with Saudi intelligence. When the jihad first erupted, the Saudis chose Sayyaf as spokesman for the mujahidin. After the Soviets were defeated and the so-called Afghan Interim Government was created, Sayyaf was named nominal prime minister, thanks in large measure to the US$26 million in bribes paid to his peers by his Saudi benefactors.

The lavish funding from Saudi Arabia also bankrolled an elaborate complex known as 'Sayyafabad', located in the town of Pabbi. It was a township of 40 000 people with its own hospital, orphanage, *madrassas* and mosques. It also boasted an institute of higher learning called the University of Dawah and Jihad, with separate colleges of science, literature, medicine, English, *shariah* law, Arabic and engineering. Pabbi had previously hosted Sayyaf's military training base as well, but this facility had moved in the mid 1980s to Camp Sadda, near the Afghan border.

In addition to staff, supporters and trainees, Sayyaf presided over a populace of some 100 000 Afghan refugees, who were nominally affiliated with his *tanzim* (organisation), Ittehad-e-Islami. When the jihad against the Soviets had first begun in 1979, the mujahidin had been a rabble of dozens of separate militias. To ensure it was able to organise and control them, Pakistan's Inter Services Intelligence (ISI) anointed just seven parties to receive money and arms. Sayyaf's was the smallest and was added last to the list purely because of his Saudi sponsors' clout. Afghan refugees arriving in Pakistan had to sign up with one of the parties to become eligible for shelter and food. The system ensured an instant constituency for Sayyaf, who commanded little support among the Afghan population because his Wahhabi dogma was alien to the Sufi-influenced style of Islam traditionally practised by the tribal Pashtun. Sayyaf was popular among the Afghan-Arabs, however, because his organisation was extremely well funded and armed, and because of the enthusiastic hospitality he offered foreigners who came to join the jihad.

The arrival of a thirtysomething, unmarried Australian woman accompanied by five children in Sayyaf's dusty desert redoubt created something of a stir, by Rabiah's account. 'People couldn't comprehend how a woman had just turned up, because the other women there came with their husbands. For a woman to just turn up with that many children saying "I'm here for the jihad, just like you", it was a concept they just couldn't get their heads around.'

Rahmah—at the time a wide-eyed eight year old—describes her first impressions of the Afghan-Arab village in Pabbi: 'It was three streets made of poor mud houses on dirt roads, all connected to each other by lanes, and situated on each end of the streets was a tent with armed Afghan guards. It was at that time known as the village of the *muhajirin* (migrants), as many of the families of the mujahidin stayed there. It was summer and 50-degree heat. The ground was extremely dry and if anyone walked on it, it would cause clouds of dust.'

Rabiah and the children were allocated half of a traditional Pashtun mudbrick house, with a kitchen, sitting room and one bedroom, which the six of them shared. The electric blankets she had brought after being warned of the severe winter cold were never unpacked. Pabbi had no electricity, just a communal generator that provided power for about two hours in the morning and two hours at night. In any event it was so hot that when they walked along the road clumps of melted bitumen stuck to their shoes, which then became caked in dirt. They used kerosene lamps for lighting and gas cylinders, called *ambooba*, for cooking. There were no telephones or television and virtually no communication with the outside world.

'Pabbi was hard core', Rabiah remembers. 'The people who lived in Peshawar had ceiling fans and electricity and running water; some of them even had CD players. Pabbi was really rugged—even by Afghanistan standards. The living conditions were shocking. The scorpions used to crawl out of the roof and the cockroaches would climb on you and the mosquitoes were so big you had to tie yourself to the mattress or they'd carry you off in the night. In summer it was 50 to 52 degrees, and in winter it got so cold the water would ice up and wouldn't come out of the taps. There was cholera and typhoid—and the dust!'

In spite of—perhaps in part because of—its privations, Rabiah remembers Pabbi as 'the best place in the world'. 'It's hard to believe you could be so happy', she says. The harsh simplicity of their existence evoked memories of her childhood in Mudgee and Wollar, except that the socio-economic tables were turned. Here poverty, frugality and sacrifice were virtues that would surely be rewarded. 'It didn't matter, because we thought after all this hardship Afghanistan will become an Islamic country and we'll all go and live there happy ever after.'

Rabiah was put to work in Sayyaf's al Jihad hospital where the inmates of Pabbi's rambling refugee camp came for medical treatment. Like everything else the hospital was made of mudbrick, with upper walls fashioned from plywood frames and mosquito wire to allow the air to circulate. The women's hospital where Rabiah worked had four wards: maternity, surgical, infectious disease and children's. There were ten or twelve beds in each ward, and often two patients to a bed. Hundreds more lined up for outpatient treatment each day, and the crowd waiting for treatment sometimes got so unruly that the hospital employed an orderly armed with a stick to whack them into line.

Like one of the 'barefoot doctors' in Chairman Mao's Cultural Revolution in China, Rabiah was trained on the job. Her superiors were an assorted collection of mostly foreign volunteers, including an Algerian vet and a Pakistani gynaecologist trained in the United States, who told Rabiah, 'I'll teach you everything I know'. She became a proficient midwife and learned to diagnose and treat common ailments such as cholera, typhoid, hepatitis and diarrhoea, and injuries caused by exploding mines, which were treated with Yemeni honey, renowned for its healing properties. The conditions were primitive to say the least.

'We used to use and re-use disposable syringes until you could literally no longer push them through the patients' skin. There was no such thing as cleaning the tables where the women gave birth. If the patients died we simply pushed them aside.' Within a few months of their arrival, Rabiah's youngest boy, three-year-old Ilyas, contracted cholera. He grew so thin that his ribcage protruded beneath his waxy skin like an African famine baby. After a few weeks in hospital, the doctors told Rabiah to take him home. 'They sent him home to die. They said, "There's nothing more we can do. Just take him home and whatever Allah has written for him will happen".' Despite her own faith, she railed against their fatalism. 'We were living a life where you realise your limitations. You become very resigned to death—but I wasn't yet.' The boy was gravely ill for three months but finally made a full recovery.

Like all the Afghan-Arabs, Rabiah was known by her *kuniya*, an Islamic nickname derived from the name of the individual's eldest child, which is at once a term of endearment and respect. Men are known as 'Abu'—which means 'the father of'—followed usually by the name of their eldest son, while women are referred to as Umm (pronounced *oom*), which means 'the mother of'. Rabiah was known as Umm Mohammed, 'the mother of Mohammed'. Because there were so many women whose first sons were named after the Prophet, she was widely known as 'Umm Mohammed Australie'. She says the patients called her Doctor Jan, which translates roughly as 'dear doctor'.

The third-world desert town of Pabbi became home for Rabiah and her children for the next three years. Her rare provenance ensured everyone knew who she was. 'People knew me because I was unusual, I was weird—an Australian with no husband and six kids who came and gave up *dunya* (worldly comfort) for the sake of Allah.' For Rabiah, her new moniker signified another milestone in her personal journey, marking her transition from a Muslim who has merely 'submitted' to Islam, to a true believer. 'The transformation from Robyn to Rabiah to Umm Mohammed has just been a natural process of progression of who I really am', she says.

'The difference between Rabiah and Umm Mohammed is that Rabiah became Umm Mohammed with knowledge and understanding of what true Islam is.'

It was a spartan life. They rose each morning at 4 a.m. as the *azan* resounded across the flat mud rooftops. After dawn prayers, the boys would run to the bakery down the street, a lean-to shack where the Afghan baker used a stick of wood with a nail in it to flick steaming rounds of flat *naan* bread from a huge wood-fired *tandoor* set in the dirt. At home they would eat the warm *naan* for breakfast with jam or honey and cream made from buffalo milk. At 5 a.m. the children boarded a bus that took them to school in Peshawar, an hour-and-half journey along a potholed road prowled by *khatta aturk* (highway bandits) who mercifully let the school bus pass unmolested.

The legendary jihadist Abdullah Azzam, founder of MAK, the forerunner of al Qaeda, had established the school they attended. Azzam's military motto was 'Jihad and the rifle alone; no negotiations, no conferences, no dialogues'. However, he also believed the children of the jihad needed a solid education, and had founded the Al Ansar school in Peshawar for the offspring of the Afghan-Arabs. His school taught a mixture of secular and religious subjects and the children were taught to memorise the Quran from kindergarten. However, Sheikh Azzam opposed rote memorisation; with every Quranic verse they memorised the children would also learn its origin and meaning, the *hadith* that explain it and the laws that derive from it. By the time Rabiah arrived in Peshawar, Abdullah Azzam was dead, having been assassinated in 1989 and his body buried in the Martyrs' Graveyard in Pabbi. His school was being administered by his wife.

Rahmah and her siblings attended the Al Ansar school for about two years. Rahmah recounts those days with fond nostalgia: 'I can still smell and feel the cold dawn breeze—well, freezing breeze—on my face, waiting for the school bus to take us on a near two-hour drive to Peshawar … and the hot bread we would buy on the way. On the way back us children would gather up the remaining school money and buy some kebabs and have a group lunch on the bus. It was something that we always looked forward to. Even though coming home was a near three-hour drive, it was one I enjoyed (because) I felt I had a purpose—and that was to grow up a good Muslim.'

As Rabiah tells it her children took to life in Pabbi 'like ducks to water'. However, 13-year-old Mohammed continued to struggle with his studies. In the highly regimented Arabic schooling system of Peshawar, where the children were whacked with sticks for misbehaviour, no allowances were made for a dyslexic foreign boy. Mohammed dropped out of the school after about six months. Rabiah suggested he switch to Sayyaf's technical school, where the director had offered him a place.

'I just can't handle their system, it's not gonna work', Mohammed protested.

'But he's a really good brother, and he knows *shariah*', Rabiah assured him.

'I don't care if he knows Ronald Reagan, I'm not going.'

Mohammed eventually enrolled to study carpentry at Sayyaf's technical college, according to Rabiah. He finally got his wish to join the mujahidin when, during school breaks, the boys were taken across the border into Afghanistan for a taste of jihad. Rabiah says they were not allowed where there was fighting but were taken to 'the backlines' where they were taught to fire an AK-47 and 'help out' around the camp.

When the children returned from school each day they would sleep until it was time for the *asr* (afternoon) prayer, which then left three hours free time until sunset. This was the time for socialising, when the women and girls visited each other in their homes, while the men sat drinking tea and discussing the news of the day. Rabiah attended lessons in the Pabbi kindergarten where the Afghan-Arab women studied the Quran and Islamic law. The older girls played mostly within the walled courtyards of their homes, while the younger ones played in the streets where the boys kicked soccer balls and built their own mudbrick forts in the dirt, playing at being little mujahidin.

Despite the war dragging on across the border in Afghanistan—and notwithstanding the poverty, dirt and disease—their life in Pabbi was a secure and ordered existence, centred on the family, and governed by a code of discipline and morality that was uniformly understood—all of which Rabiah had longed for. 'It was a society built on the belief that everybody had a place and everybody had a time. The children were very independent in their lifestyle and they had the security of their homes. They had very few chores because we had so few material possessions. You sweep your house, wash your clothes, cook your food, and that's it. Because it was such an ordered life, you always knew where your children were; they had freedom, they were safe, everybody knew each other, there was no fear of child molesters. It was very safe and secure.'

Her daughter Rahmah's memories are similarly rosy: 'As a child growing up in Pabbi there was always something to do, even though to most people if they ever saw Pabbi they would say, "What on earth could anyone do here?" It was a very tight-knit community, everybody knew each other and everybody helped each other ... From a very young age we were taught the oldest took care of the youngest, the strong protected the weak, and women were always put first. Boys were taught that the girls took first preference, like for example when (the Muslim festival) Eid came and we would all go to the little hut they called a store, the girls would always be allowed to buy first while the boys stood outside and waited.'

As the dust settled and the harsh light of day softened, the *azan* would ring out again to summon the menfolk to the mosque for the *maghrib* (sunset) prayer while the women retreated to the privacy of their homes or high-walled courtyards.

'My best memories of Pabbi was when the electricity was cut off at night in summer for a few hours', Rahmah recounts. 'We children would all play in the streets, the boys usually playing their own game, and the girls, we would play our own games. But the best of all times was when a group of uncles would be in town from Afghanistan, they would gather us around and tell us stories of the miracles they had experienced in the battle field. I can remember listening with all my heart and would always pray the electricity stayed cut off for longer.'

The women of Pabbi formed a kind of exclusive society of their own, in which their integral role was only enhanced by their separateness from the men. It was communally based, so that everything was shared; when a new *muhajir* arrived, the *ansar*—the resident Muslims whose duty it is to welcome them—would chip in to donate cooking pots, clothing, bedding and whatever else the newcomers needed. When a woman had a baby the others would draw up a roster to share her cooking, cleaning and washing. Just like in Mudgee, everyone knew everyone else and there was a palpable sense of community. But here there were no 'haves' and 'have-nots'; and the dirt and deprivation only intensified the sense that they were part of an exclusive elite, united by their unyielding faith, their disdain for material wealth and their righteous sense of mission. And unlike in Indonesia, where she had always felt a foreigner, here it also didn't matter where you were from. It was like a little United Nations of Muslim fundamentalists.

'It didn't matter what colour, size or shape you were, you were judged on your piety and knowledge', Rabiah says. 'I had American friends, French, German, Chinese, Indonesian, Malays, Filipinos. The majority of the sisters were very well educated; there were vets and an engineer; one was a professor of maths, another was a biochemist; there were numerous graduates from Islamic faculties. Most were bi- or tri-lingual, many spoke French or English. The idea that Muslim radicals are poor, downtrodden and uneducated is a myth. They were exceptionally intelligent women.'

The men and women of Pabbi modelled their behaviour on the first generations of Muslims known as the *Salaf al-Salih*. 'Pabbi was like a little Islamic state in Pakistan', says Rabiah. The men wore the trousers of their *shalwar kameez* above their ankles and their beards at least the length of a man's fist. The women wore flowing black gowns like the Prophet's wives and covered their faces in the company of men who were unrelated to them. There was no music, because music was regarded as the *azan* (call to prayer) of *Shaytan* (Satan). There were no two-storey houses, so no one could look down on unveiled women in the courtyards of their homes. Their adjoining walled courtyards were connected by doorways built into the mudbrick walls; when the men were away fighting or training, the doors would be left open so the children could run from house to house and the women could mingle freely with their neighbours; when the men were at home, the doors would be locked.

A strict formality governed all social relations, and elaborate customs were followed to preserve the women's honour, which included preventing face-to-face contact with men other than their husbands or male relatives. If a man went to visit the home of a friend, he would knock on arrival; if the man of the house was not at home his wife would knock back from the inside to signify that she was there alone (because even speaking to an unrelated man was unseemly) and the visitor would go away. If a woman walked past a group of men in the street, the men would turn their backs in order not to gaze on another man's wife, even though her face was veiled. A man would never ask a 'brother', 'How's your wife?' because such an inquiry could cause offence; instead, he would ask 'How's your family?' even if the man he was addressing had no children. If Rabiah's sons came home to find the doors locked, they would never yell out 'Mama!' or 'Rahmah!' because it would be disrespectful to their mother and sister to stand in the street shouting their names. Instead the boys would call out their own names to signal that they wanted to be let in.

The social regime precisely prescribed the roles of males and females, and enforced a respectful distance between the two. For Rabiah it was a welcome alternative to the chaotic domestic life she had known as a child and teenager. The role of women was strictly circumscribed, in a way that both tightly defined their activities and ensured their honour was sacrosanct. 'It might be seen by non-Muslims as oppressive but for us that's one way that you honour somebody and you show you hold this woman in the highest regard', says Rabiah. 'In Islam jealousy is a positive—protecting your women means you're jealous over their honour.'

Segregation between the sexes extended to the hospital where Rabiah worked, which treated only female patients and was staffed entirely by women. 'It was an all-woman environment so it was very working-woman friendly', she says. The hospital had a crèche where the female doctors' children could be cared for while they worked. Male specialists were summoned as required, in accordance with a specially devised ritual. Outside the entrance to the women's hospital was a bell. When the male specialist arrived he would ring the bell to signal his arrival. The female medical staff, who normally went about their work uncovered, would hastily don their veils and then ring another bell on the inside to let the doctor know it was safe to enter. The women staff would remain covered until the male specialist had left, when they would resume their work unveiled.

In a polyglot community with such stringent social mores, it was easy to unwittingly cause offence. One day Rabiah heard a knock at her door and a man's voice calling urgently 'Umm Mohammed Australie!' She knocked back to signify that there were no males at home, but instead of going away the visitor continued to call out. It was the husband of a Malaysian woman who had recently given birth to a girl. He spoke in Malay while Rabiah replied in Indonesian, the two languages similar enough to enable them to converse.

'Umm Mohammed, it's Abu Khadijah. I'm very sorry but my wife has sent me down here. She wants to know if you can come up because there's something wrong with the baby.'

'OK, tell me what the problem is', Rabiah replied from behind the door.

'The baby hasn't stopped screaming for five or six hours, and she keeps pulling her legs up, as though she's in pain.'

'It sounds like gas in the stomach', said Rabiah. 'I'm busy at the moment but I'll be there in half an hour. In the meantime, just turn her over and rub some aniseed oil on her backside.' This was a popular remedy for releasing wind.

There was silence behind the door.

'Abu Khadijah? Are you there? Do you understand?'

But the man had gone.

When Rabiah had finished what she was doing she walked up the street to her friend's home. 'As soon as I got into their house and saw his wife I knew there was something wrong. Malays are very polite people, never rude, but she was averting her gaze and answering in monosyllables. At the end of the day I am an Australian and I couldn't stand it.'

'Is there some sort of problem?' asked Rabiah.

'Umm Mohammed, I can't believe you did what you did', her friend blurted out. 'The way you spoke to him—why would you say such a terrible thing?'

Rabiah was totally nonplussed. 'I was looking at her as if she was from Mars.'

'What do you mean? I told him to rub some aniseed oil on the baby's *pantat*', she said, using the Indonesian word for 'backside' and rubbing her own posterior by way of demonstration.

The other woman gasped. 'Umm Mohammed, what does *pantat* mean in Indonesian?'

'It means backside.'

'Oh, Umm Mohammed, in Malaysian it means the exact opposite.'

Rabiah's advice, which the father had taken as an instruction to rub oil on his daughter's private parts, had caused grave offence. Among the multilingual Afghan-Arabs, such misunderstandings were common. Another conversation in which an Algerian man boasted about his wife's couscous almost led to a shoot out. The name of the popular African dish is identical to an Afghani slang term that refers to a woman's genitalia.

Despite the occasional misunderstanding, Rabiah was in her element. 'Pabbi was the best place I've ever been in my life. It was the closest thing to the implementation of Islam to the fullest extent, and it was a place that consisted only of people who had all gone there for the same reason. They were people who'd given up everything because they wanted to live under Islamic law. There were doctors, teachers, engineers, nurses, people from all over the world—every Arab country, Somalia, China, Tajikistan, Uzbekistan, some Sunnis from Iran, there was even a Japanese, French, Germans, Americans, any country you can think of—but no Australians, just me.'

The only other Australian she encountered in Pabbi was her friend Aisha, the Aboriginal convert whose husband had arranged Rabiah's entrée into Pakistan. By now the couple were living in Peshawar and Aisha came to visit, bringing a jar of Vegemite to replenish the family's exhausted supply.

'What's that you're eating?' asked an American friend who found her tucking into a piece of *naan* toast daubed with the spread.

'It's called Vegemite. It's an Australian food. Would you like to try some?'

The visitor screwed up her face in disgust at the taste of it. 'Are you sure this is *halal*? I can't believe something can taste so bad and be *halal*.'

* * *

A familiar figure in the dusty streets of Pabbi was a tall, aristocratic-looking Saudi in his early thirties, who was fast becoming an icon among the Afghan-Arabs. Osama bin Laden had left his homeland of Saudi Arabia to join the jihad against the Russians after the Soviet invasion of Afghanistan in 1979. The devoutly religious seventeenth son of a billionaire construction tycoon, bin Laden had been eager to make his mark by volunteering his services and wealth to support the Afghan cause. Arriving in Peshawar he teamed up with the Palestinian scholar Abdullah Azzam, who had been a professor at the Jeddah University, where bin Laden studied business administration. By this time Azzam was heading up the Islamic Co-ordination Council in Peshawar, which united twenty organisations there to support the Afghan struggle. It was Azzam who established MAK to co-ordinate the influx of foreign fighters, and bin Laden who provided the funds to cover accommodation, living expenses and a monthly *khafalla*, or stipend, for every foreign volunteer. Together in 1988 they formed a new organisation to keep the jihad alive after the Russians had gone, which they called simply 'the base'—in Arabic, al Qaeda.

After Abdullah Azzam's death in 1989, bin Laden had taken over the mantle of *emir* (leader) of the Afghan-Arabs and their new organisation, al Qaeda. He worked closely with Pabbi's supremo, Sayyaf, who shared his Wahhabi creed and close working relationship with the Saudi establishment. Bin Laden provided the funding for Sayyaf's military academy at Camp Sadda and his University of Dawah and Jihad in Pabbi. In return Sayyaf provided military training for the majority of the foreign volunteers, until bin Laden began to set up his own network of training camps under Sayyaf's protection and in his territory.

After the defeat of the Soviets, bin Laden had left Peshawar and returned to Saudi Arabia, where he was at first lauded as a minor hero for his role in the Afghan struggle, but later had a bitter falling out with the House of Saud when he opposed the arrival of US troops to defend the Saudi peninsula after the Iraqi invasion of Kuwait. Bin Laden's passport would soon be seized by the Saudi authorities, his citizenship cancelled and his assets frozen. But for now he maintained a guesthouse and office in Peshawar from where payments were dispensed to the foreign volunteers and continued to visit Pabbi, the stronghold of his comrade Sayyaf.

Rabiah remembers bin Laden's visits, when he would leave his wives at home in Jeddah and stay in the modest quarters reserved for the *shabab* (young men) in Sayyaf's compound where he was much admired. 'Osama would stay at the *shabab* house all the time when he came to Pabbi. He was known because he was rich. He was someone who had sacrificed his wealth, his lifestyle, his family connections and stood up for what he believes in.' Bin Laden was not yet a major leader in the jihad movement; at this stage he was principally a financier and supporter of the Afghan cause, and was little known outside Islamist circles in Pakistan and Afghanistan. He was not yet on the radar of foreign agencies such as the CIA and the FBI, nor regarded as 'someone who was anti-American', in the words of the former CIA station chief in Islamabad, Milton Bearden.

Bin Laden's munificence helped to ensure that Sayyaf was still handsomely bankrolled, even after the multibillion-dollar pipeline from the United States to the mujahidin groups began to dry up after the Soviets were defeated. Belatedly wary of the consequences of supporting Islamic militants, in the early 1990s the United States stopped funding Islamist warlords such as Sayyaf and Hekmatyar, under a new policy of 'sidelining the extremists'. Sayyaf's relationship with the Saudi establishment had also soured because of his opposition to US forces on the Saudi peninsula during the war against Saddam Hussein. But despite dwindling support from the US and Saudi governments, the money from private Gulf donors such as bin Laden was still pouring in.

'It would come in truckloads, I'm literally talking about boxes of it— boxes of US$100 bills', says Rabiah. 'It would be unloaded off the trucks and they would throw it in the tent like it was baked beans, and they would take bundles out as they needed it. I don't think it was even counted.' Most of it went towards weaponry and the cost of running Sayyaf's military training regime. What funding did make its way to the orphanage and hospital was spent on expensive hardware rather than maintenance, personnel or training, to Rabiah's dismay. 'We had warehouses with the most amazing medical equipment—incubators, ultrasound machines; things that were never used, because no one knew how to use them.'

It didn't take long after Rabiah's arrival in Pabbi for bin Laden to learn of the presence of the foreign mujahidah with six children, known as Umm Mohammed Australie. As Rabiah tells it, bin Laden was walking down the street past her house with a companion, an Algerian known as Abu Abdul, when he spotted her children playing in the street. Their conversation was related to her afterwards by Abu Abdul's wife, who was Rabiah's best friend in Pabbi.

'I bet you can't guess where those children are from', Abu Abdul remarked.

'They look sort of Arab', bin Laden replied, noticing the children's olive complexions inherited from their Indonesian fathers.

'No, they're Australian.'

'*Subhan* Allah (Praise Allah)!' bin Laden is said to have exclaimed. 'Australian—that must be a first!'

'It's a woman on her own', Abu Abdul continued. 'She came with her children, she works in the hospital, she doesn't have anything, they don't even have air conditioning.'

'Well they do now', bin Laden replied.

A few days later, an emissary delivered a brand-new air conditioner to her home—courtesy of Osama bin Laden, Rabiah was told.

The encounter with the black-haired, olive-skinned Australian children who spoke fluent Arabic piqued bin Laden's curiosity, according to the account related by Rabiah's friend. 'It fascinates me, I like to hear those kids talk', bin Laden said. 'If you hadn't told me they were from Australia and their parents were not Arabs I wouldn't believe it. They speak such good Arabic.'

Not long after, bin Laden ran into Rabiah's children in the street again while walking with his companion Abu Abdul. Eight-year-old

Rahmah would remember the occasion vividly many years later, although at the time she didn't know who the bearded stranger was. 'All I remember was I was walking with my brother to the bakery and we came across two uncles. One I knew as he was the husband of my mother's friend and the other I had not seen before and did not know his name.' The two men called the children over.

'Rahmah, do you know who this is?' asked Abu Abdul.

'No', she replied.

'This is the uncle that bought your air conditioner for you.'

Bin Laden knelt down and put his hand on Mustafa's shoulder, gave them some Afghani coins, then spoke to them in Arabic.

'What are your names?'

'My name is Rahmah, and this is my brother, Mustafa.'

'And where are you going?'

'To the bakery.'

'We shall accompany you then.'

Rahmah recounts that bin Laden walked with them to the lean-to bakery, where dozens of families from Sayyaf's refugee camp were queuing for *naan*, the main staple of the Afghan diet.

'Why are these people lined up here?' bin Laden asked. Abu Abdul was about to explain but bin Laden interjected, 'Let the children answer'.

'It's for the poor families, because they can't afford to pay for their bread', Rahmah explained. The baker had devised a credit system under which each family was given a stick of wood. The baker would carve a notch in the stick for every *naan* he gave them; later when they received their monthly *khafalla* (stipend) they would bring their sticks to the bakery and pay whatever they owed. According to Rahmah, bin Laden's reaction was to hand the baker enough money for a year's supply of bread: 'ten loaves for the morning and ten for the afternoon for everybody that stood in the line'.

Bin Laden's gesture caused quite a scene at the crowded bakery, by Rahmah's account. Women began chanting '*Allahu Akbar!*' and uttering prayers of thanks while young boys mobbed him trying to kiss his hands. Rahmah says bin Laden was so embarrassed that he raised his hands above his shoulders so they couldn't be grabbed and kissed, while he retreated from the crowd.

Stories like this about bin Laden's generosity and self-effacing manner abounded among the Afghan-Arabs, and helped cement his iconic status. His mentor Azzam described him as 'a heaven-sent man, like an angel'. American author Peter Bergen, a former CNN journalist who met bin Laden in 1997, likened him to 'a turbaned Robin Hood, hiding out not in the forests of Nottingham during the Middle Ages, but in the mountains of almost mediaeval Afghanistan'. Bin Laden's good works in this early period were even acknowledged by the former CIA chief in Islamabad, Milton Bearden, who co-ordinated US support to the mujahidin. Bin Laden 'actually did some very good things', Bearden noted. 'He put a lot of money in a lot of the right places in Afghanistan.'

The Afghan-Arabs benefited directly from bin Laden's largesse through the monthly *khafalla* paid to foreign volunteers by MAK.

'ASIO asked me, "Did Osama bin Laden ever give you money?"' says Rabiah. 'And I laughed—he probably did. Maybe it (MAK) is where the *khafallas* came from, I don't know. We never asked questions, especially the women, because we didn't need to know. Women didn't know these things.'

Rabiah's family received an allowance of US$150 per month. She says it was always paid to her by Umm Mohammed Azzam, the widow of the MAK founder, Abdullah Azzam. Umm Mohammed Azzam was an illustrious character in her own right, admired as a 'mother figure' in the jihadist movement in Peshawar where she lived. After her husband's death she took over the administration of a range of humanitarian services in the Afghan refugee camps in Pakistan. She ran ten schools, a nursery and a charity called Darul Khayat—the 'house of sewing'—which provided sewing machines, fabric and thread to Afghan war widows so they could earn an income from making clothing. She also ran the girls section of the Al Ansar school in Peshawar, which Rabiah's children attended.

Umm Mohammed Azzam herself was no great fan of bin Laden, who had fallen out with his mentor before Azzam's death. Azzam had believed the Arab volunteers should integrate and join forces with the Afghan mujahidin, whereas bin Laden purposely kept his men apart to create a separate fighting force. (It was rumoured that bin Laden might have played a role in his mentor's 1989 assassination; although this was never proven, it may also have influenced Umm Mohammed Azzam's view.) 'Bin Laden sought to pamper Arab fighters—even their food was different from that of Afghan mujahidin', Azzam's widow said in an interview. 'We owe bin Laden our respect; he took part in jihad with his money, effort and sons. He sacrificed himself and his money. However, in truth, he is not a very educated man … He holds a high school degree. He enrolled in university but soon left. It is true that he gave lectures to *ulema* (Islamic scholars) and sheikhs but he was easy to persuade.'

During Rabiah's four years in Pakistan, Azzam's plain-speaking widow became her friend and benefactor. 'Let's say I needed $200 for sheets in the hospital. I would go to Umm Mohammed or she would come to visit the hospital and ask me, "Do you need anything?" And I would say, "Yes, we need sheets". I wanted coloured ones, not white, because the old white sheets were very grotty. They were washed by women out the back but they had blood and guts stains all over them and they always looked disgusting. I wanted coloured sheets to hide the bloodstains. She asked, "How many beds?" and I told her the number of beds.'

Rabiah was pleased when Umm Mohammed Azzam returned with piles of linen dyed a dark maroon. 'When she brought the sheets I had no idea where they came from. It wasn't necessary for me to know.'

Not long after the incident with bin Laden at the bakery, Rabiah received an intriguing proposal. Within the Afghan-Arab community, the societal pressure on a middle-aged single mother to marry was intense. Rabiah's marital status had been an ongoing issue since her arrival, with 'the brothers' insisting that if she wanted to stay in Pakistan she would have to get married. The proposition was relayed to her by bin Laden's frequent companion in Pabbi, Abu Abdul.

'Umm Mohammed, there is a Saudi man who has inquired about you. He has other wives but they are in Saudi Arabia. He travels backwards and forwards, he is very well off, and he is interested in marrying you.'

Rabiah says she didn't ask the Saudi's name but agreed to consider his proposal. This was passed on to her suitor who was due to return to Saudi Arabia shortly and reportedly replied, '*Inshallah* (God willing), if it's my fortune, good'. However, the anonymous propositioner never came back to press his offer. This was around the time that bin Laden's passport was seized by the Saudi authorities and, after a final trip to Pakistan, he fled into exile in Sudan. While it was rumoured that the mysterious Saudi who had proposed to Rabiah was indeed Osama bin Laden, she says she never found out for sure.

Rabiah received numerous such offers. Another came from a well-known sheikh who was head of the Rabitah al-Islamiyya in Peshawar, a Saudi-sponsored organisation for the promotion of Islam. Eventually she accepted one of these proposals and married. She refuses to disclose the identity of this fourth husband or the details of this marriage. It is one of three marriages she would not discuss for the purpose of this book, insisting they were 'not important'.

* * *

While Rabiah was in Pabbi her old mentors, Abdullah Sungkar and Abu Bakar Ba'asyir, were still in exile in Malaysia where they would soon form their new organisation Jemaah Islamiyah (JI) to fight for an Islamic state in Indonesia and beyond. Starting in the mid 1980s, the pair sent about 200 recruits from Indonesia, Malaysia and Singapore to train in Sayyaf's Camp Sadda.

'All the non-Arab Afghan-Arabs were trained by Sayyaf', Rabiah says. 'His academy was a real academy, a military academy with privates, lieutenants, captains and sergeants. They did book study, and had passing out parades and uniforms.' The rookies who passed through Camp Sadda would later become the shock troops of JI. They included leaders such as JI's long-time military commander, Zulkarnaen, its future secretary, Abu Dujana, and Abu Rusdan, who would serve as a caretaker *emir*. Also trained there were footsoldiers such as Imam Samudra, Dulmatin, Ali Imron and

Mubarok, who would later kill 202 people in the Bali bombings of October 2002; and Rabiah's former fellow teacher from the Ngruki school, Ali Gufron, also known as Muklas, who was executed with Amrozi and Samudra in 2008 over the Bali bombings. Rabiah says that as far as she knows Muklas and his cohorts never came to Pabbi and she never met them.

'There were women there who didn't know what their husbands were doing', she says. 'Men's and women's roles were very separate. You wouldn't even ask a woman about her husband—I probably could have got myself killed by doing that. No respecting woman would want to know that much detail about a man who was not part of her own family. I'd be either a woman with loose morals or a spy or at the very least someone who was so stupid and ignorant that I was dangerous. It was done on purpose because the less you know, the less you can say.'

Another habitué of Camp Sadda who would later achieve infamy was a Pakistani, Khalid Sheikh Mohammed, who had graduated with a degree in mechanical engineering in North Carolina, and worked in Peshawar as Sayyaf's secretary and served on the 'media committee' that published his organisation's magazine. A decade later, Mohammed would gain infamy as 'the Brain'—his al Qaeda nickname—behind a string of diabolical schemes that culminated in the September 11 attacks on the United States. As with many of the rising stars in the jihadist firmament, Rabiah knew Mohammed only through his wife, who was known by her *kuniya* as Umm Hamza. They met at the hospital in Peshawar while Rabiah was acting as midwife for a mutual friend. Later, when 10-year-old Rahmah needed to travel from Pabbi to visit an eye specialist in Peshawar, Umm Hamza invited her and Rabiah to stay at their home. Rabiah says Khalid Sheikh Mohammed was not home at the time. Beyond that, she says she knew the infamous 'KSM' only by his fearsome reputation: 'He had a fierce temper. He was known to be very scary and very staunch.'

Among the Indonesian contingent in Pabbi was Rabiah's brother-in-law, Abdul Rahman Ayub, who was now teaching Arabic at Sayyaf's technical school. About two months after Rabiah's arrival, Abdul Rahman announced that he wished to renew his marriage to her eldest daughter

Devi, which had been dissolved a year earlier without them having lived together as man and wife. Devi was now fifteen and was still in Malaysia studying at Sungkar and Ba'asyir's boarding school. Eager to have her firstborn reunited with the family in Pakistan, and believing she was now old enough to marry, Rabiah agreed to Abdul Rahman's proposal.

'When he spoke to me about it, I thought—he was a good person, he was not like Abdul Rahim, he was good with the children, and he was responsible.' Her agreement was conditional on Devi coming to stay with her in Pabbi and not beginning to live with Abdul Rahman as his wife until she was seventeen. When Rabiah contacted Sungkar and Ba'asyir in Malaysia to arrange her daughter's travel to Pakistan, Abdullah Sungkar was adamantly opposed to it. He thought the idea 'ridiculous' and argued she should stay and finish her schooling. But Rabiah typically ignored Sungkar's protestations—and her daughter's own reluctance—and Devi soon joined them in Pakistan. The result was a disaster. When Devi arrived Abdul Rahman decided he wasn't prepared to wait for a year after all to claim his new bride and insisted she move in with him immediately, to Rabiah's fury. When Devi announced she didn't want to be married to him, their union was once again annulled on the grounds that he had reneged on the agreed conditions. Abdul Rahman's failure to subdue his defiant bride and her obstreperous mother was the source of much gossip in Pabbi, according to a colleague, and soon afterwards he left Pakistan and returned to Malaysia, 'embarrassed and ashamed', says Rabiah.

Devi's ill-conceived mismatch was a source of lingering bitterness in the life of Rabiah's family. She is not a woman prone to regret, but this is one exception. 'If I had the ability to change anything I've done in the past, that would be the thing I would change. I sincerely regret that that happened, although I believe that everything happens for a reason. I just didn't have the wisdom to be able to think of the long-term consequences. Whatever possessed me, I really thought it would be a way to keep the family together. Stupid me.'

A year or so later, Devi married an Iraqi man who was working at an orphanage in Peshawar, a union her mother played no part in arranging.

Nine months later, she gave birth to Rabiah's first grandchild, a girl named Huda Jehad.

* * *

In April 1992 the Afghan mujahidin claimed another historic victory, with the collapse of the despised Najibullah regime that the Soviets had left behind in Kabul. An Islamic government was hastily constituted by the mujahidin groups to take power in Afghanistan. But the promise of peace and stability proved illusory. The rival factions remained deeply divided by ethnic, tribal, religious, political and personal enmities, and a bloody power struggle soon erupted between the two strongest warlords, the legendary Tajik commander Ahmed Shah Massoud and his bitter enemy, the Pashtun, Gulbuddin Hekmatyar. In an attempt to broker a reconciliation, Osama bin Laden flew to Peshawar and arranged a telephone conference between the two chieftains, but his efforts at peace-making failed. While Massoud's forces occupied the capital, Hekmatyar's troops massed on the outskirts of Kabul in readiness for a bloody showdown.

For a while, life continued much as normal in Pabbi, which remained largely cut off from the outside world, its citizens unaware that their holy struggle was about to descend into a vicious civil war. Two years after her arrival, Rabiah was offered a new job in a school being established for orphaned Afghan girls. It was a project initiated by an Afghan woman whom Rabiah knew as Umm Abdullah, the niece of a leading Pashtun politician, Sebghatullah Mojadiddi, who had been named president in the transitional government in Kabul. Umm Abdullah had lived in Saudi Arabia for fifteen years and had a PhD in mathematics, by Rabiah's account, while her husband, who held a masters degree, taught English at Sayyaf's university. A feisty feminist by Afghan standards, with an uncommonly accommodating husband, Umm Abdullah believed all girls had to be educated in order to play a meaningful role in the new Afghan state, including girls whose fathers had been 'martyred' in the war. (Any child without a father was deemed to be an orphan, even if his or her mother was alive, because in Islam fathers are deemed financially responsible for their children.) Umm Abdullah's project faced trenchant opposition from the Pashtun patriarchy who saw little need to educate girls and resented the spread of Saudi-funded Wahhabi orthodoxy in Afghanistan. In the face of their hostility, Umm Abdullah had raised the funds and succeeded in persuading Sayyaf to back her project.

Rabiah was assigned the position of 'medical officer' at the school, with responsibility for the health care of several hundred girls. 'I was for all intents and purposes the doctor there. I diagnosed them and prescribed the drugs that were needed', she says.

The school offered an extremely limited curriculum. The girls were taught to read and write the Quran in Arabic and the Afghan language, Dari, which meant that in the process they learned to read and write. In addition they were taught domestic skills such as sewing, beading and embroidery. Given the profound conservatism of the Pashtun culture, it seemed like an achievement at the time. But Rabiah would later conclude that limiting girls' education to religious studies and basic literacy was a tragic failing. 'We made a mistake in Pakistan in the 1980s. The women's schools opened by the Arabs were only for religion. They didn't have the foresight to educate Afghan girls on a broader level. Sayyaf did have a school that taught secular studies, but it was only for boys; the only girls section was a nurses college and a female medical faculty. The orphanages taught Quran, reading and writing, and manual skills. But there was no broader education. It was a very, very big mistake. A whole generation was lost—not just girls, because even boys were not educated in general either.'

But these criticisms are made with hindsight. At the time, like most of her cohorts, Rabiah was swept up in the revolutionary fervour of forging an Islamic state. And suddenly, it seemed within their grasp. 'We honestly thought we'd obtained the objective and the difficult days were over. There was an expectation that we would all move to Afghanistan and live happily ever after.'

But in August 1992 the short-lived elation over the mujahidin victory was shattered when the Pashtun warlord Hekmatyar launched a barrage of rocket fire against Kabul, aimed at dislodging his bitter rival, Massoud. The attack precipitated a savage new contest for power. Over the next eighteen months, Kabul was subjected to the most ferocious bombardment it had ever endured, which killed 25 000 people and destroyed half the city.

It was events on the other side of the world, however, that would finally spell an end to the Afghan-Arab idyll in Pabbi. In February 1993, a Ford van carrying a 540-kilogram bomb was detonated in the underground carpark of the World Trade Center in New York. The bombers had hoped to topple the twin towers, but on this first attempt they succeeded only in ripping apart five lower floors, leaving six people dead and more than 1000 injured. The perpetrator was a Kuwaiti-born engineer, Ramzi Yousef, a nephew of Sayyaf's secretary, Khalid Sheikh Mohammed. Yousef had travelled to Peshawar in the late 1980s, stayed at bin Laden's guesthouse and trained in Camp Sadda, according to a fellow militant who later testified to having seen him there between 1989 and 1991. Yousef's attempt on the World Trade Center was the forerunner for his uncle's successful destruction of the twin towers eight years later on 11 September 2001.

Yousef's attack concentrated world attention for the first time on the looming 'blowback' from the Islamic militants who had flourished in north-west Pakistan, thanks in large measure to US and Saudi support. It also brought Osama bin Laden onto America's radar, although there was no clear connection between him and the World Trade Center bombing, and little was known at this stage about who bin Laden was or what he was doing. The FBI was told in 1993 that a 'Saudi prince' was supporting radical Islamists plotting attacks in New York. A CIA report that year named bin Laden as an 'independent actor (who) sometimes works with other individuals or governments' to promote 'militant Islamic causes'. However, when the Congressional Taskforce on Terrorism published the names of several dozen 'prominent figures in Islamist terrorism' in September 1993, bin Laden's name was not on the list. This was not because he was operating in secret, but simply because he remained a marginal player at this time.

However, investigations into Ramzi Yousef's bombing would gradually focus keen attention on activities in the militant training camps of Pakistan and Afghanistan, including Sayyaf's Camp Sadda where Yousef had trained. A US State Department report in 1995 asserted that 'all the factions' including 'the regime in Kabul' are 'involved in harboring or facilitating camps that have trained terrorists from many nations who have been active in worldwide terrorist activity'. It singled out Sayyaf for 'continuing to harbor and train potential terrorists in his camps'.

Under pressure from the United States, the Pakistani government of Prime Minister Benazhir Bhutto launched a crackdown aimed at expelling the foreign fighters entrenched in the North West Frontier Province and along the Afghan border.

'Benazir Bhutto wanted the Afghan-Arabs out in no uncertain terms', Rabiah recounts. 'She started having the security forces round people up, imprison them, and send them back to their own countries. She threatened to clean Pabbi out if people didn't give up and leave.'

Sayyaf and his lieutenants had left already, relocating to Afghanistan to fight it out for control of their ravaged country. Their former benefactor, bin Laden, had gone as well, expelled from his native Saudi Arabia and now living in exile in Sudan. With his departure, the flow of money to the Afghan-Arabs had stopped.

'Times got really tough', Rabiah remembers. 'We couldn't run the generator any more because there was no money. So we had no electricity. The hospital had no medicine, we didn't even have antibiotics.' A Saudi princess had donated US$100 000 to buy milk for Afghan children—so there was milk, but not much else. 'I remember because I asked a sheikh if we could use the money for antibiotics and he said it wasn't permitted because she'd given it for milk. It used to frustrate me—what, are you gonna fatten them so they can die of infection?' Even food was running short. 'Just before we left Pabbi, all we had left was half a cup of old oil and some lentils. We'd been eating lentils and bread, lentils and bread, lentils and bread. My children hate lentils.' There were family problems as well. Rabiah's eldest son, Mohammed, who had grown into a rebellious fifteen year old, had tired of life in Pabbi and run away to Peshawar to stay with a friend whose father worked for the United Nations, according to Rabiah.

Rahmah—who was ten years old by this time—remembers the day the family's food ran out in Pabbi. 'My mother at that point was working in the hospital with no pay as they could not afford to pay her any more. It came to the day that we had spent our last rupiah on bread and we had nothing. My mother had used the last grain of lentils in the house and we had no more kerosene. *Subhan* Allah (Praise Allah), I remember this day very clearly ... We had just prayed *thuhr* (midday prayer) when my mum called us and sat us down and explained to us that we had made *hijrah* and Allah will not leave us, but at the same time we must face hardships as the *sahbah* (companions of the Prophets) did. I could see my mother was holding back her tears as she continued to tell us how we had spent our last rupiah and that she did not know how and when our next meal would be. So she told us to make *dua* (prayer) and she held us all ... My siblings were too young to understand, but I was old enough and I began to cry.'

Rahmah recounts that suddenly they were startled by a knock at the door. It was strange, as usually no one left their houses at *thuhr* time because it was so hot. Rahmah and her brother ran and opened the door, to find a man in a turban dressed all in black, standing in front of a shiny new pickup truck.

'Is this the house of Umm Mohammed Australie?' asked the stranger.

'Yes it is', Rahmah replied.

'Can you give her this', said the man, handing Mustafa a white envelope.

'We ran inside and gave it to my mother', Rahmah's account continues. 'And when she opened it she found enough money to last us five months, *Allahu Akbar*.'

'Who was that man?' Rabiah asked the children.

'We don't know, we've never seen him before.'

'Quickly, run out and ask who he is and how did he know of us.'

But by the time they got outside there was no sign of the man or his shiny car, not even a cloud of dust.

Rahmah was sure it was a miracle that had saved them. 'Until this day I believe that Allah sent that man, and if I close my eyes I can still see his face and exactly what he wore and the car ... and I can remember thinking, *masha Allah* (thanks to Allah) what a big new beautiful car.'

As the months passed, the Pakistani government stepped up the pressure to force the foreign jihadists out. It faced stiff resistance, not least because the Pashtun code of honour known as Pashtunwali insists that hospitality and protection must be extended to their *maymon*, or guests. Furthermore, the Afghan-Arabs enjoyed the status of *muhajirin,* Muslim pilgrims who had migrated for the sake of Islam and must be given sanctuary. And the foreigners had no intention of simply walking away, according to Rabiah: 'The Afghan-Arabs said, "We'll fight, we won't go peacefully"'.

By Rabiah's account she and her family were among the last holdouts who refused to leave, even when they heard that Benazir Bhutto was sending army tanks to surround Pabbi. As the tanks moved in to block-ade the road to Sayyafabad, the mujahidin prepared to defend their ground, ordering the women and children among them to take shelter with Afghani families in the nearby refugee camp.

'They took all the Afghan-Arab women and children and put us with the Afghans. We hid inside the Afghans' houses for three days, we weren't allowed to talk, we were in hiding.' Rabiah was handed an AK-47 and given instructions on how to use it, which she was quite prepared to do if there was a fight. 'I grew up in Mudgee, I used to go rabbit hunting with my brother when I was four and used to shoot cans with a telescopic rifle as a kid. Kalashnikovs are even easier. If you put them on *roosh* (auto-matic) you don't even have to aim.'

Rabiah says she never got the chance to test her skills with a Kalashnikov; the foreigners remaining in Pabbi had no choice but to leave.

'When we had to leave Pabbi, it was like someone ripped your heart out. My kids and me, we feel like our life stopped when we left Pabbi. It was devastating—insofar as a Muslim can be devastated, because in the end it was what Allah planned.'

Rabiah and the children left Pabbi in convoy with the remnants of Sayyaf's Afghan-Arabs and returned to Peshawar where they were 'swal-lowed up' among the vast human sea of Afghan refugees, which was once again swelling daily due to fierce fighting around Kabul. Rabiah's friend Umm Mohammed Azzam found her a house in Hayatabad and a job running the dispensary in a Saudi-funded hospital. They stayed on for about a year, but it was clear the Afghan-Arabs' previous safe haven was coming to an end, at least for the time being. The foreign jihadists were no longer welcome in either Pakistan or Afghanistan, where the mujahidin leader Ahmed Shah Massoud had announced: 'The reality is the jihad is over in Afghanistan. We do not need armed Arabs going around our country. It is better for them to leave.'

'The time in Peshawar was horrible, I hated it', says Rabiah. 'It was just a very terrible time. We were being harassed. People started being asked, "Why are you here? Have you got a visa?" The army would come and pick up brothers when they were at the mosque. And the support of the Pakistani people had fallen because of all the infighting.'

Their financial situation was once again desperate. With bin Laden and al Qaeda now headquartered in Sudan, the payment of a monthly stipend to foreign volunteers in Peshawar was a luxury of the past. Rabiah's benefactor Umm Mohammed Azzam had run out of funds as well. 'Things were really bad, the money had dried up, the *khafalla* had stopped. We didn't have money. I'd been working for two or three months at the hospital without payment. We were literally eating once a day. Things were falling apart.'

In a last-ditch effort to find new sources of funding, Rabiah was delegated by the Afghan-Arab community in Peshawar to travel to the United Kingdom, Europe and the Middle East to solicit donations. She is unclear about exactly who sent her, except to say she was assigned the task by a friend named Umm Mahmud whose husband was on a 'committee' responsible for financing projects such as the orphanage, hospitals and schools. (It may have been the Islamic Co-ordination Council, an umbrella group of Peshawar-based charities established by Abdullah Azzam.) She was given a ticket, itinerary and a list of people to see in the United Kingdom, France and Yemen, who might be willing to contribute. She believes she was chosen 'probably because of the places I was being sent, and the novelty value of a "revert" who'd lived and worked with the Afghans. And I can speak multiple languages.' The trip was almost aborted at the last minute because of consternation among the male committee members about a woman travelling the world alone without a *mahram*, or male relative, to escort her. In the end they decided the urgency of the task made it Islamically acceptable.

She left the children behind with a 'sister' in Peshawar and set off, flying first to London where the expedition got off to a disastrous start. 'I got to the United Kingdom and they wouldn't let me speak or go to the mosques, because I was a woman.' The London stop improved somewhat with a private audience that had been pre-arranged with Yusuf Islam, the former 1970s pop music idol known in his heyday as Cat Stevens. The British-born Muslim convert was renowned as a passionate advocate of the Afghan cause and benefactor of a range of Islamic charities. Rabiah visited him and his wife at an Islamic school they had recently established in London. To her mind, he was no longer the pop icon whose songs had been veritable anthems for the teen surf crowd on Sydney's northern beaches. 'Cat Stevens was the same as Robyn Mary Hutchinson. He had ceased to exist', she says. 'I spoke to him about the project and said we were in need of help because that was when things were starting to fall to pieces. Yusuf Islam just listened. I don't know if he gave money because I didn't actually collect the money. But he seemed very kind, concerned and genuinely interested, and he did say that maybe he could help out with books and school equipment.'

From London, she continued on to France and Yemen to lobby Muslim communities for donations. She also took a detour to Australia, where she stayed with her younger sister Susan on Sydney's affluent and leafy north shore—a starkly surreal contrast to the parched poverty of Peshawar. While there she rang some old friends to say hello after Susan urged her, 'You don't know how many people have said to me, "What happened to your sister? Did she die or fall off the world?"'

Rabiah had hoped to secure money from her former husband, Abdul Rahim Ayub, for the upkeep of their children, and donations from the Muslim community so they could stay in Peshawar. But her efforts were fruitless on both counts, leaving her flummoxed that neither her former spouse nor her fellow Muslims viewed her continued stay in Peshawar as a cause worth supporting. 'All I needed was $150 a month and I could have stayed. One hundred and fifty dollars a month was enough to support a family of six. The Muslims here spend more than that on their Tim Tam biscuits and smelly things for the toilet. I just wanted to be supported. But I didn't get any support.'

Rabiah returned to Peshawar empty-handed. 'The whole thing was a pretty dismal failure. It only raised about $10 000 or $15 000—enough to keep a hospital going for about a week.' The disappointment over her own failed efforts as a fund-raiser was overwhelmed by the realisation that the much vaunted Afghan jihad was coming to an inconclusive end. The victory over the Russians had been squandered, the rival mujahidin factions were continuing to tear Afghanistan apart, and there was still no prospect of an Islamic state.

'It was a sadness that hit you at the core of your being', says Rabiah. 'Where had we gone wrong? Because Allah promises victory for Muslims, but it was just a mess. We had to look at ourselves—what had we done wrong?' Her conclusion was: 'What had gone wrong was that we hadn't obeyed Allah. We started infighting. Allah will only give the Muslims victory when they are united.'

She also felt betrayed by long-time Islamists such as Sayyaf, who she believed had sold out on their commitment to an Islamic state in return for a share of power in Afghanistan. 'They were setting up a democracy, they were having elections, Sayyaf was part of it. It was wrong.' For Rabiah, the objective was not democracy for Afghanistan, but securing an Islamic state. 'I became a Muslim because I wanted to live Islam, not because I wanted to be a democratic Afghan or a republican American or a Pancasila Indonesian. If I wanted to live in a Western democracy system with the rule of law, I'd live in Australia.'

The realisation that their struggle had foundered was a watershed—for Rabiah and the wider jihadist movement. She describes how at this point the movement polarised between those who felt that jihad had failed and those who believed the military struggle must continue. 'After Peshawar they actually split into two distinct groups', says Rabiah. On one side were the 'Ikhwanis', flag-bearers of the original Muslim Brotherhood, the *Ikhwanil Muslimin*, which had begun in Egypt and spread through the Muslim world. The pragmatists of the Brotherhood now believed that military jihad was futile and that their best course henceforth was to work within existing political systems to achieve Islamic law. The other camp, loosely termed 'Salafi Jihadists', believed that events in Pakistan and Afghanistan were merely a temporary setback, and that—like any revolution—the struggle must go on. This group completely shunned Western-style political systems and believed that military struggle was justified in order to establish Islamic law. It was in this camp that Rabiah's allegiances lay.

The Salafi Jihadists included the adherents of Osama bin Laden, now based in Sudan, and the remnants of Sayyaf's Afghan-Arabs who were fleeing in all directions from Peshawar. In the coming years they would take their fight to Somalia, Chechnya, Bosnia, Indonesia, the Philippines, and eventually further afield to the 'far enemy', the United States and its allies.

But for Rabiah and her family the Afghan jihad had come to an end, at least for now. Dispirited and penniless, she had no option but to return to Australia. 'It was just one of the many times that I came back when it wasn't really a choice. I didn't want to come back, but there wasn't any money for wages any more in Peshawar. I couldn't support myself, the money had run out, the hospitals were closing down, everyone was leaving.'

She sold all her belongings—blankets, beds, whitegoods, cooking ware, and the air conditioner bought for her by bin Laden—to raise money for their airfares home. But she knew they would not be back in Australia for long.

'It was not the end of the dream. Allah had something else in mind.'

11

'WAHHABI'

Australia & Egypt, 1995–1999

The culture shock of returning to Australia after four years with the mujahidin in Pakistan was worse than anything Rabiah's young family had encountered when travelling abroad. The children had all been born or lived for much of their lives in third-world conditions in Indonesia or Pakistan. Five-year-old Aminah had been a baby when they left Australia and didn't speak English. The two youngest boys, Mustafa and Ilyas, had forgotten much of their native tongue and conversed more readily in Arabic and Dari. Eleven-year-old Rahmah would later describe a recurring dream; she was twenty-one years old, spoke twenty languages and was still in fourth grade at school.

They were picked up at the airport by Rabiah's former husband, Abdul Rahim Ayub, who took them to stay at his two-bedroom flat at Dee Why on Sydney's northern beaches. After a week there they moved to a refuge run by the Muslim Women's Association at Yagoona in the city's outer south-western suburbs.

'For my children, it was almost like I'd picked them up and I'd put them on another planet', Rabiah remembers. 'Everything they'd learned in their lives—this is right, this is wrong, this is how you do and don't behave—it was absolutely 180 degrees the opposite. And some of it was funny, but some of it was terrible.'

The first morning in the communal dining room—where even sitting up at a table for breakfast was an oddity—Aminah couldn't recognise anything that looked to her like food.

'Mama, what's for breakfast?' she asked.

'Have one of these—this is what they eat here', Rabiah replied, pointing to the miniature cardboard packets of cereal on the table.

'But they're boxes.'

'No, there's stuff in them you can eat—here, have this one.'

'What is it?'

'It's called Rice Bubbles.'

Aminah stared with dismay at the contents of the little box, which resembled no food she'd ever seen.

'*Mumkin ruz bidoon bubbles?*' she asked plaintively in Arabic. ('Can I have the rice without the bubbles?')

At night in the refuge the children were put in a room with bunk beds, another disconcerting novelty after four years of sleeping on wooden pallets on the floor. Eight-year-old Mustafa fell out of the top bunk, sustaining concussion, and was taken to Sydney's Westmead hospital where a doctor proceeded to ask him a series of standard questions to assess whether the blow to his head had caused any serious damage.

'What's your name?' the doctor asked.

'Mustafa', the boy replied.

Checking the paperwork, which showed the child's given name was Abdullah, the doctor frowned.

'When is your birthday?'

'I don't know.' Like many Muslim families, Rabiah's did not celebrate birthdays.

'Who is the prime minister of Australia?'

'I don't know.'

'What did you get for Christmas?'

'Nothing.'

The doctor concluded the boy had severe amnesia. In fact he just had a bump on the head, but the questions the doctor assumed any child would be able to answer were entirely foreign to his life experience.

Within a short time the children fell ill with a range of ailments including the common cold, gastroenteritis—apparently from the strange bugs in the food and water—and asthma. On doctor's orders Rabiah bought them regular beds, a precaution against the dust mites that make asthma endemic in Australia. They had trouble adjusting to the food and all lost weight. Rabiah believes they were homesick for their mudbrick house in Pabbi. 'For the next year all they said was, "Can we please go home? We don't like it here".'

The children were enrolled in the local state school, a condition of their accommodation at the women's refuge. Five-year-old Aminah, a bright and inquisitive pupil like her older sisters, was eager to begin, until they pulled up at the school on day one to be greeted by a female teacher in a sleeveless top and three-quarter-length shorts. Aminah was accustomed to female teachers being covered from head to toe in black.

'Please, what have I done? Why are you going to give me to these people?' she shrieked at her mother.

'Aminah thought I'd gone completely mad, handing her over to the *kafr* (non-believers)', Rabiah recalls.

Her predicament worsened at morning assembly, when Aminah and her siblings were called up onto the stage in the school hall for an official welcome. By this stage Aminah was trembling with fright, Rabiah recounts: 'She doesn't know if she's going to be executed or not, so she's shaking and crying'. After the principal introduced the newcomers, a boy of Aminah's age stepped forward to give her a hug and kiss of welcome. It was all too much for her brother Ilyas. He and his siblings had grown up attending a segregated school; they had never played with children of the opposite sex who were unrelated to them—let alone been hugged and kissed in public by complete strangers. Ilyas jumped on the boy and dragged him off, shouting, 'Anyone touches my sister and I'll kill them'.

For the two eldest children, Devi and Mohammed, now aged nineteen and seventeen, returning to Australia presented the possibility of a life radically different from the austere Islamic lifestyle their mother had chosen. Both of them seized the alternative. Mohammed, who in any event was too old to stay at a women's refuge, went to stay instead with Rabiah's sister, Susan, at her home on Sydney's northern beaches. He got a job as an oxy-welder, stopped praying and got his ear pierced. Another man who met him at the Dee Why factory where he was working says, 'I wouldn't say he was anti-Islam but he had ceased to practise and he didn't associate with the Muslim community'. After a couple of weeks at the refuge, Devi left with her two-year-old daughter Huda and went to stay with Susan as well. (Huda's Iraqi father, who had intended following them from Pakistan, never got a visa and didn't make it to Australia.) Susan, who had three children of her own and doted on her niece and nephew, was happy to offer them a home, and made no secret of her disapproval of their unsettled life, being dragged by their mother on her travels around the world.

'She thought she was saving them', says Rabiah. 'She thought she was giving them the chance of a normal life, rather than the indoctrination they'd had with me.'

Like her brother, Devi soon shed her Islamic attire, abandoning the shapeless robe she had worn in Pakistan for jeans and t-shirts, which she initially teamed with a headscarf. She moved with baby Huda into a flat in beachside Harbord, where Rabiah had hung out with her friends as a teenager smoking marijuana joints in the sand dunes. Eager to continue her curtailed schooling, Devi enrolled in a TAFE course to complete years eleven and twelve of secondary school, intending to go to university to study sociology or languages, according to Rabiah.

'There's something I've got to tell you', Devi announced one day when her mother rang to say she was coming to visit. 'I'm not wearing hijab any more.'

For Rabiah this was a crushing blow. Devi's simple act of discarding the headscarf felt to Rabiah like a massive rejection of all that she believed in and had instilled in her children. 'I felt extreme sadness. She's my first-born child and she was letting go of something that I believed would bring her eternal happiness.' She was referring not simply to the garment, but to the faith it symbolised. She believed that for a woman to go out without being 'properly covered', which meant at least concealing her hair, was a 'major sin'. 'I'm a mother and I believe in the laws of Allah. Obviously any mother doesn't want her daughter to do something that will bring the anger of Allah upon them.'

In a later conversation, Devi asked her: 'Mama, can we leave Islam out of our relationship? Can you just be my mother and I be your daughter and let me find my own way? Will you agree that we will put Islam aside in our relationship?' Rabiah's response was: No, she could never put Islam aside.

After a few weeks at the women's refuge, Rabiah was deemed eligible by the government for subsidised accommodation at a new housing estate on the south-western outskirts of Sydney. She was taken to a brand-new, four-bedroom, split-level home, with a playground where boys and girls romped about together and a communal park where residents attended weekly 'BYO' ('bring your own' alcohol) barbecues. But the prospect of life in such a quintessentially Australian setting was now so foreign that it filled her with dread. 'It was just so impossible for us to live like that. It was a lifestyle that was just so void of anything Islamic. How could I have gone to barbecues with music and drinking?' Instead she found a two-bedroom house in her old stamping ground, Lakemba. The rent was cheap because the street was a known haunt of drug dealers and criminal gangs, but at least it was near the mosque.

Rabiah enrolled the children in the Al Noori Islamic primary school at nearby Greenacre, which had been set up by her former friends Silma and Siddiq Buckley. The couple had since divorced and the school was being run by a board chaired by the respected community leader and former president of the Islamic Council of New South Wales, Sheikh Khalil Chami. Sheikh Chami had known Rabiah in her days as a voluntary scripture teacher and had always been impressed by her seemingly inexhaustible energy. He appointed her to a committee to choose a new principal and she later joined the school board.

'She was very, very active—a very, very good worker', says Chami. 'She was the best in that time. She could achieve anything. If we wanted something done she'd do it. We were a very good team.' Chami recalls Rabiah was 'very frank and outspoken' but says he saw 'nothing radical or extreme' in her behaviour or views.

The new principal of the Al Noori school, Siddiq Buckley, who had known Rabiah when she first moved to Lakemba in the early 1980s, found her as dedicated as ever—'she was a very concerned person, concerned about following Islam'—and just as abrasive. 'She was just an opinionated person. That's the way Rabiah was—black and white. Her opinions didn't bother me a bit, that's just the way she was.'

Siddiq took exception on one occasion when Rabiah remarked that she wouldn't send her children to a *kafr* school. The word *kafr* means 'non-believer', but is sometimes translated into the more pejorative 'infidel'.

'Don't call them *kafr*', Siddiq reproved her.

'What should I call them?'

'Call them "non-Muslims".'

'Isn't that the same as saying that a table is a "non-chair"?' Rabiah objected.

'I was a bit too radical for them', she would later reflect.

Rabiah threw herself into Islamic community life in Sydney. In addition to serving on the school board, she was active in the Muslim Women's Welfare Association, a converts group that published a book about women in Islam, and set up a charity to distribute relief to needy Muslims.

By this stage a new 'holy war' had erupted in Bosnia, creating a fresh *cause célèbre* for the international jihadist movement. After the collapse of the former Yugoslavia, Serb and Croatian forces had moved to expand their territory into neighbouring Bosnia and Herzegovina, unleashing a vicious series of struggles in which Bosnian Muslims were targeted in mass killings, systematic rape, torture and ethnic cleansing. Bosnia invigorated the Islamic community as Afghanistan had done a decade before. Rabiah and some 'sisters' launched a drive to raise funds in conjunction with the international Muslim charity, Human Appeal International (HAI), and used the proceeds to send shipping containers of food, medicine and clothing, along with money. HAI was later named in a CIA report on terrorist financing, which alleged the charity 'probably acts as a fundraiser for Hamas', the Palestinian militant group. But Rabiah says that in the mid 1990s there were no such qualms.

'In those days everyone agreed with jihad. I'm talking about Afghanistan, Kashmir, Bosnia. I never met any Muslim—or even non-Muslim—who was against it.'

The jihadist wave sweeping the world had reached Australia as well. In Sydney it centred on a new *musalla* (prayer room) in Haldon Street, Lakemba, which was the hub of a burgeoning Salafist community. It was established by a group of renegades from the Lakemba mosque who had broken away from the mainstream congregation led by the so-called Grand Mufti of Australia, Sheikh Taj al Din al Hilali. The rebels' spiritual guide was Rabiah's former teacher Sheikh Mohammed Jamal Omran, leader of Australia's largest Salafist group, the Ahlus Sunnah Wal Jamaah Association. Like the Afghan-Arabs in Pabbi, the men were conspicuous by their long beards, robes and trousers above their ankles, while the women were garbed all in black. Hundreds of people turned out for the fiery Friday sermons delivered by Omran's lieutenant, Sheikh Abdul Salam Zoud. As the years passed, the Haldon Street *musalla* would attract intense scrutiny from the Australian Security Intelligence Organisation (ASIO). But back in the early to mid 1990s, Sheikh Zoud's exhortations that Muslims must live by the *shariah* aroused no controversy. 'To say then that all Muslims should live under Islamic law was completely acceptable, because we were talking about Muslims in Muslim lands', Rabiah says.

Foreign sheikhs on the Islamic speakers circuit who ventured to Australia received an enthusiastic reception. Sheikh Omran hosted one such visit by the British-based cleric Abu Qatada, who had been in Peshawar for the jihad against the Russians in the 1980s and was granted asylum in the United Kingdom in 1993. Years later he would be convicted of terrorism charges in his homeland, Jordan, and accused of being 'Osama bin Laden's right-hand man in Europe'. His visit to Lakemba in 1994, well before he gained notoriety, was no clandestine affair. 'They held it in the bloody council hall', Rabiah recounts. The public hall near the Lakemba train station was packed with dozens of men and about thirty women who sat at the back behind a curtain. Rabiah says the discussion centred mainly on 'correct' Islamic observance.

The surge in jihadist activity had also galvanised the Indonesian migrant diaspora, which now boasted its own chapter of JI, the organisation formed in Malaysia in 1993 by Abdullah Sungkar and Abu Bakar Ba'asyir. During one of their visits to Sydney the two clerics had resolved to establish an Australian *jemaah* (community) and appointed Rabiah's former husband, Abdul Rahim Ayub, as its *emir*. As Rabiah tells it, Abdul Rahim was chosen because 'he was the only one with prior connections— he met them through me'. Rabiah maintained regular contact with Abdul Rahim, the father of her three youngest children, Mustafa, Ilyas and Aminah. He had married again, to the same Indonesian woman whom Rabiah had suggested a few years earlier as her 'co-wife', and had a baby son.

Throughout the 1990s, Sungkar and Ba'asyir visited Australia eleven times. Their *jemaah* came to number about 130 members in Sydney, Melbourne and Perth, about thirty of whom swore the *bai'at* to one or other of the pair. The principal role of JI's Australian branch was to raise funds through lectures, prayer meetings and *zakat* (alms) donated by its members and remitted to Sungkar and Ba'asyir in Malaysia.

'So-called "JI in Australia" was just a group of Indonesians', says Rabiah. 'There were lots of Indonesian students, mostly illegal, and a lot who got amnesty in the 1980s. Most weren't practising Muslims when they came. When Abdullah Sungkar and Abu Bakar Ba'asyir came, it wasn't to recruit them; they just preached to them, and brought them back to their *deen* (religion). They told them that now they lived in a country of such wealth, it was their duty to give something back. The only function that people served in Australia was to raise money to support the schools and other projects in Malaysia. They got more money in a week here than in a month in Indonesia.'

Over the years, Sungkar and Ba'asyir grew bolder and more vociferous in their denunciations of the Suharto regime. They were equally contemptuous of democracy, and urged their followers in Australia to obey only Islamic law, arguing that man-made laws usurp Allah's rightful authority and constitute 'an open declaration of disbelief'. The clerics had also become stauncher in their own observance of Islamic practice. Rabiah recalls attending a lecture given by Ba'asyir at the Dee Why mosque around this time; afterwards, when she went to speak to the mentor whose home she had visited so often at Ngruki, she was obliged to converse with him from behind a curtain.

Rabiah herself was by now a well-known figure in international Islamist circles, by virtue of her years in Indonesia and Pakistan, her linguistic range, and her close association with jihadist icons such as Sungkar, Ba'asyir and Sayyaf. Her fund-raising for Bosnia became known abroad, and in 1995 she received a job offer from an Islamic propagation centre in Kuwait. The position at its headquarters in Kuwait City came with a salary of US$5000 per month, plus airfares, accommodation and Islamic schooling for her children. She leapt at the offer.

The week before she was due to leave for Kuwait, Rabiah's brother George drove her son Mohammed over from the northern beaches to farewell his family. The visit was strained. Rabiah's relations with George had been cool for many years. Mohammed had evidently abandoned Islam and was wearing a beanie pulled down low over his head to hide an earring, which George seemed to enjoy pointing out to Rabiah, and which she pointedly ignored. Before they left, Mohammed asked his mother exactly when she was flying out to Kuwait, so he could come and say goodbye to her and his siblings.

But the trip to Kuwait never eventuated. When Kuwaiti officials got their hands on Rabiah's passport and apparently saw the visa stamps revealing her four-year sojourn with the mujahidin in Pakistan, she says the job offer was suddenly withdrawn. By way of compensation they paid her US$5000, the equivalent of one month's salary.

A few days later, Devi rang her mother, fuming. Unaware that the trip had been cancelled, her brother Mohammed had got up at dawn on the day of their scheduled departure and taken a bus to the airport to see his family off. He had sat waiting for them for hours. The family had been unaware that Mohammed was coming to farewell them, and no one had thought to tell him they weren't going.

'How could you do that to him?' Devi railed at her mother. 'It just reinforced in his mind that you don't care about him.' Rabiah would later describe Mohammed's reaction as that of a 'disappointed little boy'.

Her own disappointment at the lost opportunity in Kuwait quickly turned to anticipation. She now had US$5000 in the bank. It was her ticket to freedom.

'I couldn't stand it in Australia any more', she says. 'The children kept getting sick. They'd developed asthma and the doctor said it was emotional. I was trying to home-school them because I'd put them into school and they hated it. And they were losing their Arabic.' Her now instinctive reaction was simply to pack up and leave. It was merely a question of where she should go.

Rabiah had a friend from Melbourne who was living and working as an English teacher in Egypt. There was also a large cohort of Indonesian students studying at the Al Azhar University in Cairo, the most esteemed Arabic language and Islamic studies institute in the world. Another friend in Jakarta who was planning to travel there reported it was easy to get visas. Sheikh Khalil Chami provided a letter of introduction for Rabiah to the authorities at Al Azhar. Before the end of 1995, she and the four youngest children were on a plane with their Chinese samsonites, three sets of clothing and jars of Vegemite, bound for Cairo.

* * *

When Rabiah and her family landed in Egypt in late 1995, the country was in the throes of a bloody Islamist insurgency. Egypt had been the crucible of the modern Islamic political revival. It was the birthplace in the 1920s of the Muslim Brotherhood, which provided a prototype for Islamic groups around the world; and of the writer Sayyid Qutb, whose conception of Islamic revolution became the underpinning philosophy of the jihadist movement. When the Brotherhood spurned the notion of violent jihad, a younger generation of militants emerged, nurtured by two new organisations, al-Gamaa al-Islamiyya (the Islamic Group) and al Jihad. The latter was led by the Egyptian physician Dr Ayman al Zawahari, who would become a driving force behind al Qaeda's turn towards terrorism.

By 1995 emergency law had been in place in Egypt for fourteen years, since the 1981 assassination by Islamic militants of President Anwar Sadat. Through the early 1990s a fresh wave of violence had rocked the country, beginning with sniper attacks at cruisers on the Nile River and the ambushing of a tourist bus, and ultimately claiming more than one thousand lives. Muslim activists were being arrested in their hundreds under draconian emergency laws, detained, beaten and tortured in the country's notorious jails, emerging often more militant than when they went in.

Rabiah and her family were greeted in Cairo by a group of Indonesian students who were enrolled at Al Azhar University, the most popular destination for Indonesians studying in the Middle East. They were boarding in a grimy tenement in the district of Al Husein, a crowded quarter of narrow alleyways and pungent market stalls not far from the main campus of the famed university.

Al Azhar boasts of being the oldest centre of Islamic learning in the world. It was founded in the tenth century and reputedly named after the Prophet Mohammed's well-educated daughter, Fatima az-Zahraa— Fatima, the brilliant—a role model for generations of Muslim women. Al Azhar was described by Napoleon Bonaparte, whose forces occupied Cairo, as the Sorbonne of the Middle East. The university adjoins the historic Al Azhar mosque, a jewel of Islamic architecture with its stately minarets, alabaster columns and vast white marble courtyard.

After a few weeks staying with the students, Rabiah and the children moved to Nasser City, a satellite town on the eastern outskirts of the capital, where they rented an apartment close to a preparatory secondary school for Al Azhar where Rabiah intended sending the children. They slipped easily into a community of expatriate students, academics and families that had sprung up in the environs of Al Azhar. Far from home, the *muhajirin* (migrants) sought each other out and, as in Pabbi, the women coalesced into an intimate society of their own. In addition to Indonesians and Malaysians, there were many English speakers—mostly Europeans, from France, Germany, Belgium and Britain, many of them married to Egyptians. The women held weekly meetings where they read the Quran together and studied the *hadith*. When it become apparent that Rabiah had studied more than most of them, she took over some of the classes. By necessity, these gatherings were kept low key so as not to arouse suspicion. Muslim activists were being kept under close surveillance and Rabiah was told the emergency laws prohibited gatherings of more than five people without a permit. Women who wore Salafi attire and veiled their faces were automatically deemed suspect. At one point she received a friendly warning from an Egyptian sheikh who was teaching her children the Quran: 'Umm Mohammed, I want to give you some advice. While you are here don't speak in Arabic, speak in English—because the Arabic you speak is Peshawar Arabic, and if the secret police hear you, they'll know exactly where you've been.'

In readiness for their enrolment at the Al Azhar secondary school, Rabiah hired private tutors to coach the children in Arabic, Quranic studies and secular sciences to ensure they would pass the entrance test. After months of tuition, she signed them up for the exam. But an unforeseen problem arose, when she was advised that the school she had chosen was open only to *ahul balad*, or 'people of the land'; the children of non–Arabic Egyptian nationals were obliged to attend a separate school for 'foreigners'. Rabiah learned of the restriction on the day the children sat the entrance exam.

'But I want them to go to this school', she announced at the school administration office.

'I'm sorry, madam, they'll have to go to the foreigners school', she was told.

'No, I want them to go here. My children speak Arabic and I want them to go here.'

When they refused to yield, Rabiah demanded an appointment with the Grand Imam, Sheikh Mohammed Sayyid Tantawy, leader of the Supreme Council that governs the affairs of Al Azhar. She tells of how she barrelled up to his office accompanied by her daughter Rahmah, now aged thirteen, sweeping past the armed guards and ignoring their request to see proof of identity.

'Go ahead and shoot me, imagine how good that's gonna look', she snorted. Inside, she was ushered into Tantawy's office, where she proceeded to lecture the man in charge of the world's highest centre of Islamic learning on the finer points of Islamic law.

'You're supposed to be the oldest Islamic learning institute in the world, but you won't accept a *hadith* of the prophet!' she berated him. 'The Prophet said, "Whoever speaks Arabic is an Arab". My children speak Arabic and I want them to go to the Arab school.' She says she refused to leave his office until he finally relented, instructing an aide: 'Give her whatever she wants, just get her out of here!' Later when Tantawy recognised Rahmah on the school campus, he greeted her: 'My daughter, any time, whatever you need, you can come to me—but please leave your mother at home'.

Rahmah and her little sister Aminah and the two boys, Mustafa and Ilyas, attended the Al Azhar preparatory school for two and a half years. It was an exacting regimen. The school day began at 7.30 in the morning and ended at 1.30 in the afternoon, followed by two hours of private tuition and then homework. Rahmah studied twenty-one subjects: the full range of secular disciplines including mathematics, history, geography and English; a suite of Islamic topics such as Quran, *hadith* and philosophy; and five Arabic courses including grammar, literature and poetry. According to Rabiah, her children were the only non-Arab pupils at the school—and the poorest. Their classmates, who included the offspring of Saudi princes and Gulf-state oil sheikhs, were deposited at the school gates by taxi or chauffeur-driven limousine. Rabiah's suggestion that her family buy a cart and donkey for the school trip was greeted with disdain by her children, like many of her ideas.

'My children were always very polite. But in the end they would just gang up on me and flatly refuse.' Despite her insistence that their objections were 'un-Islamic', they were adamant: 'May Allah forgive us, Mama, but we refuse. We will not ride on a donkey.'

After six months in Cairo, Rabiah received a phone call from Sydney. Her eldest daughter, Devi, was struggling to complete her studies while bringing up a child on her own, and wanted to know if three-year-old

Huda could join the family in Egypt. Rabiah and the children were delighted at the prospect of having their little 'sister' back with the family. A friend came up with the money for an airfare, and not long afterwards Huda arrived in Cairo clutching a teddy bear named Benny that she'd not let go of since leaving Australia.

As the children continued their studies at the Al Azhar preparatory school, Rabiah decided that, by her standards, the venerated institution did not merit its reputation as a bastion of Islamic excellence. She was incensed by the school's practice of punishing a child for misbehaviour by caning the entire class on the soles of their bare feet. She marched up to the school office to complain that this was 'unacceptable and un-Islamic', because Islam teaches that an individual is only responsible for his or her own actions, and to announce that she would be forced to withdraw her children unless the policy was changed. Unlike the Grand Imam, the headmistress was unmoved. 'She was looking at me as if to say, "And you think I care?"' Rabiah recounts. There were many such visits to the school to lambast teachers and administrators over its failings. Her children would groan in anticipation of her rampages, which they referred to as 'doing a mama'. 'You'd see the looks on my kids' faces—"Oh no, here we go"', Rabiah remembers. Sometimes they would recount the events of the day to her only after she promised not to storm up to the school office to complain.

Mass canings for misbehaviour were not the only feature of their school life that Rabiah found 'un-Islamic'. Funded and controlled by the Egyptian government, Al Azhar prized secular studies and propagated a conservative, apolitical style of Islam and a determinedly Western outlook. Any display of 'radical' Islamic dress or behaviour was discouraged; female teachers wore make-up and shunned the hijab, while the men eschewed long beards. At Easter the children painted colourful designs on eggs in class to mark the Christian festival. Rabiah recalls a plan to reduce the hours spent studying the Quran so French could be added to the curriculum, a proposal she found ridiculous.

But what most disturbed her was the reliance on rote memorisation for which Al Azhar was famed. One day she caught Ilyas doing his English homework, reciting rhythmically the names of the days of the week:

'Mon-a-day, Tues-a-day, Wed'ns-a-day, Thurs-a-day …'

'What on earth are you doing?' she demanded.

'That's how they told me to do it', he explained.

Another child they knew, while discussing Shakespeare in an English class, prefaced an answer with, 'Well I think …' The teacher threw a book at her, bellowing, "I don't care what you think—I want to know what I told you!"'

The technique of rote learning was applied methodically to study of the Quran. Every student was expected to have committed the entire book to memory by the completion of primary school. They were regularly tested on the *ayats* (verses) they had most recently learned, by which time they had usually forgotten all the ones they had previously memorised. Rabiah believed this 'parrot fashion' learning was pointless, apart from which it is considered sinful to memorise the Quran and then forget it. 'There's very high regard for memorisation of the Quran but it has to be done with appreciation and love and knowledge', she says. 'Rote learning is fine as long as it's coupled with knowledge, but without that it's against the principle of what the Quran was sent down for. The Quran is a guide, a way of life. I have seen people who are *hafiz*, they've memorised all thirty parts of the Quran, and they don't understand a word. Rote learning—of the Quran or anything—is bad, because it stops people thinking.'

Like her mother, the now 14-year-old Rahmah took a dim view of the lax standards at Al Azhar. The girl had grown into a mature and forthright young woman who combined her mother's penchant for speaking her mind with an unfailing politeness and a tact that Rabiah lacked. 'I had to do a mama today', she would announce after holding her ground in an argument; 'only without the shouting and banging on the counter', she would usually add. 'Rahmah is the complete opposite to me', says Rabiah. 'The more irate or upset someone gets, the calmer she becomes. Rahmah is a negotiator. I think it's all the years of having to deal with me—like when we were in Egypt. There were so many times when I could have been shot or thrown in jail, but Rahmah has an ability to defuse the situation.'

Like her mother, Rahmah habitually wore the *niqab*, which was frowned on by the school authorities. She had little regard for the female *hadith* teacher who wore a midi-skirt, red lipstick and a hat instead of hijab, while lecturing her young charges on the need to live by the *Sunnah* of the Prophet. Rahmah hoped to go on to university to become a scholar in Islamic jurisprudence, but found the standards at the Al Azhar school uninspiring and told them so.

'Azhar was a joke', says Rahmah. 'From being the first Islamic university that was founded on pure Islamic teachings, it has become a place ruled by a system that is all about the powerful rule, and the weak—well, who cares. Totally opposite to what I grew up with in Pabbi. I was made to repeat a year only on the basis that I disagreed with many of the things that they taught … I was told that if I knew what was best for me and my future then I should learn to sit and shut up. And that is something that is not taught in our religion; no matter how young you are, if you are saying the truth, then you (should be) listened to. So to come into a system where you are muzzled from even saying the smallest things was a tremendous shock to me and I had great difficulty accepting it.'

As Rabiah tells it, Rahmah's patience finally snapped during a lesson on biological evolution, when she stood up and announced to the rest of the class: 'Listen, if you want to be descended from a monkey, a gorilla, a giraffe or any other animal, that's up to you. But me—I was created by Allah, and my first ancestor was the prophet Adam.' She walked out of the classroom, went home and confronted her mother.

'Mama, I want to ask you a question and I want you to just answer me yes or no. Does the curriculum and methodology of Al Azhar follow the Quran and *Sunnah* in their entirety?'

'Well …' Rabiah began.

'Mama—yes or no?'

'No', Rabiah replied. After that, Rahmah never went back to the Al Azhar school. Not long afterwards, 10-year-old Ilyas followed his big sister's example.

'Mama, didn't you teach us that the Prophet said you're not allowed to learn your *deen* from liars and hypocrites?'

'Yes, Ilyas.'

'Well why do you send me to Al Azhar then?'

'I couldn't answer him, so I took all the children out', Rabiah says. 'There is no learning institution anywhere that compares to the high level of Arabic at Al Azhar. A lot of people attend for that alone. But my children were brought up (with the belief) that you never compromise your religion.'

The withdrawal of the children from the Al Azhar school left Rabiah and her family in a precarious situation, because all of their visas hinged on their student status. Moreover, after three years, living in Egypt had become expensive, and the political climate had deteriorated. In November 1997, the Islamist upheaval climaxed in the massacre of fifty-nine foreign tourists and four Egyptians at the temple complex at Luxor by terrorists from the Islamic Group and al Jihad. The atrocity triggered a wide crackdown with hundreds of arrests, and turned Egyptian public opinion decisively against the extremists. Rabiah and her friends had to stop their weekly meetings after the secret police paid a visit to the apartment block where they gathered. 'I was more or less told indirectly that if I wanted to say in Egypt, I should stay at home and mind my own business, so it all became complicated and a little bit iffy', Rabiah recalls.

The decision about their immediate future was made for them when Rabiah took Aminah to see a heart specialist in Cairo for an annual check-up. The child had previously been diagnosed with a hole in her heart, a condition that Rabiah was told was not life threatening but required regular monitoring. The Cairo specialist's opinion was that Aminah needed open heart surgery, a procedure that Rabiah was told would cost US$15 000 in Egypt. So, in the winter of 1998, Rabiah decided there was no alternative but to return to Australia. 'We came back for the same reason we always came back—there was no other option.'

* * *

On her return to Sydney in 1998, Rabiah's friends and acquaintances saw a conspicuous change. Previously in Australia she had discarded her black *niqab*, in deference to the advice of her teacher Sheikh Omran that it was unnecessary and provocative. She no longer cared what people thought, and now chose to keep it on. The spectre of a woman shrouded from head to toe in black with only her eyes visible behind a slit in the fabric was a rare sight on the streets of Sydney. It provoked a range of reactions, although not yet the naked contempt it would later arouse.

'In those days the resentment was because it was seen as cultural garb', says Rabiah. 'It was viewed like someone wearing a kilt. People objected because it was not the Australian thing to do. They'd make fun of you, rather than spit at you.'

'Go back to where you came from!' the occasional heckler would call out in the supermarket; at which a strident Australian accent would snap back: 'Shut up, you idiot! I'm from Mudgee, I don't want to go back there!'

In the mainstream Muslim fraternity, Rabiah's garb occasioned mild alarm. Her long-time supporter, Sheikh Khalil Chami, saw the *niqab* as an emblem of Wahhabism, the rigid strand of Islamic orthodoxy pioneered by the eighteenth-century Saudi desert preacher Muhammad ibn Abd al-Wahhab. 'I wasn't happy when I saw her in *niqab* because I know then she's turned from the mainstream. I said to myself inside, "We lost this girl". From her talk and her actions I think she's with the Wahhabis. We don't need those groups here in Australia. We need unity of Muslims, we have to work together. Wahhabis give a bad face to Muslims.'

Silma Buckley was unsurprised to see her former friend in full Salafi regalia. 'It was predictable for somebody like Rabiah, who went to extreme lengths. If she thought anything was required, she did it.' Silma herself disapproved of women concealing their faces. 'Practically, academically, theologically, I don't believe it's sound. And it's a destructive influence because you can't communicate with people.'

For Rabiah, however, it was simply a personal choice. She believed it was ideal (though not compulsory) for a woman to conceal her face from unrelated men, and wasn't prepared to compromise simply because it caused onlookers offence. To her it was simply a case of practising Islam in its 'purest' form, and she couldn't fathom that anyone would disapprove of that. 'There's no such thing as "radical" and "non-radical" Islam. There is just pure Islam—and then there are degrees of corruption. People say, "But that's the puritanical interpretation of Islam". I say—

"Isn't pure good?" People nowadays use the word "Salafi" as a term of abuse. But how can the word "pious" mean something bad?'

As for being branded a 'Wahhabi', she says: 'I'm not a Wahhabi and I take great offence to that, because it indicates that you are a follower of a human being. The only reason I accept the teachings of Imam Abd al-Wahhab is because they're in keeping with the Quran and *Sunnah* as taught by the Prophet Mohammed. But it's totally unacceptable to be called anything other than a Muslim, because that's the name Allah gave to people who accepted Islam.'

Despite her peripatetic habits and wish to live in an Islamic country, for Rabiah there were ways in which Australia still felt like home. She remained an 'Aussie' girl in much of her behaviour, mannerisms and mode of speech. She had an essentially love-hate relationship with her homeland. 'People might say, for someone who hates Australia so much, she keeps coming back. But it's not Australia I hate. Australia is one of the most beautiful countries in the world and I've travelled all over the world. It's not Australia I hate—it's the system.'

While she could move with ease in and out of Australia, for her children it was a difficult transition. After four years in Egypt, they felt more than ever like strangers in their native land, their upbringing and experience almost entirely foreign to that of their peers. 'My children are like aliens—they don't fit in here', Rabiah says. 'Even children who've been brought up here with a relatively strict Islamic upbringing—they can't relate to my children and my children can't relate to them.'

Rabiah now bypassed both the state education system and the local Islamic school and registered the children for home-schooling. For the next year she tutored them herself, following the compulsory New South Wales public school curriculum combined with a Saudi program of Islamic studies. She also opened another weekend Islamic school, which she ran from her home in Lakemba, attended by about twenty-five children from local Muslim families. They sponsored an orphan in Sudan through Human Appeal International, and once a month Rabiah would shepherd her flock up Haldon Street to deliver their donation.

'I used to march them up the street singing Islamic songs', she remembers. They became a familiar sight in the Haldon Street shopping strip: a horde of children in Muslim caps and headscarves marching and chanting in unison: 'Allahu Akbar! Allahu Akbar! (God is Great!)' Passers-by would stop and wave while motorists tooted their horns at the odd procession. Rabiah's own children recoiled with embarrassment at the spectacle.

After studying for more than a decade in Indonesia, Pakistan and Egypt, Rabiah was by this stage widely acknowledged in the Muslim community as a minor authority on matters Islamic, particularly on the *Sunnah* (customs) of the Prophet Mohammed as recorded in the *hadith*. Sheikh Chami concedes she was 'very knowledgeable in Islam'. She began giving weekly lessons on Islamic parenting at the Salafist *musalla* (prayer room) in Haldon Street, and sessions on Islamic faith and practice for women at her home. 'The lessons were more like gatherings, to pass on to them what I had learned', she says. 'They were talks that would encourage people to come back to the true Islam and remind them what the *shahadah* (declaration of faith) means, and to encourage them to seek knowledge.'

Women from the Muslim community flocked to her classes, and she became the mentor and spiritual guide for a widening circle of young women, drawn by her knowledge, charisma, experience and passion. Her students gradually took to wearing the *niqab*, and the all-enveloping black shroud became an increasingly common sight on the streets of Lakemba. Some of the men found her far too confronting. A male convert who met her in this period says, 'Rabiah was very big on women's rights in Islam. She was always demanding her rights as a woman and rights for Muslim women in general.' This man, a friend of her former husband Abdul Rahim, found her 'too pushy' and 'extreme'.

With a friend, Rabiah created a Muslim 'prayer kit' consisting of a book, DVD and calico prayer mat printed with step-by-step instructions on how to perform the ritual *salat* (daily prayers). The prayer mat was a great success according to Rabiah, with thousands sold in Australia and overseas and the funds channelled back into a charity she ran that provided assistance to needy Muslim families in Sydney and donations to Islamic charities abroad. She was often consulted for advice and direction on points of Islamic law and behaviour. People who sought her advice— or received it unsolicited—were often shocked by her bluntness. On one occasion she chastised Muslims for adorning their walls with pages from the Quran, telling them they might just as well hang up strips of toilet paper. Some took deep offence, missing her point that it is not the paper the Quran is printed on that should be revered, but the knowledge contained in it. 'It would be like going to a doctor, getting a prescription, and then instead of taking it to the chemist to have it filled, hanging it around your neck', she explained.

Eight months after their return to Australia, the four-bedroom house they were renting in Lakemba was sold. The new owner was perturbed to learn that his tenant was a veiled 'Wahhabi' with a horde of children. 'It would have been better if I'd had an elephant as a pet', she later mused. The lease had expired and the owner announced it would not be renewed. Rabiah was served with an eviction notice and told that if she did not leave voluntarily the police would be called.

Not for the first time, Rabiah and her brood, which now included her granddaughter Huda, found themselves with nowhere to go. Devi and Mohammed had made their own lives on Sydney's northern beaches and had little contact with the family; likewise Rabiah's brother and sister, George and Susan. She could not turn to her former husband Abdul Rahim, who had left Sydney and moved to Perth in Western Australia, after a power struggle for control of the Dee Why mosque ended in a fist fight. The imam, Zainal Arifin, had taken out an apprehended violence order against Abdul Rahim and his twin, the Afghan veteran Abdul Rahman, who had also migrated to Australia.

Rabiah received an offer of accommodation from a friend named Jamilla, a fellow Australian convert who lived with her husband on a large block of land surrounded by market gardens at Lidcombe, in Sydney's south-west. They had a large garage, which her husband had carpeted and turned into an office and library, and which Jamilla now invited Rabiah and the children to stay in until they found somewhere else.

Jamilla's husband was Sheikh Mohammed Feiz, a rising star of the Salafi set in Sydney. He was a former drug-taking street punk who had first made his name as a body-builder and teenage boxer, fighting under the moniker 'Frank the Beast'. Like so many other troubled souls in search of fulfilment, he had explored Christianity, Buddhism and even Judaism, before discovering Islam. Then, as Feiz himself puts it: 'I found the truth'. Like Rabiah, he was drawn to the stark clarity and prescribed life guide offered by Islam. 'I don't believe in unclear concepts. Everything divine must be clear', he later said. Feiz had become a student of Sheikh Omran, who recognised the young man's zeal and potential and sent him to Saudi Arabia to study Arabic and Islam in the holy city of Medina. He returned seven years later as Sheikh Feiz, and became the star attraction at the Haldon Street prayer room, where his charismatic persona and electrifying delivery drew large crowds to the weekly sermons in which he denounced the 'Zionist pigs' and Christian Crusaders bent on destroying Islam.

Rabiah and the five children moved into Feiz's carpeted fibro-cement double garage. It had a fridge, microwave, computer, and mattresses on the floor for sleeping on. 'The kids loved it', says Rabiah. 'They said, "This is great, it's like living in Pabbi again".'

In early 1999, Rahmah—who was now sixteen years old—became engaged to be married. The husband chosen for her by Rabiah and Sheikh Omran was a young man named Khaled, the son of a devout Lebanese family in Lakemba. He was one of Sheikh Omran's followers and a regular at the Haldon Street prayer room. The Islamic marriage contract signifying their betrothal stipulated that Rahmah would stay with her family for another year before going to live with Khaled, at which time the formal wedding celebration known as the *walima* would take place.

Not long after this, tragedy struck when Rabiah's close friend Khadija, the wife of Sheikh Omran, was diagnosed with an aggressive cancer. The entire community was shocked. Khadija was much loved; moreover, she had been a devotee of organic food who had made her own bread and kept bees for honey, yet suddenly her body was riddled with cancer. To compound the tragedy, Khadija and Sheikh Omran had five children.

Distressed by her friend's illness, Rabiah left her children in Sydney and went to stay with Khadija at her family's home at Cooronbong near Newcastle, where Khadija's mother had taken her daughter to nurse her through her illness. They tried all manner of treatments, from conventional drugs to new-age elixirs, but it was soon apparent that the cancer was terminal. It was a traumatic and emotional time for all who knew her. Some among Khadija's friends and family resented Rabiah's black-veiled presence and her strongly stated opinions about her friend's treatment, which included objecting to the natural remedies that were failing to alleviate Khadija's intense pain. Nadia Aboufadil had not seen Rabiah since she had left Melbourne for Pakistan a decade earlier. Nadia was grief-stricken by Khadija's illness and incensed at Rabiah 'taking over' her treatment.

'She was not human any more when she came back', says Nadia. 'She just didn't seem to be a person any more. She had changed so much. I didn't like the new Rabiah at all—but I could see it was a progression of the original Rabiah. I hated her. I wanted to beat her up.'

Khadija's brother, the soccer star Craig Johnston, who had flown from the UK after learning of his sister's illness, had never met Rabiah before. A life-long surfer, Johnston recalls Rabiah chatting at Khadija's bedside about her days on the surf scene. Johnston remembers her as 'a strong-willed person', but says: 'Charmaine's condition was dreadful and it was a very emotional time for us all. As far as I knew this lady was just there to help my very sick sister with her religious beliefs and her pain.'

While the family clung to hopes of a miracle, Rabiah could see that her friend was dying. She was constantly at her bedside, urging her to pray and seek Allah's grace.

'For God's sake, will you shut up—can't you see I'm dying?' an exhausted Khadija snapped at her more than once, Rabiah recalls.

After Khadija passed away in December 1999, rumours circulated that Sheikh Omran and Rabiah would marry. 'It got really nasty', Rabiah remembers. 'People were gossiping that I'd only gone to look after her from ulterior motives, because I wanted to marry Abu Ayman. I think it was just that people can't mind their own business, and they wanted to put an ulterior motive on me staying with Khadija when she died.' Rabiah says Sheikh Omran never proposed and that she would not have married him even if he had. 'Abu Ayman wouldn't marry me—I was his student, he respected me. And I was so far removed from the type of woman Khadija was. The wives of sheikhs are usually simple, undemanding women, who are able to sacrifice themselves.'

In the aftermath of Khadija's death, Rabiah felt the familiar need to get away. And at the end of 1999, the opportunity arose. A couple of friends who had recently married were planning to do the *haj* pilgrimage to Mecca. The pilgrims were Maryati Idris, an Indonesian woman whom Rabiah had met in Jakarta and had also known in Cairo, and her husband, Jack Thomas, a Muslim convert from Melbourne. Rabiah had met Thomas when the couple attended Rahmah's wedding in Sydney. Maryati rang Rabiah a few months after the wedding to announce that the couple were going to 'do *haj*'.

'*Inshallah* I'll be able to go next year', Rabiah said.

'Why don't you come this year? It would be awesome if we could go together', Maryati suggested.

'I've saved enough money for myself to go, but I need enough for my son because I can't go alone. By next year I'll have enough for Mustafa to come with me.'

Maryati rang back a few days later.

'We want you to do *haj* with us. If you come with us, we'll pay for Mustafa.' It was a calculated act of generosity as Muslims believe that enabling someone else to make the pilgrimage will be specially rewarded by Allah.

Rabiah accepted their offer, then did some calculations of her own. She had wanted to do *haj* ever since converting to Islam. But for the same cost as two people taking the expensive package tour to Mecca, her entire family could travel abroad to live in an Islamic country. She rang Abu Bakar Ba'asyir in Indonesia to seek his advice on whether she should do *haj* or *hijrah*, migration for the sake of Islam. Ba'asyir gave the advice she wanted to hear: doing *haj* would benefit only her and Mustafa, while doing *hijrah* to a Muslim country would allow her whole family to reap rewards. Maryati was surprised by the change of plan, but Rabiah assured her that donating towards *hijrah* would also earn Allah's pleasure.

The children were startled when Rabiah came home from the travel agent with return tickets to Pakistan for herself, 14-year-old Mustafa, 12-year-old Ilyas, 10-year-old Aminah and her granddaughter Huda, now aged seven, who had been living with them since Egypt.

'But Mama, we don't have any money or anywhere to go. Where are we going? And what are we going to do?'

As always, Rabiah had a plan. They would travel to Peshawar to look up her old friend Umm Mohammed Azzam and reunite Huda with her father, who Rabiah believed was still in Pakistan. Rahmah and her husband Khaled would join them there later.

At this point Rabiah insists she had no thought of going to Afghanistan, where the black-turbaned zealots of the Taliban had swept to power three years before. 'I didn't support the Taliban at all. I had heard a lot of negative things—that they were beating women up, women had no rights, they weren't allowed to be educated. I thought they were a bunch of uneducated Afghans who had a very flawed concept of Islam and they were imposing it on the people of Afghanistan.'

12

A LETTER TO OSAMA

Afghanistan, 2000–2001

ATTENTION: ENTRY OF FOREIGNERS
IS PROHIBITED BEYOND THIS POINT

The big black lettering on the sign outside Peshawar hinted at the perils of the journey ahead, as a dilapidated taxi carrying Rabiah and the four children rattled along the Jamrud Road, west towards the Afghan border. Dawn broke and thin spirals of smoke rose from the roadside teashops and kebab stands as they drove past the Smugglers Bazaar and the vast squalor of the Kachagari refugee camp. As they entered the Khyber Agency, an autonomous tribal zone barred to foreigners except with an armed tribal escort, the guard at the checkpoint took a cursory glance and waved them through. The woman in the sky-blue *burka*, two girls in hijabs and a pair of swarthy youths in faded *shalwar kameez* must have looked like any Pashtun family.

On either side of the bumpy bitumen, vendors squatted beside pyramids of tomatoes and beckoned from stalls selling bottled water and guns; the sheep tails hanging in some stores signified hashish for sale. As the road ascended through the Suleiman Ranges, small stone forts and mudbrick Pashtun houses dotted the barren hillsides, dwarfed by the grand fortified compounds of opium and weapons smugglers. The girls gripped hands as they passed under the stone archway of the Jamrud Fort, a relic of a bygone Sikh empire, which marks the entrance to the legendary Khyber Pass.

The ribbon of tarmac—once reputedly so narrow that two fully laden camels could not pass abreast—climbed higher until they reached the final checkpost. After a muttered exchange of cigarettes and *baksheesh*, they were again waved on. Then, through the dusty windows of the taxi, a breathtaking vista spread out before them—the majestic Hindu Kush mountains enclosing the treacherous switchback leading to Afghanistan.

Rabiah clutched the children tightly and whispered, '*Inshallah* (God willing), today we will be going in'.

They had arrived in Peshawar a few months earlier—Rabiah; her two younger sons Mustafa and Ilyas, now aged fourteen and twelve; 10-year-old Aminah; and granddaughter Huda, aged seven. They were met by Huda's father, an Iraqi refugee who was now teaching Arabic at a Peshawar university. He had remarried and had three young children. He found Rabiah a downstairs apartment in a house owned by another Iraqi family in the old 'Afghan-Arab' enclave of Hayatabad. Rabiah enrolled the children to resume their studies at Abdullah Azzam's Al Ansar school, but when she went to look up her old friend Umm Mohammed Azzam, she discovered the jihad pioneer's widow had returned to her native Jordan and was not expected back for several months. Most of the people Rabiah had known in 'the first jihad' were also gone. When she got her son-in-law to drive her to Pabbi she found a ghost town, its mudbrick houses crumbling and taken over by Afghan refugees. In keeping with the ever-shifting realignments of Afghan politics, Pabbi's former patron, Sayyaf, had abandoned his old base to join forces with Ahmed Shah Massoud and the Northern Alliance and was now living in a modest compound outside Kabul.

While the politics had changed, there was a new buzz about Peshawar. Throughout the 1980s it had been the launching pad for the jihad against the Russians. Now it was the staging point for a new wave of would-be mujahidin, arriving to join the Taliban in Afghanistan.

'I got there and people were flocking into Afghanistan', says Rabiah. 'People were arriving constantly, weekly, from all over the world to cross over.' Rabiah maintains she was surprised. Her impression at this point was that the Taliban were a bunch of bearded hoodlums 'who wanted to keep Islam in the dark ages'.

There was intense debate in Peshawar about the kind of Islamic state the Taliban had enforced. The black-turbaned warriors had swept to power in 1996, to the initial relief of a populace brutalised and desperate after seven years of savage civil war between the rival mujahidin factions after the defeat of the Soviets. The puritanical *taliban* (students) raised in the *madrassas* along the Pakistan–Afghanistan border had vowed to restore security and order, based on Islamic law. As the Pakistani author Ahmed Rashid wrote:

> They saw themselves as the cleansers and purifiers of a guerrilla war gone astray, a social system gone wrong and an Islamic way of life that had been compromised by corruption and excess ... From their *madrassas*, they learnt about the ideal Islamic society created by the Prophet Mohammed 1,400 years ago and this is what they wanted to emulate.

And so they did, starting with the announcement on Radio Shariat: 'Thieves will have their hands and feet amputated, adulterers will be stoned to death, and those taking liquor will be lashed'.

The *muhajirin* (migrant) community of Peshawar was polarised—as was the broader jihadist movement—over the Taliban's draconian methods. Some had branded them 'Islamically deviant' and puppets of the Pakistani ISI (Inter Service Intelligence), which sponsored their meteoric rise. Others sympathised with their 'year zero' approach, and believed the excesses of their early years were short-term aberrations that would ultimately give way to the creation of a perfect Islamic state. Rabiah decided to go and find out for herself.

When her daughter Rahmah arrived in Peshawar, heavily pregnant and accompanied by her husband Khaled, they were stunned to learn that Rabiah had decided to 'go over the mountain'—local parlance for crossing into Afghanistan. Not long after their arrival Rahmah gave birth to a son named Zubair in Peshawar. From all that she and Khaled had heard, Afghanistan was no place to take a newborn baby. The infant mortality rate was 18 per cent, the highest in the world; a quarter of all children would die before their fifth birthday. Only 29 per cent of the population had access to health care, and only 12 per cent to safe water, so children were dying of preventable diseases such as measles and diarrhoea. Rahmah and Khaled refused to take their infant son to such a place. Rabiah was dismissive of their concerns and angrily announced she was taking the other children and going without them.

But getting to Afghanistan was no simple enterprise. The border was closed to foreigners. Only the tribal Pashtun—most of whom had no personal documents, let alone passports—were allowed to cross freely. Rabiah knew, however, that there was a well-worn route. Their Iraqi host put them in touch with a people smuggler who could make the arrangements for a fee of $200—whether or not they made it across.

When they arrived at the border crossing at Torkham, 58 kilometres west of Peshawar, the scene before them was bedlam—a jostling melee of heavily laden camels, donkeys, horse-drawn carts, ancient Mercedes buses, trucks belching diesel fumes, and a river of humanity on foot. Merchants hawked kebabs, tobacco, carpets, clothing and foodstuffs from a grimy metropolis of roadside stalls. Overhead, the trees and lampposts were festooned with garlands of black tape, ripped from music cassettes banned by the Taliban and confiscated on the spot from unwary travellers.

The border was marked by a crude metal archway over the road, and more signs in Urdu, Arabic and English: 'Warning—no foreigner is allowed beyond this point. Anyone passing will be prosecuted.' From raised platforms on either side, soldiers from the Pakistani Frontier Scouts with rifles slung over their shoulders scanned the crowd for anything out of the ordinary—such as foreigners attempting an illegal crossing.

Rabiah adjusted her *burka* and surveyed the scene from behind the blue mesh that concealed her eyes. She whispered a prayer and pulled Aminah's and Huda's hijabs tightly around their faces. Huda clung to her beloved teddy bear, which had been renamed Beniah and given a ribbon and a thatch of sewn-on woollen hair, after Huda decided she was too old to have a boy teddy. Mustafa and Ilyas unloaded their few bags and an Esky cooler carrying drinking water from the taxi. They would have to cross the frontier by foot.

'OK, we're going to split up now', Rabiah instructed them. 'Ilyas and Aminah, you walk ahead. Huda will come with me. Mustafa, you walk separately on the other side. And no matter what happens, don't look back. Even if one of us gets caught, you just keep walking.' Nervously they slipped into the crowd and walked to the crossing.

'I sent Ilyas and Aminah ahead, and I saw them cross', Rabiah remembers. 'Huda and I were just ahead of Mustafa. He was alone on the side.'

A moment later, Rabiah and Huda were through. A few steps behind them, Mustafa was about to cross when a Pakistani soldier, whose attention was apparently drawn by the large Esky he was carrying, singled him out. The soldier barked a question at him in Pashto, a language Mustafa didn't understand; he caught only the last word, 'Kabul'. Guessing that the guard was asking where he was going, Mustafa grunted 'Kabul' back. The guard was apparently satisfied and motioned him through.

On the Afghan side of the border they regrouped, Mustafa still sweating from his brush with capture, Rabiah and the girls weeping with sheer relief. Looming over them was an enormous sign in Arabic: 'May the peace and blessings of Allah be upon you. You have now safely entered the land of the Islamic Emirate of Afghanistan.'

'I'll never forget it, we stood there and the tears rolled down our faces', Rabiah recalls. 'You will never be able to put it down on paper, the feeling of crossing over and knowing that you had entered the place where you belonged. That was the best day of my life.'

From there they took another taxi to the city of Jalalabad, about 60 kilometres west of the border on the road to Kabul. Laid out in the sixteenth century as a winter resort for the aristocrats of the Mughal Empire, Jalalabad lies on the southern bank of the Kabul River on a fertile floodplain that irrigates a vivid patchwork of orange groves, rice fields and sugar cane. Rabiah had a friend from Peshawar who was now living in Jalalabad and had invited them to stay. 'I simply asked, "Where do the foreigners live?" And we were pointed in the right direction.'

Rabiah's friend, an Austrian woman known as Umm Sofia who was married to a Moroccan, lived in a compound of mudbrick houses surrounded by rice fields and connected by dusty alleyways, which turned into a muddy mire in the rain. There was no electricity or running water, and diseases such as cholera, typhoid and malaria were endemic. Rabiah loved it. 'Afghanistan was incredibly beautiful, it used to take my breath away. Every time I left the house, looking at the mountains and the rivers, I always felt the most breathtaking beauty. At night, standing on your roof and just looking up at the stars when there's no electricity, they were so bright it was like you could put your hand out and touch them. Or standing on your roof looking at the mountains covered in snow, it was breathtaking, I could feel it in my chest, my heart would expand.'

Jalalabad was home to a small cohort of Muslim émigrés from Europe, North America, the Middle East and Africa. Some were veterans of the jihad against the Russians; others were newcomers drawn by the utopian vision of an Islamic state. A few had followed Osama bin Laden when he relocated from Sudan to Afghanistan after the Taliban's rise to power. Bin Laden had moved to Afghanistan four years before, in 1996, after US pressure on the Sudanese government forced him from exile in Khartoum. After arriving by chartered jet with three wives (a fourth refused to accompany him to Afghanistan), innumerable children and a retinue of staff and fighters, he was given the use of a farm south of Jalalabad, where his followers set up tents for the wives and dug latrines and drainage ditches in a complex enclosed by barbed wire. By the time Rabiah arrived in Jalalabad, bin Laden's base had been deserted except for a handful of families whom she visited there once to treat a sick child. Bin Laden and his entourage had relocated to the desert city of Kandahar, headquarters of his Taliban hosts.

The foreign jihadists in Afghanistan still called themselves 'Afghan-Arabs', the term coined in the 1980s for those who joined the jihad against the Soviets. They regarded bin Laden as their *emir*. But according to Rabiah, most were there simply because they wanted to live in an Islamic state. 'I don't want anybody to read this book and think, who's she trying to kid—they're just nice, sweet, innocent people who reach out to the stars. People like me went through hardship that you can't imagine simply to live under Islam. The picture that's painted of Afghanistan is one of a seething mass of deranged people who went there because they wanted to take over the White House or stop people wearing bikinis on Bondi beach. It's absolutely ludicrous. We were normal people who lived normal lives and did normal things. Going to Afghanistan was not some diabolical plan to take over the world. It was simply a choice.'

In rural Jalalabad, which was populated largely by ethnic Pashtun accustomed to an austere tribal lifestyle, the transition to Taliban rule had been relatively calm. Unlike in cosmopolitan Kabul, there were no cane-wielding zealots from the Promoting Virtue and Preventing Vice squad patrolling the streets, lashing out at men caught with Western-style haircuts, or women who rode in taxis unaccompanied by a *mahram* (husband or male relative) as chaperone. In Jalalabad a more benign order prevailed. While the international community was denouncing the Taliban over practices the West deemed barbaric, in Rabiah's view it was just as an Islamic state should be. 'You walked out on the street, and there was nothing that offended you as a Muslim—no nakedness, no music, nothing that was forbidden. When you walked out on the street you were respected and men would avert their gaze. If there was a group of men talking on the street and they saw a woman approaching, they would move out of the way. It was where a Muslim belonged.'

Using a rudimentary kit she had brought from Australia and medicines imported from Pakistan, Rabiah set up a makeshift clinic in her friend Umm Sofia's home. Word got around that a new 'doctor' had arrived and women began turning up for treatment. As a result Rabiah was offered a house by the local Taliban leadership and work in the city's hospital, a Saudi-built facility that had been handsomely equipped but had long since run out of funds for maintenance or staff wages.

But Rabiah had no intention of making her Afghan home in Jalalabad. With no husband to support her, she needed to earn an income. The relatively affluent foreign population of Jalalabad was too small to support her and the native Afghans could not afford luxuries such as penicillin and anti-malarials. Moreover, the summer heat in Jalalabad was severe, and there was no school. On coming to power the Taliban had shut down schools across the country—boys and girls schools—claiming they had to introduce a segregated system and educate a new generation of teachers with proper Islamic training. The Afghan-Arabs had begun to open their own schools but there were none in Jalalabad and home-schooling the children was occupying most of Rabiah's time. Mustafa and Ilyas attended Quran lessons but spent most of their days swimming in the river, riding bikes and hunting snakes with their air rifles. To Rabiah, Jalalabad felt like a backwater, remote from the real work of building an Islamic state, which was being done in the political capital Kabul and the Taliban stronghold of Kandahar in the country's south.

Seeking guidance on how she could be most useful, Rabiah composed a letter to the *emir* of the Afghan-Arabs—her former benefactor in Pabbi, Osama bin Laden:

Dear brother, (*she wrote*)

I don't know if you remember me. My name is Umm Mohammed Australie. I used to live in Pabbi. I have now returned to Afghanistan and would like to continue my work in the medical field. I don't know whether it would be more beneficial for me to be in Kabul or Kandahar and I ask for your guidance.

Your sister in Islam,
Umm Mohammed Australie.

By 2000, when Rabiah penned her missive, bin Laden was no longer a mere humble supporter of the Afghan cause. Shortly after arriving in Afghanistan he had announced his Declaration of Jihad against the United States, followed in 1998 by the formation of the World Islamic Front for Jihad against the Jews and Crusaders. In February of that year he declared a *fatwah* decreeing it was the duty of all Muslims 'to fight and kill Americans and their allies, whether civilians or military'. He instructed his followers: 'Tear them to shreds. Destroy their economy, burn their companies, ruin their welfare, sink their ships, and kill them on land, sea and air.' Nine weeks later al Qaeda staged its first major attack, when simultaneous truck bombs destroyed the US embassies in Kenya and Tanzania, killing 224 people and injuring hundreds. In November 1998 bin Laden was indicted by a US Grand Jury on terrorism charges and a US$5 million bounty was placed on his head.

Rabiah claims that when she composed her letter to bin Laden, she was offering her services not to the accused terrorist, but to the benefactor and financier who had the funds and wherewithal to facilitate the creation of an Islamic state. 'The reason I wrote to Osama was because he was known as the leader and organiser of the Afghan-Arabs, it's as simple as that. It wasn't a case of "Osama, you are my leader, direct me to where I have to go". It was a case of how can I be most useful.'

She says she can't recall being aware at this stage that bin Laden had been blamed for the African embassy bombings. However, she does recall the cruise missile attacks carried out in retaliation by the United States, which killed sleeping villagers in Afghanistan and wiped out a medicine factory in Sudan, helping to transform bin Laden from a little-known jihadist into a popular hero throughout the Muslim world. Rabiah shared the widely held view of bin Laden as a courageous champion of oppressed Muslims, standing up to the West. 'There is a *hadith* that says the greatest jihad is speaking the word of truth to a tyrannical leader—that's how I saw the declaration of war that Osama made. I saw it as a warning to the United States.'

Rabiah gave her letter to a 'sister' in the Afghan-Arab community whose husband presumably arranged for it to be forwarded to Kandahar. A fortnight later, bin Laden's response arrived. She doesn't recall whether it came in the form of a letter or simply a message, but the gist of it was this:

> Yes, sister. I remember you. Welcome to Afghanistan. My advice to you if you want to open a clinic is that you will probably find Kabul is the best place for you to go, because the majority of Afghan-Arabs are there and would benefit from what you want to do.

241

Within days of receiving bin Laden's reply, Rabiah and the children were in another battered taxi lurching along the treacherous gash of highway carved through the peaks of the Hindu Kush. In the 1970s when Afghanistan was a leg on the hippy trail that took Western backpackers from India to Europe, the journey from Jalalabad to Kabul took two and a half hours. But two decades of war had pounded the route to rubble, and in 2000 the trip took five times that long. Old men and boys with shovels waited by the roadside to heap mounds of gravel into the gaping holes in the road, in return for a few coins thrown from the windows of passing cars. 'That's a journey I wouldn't wish on my worst enemy', Rabiah recounts. 'It's not a road with potholes, it's potholes with a road—and I'm talking about craters. The road was as wide as this carpet (indicating a modest rug in her Lakemba home) and if you looked out the window, the door of the taxi was almost level with the edge of the cliff, and there was a drop of thousands of metres to the bottom of the valley. That was scary. That's when you know if God has written that you are going to die— because if he hasn't, then you survive that road.'

Their destination in Kabul was the home of an Iraqi family whom Rabiah had known in her Pabbi days when their children had been classmates at Abdullah Azzam's Al Ansar school. They stayed with this family until they found what passed for a home of their own; a vacant house in the relatively new suburb of Karti Parwan that had been evacuated and apparently ransacked amidst the civil chaos in Kabul. The windows had been smashed and the doors jemmied off their frames. There was no electricity or running water but there was a well in the yard, and Rabiah sent the boys out to collect discarded plastic sheets and hessian bags that she used to seal the windows. For Rabiah it brought back fond memories of her dirt-floored childhood home at Wollar, but her children found little to relish in their new circumstances. Petite Aminah was distraught, recalling later, 'If it was left to me I'd just sit in a corner and cry till someone took me out of here'.

Their street in Karti Parwan was home to a cluster of foreign families who had congregated in Kabul since the Taliban's takeover. Among them was an Egyptian-Canadian aid organiser, Ahmed Khadr, known by his *kuniya* as Abu Abdurahman al Kanadi ('the Canadian'). Khadr was a well-known figure in jihadist circles, and now became Rabiah's patron in Kabul.

Khadr had grown up in Egypt but migrated to Canada in his twenties to study computer programming at the University of Ottawa, where he obtained a masters degree. After the Soviet invasion of Afghanistan he travelled to Pakistan to work as a volunteer in the Afghan refugee camps, joining a Canadian-based charity in Peshawar, Human Concern International. In the mid 1980s Khadr and his wife Maha Elsamneh moved their family to Peshawar, but returned regularly to Canada to raise funds for their projects, which included a hospital in Afghanistan, seven medical clinics in the refugee camps and an orphanage for 400 children called 'Hope Village'.

In Peshawar, Khadr worked with al Qaeda co-founders Abdullah Azzam and Osama bin Laden, and became a close friend and ally of bin Laden's eventual deputy, the Egyptian doctor Ayman al Zawahiri, who was working at the Red Crescent hospital where Khadr's wife also worked as a volunteer. Khadr would later be described as a 'founding member' of al Qaeda. However, most accounts suggest the politics of the jihad was not his first interest. A journalist who met Khadr at this time described him as 'a man of respect' who seemed 'entirely humanitarian and not ideological at all'. Khadr was arrested in 1995 after his son-in-law was linked to a bombing at the Egyptian embassy in Pakistan. Khadr was charged with aiding terrorism but investigators admitted they 'did not have much evidence' against him, and under pressure from the Canadian government Pakistan dropped the charges and released him.

Rabiah had first met the Khadr family in Peshawar while she and they were living in Hayatabad in 1994, and their children were all attending Abdullah Azzam's school. Inspired by Umm Mohammed Azzam's 'house of sewing', Khadr's wife, Maha, had set up her own charity for Afghan war widows, providing sewing machines and fabric so they could earn an income making quilts and clothing.

After the rise of the Taliban, the 'Kanadis' shifted to Jalalabad where Khadr established an orphanage for Afghan boys. His family moved into the bin Laden compound where Khadr's daughter Zaynab played with bin Laden's girls while their brothers rode horses. Khadr's sons were later sent for military training in an al Qaeda camp; one of them, Abdurahman, testified in a subsequent court case in Canada that the intention was not to 'go after America' but to defend Islamic countries from attack.

When bin Laden moved to Kandahar, the Khadr family shifted to Karti Parwan in Kabul, from where Khadr ran his new charity, Health and Education Projects International, which built wells, schools and orphanages. Rabiah was especially drawn to the Khadr women, who were oddities like herself. 'None of the Arab women worked. The only ones I knew who worked were me, the wife of Ahmed Khadr, and Zaynab, his daughter.' Zaynab was a strong-willed twenty-one year old who wanted to study medicine and wouldn't leave men's work to the men, by Rabiah's account. 'I remember once in Kabul we were trying to light the *bukhar* (stove), and we didn't know the pipe that takes the smoke out was blocked. Zaynab threw petrol in, and the fire exploded outwards and burned off her eyebrows.'

Rabiah's family often visited the Khadr family's home. On one occasion the Khadr boys invited her sons to watch a DVD of the Hollywood blockbuster *King Kong*, which would certainly not have been deemed *halal* (permissible) by the Taliban.

'Why are you letting your children watch that rubbish?' Rabiah demanded of Ahmed Khadr.

'Give me an Islamic reason why they shouldn't', Khadr replied.

'Because it's *shirk* (disbelief). What is this—a giant gorilla saves the world? It should be Allah that saves the world!'

Ahmed Khadr laughed. 'Yeah, yeah, Umm Mohammed. It's just imagination. It's not reality. If they're not allowed to use their imaginations, how can they tell the difference between what's real and what's imagined?'

Rabiah couldn't fault his explanation, but in her household *King Kong* remained *haram* (forbidden).

Under the auspices of Khadr's Health and Education Projects International (HEP), Rabiah began work on a range of proposals, such as the construction of wells for fresh drinking water and a medical clinic to be set up in a new girls school that the Khadrs were planning to open near Kabul, despite the Taliban's objections.

Khadr gave Rabiah a letter of introduction; or, to be more precise, he gave her a blank letterhead and she later filled it in herself:

To whom it may concern,

Subject: Employment with HEP

This is to certify that Ms Rabiah Hutchinson is working as a medical officer in HEP's Afghanistan Program. Her duty includes:
- co-ordinating HEP Medical Programs
- liaising with other NGOs and government departments
- representing HEP in all designated tasks, e.g. Public Education, Fund Raising, etc.

We request that you extend all possible assistance to facilitate her assignment.

(Signed:) Mr A Khadr, Director

Ahmed Khadr was by this stage well known to the international authorities, because of his connections with al Qaeda and his channelling of funds to Afghanistan. In 1999 the British government urged the United Nations to add Khadr's name to a list of individuals believed to finance terrorism. American prosecutors would later allege that some of the money raised in Canada—which Khadr's son estimated at C$70 000—was used to support military facilities such as al Qaeda's Khalden training camp. Abdurahman Khadr testified that clothes and medicine bought with donated money were sent to the Khalden camp, but denied his father's charity financed military training.

Ahmed Khadr was killed in the aftermath of September 11 when Pakistani security forces attacked a safehouse where he was staying in the tribal zone of South Waziristan in October 2003. One of his sons, Abdul Karim, was shot in the spine and paralysed. Another son, Omar, was captured in a separate raid by American forces and accused of throwing a grenade that killed a US serviceman, although documents released by the Pentagon showed there was no proof that it was he who threw the grenade. Fifteen years old when he was captured, Omar Khadr was later transferred to Guantánamo Bay where he was detained for more than six years, charged with war crimes and supporting terrorism. At the beginning of 2009, he was reportedly the youngest detainee still being held at Guantánamo Bay.

Rabiah rejects the assertion that her patron Ahmed Khadr was an 'al Qaeda financer' as accused. 'I had access to that money. It was not "al Qaeda financing". It was for building orphanages and clinics and wells. Anyone who had a project, they would finance it.'

In late 2000 the Khadrs were about to leave on an extended trip to Peshawar, and invited Rabiah and her family to stay in their Karti Parwan home in their absence. Rabiah and the children moved in after Khadr and his wife Maha left for Peshawar. Their daughter Zaynab was still in the house, preparing to travel to Peshawar separately with her daughter Sofia, who was about ten months old. However, their plans were thrown into confusion when Rabiah noticed that the child had a serious medical problem.

'As soon as I saw the little girl I knew there was something wrong', she says. 'She had an enlarged head. The family didn't know there was anything wrong with her. The grandmother said, "It's hereditary, big heads run in the family". But I could tell by the circumference of her head that the actual growth was above the eye sockets. It wasn't just a big head, it was abnormal growth in particular areas of the head.'

Rabiah believed Sofia had either a tumour or fluid on the brain. She knew that neither tests nor treatment for these were available in Afghanistan. The child would have to be taken abroad. On her advice, Zaynab took the baby to a Peshawar paediatrician who diagnosed fluid on the brain and recommended extensive tests, a biopsy and surgery.

'When the family got back, we spoke about it and I decided I thought it would be better for them to take the child to Canada', says Rabiah. This was problematic as Zaynab and Sofia would have to fly to Canada alone without a *mahram* (husband or male relative) to escort them. Zaynab was divorced from her husband, and the family now feared that Khadr and his sons might be detained if they set foot on Canadian soil. Normally Zaynab would be forbidden from travelling alone. But the family believed the urgency of the child's condition warranted an exception and resolved to seek a ruling from an Islamic cleric to that effect.

First they decided to get a second medical opinion. The opinion they sought was that of Ahmed Khadr's friend and fellow Egyptian, Dr Ayman al Zawahiri, Osama bin Laden's personal physician and key lieutenant, who was regarded in al Qaeda circles as a 'medical genius'. A conference was arranged at the Khadr family's home so that Rabiah could brief Zawahiri on the child's condition. Zawahiri is described elsewhere as a 'cerebral, taciturn man in his early fifties, his face framed by heavy glasses, a beard and a white turban'. In keeping with Salafi practice, Rabiah did not see his face.

'When he came, I was behind a curtain and he was on the other side. Some of the women sat with me, and some men sat with him', she recalls. Their meeting lasted about ten minutes, with Zawahiri speaking polished English throughout. 'He was very professional and soft-spoken. We spoke about the case and he agreed with my findings.'

Rabiah was well aware that Zawahiri was no ordinary doctor. 'Of course I knew who he was—everyone knew who he was. By this time there had already been an amalgamation of (his organisation) al Jihad with al Qaeda and he had taken the *bai'at* to Osama bin Laden.' It was Zawahiri who had penned the 1998 *fatwah* authorising the killing of Americans and their allies, which heralded the onset of al Qaeda's war on the West. However, on this occasion and for Rabiah's purpose, he was simply a doctor—and a real one, at that.

'I remember him saying something like, "Umm Mohammed, I think you have more expertise than I in this field"', says Rabiah. 'I remember being really embarrassed—he was a real doctor and I was a fake one, but he was treating me as if I was a colleague. I felt like digging a hole and burying myself.' At the end of their discussion, Zawahiri endorsed Rabiah's view that the child should be taken to North America for treatment. The family obtained the required religious ruling and Zaynab left soon afterwards with Sofia for Canada.

Rabiah's conferral with Ayman al Zawahiri cemented her status as a trusted insider in the jihadist elite, whose expertise was valued and sought by the Taliban and al Qaeda. The Taliban regime now provided her and her family with their own house in Karti Parwan, in a tree-lined street with open drains and turbaned vendors squatting in the dust selling plump oranges from wooden carts. The house was a former colonial-era three-storey mansion, commandeered by the Taliban and divided into apartments. Whatever grandeur it might once have possessed had long since faded, its walls now pockmarked with shell holes and the scars of automatic rifle fire and most of its windows smashed, although the interior still boasted 6-metre-high ceilings and black-and-white chequerboard ceramic tiles on the bathroom floor. It was occupied by three families of Taliban sympathisers and known among its neighbours as 'Beit al Arab'—the house of Arabs. As in the 1980s, any foreigner who came to join the jihad was automatically classed as 'Arab'.

'Someone had gone to the Taliban and said, "There's this woman who's come from Australia, she's a single mother, she's a *muhajir*, she has four kids, she needs somewhere to stay"', says Rabiah. 'I was given a house, not because I was some important terrorist on the al Qaeda hierarchy but because it's Islamic law. I was a *muhajir*. I was a woman alone with children who had left wherever I was for the sake of Allah, and it was incumbent upon them to house me.'

Rabiah and the four children were allotted five rooms for themselves, palatial compared to much that they were used to, as well as use of the third-storey rooftop, which afforded scenic views of the city and mountains. 'In winter you could see the snow-covered mountains all the way to the Hindu Kush, it was absolutely beautiful', Rabiah recalls.

In the back garden were fruit trees whose branches were festooned with magnetic tape ripped from videocassettes seized by the Taliban. Nearby was a pile of television sets that had been confiscated and smashed, leaving empty shells the smaller children liked to climb into and play at being actors on television, to the delight of those who sat around watching. Another television set dangled from the branch of a tree. Rabiah found all this funny and thought the tape in the trees looked 'pretty' as it glittered in the sunlight. Not so amusing was a dank, spider-infested cellar under the house, which was said to have been used as a prison by the Taliban when they first swept to power. Graffiti were daubed in blood on the walls: 'May Allah forgive me'; and next to it, scrawled in another hand, 'There is no Allah'.

Because it was in 'a good area', the house had electricity for about four hours a day but the current was so weak that in the evenings it flickered like candlelight. Sometimes when they switched on the Soviet-era washing machine, it would merely groan and refuse to operate, as Rabiah recalls. 'You were always getting electrocuted, you'd put your hand on it and "zzt!" It was quite common that there would be no on-off switch and no plug on the electricity cord. You would just poke the cord with the wires sticking out of into the wall.' They had a pump known as a 'sanyo' (whether or not it was that Japanese brand) to pump water from an underground well to a tank on the roof that fed taps in the kitchen. But the water was so rank it could only be used for washing and cooking. The boys had to travel half an hour by taxi with jerry cans twice a week to get drinking water from a spring outside Kabul.

Rabiah made curtains and matching bedspreads and bought wooden bases to keep their mattresses out of the dust, and they soon settled in. 'We were there in that house for a year. Apart from the hardship of living in one of the poorest places on Earth, it was like when you get off a plane in Australia and think, it's good to be home—that's how we felt about Afghanistan. It was the place where we belonged. We forgot who we were for a while. Immigrants should never forget that that's what they are. I broke a rule, an unwritten rule, that a *muhajir* doesn't ever settle down.'

Rabiah set up a basic medical clinic in a room of the house to cater to the 'Arab' community of Kabul, which she says numbered more than one thousand families. She did pregnancy tests, checkups and pre-natal care, using a Doppler she had brought from Australia to monitor the unborn babies' heartbeats. She prescribed and dispensed treatments for diarrhoea, malaria, cholera, hepatitis and gastric diseases, all of which were endemic in Kabul. 'I became a very good diagnostician, but I was very aware of my limitations', she says. 'If I didn't know what was wrong or they needed a consultation or a follow-up with a real doctor, I would take them. I would always refer things that I didn't know about, or if they needed specialist attention.'

When Rabiah's pregnant patients were ready to deliver she accompanied them to the Saj Gul women's hospital, a grimy sprawl of cement-block buildings south of the Kabul River. She doubled as translator for many of the Arab women who spoke neither English nor Dari, and frequently delivered the babies herself. The hospitals were starved of funds and supplies, but the relatively affluent foreigners could afford to bring their own, and Rabiah would brief them ahead of time: 'Right, you've got to have an operation tomorrow. You have to bring three packets of gauze, a saline drip, a canula, and a bottle of Savlon.' At one point she had to go into hospital herself for an appendectomy. The conditions were so gruesome that when the time came to have her stitches out she refused to go back, instead giving her granddaughter Huda a scalpel, tweezers and step-by-step instructions on suture removal.

The foreigners known as 'the Arabs' formed an exclusive society of their own, which held itself largely aloof from the broader Afghan community, reflecting tensions that dated back to the jihad against the Russians. Many Afghans resented the intrusion of these 'Wahhabis' with their alien dogma, language and customs, while the newcomers, especially those from Middle Eastern countries, often looked down on the Afghans as peasants with an inferior understanding of Islam. Rabiah was annoyed by this divide and mostly blamed the Arabs for failing to appreciate their Afghan hosts.

Later, during the 'war on terror', the people who called themselves 'Afghan-Arabs' in Afghanistan in this period would be classified *en masse* as 'al Qaeda'. The reality is somewhat less clearcut. They were certainly close to al Qaeda, but not necessarily al Qaeda members themselves, and not necessarily involved in bin Laden's jihad against the West. 'The majority of people we knew weren't al Qaeda—whatever "al Qaeda" is supposed to be', says Rabiah. 'They weren't opposed to it, but they weren't necessarily a part of it. They were just people who had gone to live in an Islamic state. Would they have fought? Most definitely—fought to hang on to what they had achieved. And anyone who was willing to fight was immediately labelled "al Qaeda".'

Since the jihad against the Russians, the Afghan-Arabs had looked to bin Laden as their *emir*. But not all of them supported his *fatwah* against the United States and its allies, which was a source of much consternation among them. Some were all for it, while others saw it as a potentially suicidal diversion from their article of faith—achieving Islamic law—and lobbied strongly against it. Many sympathised with bin Laden's vendetta but had no personal stake or involvement in it. Rabiah's view—as she states it (and in two years of research I have found nothing to disprove this)— was that the jihad against America was 'Osama's war'. She had some sympathy for it, but regarded it as a quite separate undertaking from her own quest to help build an Islamic state. Like all the Afghan-Arabs, notwithstanding their differences, she admired bin Laden's dedication and relied on his largesse. 'I don't know anyone who opposed him', she says. 'What was there to oppose? He was building roads, and the school—he probably paid for half of it. No one was against Osama, there was nothing to be against.'

By the time Rabiah arrived in Kabul, the Arabs had established their own school, funded by bin Laden and run on a Saudi curriculum. The Abu Bakr school catered only for boys but a girls school soon opened as well, named after the Prophet's first wife Khadija and situated in the former embassy district of Wazir Akhbar Khan, where entire streets of former diplomatic missions had been taken over by the Taliban and al Qaeda. The school went from kindergarten to year ten and pupils attended six days a week, studying a mixture of secular and Islamic subjects. After months of studying at home, Aminah and Huda were delighted to be back at school. 'It was so exciting, the girls were so happy', Rabiah remembers. Huda, who had her grandmother's bent for mischief, earned the ire of the school authorities by encouraging her entire class of 9-year-old girls to climb a large tree in the schoolyard, barefoot except for their mandatory white socks, which became caked in mud and tree bark.

The school was established by a group of women in Rabiah's circle who called themselves the 'women's committee' of the *muhajirin*. The committee—of which Rabiah says she was 'too busy' to be a member— also arranged classes for the women to study the Quran, *hadith* and Islamic law. Rabiah herself took charge of a class on *tafsir* (interpreting the Quran) for the English-speaking women. The committee had had to lobby bin

Laden to secure funds for the school, as Rabiah recalls. 'Sheikh Osama thought that all the girls could study to year six and that would be enough, because he felt that by year six they'd have command of the Arabic language, enough to bring up their children and learn about Islam.' This was apparently not bin Laden's blanket opinion on education for women, but his view on what was appropriate in Afghanistan at the time. However, the women's committee vehemently disagreed. (Bin Laden's own wives probably disagreed with him too; one of them had a PhD in child psychology, while another had a doctorate in Arabic grammar.) The women resolved to persuade bin Laden he was wrong. As Rabiah tells it: 'One of the older women marched over there and said it was ridiculous, what was he thinking? If all the women only studied to year six—what about doctors? Dentists? Teachers?' Bin Laden was reportedly persuaded and the girls school was extended as far as year twelve.

Bin Laden and his wives lived in the desert city of Kandahar and rarely ventured to Kabul. (Contrary to a report that Rabiah was the midwife for one of his babies, she says she never met or treated any of bin Laden's wives.) However, stories of the Sheikh's benevolence, humility and ascetic lifestyle were swapped eagerly among the women in Kabul. It was said that each Friday bin Laden would gather his wives around him and ask if any of them had a complaint about how he was treating them. The al Qaeda women would roll their eyes and bemoan their own husbands' lack of such consideration. There were stories of how bin Laden would not allow his children to drink refrigerated water for fear it would 'soften' them—Rabiah adopted the same habit—and of how, when he was travelling, he would insist that his elderly Afghani cook sleep in a bed while he slept with only a blanket on the bare floor of his tent. At the festival of Eid al Fitr, which marks the end of Ramadan, bin Laden would send a live sheep to every family so they could celebrate the feast. He had done the same thing in Pabbi, according to Rabiah.

'Osama would buy a truckload of sheep and send them around to people like me. I think I ended up with about three. I didn't want to kill them, they were so cute. But my son convinced me they wanted to sacrifice themselves for Allah.'

The women's circle in Kabul included at least one al Qaeda lumi-
nary—the wife of Dr Ayman al Zawahiri, whose name was Azza Nowair,
though her friends called her Umm Fatima. She was the daughter of a
wealthy Egyptian clan and a philosophy student at Cairo University where
Zawahiri studied medicine. They married at Cairo's Continental-Savoy
Hotel and later had five children, including a girl with Down syndrome.
Umm Fatima was a member of the women's committee that had established the new school, and a trusted friend to Rabiah.

'Umm Fatima was an amazing woman and the epitome of a lady',
Rabiah says. 'She was very intelligent, she was funny, very dry humour,
and always positive. She could be speaking to a group of women, and she
had this uncanny ability to make you feel she was speaking directly
to you.'

Zawahiri and Umm Fatima lived in an expansive but run-down
colonial-era manse—probably a former diplomatic house—in the embassy
quarter of Wazir Akhbar Khan. They shared the house with another family
who lived in the section upstairs. The house had double-glass doors that
opened onto an overgrown English garden, but like most of the Arab
houses it was virtually empty inside. Rabiah recalls that the Zawahiris were
the only Arabs in Kabul with security guards. (After the al Qaeda bombing of the American warship USS *Cole* in Yemen in October 2000, bin
Laden separated his key leaders so that in the event of an American attack
they could not all be eliminated at once. His military chief, Mohammed
Atef, was moved to another location in Kandahar, while his deputy
Zawahiri was headquartered in Kabul.)

Zawahiri was never there when Rabiah visited Umm Fatima at home.
She remembers arriving on one occasion to find her friend dressed 'the
way Arab women usually dress up when their husbands are at home—like
how Western women dress when they go out'.

'Is your husband home?' Rabiah asked in surprise.

'No', Umm Fatima sighed.

'Are you expecting him?'

'I always expect him.'

'That must be hard. If he doesn't come, don't you get disappointed?'

'Well I guess I'd rather have him not come and be disappointed, than have him come and find me looking like something the cat dragged in.'

Like many in their circle, Umm Fatima was perturbed at Rabiah's marital status. Rabiah was a woman of forty-seven with six children. Being unmarried was considered an unnatural state, which detracted from one's practice of Islam. Rabiah's friends were constantly trying to rectify the anomaly, and Zawahiri's wife raised it at one of their get-togethers.

'There is someone interested in marrying you', Umm Fatima announced.

Rabiah laughed. 'I'm too old for that sort of thing.'

'Don't be ridiculous, Umm Mohammed. You and I are the same age and I'm certainly not too old for it!'

Rabiah politely rejected the advance. She still wonders who her friend had in mind.

* * *

We are opposed to the Taliban because of their opposition to human rights and their despicable treatment of women and children and great lack of respect for human dignity.

US Secretary of State, Madeleine Albright, 18 November 1997

Initially welcomed by the international community as a force for stability, the Taliban had swiftly become a pariah regime, denounced by Western governments and subjected to United Nations sanctions, principally because of its stance on education, the treatment of women and—increasingly—its protection of the fugitive bin Laden.

On coming to power, the Taliban had declared, 'We want to live a life like the Prophet lived 1,400 years ago … We want to recreate the time of the Prophet.' And so they banned television, music, videos, cards, chess, football, high heels, the shaving of beards, flying of kites and keeping pigeons. Women were banned from working except in the medical field and from leaving their homes without being covered in a *burka*. A Taliban decree explained that 'Islam as a rescuing religion has determined specific dignity for women', while the governor of Herat announced: 'We have given women their rights that God and his Messenger have instructed, that is to stay in their homes and to gain religious instruction in hijab'. (The word *hijab* is used here to mean 'seclusion'.)

After capturing Kabul, the Taliban had shut down 63 schools, affecting 103 000 girls and 148 000 boys. By December 1998 UNICEF reported that nine in ten girls and two in three boys were not enrolled in school. (Most of the boys in school were attending religious *madrassas*.) The Taliban leadership claimed it would reopen schools once a segregated system was in place, because 'women must be completely segregated from men'. By 1999, schools had begun reopening, mostly in rural areas. A Western aid agency reported that 30 000 female students were enrolled at 600 schools it sponsored, and that 'there are parts of rural areas in Afghanistan today, where there are more girls in school than ever before in Afghan history'. Education for girls still ended at the age of twelve.

For Rabiah, the hardships of life under the Taliban were simply part of the sacrifices required to build an Islamic state. The restrictions that others found unbearably oppressive were for her a minor inconvenience at worst. She was quite comfortable going about veiled, and as a 'medical officer' she was exempt from the ban on women working. She regarded the regime's brutal enforcement as the somewhat overzealous application of means to a worthy end.

'There are many things the Taliban were doing that were wrong, for example walking around with bamboo sticks and if they saw someone smoking giving them a good whack—that was not practised in the time of the Prophet. Some of the Taliban were illiterate farmers who couldn't read or write; they were just Afghans who put on black turbans, and often what was implemented was the footsoldiers' interpretation. That's what the Western press picked up on—people who did things that were unacceptable. But it was not something I saw as a major problem because it was temporary.'

Rabiah saw the Taliban's Afghanistan as the embryo of an Islamic state, which would necessarily be perfect once it was in place. To that end, she had no problem with the severe *hudud* laws, which provided for the stoning of adulterers and severing of the hands of thieves. She believed simply that these were punishments prescribed by God and therefore must be enforced. And she saw definite upsides to the Taliban's rough justice and its enforcement of women's 'rights'.

'What was evident in the time of the Taliban was how much safer it was, and how much more women were respected. Previously women couldn't even walk from A to B without fear of being raped or kidnapped or killed. They wouldn't even go to the markets. In the time of the Taliban, all that disappeared.' She was not alone in this view. A Swedish aid worker reported to a conference on Afghanistan held in Stockholm in 1999: 'The majority of Afghans south of Kabul would most probably agree that the Taliban, although not as popular today as when they came, are better for the people, their security and welfare, compared to what was there before them and that there is no real alternative but anarchy'.

However, after five years of Taliban rule, Afghanistan remained a humanitarian disaster zone. It had the largest refugee population in the world with 3.6 million people displaced. Renewed fighting and a long drought had destroyed 70 per cent of the country's livestock and half its arable land, leaving people in some areas reportedly eating grass and rats, or selling their daughters for food. Its plight was compounded by sanctions imposed on the Taliban for harbouring bin Laden. The United Nations and many Western NGOs had shut down or curtailed their aid programs in protest at the Taliban's policies towards women. Islamic NGOs such as Ahmed Khadr's Health and Education Projects were left to fill the void—which they did with unconcealed disdain for the UN.

'They used to live in air-conditioned compounds and drive around in $40 000 four-wheel drives which they had trucked in', says Rabiah. 'Their wages were astronomical. They had a whole street of shops—they called it Supermarket Street—where they sold Rice Bubbles, Worcestershire sauce, toilet paper and bottled water. With the amount of money the UN had, you could have rebuilt Afghanistan fifty times.'

Rabiah worked closely with the Taliban regime, mainly through the Public Health Minister Mohammed Abbas, an English-speaker whom she met in hospital while having her appendix out. Like many of his govern-ment colleagues, Abbas had little time for his ministerial work. The Taliban was still fighting to defeat Ahmed Shah Massoud's Northern Alliance, and Abbas was a member of the military *shura* (council) and thus was needed on the battlefield. The aid workers who dealt with him found he would dis-appear on military duties for months at a time, then return to resume his supervision of the country's appalling health system. Rabiah proposed to Abbas that she would teach English to the female hospital staff, and then enlist them in voluntary literacy programs to promote the education of women and girls. She says the curriculum she began devising drew Abbas's enthusiasm because it would also include a course in Islamic studies, based on the Taliban's preferred Hanafi school of jurisprudence. Rabiah says her role as an 'honorary doctor' gave her easy access to the powers that be. 'I could see the directors of hospitals whenever I wanted to, and through them I could submit proposals to the Taliban. I would initiate projects, raise funds, try to get support for them. I didn't actually work "for" the Taliban—I didn't work for anybody. There were lots of aid agencies doing projects. If you put up a proposal and a plan you could get funding.'

Despite the withdrawal of most Western NGOs in protest at the Taliban's policies, there were still funds available from other sources. The Saudi charity Al Haramein—which was later listed by the UN as an affiliate of al Qaeda—approached Rabiah to establish a state-of-the-art medical clinic. Separately a Libyan group proposed that she help set up a new hos-pital. However, both projects were for the Afghan-Arabs rather than the Afghan people, and Rabiah opposed the idea of a two-tiered service that would provide superior health care for the well-heeled immigrants while leaving the Afghan system destitute. She calculated that if every Arab family donated US$10 per month, they could raise enough to transform the standard of care for foreigners and Afghans alike. 'Instead of the Arabs having their own hospital, which was what tended to happen, I wanted to have them pay their money to utilise the existing facility, so they would be entitled to a better standard of care, but the money would then go back into the hospital and would raise the level of care for the Afghans too. Otherwise, what were we giving back to Afghanistan? Sure, we were *maymon* (guests), but were we going to remain guests forever? And isn't it one of the principles of setting up an Islamic state that it belongs to all Muslims regardless of race, colour or economic disposition?'

For Rabiah, Afghanistan was not a desperate basketcase, but a perfect society in the making. She had finally found the place where she felt she truly belonged and could play a useful and valued role. She was so sure of this that she planned to apply for Afghan citizenship as soon as the Taliban started issuing passports to foreigners.

Little did she know that life in Afghanistan was about to be turned upside down. In these months before September 2001, Rabiah and her cohorts lived an insular life, largely cut off from the outside world, and either oblivious or in stubborn denial about the historic tide that was about to overtake them. 'It was very easy to shut out the outside world—we had no television, no internet, no telephone. We used to get an English newspaper once a week from Pakistan, and sometimes the *Times* magazine. It was really your own world. It was easy to forget about all the hostility to Afghanistan, that there were people who'd like nothing more than to wipe it off the face of the Earth. We were always aware Afghanistan could be attacked at any time, my son was always reminding me, but I chose to forget it.'

* * *

In March 2001, Rabiah was at home in Karti Parwan when an unexpected visitor showed up. It was mid morning and she had gone next door to a neighbour's house to listen to a favourite CD of Quran recitations. The rhythmic chanting was suddenly interrupted by a loud voice in the street outside: 'Yeah, I think this is the one!' a man with an unmistakeable Australian twang was calling out.

'I thought I was going mad—I could hear this Aussie accent', Rabiah recounts. 'And I thought, I know that voice.'

The house's windows were painted white on the inside in keeping with a Taliban edict to ensure women could not be seen through the windows of their homes. Rabiah scratched a hole in the white paint and peered down at the street. There, conversing loudly with an Afghani taxi driver, was Jack 'Jihad' Thomas, the husband of her Indonesian friend Maryati.

'I looked out through this little bit of paint I'd scratched off, and there was Jack in one of those hats, singing out at the top of his voice— I could not believe my eyes.' Thomas was wearing an Afghani *pakul*, the large flat cloth hat that had once been de rigueur for aspiring mujahidin. 'In the first jihad everyone wore them. But in the time of the Taliban they were the hats that Ahmed Shah Massoud and the Northern Alliance wore, and no one in their right mind would wear one in Kabul. How he didn't get himself killed I'll never know.'

Rabiah went up to the rooftop to find her sons.

'Mustafa, Aamu (uncle) Jihad is outside!'

'Who?'

'You know, Aamu Jihad—Maryati's husband. And you'd better get him off the street because he's got a Massoudi hat on and he's screaming at the top of his voice.'

When they brought him inside, Thomas explained that Maryati and their baby daughter were waiting in Pakistan. His plan was to go back and get them and bring them to stay with Rabiah and her family in Kabul. (Thomas had stopped on his way in Jalalabad and met Rabiah's patron Ahmed Khadr, who presumably provided directions to her house.)

'You can't stay with me because I'm a woman alone', Rabiah told Thomas.

'What are you talking about? We've come all this way to show you the baby!'

'OK, go back and get Maryati and I promise I'll find you somewhere to stay.'

When Thomas returned with his wife and daughter, Rabiah arranged for them to stay at a Turkish guesthouse nearby. Thomas was still offended that after travelling across the world from Australia they were seemingly not welcome in their friend's home. 'Jack didn't get it. He wasn't impressed. He thought I'd disrespected them', says Rabiah.

A naive adventurer from the western suburbs of Melbourne, Thomas was eager to fight with the Taliban, to help fortify the new Afghan Islamic state. At this stage the Taliban controlled 90 per cent of the country but Massoud's Northern Alliance, which was bolstered by Western backing, had stubbornly clung to its stronghold in the Panjshir Valley, north of Kabul, where fighting continued. Rabiah wrote a letter to vouch for Thomas and introduced him to one of her neighbours, who Thomas says was a commander with the Taliban at Bagram and 'seemed to know Osama bin Laden'. Thomas was dispatched to al Qaeda's Camp Faruq near Kandahar for the three-month beginners training course, which was mandatory for foreign volunteers. His wife and daughter stayed with Rabiah while he was away. After completing his training, Thomas visited Kandahar to seek assistance with accommodation and living costs for his family. He met with bin Laden's lieutenant, Dr Ayman al Zawahiri, to ask his advice on obtaining work in Afghanistan. Zawahiri suggested he apply to Ahmed Khadr for a job at his orphanage.

During their meeting, Zawahiri took the opportunity to ask Thomas about his friend Umm Mohammed Australie. The al Qaeda deputy and chief physician had an important project, which he needed to delegate to a skilled and trusted woman.

'They wanted to organise a women's hospital', Thomas later explained, and Zawahiri wanted Rabiah to run it. The first Rabiah learned of this proposition was when she received a message from her friend Umm Fatima, Zawahiri's wife.

'She sent a message for me to come and visit her. When I got there she said they wanted to build a hospital in Kandahar, and her husband had said he would like me to be involved, and that I should apply in writing.' She subsequently received a letter from Zawahiri himself, setting out his idea for a 'state-of-the-art facility' in Kandahar, with Rabiah to be assigned the position of director.

However, Rabiah was unenthusiastic about Zawahiri's plan. Like the earlier concepts put forward by Al Haramein and the Libyans, the idea was for a top-flight health service for the relatively well-off foreigners in al Qaeda's circle, while providing nothing for the more needy Afghans.

Moreover, Rabiah was reluctant to move to Kandahar because there was no school there. She says she didn't reply to Zawahiri's letter and the hospital never eventuated because the September 11 attacks occurred about three months later.

The job offer from Ayman al Zawahiri was powerful evidence of Rabiah's status as a trusted confidante of the al Qaeda leadership, and would later make her a high-priority target of the Australian Security Intelligence Organisation. (The Australian authorities learned of it from Jack Thomas during his interrogation in Pakistan after his arrest there in January 2003.)

Around the same time as Zawahiri's job offer, Rabiah received another proposal, of the marital kind. In keeping with the custom, the proposition was not made to her directly but relayed by a neighbour through her son.

'Someone's interested in marrying your mother', the intermediary announced.

Mustafa knew already what Rabiah's response would be. 'No thanks, she's right', the boy replied.

But her wooer proved persistent, sending the intermediary back, until finally she agreed to entertain his proposal.

Rabiah's suitor was a legendary figure in jihadist circles—a veteran mujahidin commander, strategist, author and intellectual who had risen to become a senior adviser to the al Qaeda leadership. His name was Mustafa Hamid but he was universally known as Abu Walid al Misri. (Al Misri means 'the Egyptian'.) Hamid was born in 1945 in Minya al-Qamh, Egypt, joined the Muslim Brotherhood Youth Scouts as a six year old, and graduated as a mechanical engineer from Alexandria University. He worked as a Mercedes Benz mechanic in Kuwait, flirted with Marxism, turned his hand to journalism, and then had his epiphany when Israel attacked Lebanon in 1978, which prompted him to join the fight for a Palestinian state. He later said he 'did not feel very religious' at this time. His religious awakening came the following year after the Soviet invasion of Afghanistan, when he became one of the first Arabs to join the Afghan mujahidin. As he put it himself, he 'dreamt of jihad spreading from Afghanistan to the rest of Islamic and Arabic countries'.

While fighting with the mujahidin in Afghanistan, Abu Walid styled himself as a war correspondent, filing regular reports for Islamic magazines in the Middle East on the Afghan struggle. He said later he saw it as a 'great opportunity to spread the word of jihad in Afghanistan around the Islamic countries'. A conscientious diarist, he later turned the extensive notes and diaries he kept in the trenches into a series of books chronicling the history of the mujahidin. His writings provide an invaluable insider's account of the jihad. Unlike many of his cohorts, Abu Walid refused to romanticise their struggle, providing a rigorous and often scathing commentary on the mujahidin groups' leadership and strategic direction, or lack thereof. He had little time for self-serving warlords such as Hekmatyar and Sayyaf and considered the movement 'full of worthless characters, outlaws, hypocrites and opportunists'.

In the 1980s Abu Walid was a senior commander and respected military strategist under the mujahidin warlord Jalaludin Haqqani, and worked closely alongside Osama bin Laden and his military deputy, Mohammed Atef (aka Abu Hafs al Misri), a fellow Egyptian and close comrade. In the 1990s, while bin Laden was in Sudan, Abu Walid was left in charge of al Qaeda's remaining infrastructure in Afghanistan, principally its network of training camps, and became the *emir* of Camp Faruq. By 1998, three years before Rabiah met him, he had been made a member of the governing *shura* (council) of al Qaeda, a committee of senior leaders who advised bin Laden. He continued to play a key role in the organisation's training program, which included a 'political course' he supervised in February 2001. Maintaining his secondary career as a media commentator and writer, Abu Walid also held the position of director of the Kandahar bureau of the Qatar-based television network, al Jazeera, perhaps explaining the easy access to al Qaeda for which the broadcaster became known.

When Rabiah learned the identity of the man seeking to marry her, she could hardly help but be impressed. 'Everybody knew Abu Walid al Misri. He was well known, he was famous. His advice especially on matters of strategy was sought constantly.'

He was also extremely personable—'well-mannered, relaxed and amusing', according to someone else who knew him. He spoke fluent English and was extremely well read, referring in casual conversation to items from Western culture or articles he had seen in the *New York Times* or on the BBC. Jack Thomas had met him and reported back to Rabiah that he was 'a really nice guy'. Thomas found Abu Walid humble and soft-spoken and thought he would be a 'calming influence' on the 'fiery' Rabiah. The al Qaeda leadership apparently considered them a good match. Abu Walid told Rabiah later that it was his friend Abu Hafs, bin Laden's military chief, who suggested they wed, though it's unclear what he knew of her as Rabiah says she did not meet either Abu Hafs or his wife.

In any event, they struck up an easy rapport when they met at Rabiah's home, she on one side of a curtain, he on the other.

'Abu Walid was the type of person that most people who knew him liked him', Rabiah says. 'He was extremely intelligent and very easygoing. He was also very liberal—very much a modernist.' Rabiah had been under pressure to choose a husband since arriving in Afghanistan, and there were good practical reasons to marry—the need for financial support, the requirement for a *mahram* so she could travel, not to mention that she was lonely. Abu Walid was an impressive candidate all round, not least because he was unlikely to get in her way. 'I thought that because he was a journalist and an intellectual, and because his first wife was known to have more freedom than a lot of other Arab women, I just thought it wouldn't be restrictive', she says.

Abu Walid already had a wife, to whom he was still married. She was his cousin, Wafa, with whom he had seven children including a son who was killed at fourteen when their home at Camp Faruq was bombed by Soviet forces. Wafa was herself a well-known figure in jihadist circles. There were stories of how Abu Walid used to leave her behind in a tent with guns and grenades to defend herself and the children while he went off to fight the Russians, with the parting advice: 'Allah will look after you'. Herself an educated woman, Wafa had refused to stay in Afghanistan under the Taliban, instead relocating with her children to

Iran so they could go to school. In her absence, Abu Walid had decided to marry again, and evidently liked what he had heard about the spirited mujahidah from Australia.

'Does your wife know you are taking a second wife?' was Rabiah's first question when they met. She had no objection to assuming the second wife position, as long as it was done openly. In her view, second marriages kept secret are 'always a disaster'. (She says another key to a successful polygamous marriage is: 'You can only live with it if you don't think about the time he's with the other wife. You can't open that door or you'll go mad.')

'She doesn't know yet, but she will', Abu Walid assured her.

And so Rabiah accepted his proposal. Like her previous marriages it was principally a pragmatic union in a society in which it was simply not feasible for a woman to remain alone. 'I got married because I had big plans and I wanted to do things, and being a woman alone in that society, you are so limited in your movement and your status in society because you don't have the protection of a husband. It's not because you're nobody if you're not married. It's a form of protection. If you are married, your status is very clear, there can be no doubt in anyone's mind, no room for anyone to doubt your intentions or your motives or your goals.'

Their marriage contract was signed with minimal formality in Kabul, and celebrated with separate small gatherings of a few male and female guests. Abu Walid did not like to socialise and spurned fancy gatherings. And having not yet informed Wafa, who was well known in the women's circle, he was nervous of become a target of the incessant gossip among the al Qaeda women. While he was in Kabul, Abu Walid lived with one of his daughters and her husband in a commandeered diplomatic house in a leafy street of high-walled compounds in Wazir Akhbar Khan, opposite what is now the Danish embassy. However, his own home was at the al Jazeera office in Kandahar, to which he was eager to return. As Rabiah's children were at school in Kabul and there was still no school in Kandahar, they agreed that she would continue to spend most of her time in the capital and they would commute between the two cities.

A few weeks after their marriage, in July or August 2001, Rabiah left the children in the care of a friend and travelled to Kandahar to spend time with Abu Walid. It was a journey of some 400 kilometres through parched mountain desert, which took more than sixteen hours on a road relentlessly pummelled by two decades of war and neglect. Afghanistan's second-largest city, Kandahar had once been the grandly laid out bastion of the Durrani dynasty, which ruled the country for 300 years. It was an important political and religious hub, home to the mausoleum of the eighteenth-century king Ahmad Shah Durrani and the shrine holding the Cloak of the Prophet Mohammed, while its numerous bazaars made it a thriving centre of commerce at the intersection of ancient trade routes between Persia and the Mughal Empire. Its irrigated fields and orchards once produced figs, peaches, mulberries and pomegranates, which were served at the table of the British Governor General of India in Delhi. But by 2001, Kandahar was a wasteland, its orchards abandoned, its fields among the most heavily land-mined terrain in the world.

The al Jazeera house where Abu Walid lived was in the centre of Kandahar, not far from the compound built for Taliban leader Mullah Mohammed Omar by his grateful guest Osama bin Laden. Bin Laden himself lived on a former agricultural co-operative called Tarnak Farm, in an isolated stretch of desert 5 kilometres from the Kandahar airport. Donated by the Taliban, his 40-hectare complex encircled by a mudbrick wall included dormitories, storage facilities, a mosque, a medical clinic and a crumbling office block. (Unbeknown to bin Laden, the CIA had detailed satellite maps of Tarnak Farm and in 1998 devised a plan to attack the facility and capture him in the middle of the night. The raid never won final approval in Washington.)

Abu Walid's modest setup at the al Jazeera house caused Rabiah to laugh at his title. 'The "bureau chief of Kandahar"! The chief of himself—that's all he was. It was just him—the bureau consisted of a satellite telephone.' His living quarters were spacious but mostly empty except for a large library of books and a mass of paperwork. Abu Walid was a voracious reader and avid student of military history, well versed in the theories of Machiavelli, Genghis Khan and the legendary Chinese military sage Sun Tzu, author of *The Art of War*. When Rabiah met him, Abu Walid was immersed in a project he said he had been working on for three years, a study with the working title 'The Third Opium War', which would document the role of the poppy trade in fuelling the Afghan wars. Notwithstanding his talents as an author and unofficial historian, it seems likely that the purpose for which al Jazeera employed him was to facilitate the network's unique access to the al Qaeda leadership.

By Rabiah's account, she and Abu Walid settled into a companionable routine, based more on their shared intellectual interests than mundane domestic needs.

'As a husband he was very easygoing, just in every way', she says. 'He's the type that, if he came home and you said, "I got engrossed in this book and I haven't cooked anything", he'd be more interested in knowing what the book was than where his lunch was. He needed a lot of intellectual stimulation. And his interests were very broad.'

She helped with his research, and they engaged in long discussions in English about politics, Islamic history and the state of the jihad. They argued about the skills of historical figures such as Genghis Khan and Adolf Hitler, both of whom Abu Walid regarded as 'great' military strategists, while Rabiah considered the former a crazy psychopath and the latter 'the devil in human form'.

Abu Walid was a man of sharp intellect and expansive knowledge. But Rabiah was startled to discover after their marriage that he had little interest in the intricacies of Islamic law and practice. 'Abu Walid studied mechanical engineering; he didn't study Islam. He didn't know anything about the *deen*. I was shocked that someone who was as famous a mujahid as he was, Islamically he had no knowledge. He was the first mujahid I had ever known who knew virtually nothing about Islam. He believed in Islam and the superiority of Islam, but more from an historical and political point of view.'

He could iterate the dates and details of any number of military engagements, but could barely recite an *ayat* of the Quran. He often chided Rabiah for being engrossed in the 'nitty gritty' of Islam, using the English phrase for what he saw as a pointless fixation with minutiae. He once rebuked her for reading a book by the fourteenth-century jurist Ibn Taymiyya, a leading exponent of military jihad.

'Why are you wasting your time reading that?' he asked her.

'It's a book on *aqida*', she replied. (*Aqida* means the Islamic creed or articles of faith.)

'*Aqida! Aqida!* That's the cause of all this *fitna* (strife) we're going through.'

Abu Walid believed with a passion that preoccupation with the technicalities of Islam, and the resulting doctrinal disputes and schisms, had become the major hindrance to progress in the Islamic world. 'He used to blame the scholars of Islam for making Islam complicated', says Rabiah. 'He believed Islam had suffered from dogmatism, and that the Quran was a very general guide for human beings and it was not necessary for a layman to be involved in study of the *hadith* or *tafsir* (interpreting the Quran). He said we had destroyed Islam by focusing on the nitty gritty.'

Abu Walid paid little heed to the distinctions between Sunni, Shia and Sufi, 'hated fanatics', according to Rabiah, and had no time for the Salafist obsession with detail. 'Telling him "Your pants are too long" or "Your beard is too short"—he wasn't interested at all. At all.'

'Allah gave human beings a brain to think with', Abu Walid used to say. 'If an Islamic practice holds you back, then you change it.' In Rabiah's view this bordered on apostasy, although she didn't say so at the time.

Despite his intimate involvement with bin Laden's organisation, Abu Walid was a free thinker and long-time internal critic of al Qaeda's management, leadership and strategy, which frequently saw him directly at odds with bin Laden and his cohorts. His extensive writings were later analysed in a study published by the Combating Terrorism Center at the United States Military Academy at West Point in New York, entitled *Cracks in the Foundation: Leadership Schisms in Al-Qa'ida from 1989–2006*. This report noted that Abu Walid's single most important characteristic is his pragmatism. While he shared the broad outlines of the Salafi jihadi ideology, Abu Walid 'approached jihad as, above all else, a military struggle'. For him, 'the foremost requirement of a jihadi strategy is that it be *effective*, not that it be ideologically pure or symbolically potent'.

His unswerving pragmatism was the spark for recurring conflict with bin Laden and others among al Qaeda's leaders who took a more doctrinaire line. Abu Walid had infuriated bin Laden during the jihad against the Soviets in 1989, by castigating the al Qaeda leadership over an ill-fated attempt to attack and seize the city of Jalalabad, which failed with extensive loss of life among the mujahidin. Abu Walid knew the operation was backed by the Pakistani ISI and the CIA, and warned that the mujahidin were being manipulated by 'international powers'. He called the operation foolhardy and ill prepared and likened it to a horde of children being led to their doom by the Pied Piper. He wrote later that had he been in charge, he would have court-martialled bin Laden and his commanders 'and sentenced them to death'. Bin Laden was furious at Abu Walid's assessment and ordered it 'torn to pieces and scattered to the wind'. This only confirmed Abu Walid's view of the al Qaeda leadership: that 'their limited mentality will always be disastrous to their operations'.

Abu Walid's unstinting critique of al Qaeda's failings continued through the years, and the fact that bin Laden put up with it is testament to the esteem in which Abu Walid was held. He criticised bin Laden's autocratic leadership as 'unhealthy' and lamented the group's incompetent administration and poor strategic planning. In 2000 he complained that al Qaeda's mode of organisation appeared to be 'random chaos'. 'Waging jihad like a rhinoceros is stupid and futile', he railed in one memorable aside. He despaired over what he called al Qaeda's 'Salafi predilections', and said its habit of choosing allies merely because they shared its ideology was 'a great calamity'. Rabiah recalls hearing much the same. 'While we were in Kandahar he would complain about them being tunnel-visioned and having closed minds.'

Abu Walid's attitude to bin Laden was clearly ambivalent, by Rabiah's account. 'Abu Walid respected Osama for his manners. He said he was very humble. He said he was so charismatic. But he hated Wahhabis. He never saw Osama as a leader. Osama was someone who could facilitate, but he never gave him the title of *emir*.' Abu Walid's personal ties of loyalty were less to bin Laden than to his fellow Egyptians, the al Qaeda military chief, Abu Hafs al Misri, and bin Laden's head of security, Saif el Adel, who was married to Abu Walid's eldest daughter. He was also devoted to Taliban leader Mullah Mohammed Omar, to whom he had sworn the *bai'at*.

Abu Walid was conspicuous among the dissidents in al Qaeda's ranks who opposed bin Laden's declared war on the United States. Rabiah recalls his anger over events such as the bombing of the US embassies in Nairobi and Dar es Salaam in 1998, and the attack on the USS *Cole* in Yemen in 2000. 'He thought it was absolute lunacy for anybody in Afghanistan to entertain the thought of taking on America. He thought it was waving a red flag in front of a humongous enraged bull. It used to make him angry.' These views were echoed in Abu Walid's writings, some of which were found by the Americans in Afghanistan, others published in Islamist websites and magazines.

Despite his idiosyncratic position, Abu Walid remained at the centre of al Qaeda's leadership and planning. The British-born Australian JI member, Jack Roche, who was convicted in 2004 of planning to bomb the Israeli embassy in Canberra, has described meeting Abu Walid in Afghanistan in 2000. Roche testified at his trial that 'Sheikh Abu Walid' was present with bin Laden's lieutenants Abu Hafs and Saif el Adel, at a meeting held at Camp Faruq to discuss possible Jewish targets in Australia. Roche says that Abu Walid opened the meeting by asking him, 'How are things in Indonesia and the Philippines?' presumably referring to the state of JI's operations in those countries. After that, Roche says Abu Walid let Abu Hafs do the talking while he 'just sat there', and 'didn't say much at all'. 'I saw him as obviously some kind of adviser', says Roche.

While Rabiah knew of Abu Walid's role as an adviser to al Qaeda, she says she was not aware—and professes surprise to learn—that he was a member of the organisation's governing *shura* council. That she could have been unaware of this is quite plausible, given the 'need to know' rule that was applied to women in the jihadist movement.

By the time Rabiah met him in mid 2001, she says Abu Walid was 'very disillusioned' with bin Laden's group: 'He disagreed with them on everything, their methodology, their goals, everything'.

Perhaps because of his own reservations—perhaps also because he had still not told his first wife Wafa about their marriage—Rabiah says Abu Walid would not allow her to make contact with the al Qaeda women in Kandahar.

'When I first came to Kandahar the women wanted to put on a party out at the *mujama*—the "place of gathering" where Osama lived. But Abu Walid said, "I don't want you to go". He didn't believe it was sincere.' Abu Walid apparently suspected that the women's motivation was not to welcome their new 'sister' but to check out his second wife. Seemingly for the same reason he would not allow Rabiah to set up a clinic in their home, or visit bin Laden's compound to treat the al Qaeda women. 'Abu Walid didn't want me to be involved. He didn't want me visiting the women and the women visiting me, because he didn't want problems.'

Tensions between bin Laden and his Taliban hosts had also been simmering for years. Bin Laden's escalating rhetorical and physical attacks on the United States and its allies had placed the Taliban regime under intense international pressure. Taliban leader Mullah Omar had repeatedly asked bin Laden to refrain from 'media encounters' such as his celebrated interviews with CNN and ABC America, which drew attention to his Afghan sanctuary. When bin Laden ignored this, it was the Taliban who shifted him to Kandahar, both for his own protection and to keep him under control. They confiscated his satellite telephones and appointed a ten-man guard to keep watch over him. In June 2001, Taliban leader Mullah Omar declared that any *fatwah* by bin Laden was 'null and void' because he didn't have the religious authority to issue them. However, the Taliban resisted taking any real action to curb bin Laden's activities and refused to surrender him.

Abu Walid described to Rabiah how he had been present at a meeting between Mullah Omar and the Saudi intelligence chief, Prince Turki al Faisal, who visited Kandahar twice to try to persuade Omar to hand bin Laden over. After a previous session, at which Omar had reportedly agreed to this in principle, Prince Turki had ordered the shipment of 400 brand-new pickup trucks from Dubai to Afghanistan as a downpayment on bin Laden. Prince Turki thought it was a done deal. But Mullah Omar's position had hardened. 'Just think of the benefits for your people. There is so much we can provide', Prince Turki cajoled the Taliban leader.

'It's not allowed. It's *haram* (forbidden)', Mullah Omar kept replying.

Several times throughout an increasingly tense conversation, Mullah Omar got up and left the room. The third time he came back he was dripping with water. When Prince Turki resumed his efforts at persuasion, Mullah Omar held a hand up to silence him and announced, '*Bas, bas* (Enough, enough)'.

'You have come and you have spoken', Omar declared. 'I felt my temper rising so I went out and I did *wudu* (ritual washing), just as the Prophet said. And I did that three times, because the Prophet said when you lose your temper one of the best ways to control it is to go and do *wudu*. But there must be something wrong with me. Because I've done *wudu* three times, and the last time I tipped the whole bucket of water over my head. But I can no longer bear to hear what you are saying.'

Mullah Omar refused to withdraw his protection of bin Laden, and Prince Turki left, empty-handed and furious. Abu Walid's description of this meeting to Rabiah is corroborated by other published accounts. Another version has Prince Turki leaving with a parting warning: 'You must remember, Mullah Omar, what you are doing now is going to bring a lot of harm to the Afghan people'.

Rabiah remained largely oblivious to Afghanistan's impending doom. Impatient as always to make herself useful, she devised a number of new projects to occupy her time in Kandahar. She planned to write articles for the Taliban magazine and hoped to broadcast a women's program in English on Radio Shariat. Abu Walid seemed to share her enthusiasm.

'It would have been just a radio program for women—in English because that was seen as educated and progressive', she says. 'We wanted them to be aware that suppression of women has no place in Islam. It would have been the same as the program to teach English in the hospital—teaching women through the English medium, but within the bounds of Islam.' Abu Walid undertook to raise these ideas with the Taliban leadership, whose support for them was far less certain. 'We were trying to figure out how to do it, because it would have been unacceptable to the Arabs—a woman being on the radio. But we were working on it', Rabiah says. There was also discussion about whether Rabiah should be sent to interview six female aid workers who had been arrested by the Taliban in Kabul in August 2001, and accused of illegally preaching Christianity. She says her task, had it eventuated, would have been 'to find out what they were doing and what they had to say'. Like the other proposals, this never came to fruition because of the world-changing events that were about to occur.

By the beginning of September 2001 there was a growing sense of peril in Kandahar, though very few knew exactly what was about to transpire. 'We did have a sense that something big was going to happen—but we thought *we* were going to be attacked', says Rabiah.

It has since been revealed that the United States was devising a secret contingency plan to oust the Taliban regime by force if Mullah Omar continued to refuse to hand over bin Laden. While this was not known publicly at the time, it was clear to those in Afghanistan that the United States was running out of patience. Concerns about the possibility of a pre-emptive US strike were raised by al Qaeda trainees at a 'political course' presided over by Abu Walid in 2001, and detailed in documents later found by the Americans. A number of trainees asked about the likelihood of a US invasion in questions that were passed on to bin Laden in a submission by Abu Walid at the conclusion of the course.

Bin Laden's determination to attack America had been the subject of increasingly heated debate and vocal opposition within the al Qaeda *shura*, of which Abu Walid was a member. It was known that Khalid Sheikh Mohammed was working on a project known as 'the planes operation', and in late August bin Laden formally notified the *shura* that a major attack against the United States would take place in the coming weeks. Taliban leader Mullah Omar was known to oppose such an attack, and a bitter split now emerged within al Qaeda's top leadership. According to testimony given by the principal architect of September 11, Khalid Sheikh Mohammed, a majority of *shura* members—including Abu Walid and his son-in-law, Saif el Adel—opposed the attacks, on both strategic and ideological grounds. Bin Laden was dismissive of their qualms, remarking at one point, 'I will make it happen even if I do it by myself'. Khalid Sheikh Mohammed said later that he would have disobeyed and carried on, even if the *shura* had ordered bin Laden to call off the attacks.

Whether or not Abu Walid knew the details of the forthcoming operation is unclear. If he did, Rabiah says he didn't share this knowledge with her.

'I want to make it clear I have absolutely no knowledge of 9/11 before it happened', she says. 'I don't know if Abu Walid knew. He never said. If he did he never told me. I can't imagine he would have agreed to it, because the one thing Abu Walid and I had in common was that both of us really wanted to see Afghanistan succeed.'

On 11 September 2001, Rabiah was watering the garden in the courtyard of Abu Walid's home in Kandahar. He had gone off to the Ministry of Information for a meeting.

'I was in the yard watering the garden, and I heard all the gunshots', Rabiah remembers. 'The whole place erupted. There was gunfire and people screaming and yelling out *"Allahu Akbar!"* and blowing their car horns in the streets, and great excitement.' Next, Abu Walid came running through the gates.

'They've attacked the twin towers!' he shouted.

'What twin towers?' she asked, amid the din and confusion.

'In New York—they've flown planes into the World Trade Center!'

'Who?'

'Who else?'

Abu Walid ran back out the door of the al Jazeera house, saying he was going to watch the satellite television coverage of the event. He returned two hours later.

'He came back and he was really white, really pale. And he looked really, really sad', says Rabiah.

'What's happened?' she asked him.

'The *shabab* (young men) have flown two planes into the World Trade Center in New York.' He paused and added, 'This is a disaster'.

Then Abu Walid put his face in his hands and wept, repeating over and over, '*Y'Allah* (Oh God), what have they done?'

13

FUGITIVES

Afghanistan, 2001

In the days after the September 11 attacks, an atmosphere of chaotic excitement and creeping dread prevailed in Kandahar. There was jubilation on the streets, but inside the al Jazeera house Abu Walid's sorrowful despair turned to anger.

'Over the next couple of days, everybody else was excited, everybody was talking about it, saying how good it was. But Abu Walid was devastated, he was angry, he didn't approve—his reaction shocked me', says Rabiah. 'Through the course of those days we had many conversations about it and he said, "You know, this is just what America was waiting for. Any excuse. The people here are not realists. America will wipe Afghanistan off the face of the map".'

Rabiah's own reaction was a mixture of confusion, shock and amazement. She still hadn't seen the televised images of the devastation in the United States, but was tuned in to the blanket coverage on BBC radio, which conveyed the enormity of the attack. On the streets of Kandahar the conspiracy theories had started—the Jews had done it, or the CIA. But Abu Walid's response left her in no doubt that this was the work of al Qaeda. 'It was all rather surreal. At first it was a sense of disbelief, and just confusion. The fact that these men had done this was unbelievable— twelve men who were supposedly from Afghanistan, with box cutters— that these simple people had carried out this thing was amazing.'

She saw it as an act of war, but doubted whether it was legal under Islamic law because of the huge civilian death toll. She claims she felt not elation, but a sense of foreboding about what would follow. 'Obviously I knew what was coming—there was no way America would let that pass. I don't think there was anyone who, the reality of what had happened didn't hit them. As soon as everyone got over their initial surprise it was like OK, they'll be coming after us.'

Abu Walid's superiors at al Jazeera were pressing him to get an interview with bin Laden, who was still in Kandahar. But Abu Walid was stalling. 'They wanted him to interview Osama. He was making excuses— he didn't want to interview Osama because he was so angry. He actually said he wouldn't be able to sit face to face with him. He believed the Afghan-Arabs had brought about the destruction of an Islamic state.'

'I am surrounded by idiots', Rabiah recalls Abu Walid muttering furiously. 'I can't believe the stupidity of these people, wanting to fight America.' Bin Laden reportedly hoped the attacks would lure the United States into an unwinnable ground war in Afghanistan. But Abu Walid knew better. 'There's no way the Americans are going to come to the ground', he told Rabiah. A devotee of the Chinese military sage Sun Tzu, who coined the adage 'know your enemy', Abu Walid knew that the war that was to follow would be fought from the air, where the Taliban and al Qaeda were powerless.

Six days after September 11, US President George Bush named bin Laden as the 'prime suspect' in the attacks and began readying for a counterstrike. The United States had plans in place already to oust the Taliban by force, and President Bush now issued a final ultimatum: 'They will hand over the terrorists or they will share in their fate'.

As bin Laden and his colleagues prepared to flee Kandahar, an order went out from the al Qaeda leadership that all the families had to leave.

'They were saying all the Afghan-Arabs had to evacuate and go to the mountains', says Rabiah. 'And I was saying, "What are you talking about? I'm going to Kabul. I want my kids".'

Apart from her eldest son in Afghanistan, 15-year-old Mustafa, who had accompanied her to Kandahar, Rabiah's remaining children—Ilyas, aged thirteen, 11-year-old Aminah, and granddaughter Huda who turned nine a week after September 11—were still in Kabul. The Afghan capital was in the grip of rising panic. The remaining Westerners were being airlifted out, while Rabiah's friends such as the Khadr family and Umm Fatima, the wife of Dr Ayman al Zawahiri, were packing up and leaving with their children. Northern Alliance troops, who had rallied after the assassination of their leader Ahmed Shah Massoud by al Qaeda agents on 9 September, would soon be advancing on the capital, backed by US and British Special Forces.

'We'll have to go and get the children', Rabiah said to Abu Walid.

'We can't. No one can go back to Kabul. Allah will take care of your children.'

'That's when I thought he was a raving lunatic', says Rabiah. 'And I thought, well OK, I'm on my own. No one is going to go and get my children and I won't be able to go and get my children, so I have to find a way.'

She persuaded an Afghani driver named Hamid who worked in the al Jazeera office to take a taxi to Kabul to get the children. With the ruinous state of the roads and people fleeing in all directions, his return trip to the capital would take three days. In the meantime Abu Walid convinced Rabiah it was too dangerous to stay put in Kandahar, as a US attack could come any day and the key Taliban and al Qaeda southern stronghold would be a prime target. He insisted they had to leave and told Hamid the driver to meet them with the children in three days' time in Afghanistan's westernmost city of Herat, near the Iranian border.

Before leaving Kandahar, Rabiah rang her daughter Rahmah in Sydney on the al Jazeera satellite phone. It was almost a year since she had last seen Rahmah in Peshawar after the birth of her son, when they had argued over Rahmah and her husband Khaled's refusal to travel with the family to Afghanistan. Now she feared she might not see them again.

'I told her I loved her and asked her—if I never see her again—to forgive me, and to ask Allah to unite us in paradise', Rabiah recalls. It was the last Rahmah would hear of her family for another two years.

As Hamid the driver set off northwards for the capital, Kabul, Rabiah and her son Mustafa boarded a mini-bus with Abu Walid to join the exodus out of Kandahar. 'It was crazy, people were going in all directions, busloads of women and children, nobody knew what they were doing.

There weren't any preparations, no one knew what was going on. We had to leave everything behind—fridges, washing machines, furniture, computers, my whole library, all my medical equipment—it just got left behind. We were only allowed to take one bag per family.'

Their trip to Herat was a 560-kilometre journey on a narrow ribbon of highway that skirts the northern edge of the Dasht-e-Mango, the 'Desert of Death', one of the hottest and most waterless wastelands in the world. The road built by the Soviets in the 1950s had been pulverised for a decade by Russian tanks and was pitted with bomb craters, which made it impossible to travel faster than 40 kilometres per hour.

'The bus trip took a day and a night, or maybe two nights', she remembers. 'It was shocking. For a start you're running and you don't know where you're going. Fourteen hours at a stretch in a mini-bus with no food, climate changes from 50 degrees to below zero, and you don't know if you're going to see your family again.'

Their destination in Herat was the Uzbek *markaz* (headquarters), the main base of the large Uzbek jihadist contingent allied with al Qaeda and the Taliban. Abu Walid had special ties to the Uzbeks. During the 1990s when he was running al Qaeda's training program, he had been responsible for training volunteers from the former Soviet Central Asian countries, including members of the Islamic Movement of Uzbekistan. They remained loyal to their former mentor and were happy to shelter him and his family. The day after their arrival, the al Jazeera driver Hamid arrived in a taxi with Rabiah's children, Ilyas, Aminah and granddaughter Huda, each carrying a single bag, and Huda clutching her constant companion Beniah, the sex-change teddy bear. Their flight from Kabul had been a nerve-racking affair. Anti-American demonstrators had taken to the streets to protest in advance against the looming US counter-attack, and the US embassy had been set on fire. Taliban troops were bolstering their defences as the Northern Alliance prepared for its assault on Kabul. The children said they'd been up on the roof watching the distant rocket fire as Northern Alliance forces moved towards the capital.

On the evening of the day Rabiah was reunited with the children, the US and allied bombardment of Afghanistan began. The city of Herat, which was the site of the largest Soviet-built airbase in the country, now controlled by the Taliban, was targeted in the first wave of US bombings.

'I can remember waking up and the walls were shaking', says Rabiah. 'They were dropping 500-kilogram bombs. We went outside to get a better look, but the US planes were so high you couldn't see them.' The Taliban were firing at the incoming jets with Soviet-era anti-aircraft guns mounted on legs. 'I said, "Why are they wasting their ammunition? There's no way they'll hit them." And so you'd watch the bombs explode. And that went on all night.'

There were three waves of bombings on the night of 7 October 2001, carried out by twenty-five strike aircraft launched from carriers in the Persian Gulf and Arabian Sea, and fifteen B1, B2 and B52 bombers dispatched from Diego Garcia in the Indian Ocean. Fifty Tomahawk cruise missiles were fired from US and British warships and submarines. As the bombing continued, the airbase at Herat was obliterated, electricity supplies in Kabul severed, and al Qaeda and Taliban training camps and communications facilities destroyed. The aerial bombardment provided cover for ground offensives by anti-Taliban fighters at strategic sites around the country, supported by CIA and US Army Special Forces.

Civilian bystanders were among the casualties. The Reuters news agency interviewed a 16-year-old ice-cream vendor from Jalalabad who was injured when a Cruise missile hit an airfield near his home.

'There was just a roaring sound, and then I opened my eyes and I was in a hospital', said the boy named Assadullah. 'I lost my leg and two fingers. There were other people hurt. People were running all over the place.'

A resident of Kabul gave this account to the BBC: 'The street next to my home was bombed, and eighteen were killed and twenty-three injured. Everything was destroyed there. The doors and window glass of our homes were broken. I have a baby child, one and a half years old. Even she is afraid of the plane sounds and bombing. The planes are going up and down and who knows what might be their goal and what disaster might happen again to the poor and innocent people.'

The next day in Herat, the Uzbek fighters constructed an underground shelter for the women and children in their encampment. They dug all day from *fajr* (dawn) until the light began to fade, then ordered the women to gather up the children and a pile of blankets and take shelter for the night.

'We went out and we walked around the back of the *markaz*', says Rabiah. 'We could see a tarpaulin with light coming out of it. I said, "What's that?" And someone said, "That's the air raid shelter". There was this dirty big hole in the ground, about as big as a kitchen, but not quite as deep. The entrance was at ground level and there was no roof on it, just wooden beams with a tarp across it.'

The Uzbek women and children were already inside the bunker but Rabiah baulked. 'I'm not getting in that. There's no roof on it.'

'We're gonna do the roof tomorrow', replied her sons, whose hands were soiled and bloodied from helping to dig without tools. But Rabiah was adamant.

'Go and tell the men I'm not getting in.'

'Mama please, we can't tell the men that', her sons pleaded.

'No way, that's not an air raid shelter—it's a bloody pit. If there's an attack we'll be trapped. We'll be sitting ducks.'

'There was a big drama because I wouldn't get in', Rabiah says. 'It was a horrific embarassment to my sons because women don't give orders.'

But the Uzbek men had no choice but to relent. 'Sometimes it had its advantages to be known as the crazy Australian woman. They'd just go, "Oh yeah, that's the crazy Australian woman".'

The following day the men constructed a skeletal timber roof over the pit and that night Rabiah, Aminah and Huda retreated to the bunker with the Uzbek women and children, while her sons stayed inside the *markaz* with the men. The women had blankets and weapons to defend themselves in case they were overrun. The bombing resumed at dusk. 'The attacks would start at *maghrib* (sunset) and they'd go all night', says Rabiah.

After five days in Herat, Abu Walid decided it was too dangerous for them to stay there any longer. The city's predominantly Persian-speaking population had no love for the Pashtun Taliban and their Arab allies and were ready to take up arms against them. The Uzbeks were evacuating women and children, and Abu Walid announced they must return to

Kandahar. They travelled in a mini-bus, which broke down in the desert in the late afternoon. The US bombings raids would resume at dusk, and once night fell the roads would be prowled by the dreaded *khatta aturk*, highway bandits.

'Isn't this exciting?' Rabiah remarked to Abu Walid as they waited by the roadside.

'Are you really stupid or are you just pretending to be?' said Abu Walid. 'Don't you realise that when the sun sets this road will be swarming with the kind of people you don't want to meet in your worst nightmare. Do you have any idea what could happen to you and your daughters?'

After a hasty repair job they made it back to Kandahar by sunset and went to stay with a friend of Abu Walid, a Taliban commander who worked in the Ministry of Religion and lived in a fortified compound. They were instructed that when the bombing resumed they should take shelter in the corners of the house, so there would be less chance of the roof caving in on them.

'It was just continuous carpet bombing from sunset till dawn', says Rabiah. 'They bombed only at night. It was like watching a fireworks display. For the first few days the boys would climb out on the roof and watch the bombing, then we became so used to it we just went to sleep. Sometimes the bombs came so close that the force of them would blow open the windows.'

One night a bomb landed two houses from where they were staying. The impact shook the walls, burst open the windows and killed an Afghan family. Thirteen-year-old Ilyas had a narrow escape when another bomb exploded on the roadside while he was going to fetch bread, throwing him off the back of a motorcycle.

A week after the US bombing raids started, the *Times of India* reported more than 300 civilians had been killed or injured and charged that the US strikes were in violation of the United Nations charter allowing the use of force in self-defence. A mosque in Jalalabad was reported to have been hit during prayer time, killing seventeen people. As neighbours scrambled to the rescue, a second bomb reportedly dropped,

killing at least another 120. Kandahar came under sustained bombardment, prompting its residents to flee *en masse*. A Kandahar merchant later
told of how he escaped to his family's ancestral village 40 kilometres to the
north, arriving just as it was attacked by US warplanes. 'I brought my
family here for safety', he told the *New York Times*. 'Now there are nineteen dead, including my wife, my brother, sister, sister in law, nieces,
nephews, my uncle. What am I supposed to do now?'

The ferocity of the US blitzkrieg confirmed Abu Walid's grimmest
fears—and his caustic assessment of his comrade bin Laden. 'Look what
you have done', Rabiah would hear him muttering.

Over the months and years that followed, Abu Walid would emerge
as bin Laden's harshest critic within the jihadist movement. In a series of
articles published after the fall of the Taliban, he blamed bin Laden's
flawed leadership, lack of wisdom and strategic myopia for the loss of
Afghanistan's Islamic state.

'The most serious issue was the extreme weakness of bin Laden's
political and military capabilities', Abu Walid wrote. 'This was no longer a
secret as bin Laden revealed this himself in his own statements, which he
released after leaving Afghanistan ... which revealed his gross ignorance
of the fundamental principles of military action.' Abu Walid cited the
Chinese sage Sun Tzu's *The Art of War* and opined: 'If you are ignorant of
yourself and of your enemy you will be defeated in every battle'. He said
bin Laden's style of leadership was like a 'disease' and flew in the face of
basic military principles known for centuries. 'This includes the idea that
the method of absolute individual command was unsuccessful, outdated,
and usually ended in defeat.' Abu Walid's view was that America's greatest
success was in the field of 'psychological warfare', because it succeeded in
'misleading bin Laden and caused him to have the illusion that he had
become a great and frightening superpower, thus his decisions and actions
were influenced by that illusion'.

Abu Walid personified the schism in al Qaeda's governing *shura,*
which would leave the organisation splintered and weakened in the aftermath of September 11. Reflecting this split, as the US bombardment

continued bin Laden and his colleagues fled in two separate directions. Bin Laden and loyalists including his deputy Dr Ayman al Zawahiri headed towards the underground Tora Bora cave complex excavated by bin Laden in the 1980s in the Spin Ghar mountains near Jalalabad, close to the Pakistan border. The dissenters including Abu Walid and his son-in-law Saif el Adel—described later by US military analysts as 'the opposition group' in al Qaeda's senior leadership—would flee in the opposite direction to Iran.

There was nothing orderly about the exodus as the families too scattered in different directions as they were told. 'They were trying to evacuate the Afghan-Arab families to either Iran or Pakistan, everything was organised by the men', says Rabiah.

It was at this point, in Kandahar, that Abu Walid bade Rabiah and her family farewell. 'He said he was leaving, he said he had things to do and he had made arrangements and we would be taken care of.' Before she could argue, Rabiah and the children were bundled into a Toyota double-cab pickup with an Uzbek driver and their faithful guide, Hamid. The van was plastered with mud to make it less visible from the air and they were told to keep the windows up so it was less likely they would be seen. Then they set off into the desert, driving on rutted tracks and along dry riverbeds, to avoid the main roads.

'I don't even know where we went, or what direction, or where we were heading, but we were in the car for three days', Rabiah recounts.

Abu Walid had instructed the Uzbek driver to take them to a pro-Taliban village north-east of Kandahar where a rendezvous had been arranged with some Uzbek families. The driver found the house and left them, promising to return the next morning. But the Uzbek contingent never arrived, and the driver didn't return. They were told later he had been killed by anti-Taliban forces who were said to be nearby and reportedly hunting down Arabs sympathetic to al Qaeda.

'So we ended up in this house, completely on our own—and we basically prepared to die', says Rabiah.

She and the boys dug a trench in the yard behind a row of sandbags and filled empty bottles with kerosene for Molotov cocktails. They had a

Kalashnikov and a grenade, given to them by some Arabs in a nearby village. Aminah and Huda were told to hide in a cavity under the stairs with the grenade. 'I told them that if we were all killed and the Northern Alliance came to take them, they should detonate the grenade', Rabiah says. But this dramatic finale did not come to pass. As they continued their preparations they heard banging on the door. Outside was an elderly Afghani man waiting beside a taxi with a nervous-looking driver ready to take them to safety. Rabiah says he told them he had heard they were in there and thought that if he didn't rescue them he would have to meet Allah with the blood of women and children on his hands.

It transpired that their lucky escape had been two-fold. The driver who never came back was to have taken them to a safehouse in Paktia province near the Pakistan border, where some al Qaeda families had taken shelter. Among them was Rabiah's friend Umm Fatima, the wife of al Zawahiri. She had fled Kabul after September 11, travelling with her children including her youngest, four-year-old Aisha who had Down syndrome. Also at the house was another family whose children had attended Abdullah Azzam's school in Peshawar with Rabiah's children. One of the girls who was there later related to Rabiah's daughter Aminah the story of what happened. She said the women and children in the house (she makes no mention in this account of any men being present) had just prayed and kissed each other good night when they heard the familiar drone of a US bomber approaching. 'The sound got closer and closer and soon it was as if it was on top of our house. Suddenly we heard the sound of rockets. I got up and ran to the corner of the room ... Suddenly the roof collapsed on us and everything went dark. I was trapped in the corner and I couldn't move. I started to call out for my mother and there was no reply.'

The two-storey house had scored a direct hit, smashing the cement roof and caving in the mudbrick walls. According to a separate account, Umm Fatima was pinned under a beam on the ground floor. Her only son was crushed, while her daughters who made it out could hear their mother and the other trapped women screaming, 'Help us, help us'. Four-year-old Aisha was dragged from the rubble with a severe open head wound and died three days later. By the time rescuers reached Umm Fatima she too was dead. Aminah's friend told her that almost everyone in the house was killed.

'The Americans lied about that bombing', says Rabiah. 'From what I was told there were about twenty women in that house with their children, and no males over twelve. The only men were the Afghani drivers. Nine or twelve women died, plus about fifteen children.'

Zawahiri later wrote that he had 'tasted the bitterness of American brutality' with his family's death: 'To this day I do not know the location of the graves of my wife, my son, my daughter, and the rest of the three other families who were martyred in the incident and who were pulverized by the concrete ceiling, may God have mercy on them and the Muslim martyrs. Were they brought out of the rubble, or are they still buried beneath it to this day?'

The elderly Afghani man who had rescued Rabiah and her family arranged for a relative to drive them into the low-lying mountains near the town of Khost, a longtime al Qaeda stronghold close to the Pakistan border. There they belatedly met up with the Uzbeks who had promised Abu Walid they would protect his family. The Uzbeks had taken refuge in a makeshift mountain camp used in spring by Afghan *kuchis*, the nomadic animal herders who roam the country's deserts and mountains in search of pasture for their sheep and goats. Now deserted by the nomads, the camp consisted of several dozen mud huts, each comprising a room divided in two by a mud wall, with dirt floors and a single window. There were no toilets or cooking facilities but each hut had a *bukhar*, a traditional Afghan stove made from an old oil can and fired by wood or coal.

'We arrived at the camp in the middle of winter', says Rabiah. 'It was freezing. I had one jumper and the children had one change of clothes. There was no wood, we had to collect these huge spiky tumbleweeds—they were needle-sharp so we were lacerated with blood and scratches.'

The Uzbek *emira*—the woman in charge of the women and children—allocated Rabiah's group a hut and supplies: five spoons, three plates, a saucepan, a box of matches and a load of wood. Like the other families, they were also given rations of rice, flour, vegetable oil, potatoes, onions, salt and tomato paste. The temperatures plunged to well below zero at night and their only heating was the *bukhar*, which belched soot that filled their hair and left a grimy coating on their skin. They were allowed to light the stove at breakfast and dinnertime but had to extinguish it at nightfall in case the fires could be spotted by the US bombers overhead. There was no water for washing and it would be more than two months before they would next have a bath. The family took to calling Huda *kuchi* because she looked like a wild gypsy.

Meanwhile the US-led coalition's bombardment of Afghanistan continued. The first stage of the offensive had wiped out Taliban air defences, al Qaeda training camps and communications facilities. The next phase, which began at the end of October, featured cluster-bombing of Taliban ground positions and the deployment of FA-18 Hornet fighter-bombers in pinpoint strikes targeting Taliban vehicles. US and British Special Forces were on the ground to help guide the attack planes in.

'The Americans would send out reconnaissance planes. If they spotted the enemy—us—they would circle', says Rabiah. 'The jets would circle three times and that would be the mark of where the bombs would drop. You would know they had sighted you because you would see them circling. Between the first sighting and when the bombs dropped, you would have fifteen to twenty minutes, maximum. I became very good at spotting the planes—the trick to it is you hear the sound before you see the plane. And what they used to do was they would bomb a place and then, to make sure nobody had a chance of getting away, they would fly around and give anybody who had survived enough time to run, and then they would come back and bomb again. They used to kill a lot of kids that way.'

International media reports documented the mounting civilian casualty toll. On 27 October, US fighter jets dropped thirty-five bombs on a village north-east of Kabul, instantly killing ten civilians according to medical workers. Britain's Sky News showed footage of an F-18 aircraft dropping bombs that struck a mud and timber family home, and reported that twenty family members were injured and another ten missing under the rubble.

On their third day in the *kuchi* camp, the children were out collecting tumbleweeds when Rabiah heard the sound of an approaching plane. She ran out, waving her arms to attract the children's attention, but they just waved back. The Uzbeks were throwing children, bags and bedrolls onto their trucks for an immediate evacuation. Rabiah says she grabbed a Kalashnikov from one of the Uzbek guards and fired it in the air. This finally grabbed her children's attention and they ran back to the camp. She and the girls jumped on the truck for women and children, which roared off down the mountain, as the drone of the attack plane grew louder.

'The driver could hear the plane coming closer and he yelled "*Allahu Akbar!*" and drove off the side of the road', says Rabiah. 'He literally drove off the cliff and into a ravine, and—*Allahu Akbar*—we made it. But I don't think my back will ever be the same.'

The truck continued down the mountain while the US bomber dropped its payload, flattening the mountain camp behind them. They eventually took shelter in a deserted school, now just a concrete shell with no windows. They had lost their luggage and the older boys including Rabiah's sons Mustafa and Ilyas had been left behind. 'I didn't even know if they were alive', she says. It was almost night time and they were in hostile terrain.

'We were in this school and we were told that the Northern Alliance were close. So we had to lie down on the concrete floor and the women had to put the babies underneath them and we had to lie across the children so no noise could get out.' The women had grenades, given to them by the Uzbek *emira* and secreted in pockets they'd sewn onto the outside of their *shalwar kameez* so they could keep them within reach. 'If you got into a situation where it's almost certain you're going to be captured, you had the option—and some of the Afghan-Arab women did it—they'd hold onto their children and blow themselves up with their children. Would I have done it? Of course. There wouldn't be much choice—die and go to paradise, or be raped. For a Muslim woman, there's not much choice.'

They stayed like that in the abandoned school as night fell.

'I have never experienced such pain in all my life', says Rabiah. 'It was below zero, lying on this cement floor. We stayed like that all night. Every time you nodded off you would dream that you were in a freezer. There were seventeen people in one room with three blankets. We took it in turns with the blankets, sleeping in shifts for three hours at a time.

At *fajr* (dawn) it was our turn, and I have never slept such a beautiful sleep in all my life as when we climbed under that blanket and fell asleep.'

For three days they heard nothing of what had happened to the boys, until finally the truck driver went back to the razed camp and found them. Mustafa and Ilyas reported that the hut they had been staying in had been bombed into the ground.

By early November the Taliban was on the run, its frontlines decimated by US gunships dropping 7000-kilogram daisy cutter bombs. On 9 November, as US planes carpet-bombed Taliban defences, Northern Alliance troops overran the northernmost city of Mazar-e-Sharif, the first major centre to fall. They were quick to exact retribution. More than 500 Taliban found hiding in a school were massacred, and suspected Taliban and al Qaeda supporters were being executed on the spot. On the night of 12 November, the last of the Taliban's fighters retreated under cover of darkness from Kabul, and by the next day the capital was in the hands of the Northern Alliance.

'After the fall of Kabul it was pandemonium', says Rabiah. 'We had to move every few days. Sometimes we'd meet up with people; sometimes we were on our own. It went from incredible heat to cold. Sometimes we travelled *en masse* with truckloads of women and children. When we separated from them, we were on our own. It was just people running with nowhere to go—women and children running like cockroaches.'

Rabiah and her family made it to a border crossing where previously the frontier guards had been willing to accept a bribe of US$250 for passage into Pakistan. That was no longer the case; now there was a bounty on the heads of Taliban and al Qaeda sympathisers. 'Even if you paid $US1000, the Americans will pay more', Rabiah's group was told.

Two weeks after the fall of Kabul, the Americans began bombing the Tora Bora cave complex where bin Laden and his lieutenants were believed to be holding out. As the cluster bombs rained down, civilian casualties climbed further. Rabiah tells of a Moroccan family who briefly travelled in convoy with her group. They were driving an old VW Kombi van, presumably a relic of Afghanistan's hippy-trail days. Eventually the ancient Kombi would go no further on the boulder-strewn mountain roads. The pickup truck that Rabiah and her children were in could take no more weight, so Mustafa and Ilyas offered to stay behind and let the Moroccan's wife and children take their places in the pickup. But the man and his family wanted to stay together, so Rabiah's group went on and left them behind. Fifteen minutes later an American bomber flew overhead. Rabiah says they looked back down the mountain to see the Kombi van in flames, the family incinerated inside it. 'We used to listen to the news on the BBC or Voice of America and my blood would boil at the lies— that they were "pursuing the remnants of al Qaeda"', she remembers. 'They were shooting women and children in the back from Apache helicopters while they were running—they were purposely killing women and children. And all in the name of "you're either with us or against us". I just couldn't comprehend that people who were supposedly the leaders of the free world and who set themselves up as champions of what is right and good in this world would commit such acts—and use the excuse that *we* had committed atrocities.'

When they weren't running or hiding, their time and energy were absorbed by the tasks of finding shelter, food and water to survive the ferocious Afghan winter. At one point they spent two weeks hiding in the underground cellar of an Afghan family's home. Later they broke into a deserted UN clinic to take refuge with another family in its two concrete rooms. 'We had nothing, no water, nothing', says Rabiah. There was no toilet and they couldn't go outside, so they would defecate in plastic bags and throw them up on the roof. 'We didn't eat much so we didn't go to the toilet much. We were living on mostly rice and water so we were all as skinny as rakes—we didn't get sick, we were just skinny.' For more than two months they went without a bath or shower and barely washed their clothes. 'The water we used to do the washing was brown. We had to leave the water to sit so the dirt would settle, then it would freeze. It was no use washing our clothes because the water was freezing and it was so dirty and there was no soap. If we hung them outside to dry it was so cold they would freeze and the fabric would split. If we took them inside to dry where the *bukhar* was, the soot would stick to them while they were wet. But it was just the ritual of washing the clothes that made you feel better.'

Finding fresh water for drinking became a major preoccupation. On one occasion they walked for an hour to find a well. As they arrived back at their hideout, Ilyas tripped on a clod of earth and dropped the buckets, spilling their entire contents.

'I can remember us all sitting there in the dirt and sobbing. Ilyas was like he had spilt the last water on the face of the Earth. He kept saying, "Please forgive me, please forgive me".'

They ate rice and wild spinach and Rabiah cooked bread in the *bukhar*. The Afghan villagers sometimes donated food, and at the Muslim festival, Eid ul Adha, someone killed a buffalo and gave them a lump of meat. Their faithful guide Hamid, who stayed with them for the duration, showed Rabiah how to make a pressure cooker using an old oil can with a lid sealed by pastry. 'You get a stick, and you have to keep poking the stick through the pastry, to make a hole to let the pressure out; otherwise they explode like a bomb.' She recalls one miserable feast. 'It was about 3 a.m. We'd been fasting, and it was so cold your nose would drip and it would freeze. We were standing in the snow and sleet, keeping the fire going. It took about an hour to cook the buffalo so it was edible. It was good, but I wouldn't recommend that method of cooking.'

It was now December 2001. Rabiah and her family had been on the run for three months—but they were running out of places to go. The Taliban had been defeated, Mullah Mohammed Omar and his loyalists finally abandoning the desert city of Kandahar and retreating into the mountains. The battle of Tora Bora had ended with the deaths of some 200 al Qaeda fighters and the underground cave complex overrun. Bin Laden and his senior aides had evaded the dragnet and vanished across the border into the tribal lands of north-west Pakistan.

Rabiah's family found refuge in a fortified Pashtun compound with a handful of other families. Also there was Rabiah's old patron Ahmed Khadr and his family from Kabul. They too had been on the run since September 11, and had also narrowly missed being trapped in the bombed safehouse where Umm Fatima and their other friends had been killed. Rabiah says the Khadrs were planning to attempt the border crossing into Pakistan. But she and her family had tried it once and failed, and considered it too dangerous to try again. Nor did she want to head the other way to Iran, where Abu Walid was now in hiding.

'I didn't want to leave Afghanistan', she says. 'Everyone else could do whatever they wanted, but I still didn't believe we'd have to leave. To me, I would survive somehow or die.'

At this point the men in the fortress received word that Taliban leader Mullah Omar had issued an order for the remaining 'Arabs'—foreigners aligned with al Qaeda—to leave Afghanistan. Rabiah recalls being told that their presence 'was being used as an excuse by the Americans to kill Afghans day in and day out', so Omar had decided 'everyone had to leave'. Still, she resisted.

'I'm not going and you can't make me. The only one who can order me to go is Abu Walid, and unless he tells me, I'm not going.'

The men in charge of the Arabs came back to her two days later.

'If Abu Walid orders you to leave, will you go?'

'Well, I won't have a choice. I'll have to obey him.'

The men had brought a satellite telephone, which they wouldn't use at the compound because they knew the Americans could track the signal.

'Umm Mohammed, we're going to take you into the desert and Abu Walid's going to talk to you on the phone', they told her. 'And if the Americans don't get you, we'll come back for you later.' Rabiah says they then drove for an hour into the desert, let her out of the car, and drove off, so that if the Americans picked up the signal and dispatched a bomber they would be a safe distance away when the bomb was dropped.

'They left me there with the satellite phone, and it rang and I picked it up and it was Abu Walid.'

Abu Walid was reasonable as always. 'I think you have to be realistic. I think it's time for you to leave.'

'Are you advising me or ordering me?'

'I'm ordering you.'

'After the conversation it was surreal', she recounts. 'I still felt like it was the worst nightmare that anyone could ever have, and I was going to wake up. It felt like my life stopped, mine and my children's lives stopped.'

For her, the significance of that moment was this: 'I gave up. I gave up to the Americans. Because that's what they wanted—they wanted to expel the Muslims from the only *dawlah*, the only Islamic state on the face of this Earth.'

The men hadn't bargained on nine-year-old Huda also refusing to leave without a fight. 'I'm not going. If you've all decided to run away, then off you go, I'll be fine here', Huda announced. One of the boys had to pick her up bodily and put her in the car. As they drove away from the fortress she was still muttering in Arabic, 'I swear by Allah, I'm not doing this of my own free will'.

Rabiah later heard that a few days after they left, the Pashtun compound where they had been given shelter was destroyed. 'The Americans came back and they flattened the village, killed every man, woman and child. They said it was a lesson—that's how they would be dealt with, anybody found helping the enemy.'

In late December 2001, Rabiah and her family set off and crossed Afghanistan again, this time continuing on past the westernmost city of Herat, which had been reclaimed by its long-time ruler, the warlord Ismael Khan, in the name of the Northern Alliance. Herat had received a relentless pounding. Unexploded cluster bombs littered the desert landscape, and children were scouring the rubble for food packages dropped by the Americans, which by some disastrous coincidence were the same yellow colour as the unexploded bomblets.

Their destination was a smugglers post beyond Herat, a few kilometres from the Iranian border. It was just a cluster of houses in the desert where someone could facilitate payment to an official at the border crossing to let people through. When they arrived, there were two other families already there, one Moroccan, the other Egyptian, waiting to make the crossing. The instructions were straightforward: the women and children would go separately because if the guards started firing they would shoot the men first; the truck carrying them would stop a few hundred metres short of the wire fence that marked the boundary; from there they would have to run.

'So we were driving across the desert, on our way to the border', says Rabiah. 'And suddenly the truck left the road and we were driving through tumbleweeds and desert plants. Then the driver put his foot on the accelerator and it took off—we were being chased by the border guards, bouncing across the desert.'

The driver managed to lose the border police and kept driving till they could see the boundary. He pulled up in the desert and pointed them towards the barbed wire fence, about 300 metres away. 'All right, out you get', he ordered, then drove off. An elderly woman from one of the other families took off first, running towards the wire. Another woman had a suitcase on wheels, which she was dragging across the sand. Next they heard firing, and someone yelled 'Leave your bags behind and run!'

They made it to the wire and wriggled under on their stomachs.

'I was crawling under and all of a sudden I saw a big army boot right in front of my face, and I thought, "I'm going to die like a dog in Iran", Rabiah remembers. But the man in the army boots was the guard who had been paid to let them through. 'Get up! Quickly!' he snapped. They were taken to an open-backed pickup truck waiting nearby. They scrambled in, the guard threw a tarpaulin over them, and the truck took off. Huda was inconsolable. In the mad scramble her beloved teddy bear, Beniah, had been left behind, and no one was going back to get it.

14

HOUSE ARREST

Iran & Australia, 2002–2009

After crossing the Iranian border they were driven to a smugglers safehouse on the outskirts of the capital, Tehran. Rabiah and the four children crowded into a small room where they cleaned themselves up as best they could. They had lost their luggage and passports, and were carrying virtually nothing. The safehouse proprietor sent in bread, tea and yoghurt, and told them to stay put and not make any noise.

The next day they were to take a bus to Tehran, but the smuggler was nervous that Rabiah would be spotted as an illegal immigrant. She had been given an Iranian *chador*, a full-length gown with a head cover that the wearer has to clutch tightly around her face, usually leaving one eye showing. But she was unused to the billowing garment, which constantly got tangled around her arms. And the smuggler worried that the police who frequented the route on the lookout for illegal border crossers would notice her fair skin and blue eyes. 'I looked like this foreigner trying to act like an Iranian, so they wouldn't let me out of the house', she remembers. The smuggler came up with what he thought was an ingenious plan— brown contact lenses to disguise the colour of Rabiah's eyes, which he handed to her just before they boarded.

'We were put on the bus and told, "Don't talk, don't make a noise, don't draw attention to yourself". We were supposed to be inconspicuous.

I was wearing these cheap, nasty brown contact lenses—it was ridiculous, every time I closed my eyes they'd move.'

The heat and motion of the crowded bus lulled Rabiah to sleep. Fourteen-year-old Ilyas, jammed in beside her, dozed with his head bouncing on her shoulder. When they woke, Ilyas shrieked in terror. 'While I was sleeping the contact lenses had moved, so it looked like I had four eyes—two brown and two blue. Ilyas had woken up and looked up at my face and thought I'd turned into some sort of alien, and he screamed like someone had cut his throat. Everybody in the bus turned around. I refused to wear them after that, I threw them out the window. I said I'd tell people my mother was a foreigner.'

At the end of the bus ride they were delivered to a house in Tehran that was sumptuous by the standards they'd grown used to—air conditioning, television, two bathrooms and thick Persian carpets underfoot. But this was to be no holiday. They were here as virtual prisoners of the Iranian Revolutionary Guards.

'It was effectively house arrest', says Rabiah. 'We were monitored twenty-four hours a day, not allowed access to phone or internet and not allowed to contact our family. We were not allowed to move from one place to another; that was where we had to stay. We could go to the shops or to the doctor and carry on with a normal daily routine, but we had no ID documents so the risk was that we could be picked up. You see there's two systems in Iran. There's the official government authorities, and then there's the Revolutionary Guards. So we were there with the knowledge of the Revolutionary Guards, but not there officially according to the state of Iran.'

Their strange confinement was not unique. In the months after September 11, hundreds of foreign fighters and families had fled across the Afghanistan border into Iran, among them some of the leading figures in al Qaeda. The exodus to Iran was later documented in US media reports and in a study by the Combating Terrorism Center at the US Military Academy at West Point. The Iran contingent included two of Osama bin Laden's sons and between eighteen and twenty-five significant al Qaeda leaders; among them Rabiah's husband Abu Walid and his son-in-law Saif el Adel, who was now described as al Qaeda's third-ranking official. Saif outlined details of their Iranian sojourn in a published memoir. They were assisted in relocating by the veteran Afghan warlord Gulbuddin Hekmatyar, who had gone into exile in Iran himself after the Taliban came to power. The Iranian authorities, who for years had sponsored Islamic militants engaging in terrorism, tolerated their presence and initially allowed them to operate as they wished. But by early 2002 when US President George Bush branded Iran part of an 'axis of evil', amidst evidence that some of the fugitives—chiefly Saif el Adel—were using their Iranian base to plan terrorist attacks in other countries, the reformist regime of President Khatami came under growing international pressure to curtail them. As the pressure mounted, some of the most senior al Qaeda fugitives were rounded up and placed under house arrest, in villas and guesthouses in and around Tehran, where they still enjoyed relative freedom, but now under the watchful eye of the Revolutionary Guards.

'There were people who crossed over who were important—in the sense of being on an international list of wanted people—and people who were not important', says Rabiah. 'If they were important al Qaeda people they would be treated very well—they were under house arrest but very well cared for. The unimportant people were put in jail—men, women and children. The reason I wasn't put in jail is because I was married to Abu Walid, even though he didn't particularly want me any more. I think the reason I was looked after was that I was married to him and I just turned up. They didn't know what to do with me—they couldn't let me go and they didn't want to keep me.'

After three months on the run in Afghanistan, house arrest in Iran was at first a comfortable novelty. 'For the first couple of months, because we had been through so much, it was a relief just to be able to shower and wash your clothes and go out and buy food', says Rabiah. 'And just the fact that we were still together and relatively safe was a very pleasant change. We weren't sleeping with rats and mice and all sorts of animals; and to be able to go to a toilet and shut the door, and turn on a tap and have clean water. For my sons it was a relief after being on the run, where any day their mother or sister or niece could be raped, and they would be unable to protect them.'

They were able to cook and eat three meals a day. They had radio, television and a computer, although they were barred from using the internet. Huda began studying English and the boys devised a daily physical fitness and martial arts routine to keep themselves occupied. (Mustafa was now sixteen years old, Ilyas fourteen, Aminah twelve, and Huda nine.)

A few days after their arrival, Abu Walid came to visit—accompanied by his first wife, Wafa. Rabiah's appearance in Tehran had clearly caused consternation in their household. Abu Walid had hoped that she would return to Australia and had suggested as much to her earlier, while Wafa had apparently only just learned of her husband's second wife.

'I can't say she was overjoyed to meet me', says Rabiah. 'I guess she just wanted to see who her husband had married.' After an awkward reunion, Abu Walid left his two wives alone to talk woman to woman. Rabiah says Wafa confided that she felt betrayed by his having taken a second wife without consulting her, after all the sacrifices she had made for him and his career. However, she accepted that it was now his responsibility to care for his second family. 'She was a lovely woman', Rabiah says. 'She said I was her sister in Islam, and she felt for my kids. She said that Allah does as he pleases and this was just another test, because she was a woman who had sacrificed a lot for her Islam.'

The upshot of their meeting was that Wafa agreed, in effect, to share Abu Walid. Thereafter, he spent half the week with his first wife and half with his second in their separate homes. As Rabiah and the children settled into the disconcerting domesticity of life under house arrest, the novelty soon wore off.

'We never saw anybody; we had no social interaction, no contact with other Sunni Muslims. The kids didn't go to school. We were allowed to go out to the market, but apart from that we spent twenty-four hours a day inside the house. Of course we felt like prisoners—we *were* prisoners.'

As Rabiah understood it, they were 'unofficial' guests of the Revolutionary Guards, but if Iranian state security got its hands on them there was no telling what might happen. As a result, she rarely left the house because she was too conspicuous to risk being seen. 'You could tell I was a foreigner. I always had trouble with the *chador* and I never picked up Iranian Farsi. It was always a trauma for the boys to take me out because for a start I couldn't keep my mouth shut, and I didn't look the part. Most of the time they refused to take me out, and quite rightly, because if we were caught we would have been put back over the border and that would have meant Guantánamo Bay.'

The Iranian newscasts were full of stories of the continuing US-led bombardment of Afghanistan. In March 2002 the United States and its allies launched a new phase of their offensive, code-named Operation Anaconda, to wipe out Taliban and al Qaeda forces holed up in the mountainous Shahi-Kot region of Paktia province near the Pakistan border. Over seventeen days nearly 3500 bombs were dropped on an area of some 165 square kilometres. An estimated 400 Taliban and al Qaeda fighters were killed, a US army spokesman announcing: 'It's a great step, the major fighting is over'. But even as the pounding continued, several hundred more jihadists evaded the US dragnet and slipped across the border into the tribal wilderness of Pakistan, among them Osama bin Laden and his deputy Dr Ayman al Zawahiri. By now the air war on Afghanistan had reportedly claimed more than 3000 civilian lives. They included the passengers in a vehicle destroyed by two US fighter jets in Paktia province on 6 March. Islam Online reported that fourteen men, women and children were killed. 'The personnel in this vehicle were believed to be linked to al Qaeda activities', said a statement issued by the US military's central command. Meanwhile hundreds of suspected Taliban and al Qaeda supporters were being captured. About 750 detainees—most lowly footsoldiers—would be sent to the US detention centre at Guantánamo Bay.

'It was very personal for us and still is', says Rabiah. 'The people in Guantánamo Bay—those people were our neighbours. Maybe I delivered that man's son, maybe they were the fathers of children my children had played with. The fact that it was OK to invade and massacre thousands of people who didn't even know about September 11 until they saw it on CNN or the BBC, and the justification for killing those people was because of September 11. How can they justify that? Men and women were put in cages, raped, tortured, humiliated … How was it all right to come and kill civilian non-combatants who had nothing to do with September 11? How in the name of Allah can that be justice?'

Abu Walid was angry too, but his ire was reserved for Osama bin Laden, whom he blamed for Afghanistan's misery. 'He was very depressed and very moody', says Rabiah. 'His dislike for Osama became greater. He used to say, "These Wahhabis have destroyed the Islamic state, they are *kha'in*—traitors. They have betrayed Mullah Mohammed Omar. He gave them a place of refuge and they took an oath of allegiance to obey him, and now they have destroyed the Islamic state of Afghanistan."'

A news report one day about the ongoing military operation in Afghanistan prompted Rabiah to remark to Abu Walid, who was lying on the bed: 'Don't forget to say *duah* (a prayer) for Sheikh Osama and the brothers'. Abu Walid's face darkened.

'Why would I say a prayer for those *mujrimin* (criminals)—look what they did to Afghanistan.'

Rabiah just glared at him. 'I was disgusted because he was talking about our brothers who were being hunted, and saying he wasn't going to say a prayer for them because they were criminals. Who did he think he was?'

Abu Walid was working on a major treatise entitled *The Story of the Afghan-Arabs from the Time of Their Arrival in Afghanistan until Their Departure with the Taliban*, which would later be serialised in a leading London-based Arabic newspaper. In this and other writings, Abu Walid continued his excoriation of his erstwhile leader. 'Bin Laden left Tora Bora disheartened by the wounds of defeat and collapse, the very wounds that broke the Taliban and brought down the Islamic Emirate', Abu Walid opined. It was, he said, 'a tragic example of an Islamic movement managed in an alarmingly meaningless way. Everyone knew that bin Laden was leading them to the abyss and even leading the entire country to utter destruction, but they continued to bend to his will and take his orders with suicidal submission.'

When Abu Walid showed Rabiah what he was writing, it invariably prompted an argument. 'I was vehemently opposed to that book', she says. 'I told him it was *haram*, he shouldn't publish it. I said, "I don't care who's made mistakes, they are your Muslim brothers". Islam says you have to make seventy excuses for your brother if he makes a mistake.'

Abu Walid's bitter criticism and Rabiah's continued loyalty to bin Laden became a source of growing tension beween them. Rabiah had also grown suspicious about Abu Walid's faith, particularly about his apparent sympathy for the Shia creed followed by the Iranians. Abu Walid had always been dismissive of the Sunni–Shia divide, which has polarised Muslims since the Prophet Mohammed's death, when the original Shiites (the 'followers of Ali') believed that Mohammed's cousin Ali should have succeeded him as caliph. Abu Walid had close connections with Iran. He had visited the country numerous times and was an admirer of the late Ayatollah Khomeini, whose 1979 revolution had spawned Iran's Islamic state. After settling in Tehran, Rabiah says Abu Walid even renamed one of his sons 'Ali'. But Rabiah began to suspect that his affiliations with the Iranians went even deeper. Whenever Rabiah made comments critical of the Iranians or their Shia practices, she noticed that Abu Walid was quick to defend them. He was surprisingly conversant with the finer points of Shia teachings, and she thought she noticed him following Shia rituals when he prayed.

'I'm not sure if I suspected yet that he was a Shia, but something was wrong', she says.

Rabiah had made her own inquiries into the foundations of the Shia faith, a move inspired by her newfound admiration for the Iranian people. Against her expectations—because she believed that Shia were not real Muslims—she found them exceedingly courteous, self-disciplined and uncommonly charitable. Donation boxes were placed along public thoroughfares in Tehran and she frequently saw Iranian citizens stopping to place *zakat* (alms) in the boxes, which she noticed were always full. Her regard for the Iranians and their pious *akhlaq* (behaviour) provoked in Rabiah a full-blown crisis of faith. Salafi dogma brands the Shia apostates who have abandoned the true path of Islam, and Rabiah found it shocking to contemplate that this might not be the case.

'I went through a crisis. It was one of the most shocking periods in my life. I was confused, I was actually doubting my most fundamental beliefs.'

Desperate to resolve her doubts, Rabiah delegated one of her sons to buy a pre-paid internet card, in defiance of the ban on internet use that was a condition of their house arrest. She logged onto the computer in their house and after a few hours of research her questions were answered, and she had reassured herself that the Shia were not correct and that their beliefs were indeed, in her view, 'outside Islam'. Her internet outing was somehow detected and prompted a stern warning from the Revolutionary Guards, but at least her crisis of faith was resolved.

The issue over her husband's beliefs came to a head when Abu Walid took both of his families on vacation to the Caspian Sea coast, north of Tehran, accompanied by their minders from the Revolutionary Guards. (The Caspian coastal town of Chalous was one of two locations where it was later reported that important al Qaeda captives were held under house arrest. Rabiah says she doesn't know if this was where they stayed.) Abu Walid was to spend one week with Rabiah and her family and another week with his first wife Wafa and hers.

Rabiah resolved to get to the bottom of her doubts over his faith. Instead of confronting him head on, however, she decided to do so by stealth, pretending that she too had been won over to the Shia creed. She had downloaded a book on Shiism from the internet, and presented it to Abu Walid that evening.

'I've been reading this book and it seems to be the truth', she said.

Abu Walid smiled broadly. 'Ah, so you have seen it too.'

Rabiah says that Abu Walid now recounted to her how he had been persuaded years before of the Shia view. 'He said that in 1990 he was in the United Arab Emirates on assignment for the newspaper he was working for, and someone had given him that book. He said he had read it for a week, and then had spent the next week crying, because it proved to him that the Shia were right and Sunnis were wrong.'

Rabiah was staggered. 'So you believe Ali should have been the rightful caliph after the Prophet died and they stole it from him?'

'Yes, that is correct.'

Rabiah believes her assertion that Abu Walid is a Shia will prompt consternation in the jihadist world, and that Abu Walid's allies will assume it was a ruse to ingratiate himself with the Iranian regime. But she is adamant it is the truth. 'I know nobody will believe me. People will say it was just a tactic. But he was a Shia—he came out and admitted it to me.' The implications of this were far-reaching: 'For me, it meant I couldn't stay with him (because) as far as I was concerned, he had ceased to be a Muslim'.

'You are not a Muslim and you have no rights over me', she recalls announcing to a stunned Abu Walid. 'I'll see you on Judgement Day and I'll stand witness that you have left Islam.'

'You're crazy', Abu Walid replied.

'That's alright, I'd rather be crazy than be what you are. You're a liar.'

Rabiah and the children returned that night to Tehran. Abu Walid left separately in the mini-bus with the Revolutionary Guards, and she says she never saw him again.

Without Abu Walid's patronage, Rabiah's family was left in an even more precarious position. It was unlikely the Revolutionary Guards would have deemed her and the children important enough on their own to warrant keeping them under house arrest, and just as likely they would be handed over to the secret police, which would have meant a far more uncertain fate.

Rabiah decided they were no longer safe in Iran. So they packed up their few belongings and left Tehran, travelling hidden under a tarpaulin in the back of a smuggler's truck to the country's southern border with Pakistan. However, they got there only to find the border crossing closed. They considered heading west and crossing into Iraq but decided that was too dangerous. Instead they turned around and headed north again, ending up in the north-eastern Iranian city of Mashhad, 900 kilometres east of Tehran, which they had passed through when they first arrived in Iran from Afghanistan.

Iran's second-largest city, with a population of 2.5 million people, Mashhad was an easy place in which to hide. It is one of the holiest cities in the Shia world, housing the mausoleum of the sainted Imam Reza, and thus a magnet for pilgrims. Close to the borders with Afghanistan and Turkmenistan, Mashhad is also a major stopping point on the main east–west highway that carves through the mountains of Central Asia. Its strategic location makes it a hub for smugglers engaged in moving drugs, weaponry and people, including—in the aftermath of September 11— fugitives from the 'war on terror'. In August 2002, the *Washington Post* reported that dozens of al Qaeda fighters were being sheltered in hotels and guesthouses in Mashhad and another border town, Zabol, further south.

But the hitherto safe haven for al Qaeda sympathisers in Iran was no longer guaranteed. Under mounting US pressure, the Iranian regime had begun rounding up the international fugitives within its borders. In 2002, sixteen detainees described as 'al Qaeda operatives' were handed over to Saudi Arabia, in an attempt to rebut the long-standing assertion that Tehran was harbouring terrorists. The *Washington Post* reported that the wives and children of some al Qaeda figures were being turned over to their home governments 'in a display of solidarity with the United States and its allies'.

Rabiah and her family rented a house, kept their heads down and managed to remain undetected in Mashhad for about six months. But in mid 2003 the Iranian secret police came knocking on their door. Whether it was a random check or they had been reported was not clear. The police were courteous but wanted to know who they were, where they had come from and why they had no passports. They left after questioning Rabiah and the boys, but she knew they would be back. So that night they packed up again, paid double the usual rate to a people smuggler, and 'made a run for it' back to Tehran.

'We had come to the end of the road', says Rabiah. 'We didn't have any money left. And after the secret service apparatus became aware of us, I was afraid they would put us over the border.'

The following morning, Rabiah and the children took a taxi with their luggage to the Australian embassy in Khalid Istambuli Avenue, Tehran.

Rabiah presented herself at the reception desk where an Iranian secretary greeted her from behind the counter.

'I want to see the consul', said Rabiah.

'No, I think you want the immigration section', the secretary replied.

'No I don't, lady. I want the consul.'

The secretary picked up a phone, dialled a number, then handed the receiver to Rabiah.

'Yes, how can I help you?' a male voice with an Australian accent inquired.

'My name is Rabiah Hutchinson. My family and I crossed the border illegally from Afghanistan into Iran and we've been here illegally for over two years. We don't have passports and we want to go back to Australia.'

By Rabiah's account, the embassy staffer was unimpressed.

'Do you, now? Well I'm afraid there's nothing I can do for you. You have broken Iranian law so I suggest you turn yourselves in to the Iranian authorities.'

Rabiah would do no such thing. She left Ilyas, Aminah and Huda with the luggage in a waiting room at the embassy and took a taxi with Mustafa to the telephone exchange, from where she rang her daughter Rahmah in Sydney. It was the first time Rahmah had heard from her mother since Rabiah had called from Kandahar in the days after 11 September 2001. For the two years since then, Rahmah had had no way of knowing if her family was alive or dead.

'I need the name of a solicitor, I'll ring you back in fifteen minutes', said Rabiah. Rahmah found her the name of a lawyer in Sydney, whom Rabiah then rang from the Tehran exchange.

'Just refuse to leave the embassy', the lawyer advised.

'We were gone about an hour and a half, and by the time I got back to the embassy I'd become VIP of the month', Rabiah recounts. 'They were calling me Ms Hutchinson and saying "Can you step this way?" … and I was escorted up to the consul's office and asked if I would like a drink or a coffee. Apparently they had been in contact with Canberra and obviously Canberra had said: "We want her back here".'

The Australian authorities had been eager to get their hands on Rabiah Hutchinson for quite some time. In January 2003, Jack Thomas had been arrested in Pakistan as he was about to board a plane to return to Australia. Under intense interrogation by the CIA, Pakistan's ISI and ASIO, Thomas provided hours of information about his movements in Pakistan and Afghanistan. His account included details of how 'Umm Mohammed' had been his first contact in Afghanistan and how she had provided an introduction to the Taliban commander who sent him for training at al Qaeda's Camp Faruq. Thomas also revealed Rabiah's marriage to the al Qaeda strategist Abu Walid al Misri, and the invitation from bin Laden's deputy Dr Ayman al Zawahiri to start up a women's hospital in Kandahar. It was enough to arouse the interest of intelligence agencies all over the world—and to ensure that once the Australian embassy staff in Tehran had been hastily briefed, Rabiah and her children received special attention. 'Instead of being sent to the nearest immigration office, they put us in the Australian embassy car with Australian flags on the front. The kids and I—after being in the backs of trucks under tarpaulins, and driving over cliffs—suddenly we're in this humongous black car with Australian flags on it, and the driver's calling me Ms Hutchinson. It was funny actually—I didn't realise the joke was on me.'

They were escorted to the Tehran Apartment Hotel—'the plushest hotel I've ever been in'—where, according to Rabiah, the Australian Department of Foreign Affairs and Trade booked a room, paid the bill and vouched for their identities, as they had no passports. She still has the embossed leather key ring she kept as a souvenir of their extended stay there.

Rabiah and the children were granted new Australian passports, issued in August 2003 and valid for just three months. But the Australian authorities seemed to be in no rush to bring them home. ASIO was eager to glean what intelligence it could from her, and had a better chance of doing so while she was still potentially at the mercy of the Iranian authorities than once she had returned home.

After their passports were issued, Rabiah says she was summoned to the embassy and ushered into the head of mission's office where the ambassador and consul were waiting to see her. She says the ambassador's tone was apologetic.

'This has got nothing to do with us, and we're not telling you that you have to talk to them, or that you should or shouldn't, but ASIO is here and they want to talk to you.'

'I don't want to talk to them', Rabiah replied. But the female ASIO officer dispatched to interrogate her was there already. Rabiah's version of their conversation is the only one available, as neither ASIO nor the Department of Foreign Affairs and Trade (DFAT) would comment on these events, other than DFAT confirming that its staff 'provided extensive consular assistance to Ms Hutchinson and her children'. By Rabiah's account, the ASIO agent gave her an ultimatum:

'I can't force you to talk to me. But I am telling you that the government is currently considering your case and your returning to Australia is under review. And it could have an adverse effect on you if you refuse to talk to us.'

'What do you mean? I'm an Australian citizen. Are you saying they're going to cancel my citizenship?'

'I can't say they will, and I can't say they won't', Rabiah recalls the ASIO agent telling her.

'They purposely gave me the impression that me and my children would become stateless if I didn't talk to them', Rabiah claims. 'And I really honestly thought I could have my citizenship revoked. I thought we were gonna be put over the Pakistani border, or put in jail in Iran, or sent to Guantánamo Bay.'

Rabiah says she was interrogated for several hours. After the first session, the ASIO agent told her that head office 'wasn't happy' with the results so far: 'Canberra reckons all you did was do *dawah* (proselytising) on me'. She was interrogated again; about her marriages to Abdul Rahim Ayub and Abu Walid; her activities in Indonesia, Pakistan and Afghanistan; her connections with Jemaah Islamiyah, Abu Bakar Ba'asyir and al Qaeda; her knowledge of Dr Ayman al Zawahiri, Khalid Sheikh Mohammed and Osama bin Laden.

'What do you think of suicide bombing?' the agent asked her.

'It's *haram* (forbidden)', Rabiah says she replied.

'So you don't agree with what they're doing in Palestine?'

'Look, I will fight to my last breath to defend the rights of the Palestinians, but if you're asking am I going to go and lob a grenade out of a bus in Lakemba or strap on a bomb on the Manly ferry, then the answer is "No".'

Two months after the issuing of their new passports, Rabiah and the children were still waiting in Tehran, puzzled at what was causing the delay. On 22 October 2003, Rabiah was handed a Deed of Undertaking obliging her to repay the sum of $5464.23 to DFAT, to cover the cost of their accommodation and expenses in Tehran and their one-way tickets back to Australia. Their departure was finally approved the following day.

'George Bush has left—you can go home now', Rabiah recalls an embassy staffer telling her. The US President had just completed a 21-hour visit to Australia with an entourage of 650 advisers and security staff, escorted by a fleet of FA-18 fighter jets, and protected by more than 450 Australian Federal Police, backed up by Air Force Black Hawks, Navy Squirrels, the Tactical Assault Group and other specialist forces. Rabiah couldn't tell if the embassy staffer was joking, or if the Australian government seriously believed she might pose a threat to the heavily guarded President Bush.

On the day of their departure, 27 October 2003, two air marshals were assigned to accompany Rabiah and the four children on the flight to Australia. Rabiah describes the pair—an Egyptian man and a Pakistani woman—'as two humongous, gorilla-like people'. 'He looked like he had taken so many steroids he could hardly turn his neck, and she was the biggest Pakistani woman I've ever seen in my life. They wanted to make me pay for them. I told them, "Yeah, in your dreams, you can carry me on kicking and screaming, gagged and in handcuffs, but I'm not paying".'

The air marshals were given custody of their tickets and positioned themselves at either end of the row of seats occupied by Rabiah and the children. When 11-year-old Huda got up to use the bathroom, the female air marshal rose to accompany her.

'I'm going to the toilet', said Huda indignantly.

'I'll come with you.'

'Well, you'll have to handcuff me then, because there's no way in the world you're coming in there with me.'

Their strange-looking party caused a commotion during a stopover in Dubai, when a nervy Englishman travelling with his wife and toddler noticed the two beefy air marshals escorting a woman fully veiled in black, with two girls in hijabs, and a pair of swarthy teenagers in *shalwar kameez*.

'Excuse me, I have a child', said the Englishman, manoeuvring his way to the front of the queue when boarding commenced.

'Well, excuse me—I have a policeman', Rabiah replied.

'Oh, no! There's terrorists on the plane!' the Englishman cried, and refused to board the aircraft.

* * *

Rabiah and her children arrived home in Sydney at the end of October 2003. In the four years they had been away from Australia, the world had changed. In the wake of September 11, the JI bombings of the Sari Club and Paddy's Bar in Bali had killed 202 people including 88 Australians, catapulting Australia into the role of willing partner in the global 'war on terror'. 'Either you are with us or you are with the terrorists', US President George Bush had declared. Rabiah found herself ostracised in her community. Former friends crossed the street rather than talk to her, and the jibes in the supermarket turned to streams of vitriole and threats of violence. The world seemed polarised. The United States and its allies had invaded Iraq. The Bush administration had covertly authorised the use of torture at secret CIA prisons around the globe against terrorism suspects. Hundreds of detainees languished in indefinite legal limbo at Guantánamo Bay. Like many Muslims, Rabiah perceived it as a war on Islam.

'Since September 11, we have become among the most hated people on the planet, to the extent that we can be detained, tortured, raped, humiliated. And you know what's so intolerable about it—the lies. If they've decided that we're not allowed to exist, at least be honest about it, don't lie about it. Don't make up all these slogans like the "war on terror". Just say, "We don't like them and we're going to wipe them off the face of this Earth".'

Rabiah had no wish to remain in Australia. But when she applied for a new passport to replace the temporary document issued in Tehran, her application was refused. The notification from DFAT cited an adverse security assessment by ASIO, which was summarised in a Statement of Grounds dated 2 August 2004, Rabiah's fifty-first birthday:

> Rabiah Maryam Hutchinson (born 2 August 1953, Australia) has extensive links to and supports the activities of Islamic extremists both in Australia and abroad. Hutchinson is directly associated with core members of the Ahel al Sunna wal Jamaah Association (ASJA); with senior members of both Jemaah Islamiyah and al-Qa'ida; and has directly supported extremist activities. ASIO assesses there is a strong likelihood that further travel by Rabiah Maryam Hutchinson will involve participation in, or support and preparation for acts of politically motivated violence. We further assess that in continued travel overseas, Hutchinson is likely to engage in conduct that might prejudice the security of Australia or a foreign country.

The ASIO assessment was typical of the pronouncements made by intelligence agencies whose job it is to determine who is 'with us' and who is 'with the terrorists'. It was part fact, part extrapolation, and part assertion of guilt by association. Some of it was demonstrably true. Rabiah indeed has 'extensive links' to Islamic extremists and supports some of their activities, though she denies this extends to supporting terrorism. She is certainly associated with ASJA. However, it is a legal organisation, whose leaders and followers remain free to follow their beliefs, regardless of the fact that many Australians consider them 'extreme'. She is undoubtedly 'directly associated' with senior members of JI and al Qaeda. By her own account, corroborated by others, she was a trusted friend and follower of JI's leaders, and shared their goal of an Islamic state in

Indonesia. And she was clearly close to al Qaeda's inner circle, by dint of her activities in Pakistan and Afghanistan and her marriage to one of its leading strategists. But she has had little direct involvement in JI since 1999, when its militant faction embraced terrorism, and there is nothing to implicate her in al Qaeda's terrorist campaign.

The assertion that there is a 'strong likelihood' that further travel by Rabiah would involve 'participation in, or support and preparation for acts of politically motivated violence' is pure conjecture. No evidence has been produced to support this, and in more than a year that I have spent investigating Rabiah's story, I have come across no such evidence. The same applies to the suggestion that she is 'likely to engage in conduct that might prejudice the security of Australia or a foreign country'. Australia now has stringent counter-terrorism laws, but Rabiah has not been accused of any crime. Nonetheless she believes she has been judged guilty and punished with what she deems to be another form of house arrest.

'They don't need to charge me with anything. They don't need to put me in jail. They've taken away everything from me that means anything to me. I have been sentenced to a life of being alone in a society that I hate and they hate me. I have been separated from my children and my grandchildren, from my people, my country. For what? What crime have I committed? What's the justification for what's happened to me?'

The cancellation of Rabiah's passport was not extended to her children, and in late 2004 her sons, Mustafa and Ilyas, by this stage aged eighteen and sixteen, and her 14-year-old daughter Aminah, left Australia again bound for Yemen to continue their Islamic studies. The three of them were enrolled at a private Islamic institute in the Yemeni desert town of Mahrib to study Islamic law.

In October 2006, Mustafa and Ilyas were detained by the Yemeni police as part of a counter-terrorism operation led by the CIA and MI6. Its targets were a group of Europeans who lived in the same apartment block where Rabiah's sons were staying with their sisters in the Yemeni capital, Sanaa, and who were reportedly suspected of funnelling weapons to neighbouring Somalia with the backing of al Qaeda. An Australian newspaper reported that Mustafa and Ilyas were detained after Australian security agencies passed on information about their whereabouts. They were held for almost eight weeks in a windowless underground cell, lit by a bare bulb dangling from the ceiling and empty except for a soiled mattress and a swarm of cockroaches. They were blindfolded and Ilyas said he was beaten on the soles of his feet by a guard with a cane. They were interrogated at length by the Yemeni secret police and ASIO. They said the ASIO agents brought newspaper clippings about Rabiah from Australia to show the Yemeni police. According to Mustafa and Ilyas, the Yemeni guards later sneered, 'Are they afraid of old women in your country?'

Mustafa and Ilyas were released without charge in November 2006. Yemeni prosecutors said seven of the eight foreigners arrested had no case to answer, and a Yemeni lawyer told the *Australian* they were freed because there was no evidence of their involvement in any conspiracy. Despite this, they were deported from Yemen after their release. They travelled to Lebanon but when the authorities there learned of their history they refused to extend their visas. So they moved on to the United Arab Emirates, but there were visa problems again, and having a 'deported' stamp in their passports had ended their hopes of going on to study further in Saudi Arabia. They now assumed that wherever they went they would be targeted. With nowhere else to go, they returned to Australia in December 2007. Rabiah bridles at their treatment.

'My sons are not allowed to exist, they are not allowed to live anywhere on the face of this Earth. Why—because I'm their mother?'

Rabiah's daughters Rahmah and Aminah, who were also in Yemen, have remained in the Middle East with Rahmah's nine-year-old son. Aminah recently married and, in August 2008, gave birth to a boy, Rabiah's third grandchild. Her granddaughter Huda is living with them and studying at an Islamic school.

Rabiah has had no contact with her elder children, Devi and Mohammed, since before she left for Pakistan and Afghanistan in 1999. She says it is they who severed contact. 'If that is because I was a bad mother or because their lives were so traumatic, then for that I am truly sorry', she says. She also remains cut off from her brother and sister,

George and Susan. Her sister never called her again after reading an article headlined 'Australian Mum Married into Al Qaeda' (written by the author) in the *Australian* newspaper in November 2006. Rabiah's notoriety brought one benefit: in 2008 she resumed contact with her half brother, Roderick, who has struggled with depression since his troubled childhood, when he rang to tell her he had been inspired to convert to Islam after seeing her interviewed on television.

* * *

It is 2009, and Rabiah is living in a rented house near Lakemba in south-western Sydney with two of her sons. Their home is a neat three-bedroom brick bungalow with patterned rugs covering a white tiled floor, upholstered cushions lining the walls, a television set usually tuned to the news, and a shelf full of mementos of her travels. A goldfish tank bubbles in a corner, under the watchful gaze of a fat fluffy cat, named Benny after Huda's lost teddy bear.

After a lifetime of journeying, nowadays Rabiah leaves her home infrequently. When she ventures out veiled in her black *niqab*, she invariably attracts harassment and abuse. People in her community are loath to associate with her lest they too are branded as being 'with the terrorists'. She has stopped holding Islamic classes for young women because her students found that they, their husbands and families were automatically targeted for attention by ASIO.

Rabiah gazes forlornly around her fastidiously kept piece of Australian suburbia, as the drone of a lawn mower drifts in through an open window. While a home on a three-quarter-acre block in the suburbs was what many of her generation aspired to, it's a far cry from the dreams Rabiah has been pursuing for much of her life.

'This is not reality to me; it's not real. Those mud houses and no electricity in Pakistan or Indonesia or Afghanistan—that's reality to me. This is just a nightmare that I hope I'm going to wake up from one day, and find it's not true.'

The ordinariness of the setting makes a surreal backdrop for the extraordinary story that has unfolded as we have met here (and in her previous flat in Lakemba) once or twice a week for most of the last year and a half. The unfolding of the story has itself been a journey, for both of us. She has wept, shouted, laughed and railed in fury as she recounted a life lived on the frontlines of an ideological war, which has seen her a witness to and participant in some of the historic episodes of our time. I have been amused, disturbed and astounded, and have grown to deeply admire her courage and sheer indomitable will. I do not share her politics or her beliefs—although she has never stopped trying to convert me—but I respect her unwavering commitment to them, notwithstanding that they are indeed 'extreme'. If it's true that her home is a prison, then in some ways it's one of her own making; a product of her unrelenting conviction and refusal to compromise on those beliefs. For this she remains fiercely unapologetic. She rejects sympathy but asks that we consider it from her perspective:

'How would you like it if the government said to you, "Right, we don't like the way you think". Then they picked you up, separated you from your children, forced you to live somewhere you don't want to live, for the rest of your life until you die—just because they don't like the way you think and your beliefs. And you have no way of refuting it. I could have come back here and portrayed myself as something other than what I am—to regain my passport, to be reunited with my family, to feather my own nest. But I can't do that. I am a Muslim, I want to live and die a Muslim. I want to defend my right to practise Islam.'

In many ways Rabiah personifies the polarisation of the world, the so-called 'clash of civilisations' between the West and Islam, which was seemingly cleaved wide open with the events of 11 September 2001. But thankfully, in early 2009, the world is changing again—the swearing in of a new US President seeming to herald a more hopeful world order, the harsh language of the 'war on terror' replaced by a new rhetoric embodied in Barack Obama's appeal: 'To the Muslim world, we seek a new way forward, based on mutual interest and mutual respect'.

This new order will face enormous hurdles in the coming years. One almighty challenge will be persuading those who have resorted to terrorism in the name of Islam to join the quest for a new way forward. Another challenge, for us in the West, will be learning to live with, tolerate and even respect people whose beliefs we regard as foreign and extreme, because those beliefs don't necessarily make them terrorists.

As for Rabiah Maryam Hutchinson, there's no telling where the next leg of her extraordinary life's journey will lead. She herself has no idea, but she is fortified by a profound conviction that *inshallah*—God willing—she is in good hands. 'I firmly believe that nothing will happen to me except what Allah permits—and in the end Allah brings good out of everything.'

ACKNOWLEDGEMENTS

Without Rabiah's decision to entrust me with her story, this book could not have been written. I thank her for the leap of faith, her children for supporting it, her daughters Rahmah and Aminah for sharing their memories of Pakistan and Afghanistan, and Mamdouh and Maha Habib for providing the introduction that made it possible.

Many people have given generously of their time, expertise, friendship and support over the year and a half it took me to write this book. Michael Doyle and Mary Neighbour provided invaluable feedback on early chapter drafts. Sarah Curnow read the entire draft manuscript and her encouragement kept me going. Sidney Jones and Greg Fealy were as generous as always, in particular by perusing the Indonesian chapters and correcting my errors. I am especially indebted to Ken Ward who read much of the manuscript and provided crucial advice on Indonesian and Arabic terminology and the history of the Islamist movement. The authors and journalists whose works I have drawn on, particularly on Indonesia and Afghanistan, are too numerous to mention here but they are acknowledged in the notes that follow. Others who helped personally include Mark Corcoran, Amanda Collinge, Stephen Hutcheon, Liz Jackson, Anthony Johns, Takeshi Kohno, Bill Maley, Brendan Maxwell, Virginia Moncrieff, Tim Palmer, Cameron Stewart, Marc Sageman, Quinton Temby, Geoff Thompson, Leigh Sales and Daoud Yaqub. (To anyone else I have neglected to mention, I apologise—and thank you!) The priceless Natalie Hurrell doubled as research assistant and child minder. My executive producers at *Four Corners*, Bruce Belsham and Sue Spencer, and ABC News management led by John Cameron allowed me the leeway without which I could not have embarked on this project.

In Indonesia, Faried Saenong proved the finest guide, translator and fixer one could hope for. For my trip to Afghanistan I am indebted to Nick Barker of the Overwatch Group who arranged safe travel, logistics, transport and accommodation, and facilitated the services of my driver and guide, Ahmad Sadiqi; and to Rory McGregor, Pat Gleeson and their colleagues at Asia Security Group who looked after me on the ground. Thanks also to Michael Dwyer, Chris Dover, Major David Harris, Heather Grace Jones, Shqipe Maloushi, Amy Corcoran and Terry Shiel, who assisted and entertained me in Kabul. Time and budget constraints prevented me on this occasion from travelling to Cairo, but I am grateful to Anthony Bubalo, James Piscatori, Linda Herrera, Malika Zeghal and Issandr El Amrani for their advice and expertise on Egypt and Al Azhar. Most of the people who assisted my research in Australia are acknowledged in the text or the notes. However, I would like to single out Sandy Sheridan at the Mudgee Historical Society, Ian Goodacre, Craig Johnston, Roderick Hutchinson and Nadia Aboufadil for their patience and generosity.

I am extremely thankful for the boundless enthusiasm of Louise Adler at Melbourne University Publishing, and for the advice and support of her colleagues Foong Ling Kong, Elisa Berg, Cinzia Cavallaro, Eugenie Baulch and Moira Anderson.

Finally, to Michael and Oscar—thank you, for everything. For what it's worth, this book is for you.

NOTES

1 Robin Merry Hood

Page 3, **Another atomic weapons test … rabbit stew**: Stories in the *Mudgee Guardian,* 3 August 1953, p. 1. Courtesy of Mid-Western Regional Council Library, Mudgee.

Page 3, **'A bonny baby daughter'**: Birth notice in *Mudgee Guardian*, 3 August 1953, and NSW Birth and Baptismal Register for 1953.

Page 3, **the birth of their son George**: I have changed the name of Robyn's brother at his request.

Page 3, **Wayne, who died at four months**: NSW Birth and Baptismal Register 1950; and author visit to Mudgee Cemetery.

Page 4, **Mudgee in the 1950s**: Information from the Mudgee Historical Society and *Mudgee Guardian*. Additional information about Mudgee in the 1950s and the life of Robyn's family provided by Mudgee residents: Sandy Sheridan, Pauline Bassingthwaighte, Lisa Gervais, Stephen Gay, Una Gay, Colin Gay, Ken Sutcliffe, Hugh Bateman, Gary Cook, Norm King, Lorna Pitt, Annmarie Hanchard, Mervyn Neal and Keith McCallum.

Page 4, **51 Horatio Street**: The house numbers in Horatio Street have changed since the 1950s and the historic home now at number 51 is not the house where Robyn lived.

Page 5, **'like infuriated soldier ants'**: 'Jim Hutchison and George Riley Win Soldiers' Bowling Club Pairs Title', *Mudgee Guardian*, 10 February 1955. Jim's family name is spelt 'Hutchison' in this article; he appears to have used both spellings.

Page 5, **The son of a Lithgow coal-miner**: Author interview with Jim's son Roderick Hutchinson, Sydney, 14 May 2008.

Page 6, **He enlisted in the army in 1943**: Australian Military Forces Attestation Form, war records held by the National Archives of Australia, and World War II Nominal Roll, Commonwealth of Australia.

Page 6, **Scotsman named Archibald Roy McCallum**: Information on Robyn's forebears is from the Mudgee Historical Society and NSW Registry of Births, Deaths and Marriages.

Page 7, **eulogised in the *Guardian***: *Mudgee Guardian*, 27 June 1949. Provided by Sandy Sheridan, Mudgee Historical Society.

Page 8, **'He was always violent'**: Roderick Hutchinson.

Page 9, **the Woolpack Hotel**: Mudgee Historical Society.

Page 10, **'a rough and tough typical Aussie'**: Interview with Stephen Gay, Mudgee, February 2008.

Page 11, **the old Mechanics Institute**: Author visit to Mudgee, February 2008.

Page 12, **a one-horse town called Wollar**: Author visit to Wollar, February 2008.

Page 13, **a baby sister named Susan**: I have changed the name of Robyn's sister at her request.

Page 14, **ended up with shit all over him**: Anecdote related by Stephen Gay.

Page 15, **a guest of the Royal Far West Children's Health Scheme**: General information provided by the Royal Far West Children's Health Scheme and Services for the Aged. They have no record of Robyn's stay, as records from that era have not been retained.

Page 18, **a pale-blue weatherboard bungalow**: Author visit to Mudgee, February 2008.

Page 21, **'I do remember her bailing me up'**: Interview with Annmarie Hanchard, Mudgee, February 2008.

2 Wild Child

Page 22, **house propped like an eyrie**: Author visit, March 2008.

Page 23, **British model Jean Shrimpton**: 'The Shrimp shocked them', *Sun News-Pictorial*, 1 November 1965, Melbourne, p. 1.

Page 23, **a corps of neatly frocked middle-class mothers**: Photograph of mothers in the SOS movement demonstrating outside the front steps of Brisbane City Hall in the 1960s, Fryer Library Online Exhibition,

University of Queensland, <www.library.uq.edu.au/fryer/worth_fighting/6_1.html>.

Page 23, **Harbord Diggers Memorial Club**: Information from Harbord Diggers Memorial Club, Sydney, courtesy Jennifer Hamilton.

Page 23, **'Modern Go Go Dancing for Teenagers'**, etc: Harbord Diggers Memorial Club newsletters from the 1960s.

Page 24, **Her brother George** and **baby of the family, Susan**: Robyn's brother and sister would not be interviewed so I am reliant on her recollections.

Page 26, **historic Hydro Majestic hotel**: Author interview with Roderick Hutchinson, Sydney, 14 May 2008.

Page 26, **Freshwater Beach**: <www.visitmanly.com.au/html/freshwater_beach_sydney.html>.

Page 26, **legendary Hawaiian Duke Kahanamoku**: 'Duke Kahanamoku and the Dawn of Australian Surfing at the "Boomerang Camp", Freshwater Beach, Sydney, in the Southern Summer of 1915', web publication by Mountain Man Graphics, Australia, <www.mountainman.com.au/the_duke.html>.

Page 27, **Manly Girls High**: Information provided by Freshwater Senior Campus (formerly Manly Girls High), Harbord; and old school magazines, courtesy Di Marik, deputy principal.

Page 27, **'She was an unreal girl'**: Author interviews with Deborah Jensen, June 2008 and 18 November 2008.

Page 30, **'She was great, she was a really nice person'**: Author interview with Ian Goodacre, March 2008.

Page 30, **a neat Edwardian bungalow**: Author visit, March 2008.

Page 31, **'They treated her like their own daughter'**: Anonymous interview, March 2008.

Page 31, **her grandfather, Archibald Roy McCallum, died**: NSW Death Registration Transcription, transcribed by Marilyn Rowan, 14 May 2008; and information at Mudgee cemetery.

Page 32, **'She smoked dope'**: Author interview with Steve Warnock, Sydney, April 2008.

Page 33, **'Their relationship was distant'**: Roderick Hutchinson.

Page 35, **A friend remembers**: Anonymous interview.

Page 36, **'She was quite a character'**: Author interview with Lynn Collins, April 2008.

3 God Is Great

Page 39, **Bali was still largely untouched**: Tony Wheeler, *South-East Asia on a Shoestring*, 1st edn, Lonely Planet, Melbourne, 1975.

Page 43, **a job with Intensive English Course (IEC)**: <www.iec.ac.id>; and author visit to IEC, Jakarta, July 2008.

Page 43, **It was seven years after General Suharto**: Adam Schwartz, *A Nation in Waiting*, Allen & Unwin, Sydney, 1999, p. 37.

Page 44, **'I just saw a *bule*'**: Author interview with Malik Sjafei, Jakarta, 7 July 2008.

Page 44, **'She had a good heart'**: Author interview with Liliek Soemarlono, Sydney, 13 June 2008.

Page 44, **'It was felt that the gang needed an identity'**: Article on Prambors website, <www.pramborsfm.com?opt=about&id=hist>; and information from Malik Sjafei.

Page 45, **held in his mansion in Jalan Borobodur**: Author visit to Jakarta, July 2008.

Page 48, **a famous Muslim intellectual known as Buya Hamka**: Information from Dr Greg Fealy, College of Asia and the Pacific, Australian National University, Canberra.

Page 50, **Raden Bambang Wisudo**: In the Javanese alphabet there is no distinction between 'a' and 'o', so Bambang's name can be rendered as either 'Wisuda' or 'Wisudo'. Rabiah says that in Indonesia his family used 'Wisuda', but Australian records show it as 'Wisudo'.

Page 50, **aristocratic *priyayi* class**: Peter Burns, *The Leiden Legacy: Concepts of Law in Indonesia*, KITLV Press, Leiden, Netherlands, 2004.

Page 50, **the title *raden ayu***: Rochayah Machali and Ida Nurhayatai, 'Challenging Tradition: the Indonesian Novel Saman', University of New

South Wales, *GEMA Online Journal of Language Studies*, published by
the School of Language Studies and Linguistics, Universiti Kebangsaan
Malaysia, <www.docstoc.com/docs/2430792/GEMA-Online-Journal-of-
Language-Studies>.

Page 51, **had to formally convert to Islam**: Certificate issued by Department
of Religion, Ubud, Indonesia, 1 February 1974. Sighted by author.

Page 56, **new organisation called Islam Jamaah**: 'Exclusivity is not our
doctrine: LDII', *Jakarta Post*, 29 October 2005; additional information
from Greg Fealy.

Page 56, **Student protests demanding price cuts**: Schwartz.

4 A Javanese Wife

Page 59, **the term *tante girang***: Advice on this and other Indonesian terminology
courtesy Indonesia analyst and terrorism consultant Ken Ward.

Page 60, **They called her Devi**: As I have reported here the girl's given name
was Devi Suni Wisudo Putri. However, the family called her not 'Devi'
but another variant on her given name. I have used 'Devi' for the
purpose of disguising her name in order to protect her privacy, because
I have not been able to contact her to obtain her authorisation.

Page 61, **last vestiges of the White Australia Policy**: Department of
Immigration and Citizenship, *Abolition of the 'White Australia' Policy*,
Fact sheet 8, Australian Government, <www.immi.gov.au/media/fact-
sheets.08abolition.htm>.

Page 62, **'They didn't get on'**: Author interview with Roderick Hutchinson,
Sydney, 14 May 2008.

Pages 62–3, **'She was certainly different'**: Author interview with Steve
Warnock, Sydney, April 2008.

Page 63, **Australia had fallen on troubled times**: 1975 Cabinet Records,
Selected documents—The Economy, National Archives of Australia,
<www.naa.gov.au/images/economy-1_tcm2-1456.pdf>.

Page 63, **'Boy was a sweet guy'**: Author interviews with Deborah Jensen, June
2008 and 18 November 2008.

Page 64, **On 23 July 1976**: Information on the drug bust is from Steve Warnock, 'Drug Family May Lose Baby', *Sunday Mirror*, 1 August 1976.

Page 66, **a letter arrived from the immigration department**: Immigration department records on this were not made available, so I am reliant on Rabiah's account.

Page 67, **expansive residential compound for customs department officials**: Author visit to customs compound at Pondok Bambu, Jakarta, July 2008.

Page 74, **They gave him the names**: At his request, I have not used the first given name of Rabiah's eldest son. The name Mohammed—which is the basis for Rabiah's *kuniya* 'Umm Mohammed', meaning 'the mother of Mohammed'—was given to him a few years later. At the time of his birth he was given a Hindu name, to which he has since reverted.

Page 75, **'She went through a really, really bad time'**: Deborah Jensen.

Page 76, **Three months later she sent enough money**: I was unable to contact Rabiah's benefactor so I am reliant on her account, which is corroborated in part by Deborah Jensen.

5 The Death of Robyn

Page 78, **'She was just relieved to be back'**: Author interviews with Deborah Jensen, June 2008 and 18 November 2008.

Page 79, **tipped a beer over her head**: Deborah Jensen.

Page 81, **Silma Buckley**: Linda Morris, 'Islamic Pioneer Still Battles for Land, Twenty Years on', *Sydney Morning Herald*, 24 June 2003; '"Justice for All" the Principal Lesson', *Manly Daily*, 26 August 2006; Silma Buckley, 'About me', <www.silmapol.blogspot.com>; Silma Buckley, *Bridges of Light: The Struggle of an Islamic Private School in Australia*, Muslim Service Association, Sydney, 1991.

Page 81, **'I remember when she came in'**: Author interview with Silma Ihram, 23 May 2008.

Page 83, **ascetic named Rabiah al Adawiyah**: *Encyclopaedia Britannica*; 'Sufism and its Influence on Europe', a lecture by Dr Anne-Marie Schimmel, delivered at Stanford University, 4 May 1997,

<www.naqshbandi.org/events/sufitalk/sufismeu.htm>; Oxford Islamic Studies Online.

Pages 83, 84, **'One night Rabiah al Adawiyah'** and **'Man, do not put yourself'**: From 'World of Tasawwuf', Sufi anecdotes and stories, <www.spiritualfoundation.net/stories.htm>.

6 Becoming Rabiah

Page 88, **an American convert named Rahmah McCormack**: From Susan Molloy, 'Two Women Converts Explain Islam's "Simplistic" Appeal', *Sydney Morning Herald*, 8 November 1980, p. 4.

Page 88, **'It was not intellectually satisfying'**: Molloy.

Pages 88–9, **built in the mid 1970s with a gift of $300 000**: Author interview with Sheikh Khalil Chami, Lakemba, May 2008.

Page 90, **Mohammed John Webster**: 'The Priest and the Prodigal', *Australian Story*, ABC TV, 27 May 1999; Tony Stephens, 'Anarchistic Demagogue Has the Last Word', obituary, *Sydney Morning Herald*, 17 December 2008.

Page 90, **Jemaah Tabligh**: Mitsuo Nakamura, Sharon Siddique and Omar Farouk Bajunid (eds), *Islam and Civil Society in Southeast Asia*, Institute of Southeast Asian Studies, Singapore, 2001; Syed Serajul Islam, *The Politics of Islamic Identity in Southeast Asia*, Thomson Learning, Singapore, 2004.

Page 91, **'She was very motivated'**: Author interview with Siddiq Buckley, Sydney, May 2008.

Page 91, **Rabiah was pictured wearing**: photograph with caption 'Islam in Dulwich Hill', *Sydney Morning Herald*, 8 November 1980, p. 1.

Page 92, **Khadija**: W Montgomery Watt, *Muhammad: Prophet and Statesman*, Oxford University Press, London, 1961; Maxime Rodinson, *Muhammad: Prophet of Islam*, Tauris Parke Paperbacks, London, 2002.

Page 92, **women's equality in religious matters**: For more on the role of women in Islam, see Sayyid Qutb, *Social Justice in Islam*, Maktabat Misr, Cairo, 1953, pp. 73–9.

Page 92, **For the women of seventh-century Arabia**: Geraldine Brooks, *Nine Parts of Desire: The Hidden World of Islamic Women*, Penguin, London, 2007, p. 186.

Page 93, **rights that were well ahead**: Brooks.

Page 95, **'I picked up the newspaper'**: Author interviews with Deborah Jensen, June 2008 and 18 November 2008.

Page 98, **to teach Muslim scripture**: Sheikh Khalil Chami.

Page 102, **banned by the Shah of Iran's father**: Brooks.

Page 102, **matched dollar for dollar**: Burke.

Page 103, **an Afghan doctor named Abdul Aziz**: Sheikh Khalil Chami.

Page 104, **She travelled to Canberra**: Amin Hady recalls assisting Rabiah with 'family matters' but has no specific recollection of this occasion.

7 An Enemy of Suharto

Page 106, **After obliterating the Communist Party**: Adam Schwartz, *A Nation in Waiting*, Allen & Unwin, Sydney, 1999.

Page 106, **Indonesians turned to their mosques**: Edward Aspinall, *Opposing Suharto: Compromise, Resistance and Regime Change in Indonesia*, Stanford University Press, 2005; Martin van Bruinessen, 'Genealogies of Islamic Radicalism in post-Suharto Indonesia', *South East Asia Research*, vol. 10, no. 2, IP Publishing, 2002. Additional information provided by Greg Fealy, Sidney Jones and Ken Ward.

Page 111, **'She was beautiful'**: Author interview with Pujo Busono, Solo, Indonesia, July 2008.

Page 111, **part of a clandestine student movement**: Quinton Temby, 'Imagining the Islamic State in Indonesia', Bachelor of Asian Studies thesis, Australian National University, 2007; Human Rights Watch, 'Academic Freedom in Indonesia: Dismantling Soeharto Era Barriers', 1998; Noorhaidi Hasan, 'The Expansion of "Salafis" and the Zeal of Islamic Resurgence', in *Laskar Jihad: Islam, Militancy and the Quest for Identity in Post–New Order Indonesia*, SEAP Publications, Southeast Asia Program, Cornell University, 2006; van Bruinessen, Schwartz.

Page 111, **'personal morality, piety and discipline'**: van Bruinessen.

Page 112, **the new movement used a cell structure**: Amnesty International, 'The Imprisonment of Usroh Activists in Central Java', October 1988.

Page 113, **Irfan Awwas**: Amnesty International, 'Indonesia—the Imprisonment of Irfan Suryahardy', July 1986; Sidney Jones, 'Al-Qaeda in Southeast Asia: The Case of the "Ngruki Network" in Indonesia', International Crisis Group, August 2002; Sidney Jones, 'Indonesia Backgrounder: How the Jemaah Islamiyah Terrorist Network Operates', International Crisis Group, December 2002.

Page 113, **'Rabiah was very famous'**: Author interview with Irfan Awwas, Jogjakarta, Indonesia, July 2008.

Page 113, **Abu Jibril**: Jones, 'Al-Qaeda in Southeast Asia'; Jones, 'Indonesia Backgrounder'.

Page 113, **featured in a JI recruitment video**: Video obtained by author in Indonesia in 2002.

Page 113, **'We were quite close'**: Interview with Abu Jibril conducted for the author by Faried Saenong, Jakarta, July 2008.

Page 115, **when she was travelling on a train**: Story recounted to author by Shabharin Syakur at MMI office, Jogjakarta, July 2008, and confirmed by Abu Jibril.

Page 116, **Darul Islam**: David J Kilcullen, 'The Political Consequences of Military Operations in Indonesia 1945–99', PhD thesis, University of New South Wales, 2000; Greg Fealy, 'Darul Islam and Jemaah Islamiyah: An Historical and Ideological Comparison', The College of Asia and the Pacific, Australian National University, 2004; Jones, 'Al-Qaeda in Southeast Asia'; Sidney Jones, 'Recycling Militants in Indonesia: Darul Islam and the Australian Embassy Bombing', International Crisis Group, February 2005.

Page 116, **covertly supported by the Indonesian intelligence**: Jones, 'Recycling Militants'.

Page 116, **Abdullah Sungkar and Abu Bakar Ba'asyir**: Sally Neighbour, *In the Shadow of Swords*, Harper Collins, Sydney, 2004. Primary sources relied on: Abu Bakar Ba'asyir, statement to Indonesian police, January 2003, obtained by the author in Indonesia; Abdullah Sungkar and Abu Bakar Ba'asyir, 'The Latest Indonesian Crisis: Causes and Solutions', *Nida'ul Islam*, July–August 1998; Abu Bakar Ba'asyir, 'Indonesia, Democracy, Priests, Parliament and Self-made Gods', *Nida'ul Islam*, October–November 1996; Abu Bakar Ba'asyir, 'System for the Caderisation of Mujahidin in Creating an Islamic Society', address delivered at the first Indonesian Mujahidin Congress, 5–7 August, Yogyakarta, 2000, trans. Tim Behrend.

Pages 116–17, **a full-scale crackdown**: Temby.

Page 117, **'The charges were standard fare'**: Jones, 'Al-Qaeda in Southeast Asia'.

Page 117, **Sungkar made an impassioned oration**: Temby.

Page 117, **The pair had begun regrouping their followers**: Temby; Amnesty International, 'The Imprisonment'.

Page 118, **There was no shortage of eager suitors**: Pujo Busono.

Page 121, **Ibnu Thoyib**: Jones, 'Al-Qaeda in Southeast Asia', 'Indonesia Backgrounder' and 'Recycling Militants'.

8 True Believers

Page 122, **On the outskirts of Solo**: Descriptions are from author visits to Ngruki in 2003 and 2008.

Page 123, **'Why have you got chairs?'**: The chair story is recounted by both Rabiah and her former husband Pujo. He says he witnessed her exchange with Ba'asyir. However, Rabiah says he was not there, that she travelled to Solo with two female friends, escorted by Abu Jibril, in which case she must have told Pujo about it afterwards.

Page 124, **'She was really enthusiastic'**: Author interview with Ecun at the Ngruki school, Solo, July 2008. (I was unable to obtain an interview with Abu Bakar Ba'asyir.)

Page 124, **'She was unemployed'**: Author interview with Wahyuddin at Ngruki school, July 2008.

Page 124, **Ecun, found her new friend a house**: Ecun.

Page 125, **community of 1000 to 1500 people**: Wahyuddin.

Page 125, **'The jihad atmosphere'**: Alan Sipress and Ellen Nakashima, 'A Quiet Voice Echoes Among Islamic Radicals', *Washington Post*, 3 January 2003.

Page 130, **The practice of swearing *bai'at***: Amnesty International, 'The Imprisonment of Usroh Activists in Central Java', October 1988.

Page 131, **Pujo remained a committed activist**: Author interview with Pujo Busono, Solo, Indonesia, July 2008.

Page 133, **Rabiah was 'very strong and very strict'**: Author interview with Sri Murtiah at Ngruki, July 2008.

Page 135, **analysis of Ba'asyir's manuals**: Amnesty International, 'The Imprisonment'.

Page 135, **rumblings of disaffection**: Quinton Temby, Imagining the Islamic State in Indonesia, Bachelor of Asian Studies thesis, Australian National University, 2007; Sidney Jones, 'Recycling Militants in Indonesia: Darul Islam and the Australian Embassy Bombing', International Crisis Group, February 2005.

Page 136, **Abdul Rahim bin Ayub**: His correct name is Abdul Rahim bin (meaning 'the son of') Ayub; however, in the Australian usage it is commonly rendered as simply Abdul Rahim Ayub.

Page 136, **Arifin remembers Rabiah**: interview with Zainal Arifin, Sydney, May 2003.

Page 137, **Activists including the son**: Temby.

Page 137, **Irfan Awwas was raided**: Amnesty International, 'Indonesia—The Imprisonment of Irfan Suryahardy', July 1986.

Page 137, **'The Indonesian government has regularly accused'**: Amnesty International, 'Indonesia—The Imprisonment'.

Page 138, **The flagpole … remained conspicuously bare**: The story of Rabiah's refusal to fly the Indonesian flag is also recounted by Ba'asyir's wife, Ecun.

Page 139, **port district of Tanjung Priok**: Amnesty International, 'Indonesia: Arrests of Muslim Activists Relating to the Tanjung Priok Incident of 12 September 1984', July 1985.

Page 140, **'Listen, brothers!'**: Amnesty International, 'Indonesia: Arrests'.

Page 141, **'prisoners of conscience'**: Amnesty International, 'The Imprisonment'.

Page 141, **convicted of supplying the explosives**: Amnesty International, 'Al-Qaeda in Southeast Asia'.

Page 143, **girls are considered mature enough**: Geraldine Brooks, *Nine Parts of Desire: The Hidden World of Islamic Women*, Penguin, London, 2007, p. 31.

Page 145, **they had fled**: Abu Bakar Ba'asyir, statement to Indonesian police, January 2003, obtained by the author in Indonesia.

9 *Muhajirin*

Page 147, **'I had to accommodate her'**: Author interview with Abdul Qudus, 10 December 2008.

Page 148, **'very outspoken'**: Author interviews with Amaluddin and Forlina Siregar, 1 August 2008.

Page 150, **he was, by several accounts, amiable and well-liked**: Author interviews with Jack Roche, Ibrahim Fraser, Umar Abdullah and Peter Wenn, 2003 and 2004.

Page 150, **'concerned and compassionate'**: Author interview with Luqman Landy (by email), December 2008.

Page 155, **'the cheapest house'**: Author interview with Nadia Aboufadil, August 2008.

Page 156, **'They loved her down there'**: Author interview with Nadia Aboufadil and additional written material provided by her. I have also relied on Cameron Stewart, 'Persons of Influence', *Weekend Australian*, 11–12 November 2006.

Page 159, **'Will you be my co-wife?'**: Nadia Aboufadil.

Page 161, **Sungkar and Abu Bakar Ba'asyir, still living in exile**: Sally Neighbour, *In the Shadow of Swords*, Harper Collins, Sydney, 2004.

Page 162, **She showed her friend Nadia**: Nadia Aboufadil.

Page 163, **arrived in Melbourne in April 1990**: Immigration records show Ba'asyir's first arrival in Australia was on 12 April 1990. There is no record of Sungkar arriving on that day, but there are numerous accounts of his presence with Ba'asyir. See Neighbour.

Page 164, **known as Abdul Halim** and **as Abdus Samad Abud**: Australian immigration department records obtained by author.

Page 164, **'a very peaceful man'**: Cameron Stewart and Colleen Egan, 'A Word from the Wise', *Weekend Australian*, 18–19 October 2003.

Page 165, **military training in Pakistan**: Author interview with Mohammed Nasir bin Abas, former leader of JI's Mantiqi 3, Jakarta, July 2008; Sidney Jones, 'Jemaah Islamiyah in South East Asia: Damaged but Still Dangerous', International Crisis Group, 26 August 2003.

Page 169, **'The myth of the superpower'**: Osama bin Laden, CNN interview, Afghanistan, 1997, <www.CNN/Programs/people/shows/binladen/profile.html>.

Page 169, **Aisha** and **Hassan**: I have changed their names at Rabiah's request as she is concerned they will be targeted by counter-terrorism agencies if they are identified.

10 Joining the Jihad

Page 173, **The tribal town of Peshawar**: For descriptions of Peshawar, I have drawn on: Christina Lamb, *Waiting for Allah*, Hamish Hamilton, London, 1991; Peter L Bergen, *Holy War Inc: Inside the Secret World of Osama Bin Laden*, Weidenfeld & Nicolson, London, 2001; Lawrence Wright, *The Looming Tower: Al-Qaeda's Road to 9/11*, Penguin, London, 2006.

Page 173, **treasures looted**: Wright.

Page 173, **'Hotel guests are asked'**: Bergen.

Page 173, **Throughout the 1980s**: For the history of the war in Afghanistan and the role of the 'Afghan-Arabs', I have drawn on: Lamb, Bergen, Wright; Steve Coll, *Ghost Wars: The Secret History of the CIA, Afghanistan and Bin Laden, from the Soviet Invasion to September 10, 2001*, Penguin, London, 2004; Steve Coll, *The Bin Ladens: The Story of a Family and Its Fortune*, Allen Lane, London, 2008; Olivier Roy, *Islam and Resistance in Afghanistan*, Cambridge University Press, 1986; Barnett R Rubin, 'Arab Islamists in Afghanistan', in John L Esposito (ed.), *Political Islam: Revolution, Radicalism or Reform?*, Lynne Rienner Publishers, Boulder, CO, 1997; Ahmed Rashid, *Taliban*, Yale University Press, 2001.

Page 174, **They were known as the 'Afghan-Arabs'**: Some authors have referred to them as 'Arab-Afghans'. Rabiah says 'Afghan-Arabs' is the term that was used when she was there.

Page 174, **'the brigade of strangers'**: Wright, p. 105.

Page 174, **'Peshawar was transformed'**: Wright, p. 121.

Page 174, **MAK had been founded ... Abdullah Azzam**: Wright; Jason Burke, *Al Qaeda*, Penguin, London, 2003; Coll, *Ghost Wars*; Bergen.

Page 175, **new suburb of Hayatabad ... where MAK had a guesthouse**: Burke.

Page 176, **Abdul Rahman Ayub**: Author interview with Nasir Abas.

Page 176, **first training camp set up for foreign volunteers**: Coll, *The Bin Ladens*, p. 255.

Page 176, **Military Academy of the Mujahidin**: Nasir Abas.

Page 176, **Sayyaf**: Sources on Sayyaf: Coll, *Ghost Wars*; Wright, Rashid, Roy, Rubin, Burke.

Page 178, **draped in colourful Afghan *batu***: Wright.

Page 178, **US$26 million in bribes**: Rashid, p. 197.

Page 178, **elaborate complex known as 'Sayyafabad'**: Burke, p. 70; Lamb, p. 220; Wright.

Page 178, **with separate colleges**: Author interview with Ahmad Shah Amadzai, former deputy to Sayyaf, Kabul, July 2008.

Page 178, **this facility had moved in the mid 1980s**: Nasir Abas: some writers have described Sayyaf's University of Dawah and Jihad as a 'terrorist training academy'. However, Nasir Abas says that from the mid 1980s all military training was done at Camp Sadda.

Page 178, **100 000 Afghan refugees**: Ahmad Shah Amadzai.

Page 178, **(ISI) anointed just seven parties**: Wright, Lamb.

Page 182, **'Jihad and the rifle alone'**: Yossef Bodansky, *Bin Laden: The Man Who Declared War on America*, Prima Lifestyles, Roseville, CA, 2001.

Page 189, **Osama bin Laden**: Sources on Bin Laden: Wright, Bergen, Burke, Bodansky; Coll, *Ghost Wars* and *The Bin Ladens*.

Page 189, **Islamic Co-ordination Council**: Rubin, p. 179.

Page 189, **established MAK** and **bin Laden who provided the funds**: Bergen, p. 59; Wright, pp. 102–3; Coll, *Ghost Wars*, p. 155.

Page 189, **Together in 1988 they formed a new organisation**: For the most comprehensive account of the formation of al Qaeda, see Wright, pp. 131–4.

Page 189, **Bin Laden provided the funding for Sayyaf's military academy**: Wright, p. 104; John Cooley, *Unholy Wars: Afghanistan, America and International Terrorism*, Pluto Press, London, 1999, p. 212.

Page 189, **under Sayyaf's protection and in his territory**: Nasir Abas; Wright, p. 111.

Page 190, **'someone who was anti-American'**: Coll, *Ghost Wars*, p. 155.

Page 190, **new policy of 'sidelining the extremists'**: Rubin.

Page 193, **'a heaven-sent man'**: Coll, *Ghost Wars*, p. 204.

Page 193, **'a turbaned Robin Hood'**: Bergen, p. 35.

Page 193, **'actually did some very good things'**: Coll, *Ghost Wars*, p. 155.

Page 193, **admired as a 'mother figure'**: Mohammed Al Shafey, 'Asharq Al-Awsat Interviews Umm Mohammed: The Wife of Bin Laden's Spiritual

Mentor', *Asharq Al-Awsat*, 30 April 2006, <www.asharqalawsat.com/english/news.asp?section=3&id=4757>.

Page 193, **She ran ten schools**: Rubin, p. 190.

Page 194, **'Bin Laden sought to pamper'**: Al Shafey.

Page 195, **bin Laden's passport was seized**: Coll, *The Bin Ladens*, p. 376.

Page 195, **new organisation Jemaah Islamiyah**: Re-formation of JI in 1993, testimony of Achmad Roihan in the trial of Abu Rusdan in Indonesia, August 2003, cited in Sidney Jones, 'Indonesia Backgrounder: Jihad in Central Sulawesi', International Crisis Group, February 2004; also confidential author interview with JI member, Sydney, 2003, cited in Sally Neighbour, *In the Shadow of Swords*, Harper Collins, Sydney, 2004.

Page 195, **about 200 recruits**: Nasir Abas.

Page 195, **They included leaders such as**: Sidney Jones, 'Jemaah Islamiyah in South East Asia: Damaged but Still Dangerous', International Crisis Group, August 2003.

Page 196, **Khalid Sheikh Mohammed**: The National Commission on Terrorist Attacks upon the United States (also known as the 9-11 Commission), *9/11 Commission Report*, July 2004, <www.9-11commission.gov/report/911Report.pdf>.

Page 197, **source of much gossip**: Nasir Abas.

Page 197, **according to a colleague**: Nasir Abas.

Page 198, **In April 1992**: Amin Saikal, 'The Rabbani Government, 1992–1996', in William Maley (ed.), *Fundamentalism Reborn? Afghanistan and the Taliban*, New York University Press, New York, 1998.

Page 198, **Osama bin Laden flew to Peshawar**: Wright, p. 161.

Pages 199–200, **a savage new contest for power**: Saikal.

Page 200, **In February 1993**: Simon Reeve, *The New Jackals: Ramzi Yousef, Osama bin Laden and the Future of Terrorism*, Andre Deutsch, London, 1999; Burke.

Page 200, **Yousef had travelled to Peshawar**: Reeve, p. 49; Bergen, p. 36.

Page 200, **fellow militant who later testified**: *USA v Usama bin Laden*, cross-examination of Jamal al-Fadl, 20 February 2001, cited in Burke.

Page 200, **'Saudi prince'**: Wright, p. 3.

Page 200, **'independent actor'**: Coll, *Ghost Wars*, p. 255.

Page 200, **Congressional Taskforce on Terrorism**: Bergen, p. 118.

Page 200, **remained a marginal player**: Burke, p. 20.

Pages 200–1, **US State Department report**: Burke, p. 20.

Page 201, **Bhutto launched a crackdown**: Burke, p. 98.

Page 201, **Sayyaf and his lieutenants had left**: Ahmad Shah Amadzai.

Page 204, **'The reality is'**: Bergen, p. 75.

Page 205, **Yusuf Islam**: Yusuf Islam did not respond to my correspondence so I am reliant on Rabiah's account of their meeting.

11 'Wahhabi'

Page 211, **'I wouldn't say he was anti-Islam'**: Author interview with Jack Roche, Perth, 24 November 2007.

Page 212, **Al Noori Islamic primary school**: Silma Buckley, *Bridges of Light: The Struggle of an Islamic Private School in Australia*, Muslim Service Association, Sydney, 1991.

Page 212, **board chaired by**: Author interview with Sheikh Khalil Chami, Lakemba, May 2008.

Page 213, **'she was a very concerned person'**: Author interview with Siddiq Buckley, Sydney, May 2008.

Page 213, **HAI was later named**: <www.terrorfinance.org>; 'Concern Charity Channelling Funds to Hamas', ABC TV, *Lateline*, 22 September 2003; Eric Silver, 'Charity Cash for Palestinian Poor Was Siphoned to Suicide Bombers', *Independent*, 28 November 2005.

Page 214, **Sheikh Omran hosted**: Cameron Stewart and Colleen Egan, 'A Word from the Wise', *Weekend Australian*, 18–19 October 2003.

Page 214, **Abu Qatada**: 'Profile: Abu Qatada', *BBC News*, June 2008; 'Preacher Abu Qatada Wins Appeal', *BBC News*, 9 April 2008; 'Government Fears Risk of Qatada Escape Has Increased,' AFP, London, 13 November 2008.

Page 215, **Australian *jemaah***: Sally Neighbour, *In the Shadow of Swords*, Harper Collins, Sydney, 2004.

Page 215, **visited Australia eleven times**: Immigration department records, cited in Neighbour.

Page 215, **'an open declaration of disbelief'**: Abu Bakar Ba'asyir, 'Indonesia, Democracy, Priests, Parliament and Self-made Gods', *Nida'ul Islam*, October–November 1996.

Page 217, **Egypt in late 1995**: Amr Shalakany, 'Tourists and Terrorists: The Governance of Political Violence in Egypt, 1981–2006', paper delivered at Radcliffe Institute, Harvard University, December 2006; Anthony Bubalo, 'Egypt: Preachers or Politicians?' in Anthony Bubalo, Greg Fealy and Whit Mason, *Zealous Democrats: Islamism and Democracy in Egypt, Indonesia and Turkey*, Lowy Institute for International Policy, Paper 25, Sydney, 2008. Additional information from Anthony Bubalo.

Page 217, **prototype for Islamic groups**: Lawrence Wright, *The Looming Tower: Al-Qaeda's Road to 9/11*, Penguin, London, 2006.

Page 217, **al-Gamaa al-Islamiyya (the Islamic Group) and al-Jihad**: Wright.

Page 218, **By 1995 emergency law**: Shalakany.

Page 218, **the most popular destination**: Bubalo.

Page 218, **Al Azhar**: <sacred-destinations.com/egypt/cairo-al-azhar-university.htmIslamfortoday.com/alazhar.htm>. Additional information provided by: Anthony Bubalo; Malika Zeghal of the Divinity School at the University of Chicago; and Issandr El Amrani, International Crisis Group, Cairo.

Page 224, **Luxor**: Wright.

Page 225, **'I wasn't happy'**: Sheikh Khalil Chami.

Page 225, **'It was predictable'**: Author interview with Silma Ihram, Sydney, 23 May 2008.

Page 227, **'Rabiah was very big on women's rights'**: Author interview with Jack Roche, Perth, November 2007.

Page 228, **power struggle**: Author interview with Gabr el Gafi, *Four Corners*, ABC TV, 'The Australian Connections', June 2003, <www.abc.net.au/4corners/content/2003/transcripts/s878332.htm>. Also Neighbour.

Page 229, **'I found the truth'**: Cameron Stewart and Colleen Egan, 'Heroes and Lost Souls', *Weekend Australian*, 20–21 December 2003.

Page 229, **denounced the 'Zionist pigs'**: 'The Enemy's Plot', videotaped lecture by Sheikh Feiz, obtained by author at Islamic bookshop in Lakemba.

Page 229, **a young man named Khaled**: At the time of publication in 2009, Rahmah's husband was facing criminal charges in Australia, as a result of which I have not used his full name and have included minimal details about him.

Page 230, **'She was not human'**: Author interview with Nadia Aboufadil, August 2008.

Page 230, **'Charmaine's condition'**: Author interview with Craig Johnston, August 2008; and (by email) February 2009.

12 A Letter to Osama

Page 233, **perils of the journey**: For the road to the border I have also drawn on Peter L Bergen, *Holy War Inc: Inside the Secret World of Osama Bin Laden*, Weidenfeld & Nicolson, London, 2001.

Page 233, **sheep tails**: Bergen.

Page 234, **Sayyaf** and **modest compound outside Kabul**: Steve Coll, *Ghost Wars: The Secret History of the CIA, Afghanistan and bin Laden, from the Soviet Invasion to September 10, 2001*, Penguin, London, 2004.

Pages 234–5, **Taliban**: Ahmed Rashid, *Taliban*, Yale University Press, 2001.

Page 235, **'They saw themselves'**: Rashid, p. 23.

Page 235, **'Thieves will have'**: Rashid, p. 50.

Page 235, **'Islamically deviant'**: The opposition to the Taliban within the Islamist movement in Peshawar is described in Vahid Brown, *Cracks in the Foundation: Leadership Schisms in Al-Qa'ida, 1989–2006*, Combating Terrorism Center, US Military Academy, West Point, New York, September 2007, <http://ctc.usma.edu/aq/aq3.asp>.

Page 236, **The infant mortality rate**: Rashid, p. 107.

Page 236, **border crossing**: For this description I have also drawn on Bergen, Rashid and Paul McGeough, *Manhattan to Baghdad: Despatches from the Frontline in the War on Terror*, Allen & Unwin, Sydney, 2003.

Page 238, **Bin Laden had moved** and **Jalalabad**: Lawrence Wright, *The Looming Tower: Al-Qaeda's Road to 9/11*, Penguin, London, 2006, pp. 225, 229.

Page 240, **shut down schools**: Rashid, Bergen.

Page 240, **World Islamic Front**: Rohan Gunaratna, *Inside Al Qaeda: Global Network of Terror*, Scribe Publications, Melbourne, 2002.

Page 240, **'to fight and kill Americans'**: Manifesto of the World Islamic Front, announced by Osama bin Laden in Afghanistan, 22 February 1998, cited in Bergen, p. 9.

Page 241, **bin Laden was indicted**: US Grand Jury Indictment Against Usama Bin Laden, United States District Court, Southern District of New York, 6 November 1998, <www.fas.org/irp/news/1998/11/98110602_nlt. html>.

Page 241, **US$5 million bounty**: Steve Macko, 'United States Puts $5m Bounty on Osama Bin Laden's Head', *ERRI Daily Intelligence Report*, ERRI Risk Assessment Services, vol. 4–309, 5 November 1998.

Page 241, **cruise missile attacks**: Bergen.

Page 241, **popular hero**: Yosef Bodansky, *Bin Laden: The Man Who Declared War on America*, Prima Lifestyles, Roseville, CA, 2001.

Page 242, **boys with shovels**: Bergen.

Pages 242–3, **Ahmed Khadr**: 'The Khadr Legacy', Khadr family website, <www.thekhadrlegacy.com>; Stewart Bell, 'FBI Hunts for "The

Canadian": Former Ottawa Man Appears on Primary List of Suspected Bin Laden Associates', *National Post*, 10 October 2001; Stewart Bell, 'Khadrs Reveal Bin Laden Ties', *National Post*, 24 January 2004; 'Review of "Book of 120 Martyrs in Afghanistan"', published by Al-Fajr Media Center, February 2008; 'The Khadr Family', *CBC News Online*, 30 October 2006; Wright.

Page 243, **Human Concern International**: <www.humanconcern.org>; '*National Post* Apologises to Human Concern International', *South Asia Partnership Canada*, 26 April 2004, <http://action.web.ca/home/sap/media.shtml?x=57414>.

Page 243, **to raise funds for their projects**: Jack Cahill, 'Pretty Toys Maiming Afghan Kids', *Toronto Star*, 25 September 1986; Michelle Shepard, *Guantanamo's Child: The Untold Story of Omar Khadr*, John Wiley & Sons, New York, 2008.

Page 243, **'Hope Village'**: 'Human Concern International, Rehabilitating and Reconstructing a Torn Land, Afghanistan', <www.humanconcern.org>.

Page 243, **close friend and ally**: Wright, p. 136. Wright refers to Khadr here by his *kuniya* 'Abu Abdul Rahman'.

Page 243, **'founding member'**: 'The Khadr Family'. For Khadr's role in the early years of al Qaeda, see Wright, p. 136. Khadr is referred to here by his kuniya Abu Abdul Rahman.

Page 243, **'a man of respect'**: Journalist Eric Margolis, in Shepard.

Page 243, **bombing at the Egyptian embassy**: US terrorism analyst Marc Sageman asserts that Khadr financed the bombing for Zawahiri's al Jihad group. See Marc Sageman, *Understanding Terror Networks*, University of Pennsylvania Press, 2004.

Page 243, **Khadr was charged**: Shepard; Theresa Boyle, 'Canadian Held in Pakistan Bombing', *Toronto Star*, 15 December 1995; John Stackhouse, 'Canadian Sought for Questioning in Car Bombing', *Globe & Mail*, 5 September 1998; Faisal Kutty, 'Canadian Relief Worker Held in Pakistan', *Washington Report on Middle East Affairs*, February–March 1996, p. 103.

Page 243, **'did not have much evidence'**: Theresa Boyle, 'Canadian Charged in Bomb Attack', *Toronto Star*, 5 January 1996.

Page 243, **and released him**: Faisal Kutty, 'Canadian Charity Claims Religious Discrimination', *Washington Report on Middle East Affairs*, July–August 1999.

Page 243, **shifted to Jalalabad**: Wright.

Page 243, **moved into the bin Laden compound**: Testimony of Abdurahman Khadr, 13 July 2004, Montreal, cited in Stewart Bell, 'A Lot of Canadians in Al-Qaeda: Vancouver Men at Terror Training Camp, Khadr Says', *National Post*, 1 August 2004; Affidavit of Gregory T Hughes, Federal Bureau of Investigation, 2005.

Page 244, **'go after America'**: Testimony of Abdurahman Khadr, 13 July 2004.

Page 244, **Health and Education Projects International**: '*National Post* Apologises to Human Concern International'.

Page 244, **'Zaynab, his daughter'**: see also Wright, pp. 251–5.

Page 244, **Taliban's objections**: 'The Khadr Legacy'; Shepard; Bell, 'Khadrs Reveal'.

Page 245, **letter of introduction**: Original sighted by author.

Page 245, **British government urged**: Stewart Bell, 'UK Intelligence ID'd Canadian as Bin Laden Aide', *National Post*, 12 October 2001.

Page 245, **C\$70 000**: Testimony of Abdurahman Khadr.

Page 245, **Ahmed Khadr was killed**: 'Canadian Al-Qaeda Suspect Dead', *CBC News*, 24 January 2004, <www.cbc.ca/story/world/national/2004/01/24/khadr040124.html>; 'Khadr has Right to Burial in Canada: Son', *CBC News*, 24 January 2004, <www.cbc.ca/canada/story/2004/01/24/khadr_son040124.html>.

Page 245, **shot in the spine**: Shepard; Amnesty International, 'Pakistan: Human Rights ignored in the "War on Terror"', 2006, <www.amnesty.org/en/library/assest/ASA33/036/2006/en/dom-ASA330362006en.pdf>.

Page 245, **Another son, Omar, was captured**: Shepard.

Pages 245–6, **threw the grenade**: Steven Edwards, 'Secret Document Casts Doubt on Khadr's Guilt', CanWest News Service, 5 February 2008, <www.nationalpost.com/news/story.html?id=285287>.

Page 246, **youngest detainee**: 'Guantanamo's Youngest Detainee Faces His Judges', *France 24 International News*, 12 December 2008; 'UNICEF Defends the Rights of a Child Soldier Still Held in Guantanamo', 5 February 2008, <www.un.org/radio>.

Page 246, **still being held**: Janice Tibbetts, 'Harper to Wait for US Decision on Khadr's Charges', Canwest News Service, 26 January 2009.

Page 247, **'medical genius'**: Wright, p. 139.

Page 247, **'cerebral taciturn man'**: Bergen, p. 206.

Page 247, **penned the 1998 *fatwah***: Wright, pp. 259–60.

Page 248, **tree-lined street with open drains**: Author visit to Karti Parwan, Kabul, July 2008.

Page 250, **Saj Gul women's hospital**: Author visit, July 2008.

Page 251, **lobbied strongly against it**: Vahid Brown.

Page 252, **Bin Laden and his wives**: Wright, p. 248.

Page 252, **Rabiah was the midwife**: Mamdouh Habib with Julia Collingwood, *My Story: The Tale of a Terrorist Who Wasn't*, Scribe Publications, Melbourne, 2008.

Page 253, **Azza Nowair**: Wright, p. 43.

Page 253, **bin Laden separated his key leaders**: Wright, p. 331.

Page 254, **Albright**: Rashid, p. 65.

Page 254, **Initially welcomed**: Bergen.

Page 254, **'We want to live'**: Rashid, p. 43.

Page 254, **'Islam as a rescuing religion'**: Decree announced by the General Presidency of Amr Bil Maruf and Nai Az Munkar (Religious Police), Kabul, November 1996.

Page 255, **'We have given women their rights'**: Peter Marsden, *The Taliban: War, Religion and the New Order in Afghanistan*, Zed Books, London, 1998.

Page 255, **shut down 63 schools**: Rashid, p. 108.

Page 255, **'women must be completely segregated'**: Maulvi Qalamuddin, head of the Taliban Religious Police, in Rashid.

Page 255, **30 000 female students**: *Afghanistan, Aid and the Taliban: Challenges on the Eve of the 21st Century*, Report by the Swedish Committee for Afghanistan, Stockholm, 1999, p. 62.

Page 255, **ended at the age of twelve**: Bergen.

Page 256, **humanitarian disaster zone**: Rashid.

Page 256, **Mohammed Abbas**: Rashid; 'UN List of Affiliates of Al-Qaeda and the Taliban', United Nations, 17 October 2007.

Page 257, **disappear on military duties**: Rashid.

Page 257, **Al Haramein**: 'US Based branch of Al Haramain Foundation Linked to Terror: Treasury Designates US Branch', The Office of Public Affairs, US Treasury, 9 September 2004.

Page 259, **Jack 'Jihad' Thomas**: Information from Thomas's trials, *Queen v Joseph Terrence Thomas*, Supreme Court of Victoria, February 2006 and September 2008; Sally Neighbour, 'The Convert', *Four Corners*, ABC TV, 27 February 2006.

Page 259, **met Rabiah's patron Ahmed Khadr**: Information provided by Jack Thomas to the Australian Federal Police.

Page 259, **Turkish guesthouse**: Jack Thomas, interview with *Four Corners*.

Page 260, **met with bin Laden's lieutenant**: Information provided by Thomas to AFP and interview with Neighbour, *Four Corners*.

Page 260, **'They wanted to organise'**: Jack Thomas, interview with Neighbour, *Four Corners*.

Page 261, **Mustafa Hamid … Abu Walid al Misri**: Vahid Brown. (The Arabic term for 'the Egyptian' is rendered variously as 'al Misri' or 'al Masri'.)

Page 261, **born in 1945**: Mohammed Al Shafey, 'The Story of Abu Walid al Masri: The Ideologue of the Afghan Arabs', *Asharq Alawsat*, 11 February 2007.

Page 261, **Muslim Brotherhood Youth Scouts**: Summary of Abu Walid's book, written in the al-Faruq camp, Khost, Afghanistan, 7 August 1994, <www.blackvault.com>.

Page 261, **He worked as**: Al Shafey.

Page 261, **'did not feel very religious'** and **'dreamt of jihad'**: Summary of Abu Walid's book.

Page 262, **'great opportunity'**: Summary of Abu Walid's book; Steven R Corman and Jill S Schiefelbein, 'Communication and Media Strategy in the Jihadi War of Ideas', Arizona State University, 20 April 2006, <www.asu.edu.clas/communication/about/terrorism/>.

Page 262, **series of books**: *The Story of the Afghan-Arabs from the Time of their Arrival in Afghanistan Until their Departure with the Taliban*, published in seven issues of *Asharq Alawsat*, December 2004; and *Chatter on the Roof of the World*, a copy of which was found by US forces in Afghanistan.

Page 262, **little time for self-serving warlords**: Vahid Brown.

Page 262, **'full of worthless characters'**: Al Shafey.

Page 262, **Abu Walid was left in charge**: Vahid Brown.

Page 262, **member of the governing *shura***: Vahid Brown.

Page 262, **'political course'**: Vahid Brown.

Page 262, **director of the Kandahar bureau … al Jazeera**: Al Shafey: according to this account Abu Walid held the position from 1998 to 2001. Also see Nibras Kazimi, 'The Caliphate Attempted', *Current Trends in Islamist Ideology*, vol. 7, Center on Islam, Hudson Institute, 2008.

Page 263, **'well-mannered'**: description by Abu Walid's sister-in-law, Safiyah al Shami, in Al Shafey.

Page 263, **fluent English …** : Vahid Brown.

Page 263, **'a really nice guy'**: Author interview with Jack Thomas, November 2006.

Page 263, **'calming influence'**: Jack Thomas.

Page 263, **Wafa**: Al Shafey.

Page 264, **a commandeered diplomatic house**: Author visit to Abu Walid's former house in Wazir Akhbar Khan, Kabul, July 2008.

Page 264, **travelled to Kandahar**: For the journey I have also drawn on Bergen and Rashid.

Page 265, **Afghanistan's second-largest city, Kandahar**: Rashid.

Page 265, **served at the table**: Rashid.

Page 265, **Tarnak Farm**: Wright, Coll.

Page 265, **a plan to attack**: Coll.

Page 267, **long-time internal critic**: The quotes that follow are from Abu Walid's writings, cited in Vahid Brown.

Page 268, **Saif el Adel**: Vahid Brown; and 'Al-Qa'ida's (mis)Adventures in the Horn of Africa', Report by the Combating Terrorism Center at West Point, based on al Qaeda documents released by the US Department of Defence, May 2007, <http://council.smallwarsjournal.com/showthread.php?t=2765>.

Page 269, **Jack Roche**: Based on Roche's testimony to the District Court of Western Australia, *The Queen and Jack Roche*, 27 May 2004; and translation by Indrawati Zifirdaus of Indonesian notebook seized from the premises of Jack Roche, exhibit 111a, entered in evidence at Roche's trial.

Page 269, **'just sat there'**: Author interview with Jack Roche, Perth, 24 November 2007.

Page 270, **'media encounters'**: Vahid Brown.

Page 270, **Taliban who shifted him**: Rashid, p. 139.

Page 270, **They confiscated his satellite telephones**: Bergen, p. 167.

Page 270, **'null and void'**: Bergen, p. 167.

Page 270, **meeting between Mullah Omar**: These meetings are also described in Rashid, p. 138; and Wright, pp. 267, 288–9.

Page 270, **agreed to this in principle**: Wright.

Page 270, **pickup trucks**: Rashid.

Page 271, **'You must remember'**: Wright.

Page 272, **aid workers who had been arrested**: Eberhard Muehlan and the Shelter Now team, *Escape from Kabul*, Strand Publishing, Sydney, 2003.

Page 272, **contingency plan**: 'US Sought Attack on Al-Qaida: White House Given Plan Days Before September 11', *NBC News*, 16 May 2002.

Page 272, **'political course'**: Vahid Brown.

Page 272, **'the planes operation'**: The National Commission on Terrorist Attacks upon the United States (also known as the 9-11 Commission), *9/11 Commission Report*, July 2004, <www.9-11commission.gov/report/911Report.pdf>.

Page 272, **bin Laden formally notified the *shura***: Based on intelligence report of interrogation of Khalid Sheikh Mohammed, 9 January 2004, *9/11 Commission Report*.

Page 272, **Mullah Omar was known to oppose**: *9/11 Commission Report*; 'Al-Qa'ida's (mis)Adventures'.

Page 272, **a majority … opposed the attacks**: Vahid Brown; 'Al-Qa'ida's (mis)Adventures'; *9/11 Commission Report*; Fawaz A Gerges, *The Far Enemy: Why Jihad Went Global*, Cambridge University Press, Cambridge, 2005.

Page 272, **'I will make it happen'**: Based on intelligence report of interrogation of detainee, 20 February 2004, *9/11 Commission Report*.

Page 272, **Khalid Sheikh Mohammed said later**: Based on intelligence report of interrogation of Khalid Sheikh Mohammed, 9 January 2004, *9/11 Commission Report*.

13 Fugitives

Page 275, **bin Laden, who was still in Kandahar**: Jason Burke, *Al Qaeda*, Penguin, London, 2003, p. xxiii.

Page 275, **'prime suspect'**: 'Bush: bin Laden prime suspect', *CNN.com*, 17 September 2001, <http://archives.cnn.com/2001/US/09/17/bush.powell.terrorism/>.

Page 275, **'They will hand over'**: Transcript of President Bush's address to a joint session of Congress, 20 September 2001, <http://archives.cnn.com/2001/US/09/20/gen.bush.transcript/>.

Page 276, **packing up and leaving**: Lawrence Wright, *The Looming Tower: Al-Qaeda's Road to 9/11*, Penguin, London, 2006, p. 370.

Page 276, **assassination of ... Massoud**: The National Commission on Terrorist Attacks upon the United States (also known as the 9-11 Commission), *9/11 Commission Report*, July 2004, <www.9-11commission.gov/report/911Report.pdf>.

Page 276, **Afghani driver named Hamid**: At Rabiah's request I have disguised the identity of the man referred to as 'Hamid' who guided her and her family from their departure from Kandahar until after their arrival in Iran. She fears he may be punished if his identity is known.

Page 277, **Dasht-e-Mango**: Ahmed Rashid, *Taliban*, Yale University Press, 2001.

Page 277, **Islamic Movement of Uzbekistan**: Vahid Brown, *Cracks in the Foundation: Leadership Schisms in Al-Qa'ida, 1989–2006*, Combating Terrorism Center, US Military Academy, West Point, New York, September 2007.

Page 277, **Anti-American demonstrators**: Eberhard Muehlan and the Shelter Now team, *Escape from Kabul*, Strand Publishing, Sydney, 2003.

Page 278, **Soviet-built airbase ... was targeted**: Rashid; additional information supplied by ABC correspondent Tim Palmer, who visited Herat in November 2001.

Page 278, **7 October 2001**: 'Afghanistan Attack Waves', Reuters News Service, 8 October 2001; 'Defense Officials: Air Operation to Last "Several Days"', *CNN.com*, 7 October 2001, <http://archives.cnn.com/2001/US/10/07/gen.america.under.attack/>.

Page 278, **CIA and US Army Special Forces**: Gary Schroen, *First In: An Insider's Account of How the CIA Spearheaded the War on Terror in Afghanistan*, Presidio Press, Novato, CA, 2005.

Page 278, **'There was just a roaring'**: Luke Harding and Paul Kelso, 'Taliban Says 20 Civilians Killed in Kabul', *Guardian*, 9 October 2001, <www.guardian.co.uk/world/2001/oct/09/afghanistan.terrorism12>.

Page 278, **'The street next to my home'**: Voices from Afghanistan, *BBC News*, 25 October 2001, <http://news.bbc.co.uk/2/hi/south_asia/1619332.stm>.

Page 280, **the *Times of India***: Siddarth Varadarajan, 'An Ignoble War', *Times of India*, 15 October 2001.

Page 280, **mosque in Jalalabad**: 'Bunker busting bombs deployed in heavy raids', *BBC News*, 10–11 October 2001, <www.news.bbc.co.uk/hi/english/static/in_depth/world/2001/war_on_terror/key_maps/strikes_10_oct.stm>.

Pages 280–1, **killing seventeen … another 120**: 'Daily Casualty Count of Afghan Civilians Killed in U.S Bombing Attacks', compiled by and excerpted from Marc W Herold, 'A Dossier on Civilian Victims of United States Aerial Bombing of Afghanistan: A Comprehensive Accounting', unpublished manuscript, Departments of Economics and Women's Studies, University of New Hampshire, December 2001.

Page 281, **'I brought my family'**: Robert Nickelsberg and Jane Perlez, 'Survivors Recount Fierce American Raid that Flattened a Village', *New York Times*, 2 November 2001.

Page 281, **'The most serious issue'**: Mohammed Al Shafey, 'The Story of Abu Walid al Masri: The Ideologue of the Afghan Arabs', *Asharq Alawsat*, 11 February 2007.

Page 282, **in two separate directions**: Vahid Brown.

Page 282, **'the opposition group'**: Vahid Brown.

Page 283, **safehouse in Paktia province**: See account of Zawahiri's wife's death in Wright, p. 371.

Page 283, **'The sound got closer'**: From account supplied by Aminah.

Page 284, **she too was dead**: Wright, p. 371.

Page 284, **'tasted the bitterness'** and **'To this day'**: Letter from Ayman al Zawahiri to Abu Musab al Zarqawi, dated 9 July 2005, obtained during counter-terrorism operations in Iraq and released by the Office of the Director of National Intelligence on 11 October 2005, <www.global security.org/security/library/report/2005/zawahiri-zarqawi-letter_ 9jul2005.htm>.

Page 285, **end of October**: David Rohde, 'Waging a Deadly Stalemate on Afghanistan's Frontline', *New York Times*, 28 October 2001. Also see Paul McGeough, *Manhattan to Baghdad: Despatches from the Frontline in the War on Terror*, Allen & Unwin, Sydney, 2003.

Page 285, **thirty-five bombs on a village**: 'US Bomb Kills 10 Civilians in Opposition-held Afghanistan: Medic', *Hindustan Times*, 28 October 2001.

Page 285, **Britain's Sky News**: Marc W Herold, 'A Dossier on Civilian Victims of United States Aerial Bombing of Afghanistan: A Comprehensive Accounting', Departments of Economics and Women's Studies, University of New Hampshire, December 2001.

Page 287, **Mazar-e-Sharif**: Muehlan.

Page 287, **were massacred**: '600 Bodies Found in Mazar-I-Sharif', *Telegraph*, 22 November 2001, <www.telegraph.co.uk/news/1363124/600-bodies-found-in-Mazar-I-Sharif.html>; Carlotta Gall, 'Conflicting Tales Paint Blurry Picture of Siege', *New York Times*, 20 November 2001.

Page 287, **Kabul**: Muehlan.

Page 287, **Tora Bora cave complex**: Burke.

Page 289, **The battle of Tora Bora**: Burke, Wright; Steve Coll, *The Bin Ladens: The Story of a Family and Its Fortune*, Allen Lane, London,

2008; Matthew Forney, 'Inside the Tora Bora Caves', *Time*, 11 December 2001.

Page 289, **They too had been on the run**: Wright, p. 370.

Page 291, **Unexploded cluster bombs**: Information from ABC correspondent Tim Palmer.

14 House Arrest

Page 294, **hundreds of foreign fighters and families had fled**: Robert Windrem, 'Al-Qaeda Finds Safe Haven in Iran, but Former Leaders Reportedly under House Arrest', *NBC News*, 24 June 2005.

Page 294, **US media reports**: Windrem; Peter Finn, 'Al Qaeda Deputies Harbored by Iran: Pair Are Plotting Attacks, Sources Say', *Washington Post Foreign Service*, 28 August 2002.

Page 294, **study by the Combating Terrorism Center**: *Al-Qa'ida's (mis)Adventures in the Horn of Africa*, Report by the Combating Terrorism Centre at West Point, based on al Qaeda documents released by the US Department of Defence, May 2007.

Page 295, **third-ranking official**: *Al-Qa'ida's (mis)Adventures*.

Page 295, **Gulbuddin Hekmatyar**: *Al-Qa'ida's (mis)Adventures*.

Page 295, **'axis of evil'**: President George W Bush, State of the Union Address, 29 January 2002.

Page 295, **using their Iranian base**: *Al-Qa'ida's (mis)Adventures*.

Page 295, **rounded up and placed under house arrest**: Windrem.

Page 295, **under the watchful eye**: *Al-Qa'ida's (mis)Adventures*.

Page 297, **launched a new phase**: 'Operation Anaconda', *Global Security.org*, <www.globalsecurity.org/military/ops/oef-anaconda.htm>.

Page 297, **estimated 400**: 'Operation Anaconda Entering 2nd week', *CNN.com*, 3 August 2002.

Page 297, **'It's a great step'**: 'US Admits Killing Afghan Civilians in Operation Anaconda', IslamOnline & News Agencies, Shahi Kot Valley, Afghanistan, 13 March 2002.

Page 297, **slipped across the border**: Lawrence Wright, *The Looming Tower: Al-Qaeda's Road to 9/11*, Penguin, London, 2006.

Page 297, **3000 civilian lives**: Marc W Herold, 'A Dossier on Civilian Victims of United States' Aerial Bombing of Afghanistan: A Comprehensive Accounting', unpublished manuscript, Departments of Economics and Women's Studies, University of New Hampshire, December 2001.

Page 297, **'The personnel in this vehicle'**: 'US Admits Killing'.

Page 298, **The Story of**: *The Story of the Afghan-Arabs from the Time of Their Arrival in Afghanistan until Their Departure with the Taliban*, published in seven issues of *Asharq Alawsat*, December 2004; Vahid Brown, *Cracks in the Foundation: Leadership Schisms in Al-Qa'ida, 1989–2006*, Combating Terrorism Center, US Military Academy, West Point, New York, September 2007.

Page 298, **'Bin Laden left Tora Bora'** and **'a tragic example'**: Mohammed Al Shafey, 'The Story of Abu Walid al Masri: The Ideologue of the Afghan Arabs', *Asharq Alawsat*, 11 February 2007; Fawaz A Gerges, 'Promising Heaven, Delivering Dust', *Foreign Affairs*, September–October 2006; Lawrence Wright, 'The Master Plan: For the New Theorists of Jihad, Al Qaeda Is Just the Beginning', *The New Yorker*, 11 September 2006.

Page 299, **He had visited the country numerous times**: *Weapons of Mass Destruction (WMD), Iran Report*, vol. 5, no. 7, 25 February 2005, *GlobalSecurity.org*; A William Samii, 'Tehran, Washington and Terror: No Agreement to Differ', *Middle East Review of International Affairs*, vol. 6, no. 3, September 2002; James Risen, 'A Nation Challenged: al Qaeda Diplomacy; Bin Laden sought Iran as an Ally, US Intelligence Documents Say', *New York Times*, 31 December 2001.

Page 300, **Chalous was one of two locations**: Windrem.

Page 302, **the *Washington Post* reported**: Finn.

Page 302, **In 2002, sixteen detainees ... handed over**: Finn.

Page 302, **the Australian embassy**: In response to my inquiry about Rabiah's dealings with the Australian embassy, I received the following response on 29 January 2009 from Angus Mackenzie, Director, Media Liaison Section, Department of Foreign Affairs and Trade: 'I can confirm that the Department of Foreign Affairs and Trade provided extensive consular assistance to Ms Hutchinson and her children in 2003. I regret that privacy considerations prevent us providing further detail on her case or the nature of that assistance'. I have therefore relied on Rabiah's account of what occurred.

Page 303, **the lawyer advised**: Rabiah says she is unable to remember the name of the lawyer so I have been unable to verify his advice.

Page 304, **Jack Thomas had been arrested**: Sally Neighbour, 'The Convert', *Four Corners*, ABC TV, 27 February 2006; and evidence presented at Thomas's trials.

Page 304, **His account included details**: Information provided by Jack Thomas to Australian Federal Police, and information obtained by the author during research for 'The Convert'.

Page 306, **Deed of Undertaking**: Document sighted by author.

Page 306, **The US President**: 'Canberra Prepares for Bush Visit', *Lateline*, ABC TV, 21 October 2003.

Page 307, **JI bombings of the Sari Club**: Sally Neighbour, *In the Shadow of Swords*, Harper Collins, Sydney, 2004.

Page 307, **'Either you are with us'**: President George W Bush, Address to Joint Sitting of the United States Congress, 21 September 2001.

Page 308, **Statement of Grounds**: Copy held by author.

Pages 309–10, **Mustafa and Ilyas were detained by the Yemeni police**: Patrick Walters, 'Indonesian Link with Yemen Terror Suspects', *Australian*, 31 October 2006.

Page 310, **detained after Australian security agencies passed on information**: Tom Allard and Cynthia Banham, 'True Blue Trio in Spy Agency Net', *Sydney Morning Herald*, 31 October 2006.

Page 310, **released without charge**: Martin Chulov and Natalie O'Brien, 'Brothers Cleared on Terror Charges', *Australian*, 4 December 2006.

Page 310, **Yemeni prosecutors said**: Martin Chulov, 'Yemen Frees Last of Aussies', *Australian*, 18 December 2006.

Page 310, **freed because there was no evidence**: Chulov.

Page 310, **refused to extend their visas**: Natalie O'Brien, 'Sons Flee after ASIO Grilling', *Australian*, 4 February 2008.

Page 311, **'Australian Mum Married'**: Sally Neighbour, 'Australian Mum Married into Al-Qa'ida: Long road from Bali to Kabul', *Australian*, 6 November 2006.

Page 311, **interviewed on television**: *Jihad Sheilas*, ABC TV, 5 February 2008.

Page 312, **'To the Muslim world'**: Inaugural address by US President Barack Obama, Washington, DC, 21 January 2009.

INDEX

Note: some names used are pseudonyms, including some of Rabiah's siblings and children, and appear here as given in the text.